THE TELEWORKING HANDBOOK

New ways of working in the information society

Sponsored by:

European Telework Development Project

UK Telework Platform

GCS Telegence

Anixter Distribution

European Commission (DGXIII/B)

Tolson Messenger

Lauder College

You bought the book... now join the club

Simply ring 0800 616008 to arrange payment details and we will send you membership information about the Telecottage Association – you are entitled to six months free membership through your purchase of this book.

THE TELEWORKING HANDBOOK
New ways of working in the information society

2nd edition
Written by Imogen Bertin and Alan Denbigh
Designed by Imogen Bertin and Sara Roberts at Cork Teleworking Centre
Proofreading by Dr Denise Rafferty
Cartoons by Colin Wheeler
Published by TCA, the Telework, Telecottage and Telecentre Association

For further information on activities undertaken by the TCA, contact:
TCA
Freepost CV2312
WREN Telecottage
Kenilworth
Warwickshire CV8 2RR
Tel: +44 1203 696986 or 0800 616008
Fax: +44 1203 696538
Email: teleworker@compuserve.com
WWW: http://www.tca.org.uk

ISBN 0 9528492 1 6

British Library Cataloguing in Publication Data.
A catalogue for this book is available from the British Library.

Printed on paper made from 100% recycled fibres
by Selwood Printing Limited 01444 236060

Foreword

*by Ursula Huws — author of numerous studies of teleworking,
director of Analytica Social and Economic Research and Associate
Fellow of the Institute for Employment Studies.*

As we move into the last quarter of the 1990s, the word 'teleworking' is
acquiring a new meaning. When it was first realised that the combination of
telecommunications and portable computing made it feasible for many
kinds of information-processing work to be carried out from a distance, the
'teleworker' was still a comparative rarity. Pioneers who worked from their
homes or from telecottages were seen as newsworthy just by virtue of the
way they worked.

This is perhaps an inevitable effect of novelty. Early users of the
typewriter or the telephone were probably regarded with similar wonder,
and maybe centuries ago it was equally remarkable to be a scribe, using the
strange new medium of pen and parchment to record and communicate.

As the millennium approaches, the use of these new technologies is
becoming increasingly widespread and taken for granted. Indeed it is
becoming as unacceptable for most businesses to be without an email
address as it became during the 1980s to lack a fax address or, half a century
ago, to be without a telephone number. As familiarity with the potential of
the new forms of communication grows, so too does teleworking, which is
beginning to be accepted, not as a strange and exceptional way to earn a
living, but as an everyday option in working life, something which opens
up new choices in where, when and how to work for anyone whose job
involves collecting, creating, manipulating, communicating or analysing
information which can be coded in a digital form.

Sooner or later, then, it seems likely that nearly seven out of every ten
people in Europe's working population will be involved in some form of
teleworking, that is to say in using a computer for handling data which is
then transmitted over a telecommunications link to a client or employer
located some distance away.

The fact that teleworking is becoming common does not mean that it is
necessarily problem-free. For people used to the unity of time and space of
a traditional office setting, with continuous face-to-face contact with
colleagues and close personal supervision, the shift to autonomous self-
management in a remote setting can be an unsettling one. New skills are
involved and new attitudes need to be forged, changes which can be both
liberating and unnerving when they are first encountered.

Novice teleworkers may not only have to acquire a range of new
technical skills, in order to select the most appropriate hardware and
software and learn how to use it; they may also have to learn new personal
and social skills. For instance, how do you motivate yourself to get started

on a bright sunny morning when the garden is calling out for your attention? How do you explain politely to inquisitive neighbours or bored children that you have a deadline to meet and interruptions are really not welcome?

How do you tell a potential new client that, yes, you are very interested indeed in his project but right now you are in the middle of cooking the family supper? How do you develop a rhythm of work which makes it possible to exploit the new potential for harmonising work with non-work activities without neglecting either family or work, while still keeping some time for yourself? How can you spot the early signs of workaholism, or social isolation, and take preventative action?

Teleworking substitutes flexible and personally-determined rules for the external forms of regulation set by such things as the daily commute, the nine-to-five-day, the regular rest-break, the formal weekly meeting with the boss, and the allocation of roles such as who answers the phone, goes to the post office, does the typing or makes the coffee. In doing so, it can fundamentally alter one's relationship with fellow workers and managers and, indeed, with the work process itself. But the changes don't just stop there.

By the same token it can also transform relationships within the home and community, throwing into question the traditional gender division of labour in the household, and patterns of interaction with other institutions such as schools and shops.

These changes bring both dangers and opportunities. At work, there is a danger that forms of protection which have been traditonally negotiated for all workers at the workplace will fall into disuse, and that unscrupulous employers may exploit the isolation of teleworkers to worsen their terms and conditions of employment. In the home, there is a danger that teleworking may trap women into a dual role: sacrificing all leisure in the attempt simultaneously to combine caring and housework with satisfying the requirements of a distant employer. Great though these dangers are, they are counterbalanced by immense opportunities: the opportunity to custom-design a way of working which genuinely enhances the quality of life and adds to individual freedom; and the possibility of breaking down the constraints which have in the past trapped women and men in the straitjackets of rigid gender roles, allowing them to negotiate new ways of sharing both the burdens and the pleasures of domestic life.

Newcomers to teleworking have a choice: they can learn the hard way, by trial and error; or they can learn from the experiences of others and avoid the common mistakes. This Teleworking Handbook is for those who want to make the second choice.

The widely acclaimed first edition brought together, in an easy-to-read form, not only the results of recent research on teleworking but also practical advice on setting up as a teleworker.

This revised second edition, which has been updated to take account of recent developments in this rapidly-changing field, forms the most comprehensive guide of its kind yet produced.

It deserves to be read widely, by those embarking on teleworking as a full-time career, by those who will be teleworking as an occasional option, and by those who are concerned that this form of employment develops in an enlightened way, which both increases individual choice and enhances the quality of working life.

Ursula Huws, August 1997

Contents

Disclaimer

While every effort is taken to ensure the accuracy of the information given in this book, no liability can be accepted by the author or publishers for any loss, damage or injury caused by errors in, or omissions from, the information given. Readers are expected to check all essential information and to seek professional or expert advice as appropriate to specific circumstances.

Introduction

by Alan Denbigh, Executive Director of the TCA

In the 18th and 19th centuries, the industrial revolution altered society entirely by mechanising physical work. It changed working methods and locations – people moved into towns in order to work in the factories where the new machines were situated. As we approach the 21st century, the "mechanisation" of information work will constitute an equally drastic revolution, but one in which the location of the work will not be determined by traditional economies of scale.

Teleworking is just one of the changes which will make up the new information society. The word teleworker means simply working at a distance, but it indicates the freedom which information workers now have, by virtue of the technology they use, to determine the how and where of their work. People are moving back to their homes to work, rather than spending up to half a day in travel to an office which may only be in active use for as little as one fifth of the day. They are working in trains, cars and airports, or in local centres and telecottages.

This book is intended to provide a comprehensive guide to teleworking. It addresses issues facing a wide range of teleworkers – the corporate telecommuter, the self-employed freelancer, managers of telework projects and those involved in telecottages and telecentres. It is a reference book, and not intended as a "cover-to-cover" read. We have cross-referenced sections and provided an index so there is no need to start at the beginning!

The information presented here began life as a set of documents provided by the ACRE teleworking project, which was then updated over a period of years to form the TCA's factsheets, and sent out to members of the Association. It has been substantially updated and expanded to provide this handbook. The pace of technology means that this second edition has requred substantial updating throughout in addition to two extra chapters – on Europe and on agreements and unions.

A guide to this guide...

Much of the research into teleworking sees the world divided into employed teleworkers and self-employed teleworkers. But in an increasingly flexible labour market, the difference becomes less evident and less important. This book is intended to deal with all aspects of remote working, providing information for a number of different needs, including employers, employees and freelancers.

Acknowledgements

We are very grateful to our sponsors, all of whom are involved in their own sphere with teleworking as you can read in the sponsorship pages – European Telework Development Project, Anixter Distribution, UK Telework Platform, GCS Telegence, Lauder College, European Commission DGXIII/B and Tolson Messenger.

Information and assistance in preparing this handbook has been received from many different sources and in many cases from information available over the Internet. The TCA wishes to thank all those who have contributed their time and knowledge, in particular:

Nick Benjamin, Lloyds TSB Bank plc
Andrew Bibby, journalist
Monica Blake, Information Consultant
Maarten Botterman, DGXIII/B, European Commission, Brussels
Lesley Carr, People, Processes and Systems
Patrick Cotter, Waterstones Bookshop, Cork
Ian Culpin, Martech, Brussels
Ashley Dobbs, former Chair of the TCA
Brian Goggin, Wordwrights
Jerzy Grzeda, Knowledge Media Institute, Open University
Roy Guthrie, Chairperson, Scottish Teleworking Association and TCA Chair
Paul Healy, Consultant, Work Research Centre, Dublin
Chris Hudson, Communications Workers' Union of Ireland
Ursula Huws, Analytica
Malcolm Lake, Effective Quality Management
Kathy Lang, writer and computer consultant
Deborah Lowe, co-editor of *Teleworker* – the journal of the TCA
Sheila McCaffrey, KITE Telecottage
Jeremy Millard, TeleDanmark Consult A/S
Horace Mitchell, Management Technology Associates
Paddy Moindrot, Development Officer, Telecottages Wales
Bill Murray, Small World Connections
Barnaby Page, former co-editor of *Teleworker*, the journal of the TCA
Geoff Preston, Britannia Building Society
Gill Price, Scottish Widows
Stephen Simmons, Cornix
Peter Skyte, MSF Union
Rhys Taylor, ACRE
Kevin Tea, Telework Europa forum
Teddy Theanne, Anixter Distribution
Peter Thomson, UK Telework Platform
Richard Warren, SteppingStones
Janet Williamson, TUC
Colin Wheeler, cartoonist
The staff of the WREN telecottage

Overview

What is teleworking?

Teleworking is working at a distance from the people who pay you, either at home, on the road, or at a locally-based centre. Teleworkers use email, phone and fax to keep in touch with their employers or customers.

Despite the continuing press interest in the subject of teleworking today, the idea is over a quarter of a century old. The terms 'telecommuting' and 'teleworking' are attributed to US academic Jack Nilles, who in 1973 worked on the first documented pilot telecommuting project with an insurance company.

Background and history

In the 1970s era of oil crises, the concept of moving the work rather than the gas-guzzling commuter clearly had some attraction. But the idea has taken some time to catch on because a number of factors have to be in place for it to work – a good reason to do it, cheap, reliable technology and organisations that are willing to change the way they work.

The recession of the late 1980s and early 1990s didn't help, dampening all economic activity and removing one of the main drivers for teleworking – the need to expand organisations without crippling increases in overheads. Both in the UK and the US early unrealised predictions were made for the potential of telework. In 1985, the Institute for the Future forecasted that 40% of US employees would be teleworkers by the year 2000.

The 1996 *TeleFutures* report takes up the story: "Despite the slow take-off, in 1994 the European Union placed the adoption of telework at the top of the Bangemann Report list of actions to make Europe more competitive. The EU even set a target of 10 million teleworkers in Europe by the year 2000. Today the European Commission's Telework 97 report estimates we may be one fifth of the way there, with over 2 million teleworkers in Europe today.

Recent figures suggest that, as with many of the 'Information Society' changes happening around us, America has stolen a lead on Europe and now has fast accelerating growth in teleworking. Jack Nilles believes that there were 'possibly a couple of thousand' teleworkers in 1970, increasing to 'about a hundred thousand' in 1980, though he admits that no one was actually asking the relevant survey questions at the time. His figures for 1990 were 2.4 million. By 1994, his estimate reached 7.8 million (against a figure of 9.1 million from Tom Miller of market researchers FIND SVP over the same period). For 1996, Nilles suggest 12.7 million teleworkers and predicts the figures will almost double to 24.7 million in the year 2000.

Ursula Huws in her publication *Teleworking: Guidelines for Good Practice* identifies five types of teleworking:

1. **Multi-site teleworking** where an employee alternates between the employer's premises and other sites such as the home or a telecottage.

2. **Tele-homeworking** where the teleworker is based exclusively in the home, and works for one employer.

3. **Freelance teleworkers** also usually work from home, but have a variety of different clients rather than a single employer.

4. **Mobile teleworkers** include sales reps, inspectors and engineers. They take advantage of laptop computers, portable faxes *etc.* to broaden the kind of work that can be done "on the road".

5. **Re-located back office teleworking** involves activities carried out in isolation from the employers' main premises such as data entry, telereservations for airline bookings, telephone banking etc.

A variety of terms are used to describe the new forms of work, including teleworking (the catch-all term for workers who use teletechnology), telecommuting (often used to describe those who work for just one employer and who spend only part of their time working from home), distance working, flexiplace and remote working.

Researchers differ regarding what constitutes teleworking, which explains the disparity between different estimates of the uptake of teleworking. Probably all that can be said about these figures is that they are useful in sketching out trends and giving some kind of guidance on how differing legal and social conditions affect the trend towards teleworking.

The UK Department of Employment 1994 Labour Force Survey estimates nearly 500,000 non-manual workers working at home but excludes part-time workers. Ursula Huws estimated in 1993 that approximately 6% of UK employers used teleworkers (*Teleworking in Britain*, Analytica), while the Henley Centre predicted that there could be as many as 3.3 million teleworkers, or 4.6% of the workforce, in the UK by the end of 1995. The Institute of Marketing came up with a figure of 20% of employers using teleworkers or other homeworkers in autumn 1994.

The UK Department of Employment's *Employment Gazette* re-analysed the 1991 census data in 1995 to estimate homeworking. According to authors Alan Felstead and Nick Jewson, around 1.2 million people in Britain (about 5% of the working population) work mainly at home or live at their place of work. The figure is constant between England, Wales, Scotland and Northern Ireland with few regional differences, although some rural areas, particularly tourist areas, reported higher figures. There was little difference between the figures for men and women. These figures include non-teleworkers such as farmers, but likely teleworkers scored quite highly – around 454,000 people were working from home in managerial, professional, technical, clerical and secretarial occupations. Around 224,000 were self-employed, with 71,000 working for an outside firm:

Nomadic boilermen? The gas man comes to call...

Over 6,500 gas fitters employed by British Gas have been equipped with laptop computers to link them with a network of seven call centres based in Staines, Swindon, Leicester, Stockport, Leeds, Glasgow and Dudley. At the start of each day, the engineer logs in and is given his first job. The list of subsequent jobs may be changed or swapped between engineers to provide better service times, so for the rest of the day the engineer is in constant touch with the call centre.

The laptop computer also contains a diagnostic software package to help determine where faults lie. If a required part is not in the van, the engineer can order it over the computer system and it will be delivered in 24 hours. According to PR officer Paul Brinkley, "the customers are very impressed".

- 7.3% of employers and managers worked from home in 1991;
- 6.0% of professional workers worked from home in 1991.

However, these figures are based on an ambiguous census question and have been queried by other researchers. The spring 1997 British Labour Force Survey, which uses reliably large samples, counted teleworkers for the first time. The questions define a teleworker as someone who works at home or uses home as a base, has worked at home at least one full day during the reference week, and who used a telephone and a computer for the work done at home. The survey reported that 987,000 people (4% of those in employment) are teleworkers as their main job. Around 70% of teleworkers are male, about one third work in the banking, finance and insurance sectors while about one sixth work in the public administration, education and health sectors. Nearly 70% fall into the occupational groups managers, administrations, professionals and association professionals.

Surveys based on equipment purchase and usage, such as those by ROMTEC and IDC, suggest figures of around 1.5 million PC-owning homeworkers in 1996. These figures by definition do not include the wide range of workers who "tacitly" telework (also known as *ad hoc* teleworking) – spending odd days working from home, or persuading IT departments to supply them with laptop PCs rather than desktops. Tacit corporate teleworking is probably the area of fastest growth in 1997.

The 1997 UK corporate telework survey by Small World Connections, in conjunction with *Flexible Working* magazine, based on 200 responses to a postal questionnaire and 20 telephone interviews found that 75% of the respondents already have some form of teleworking. Of these, 62% report *ad hoc* or tacit teleworking, 42% use nomadic teleworkers and 17% have home-based teleworkers, though a whopping 69% expect to be using home-based teleworkers in future. Larger organisations were particularly likely to forecast growth in their teleworking, and the healthcare and finance sectors stood out as enthusiasts for teleworking. The authors also note that, in comparison to their similar 1992 survey, the variety of jobs being teleworked had broadened considerably from an initial focus on IT. However, the questionnaire sample was made up of firms with a known interest in teleworking – it was not a random sample.

In the US, a 1997 report by market research company FIND/SVP found that over 11 million people now telecommute, up 30% on 1995 figures. The number of US telecommuters is expected to grow to over 14 million by the year 2000 (http://www.gilgordon.com).

Teleworking seems to be clustered around the south-east of Britain, or in areas with large service sector employment, according to Ursula Huws in her 1993 survey. In addition, Huws found companies between the sizes of 20 and 200 employees had very few teleworkers – the phenomenon was limited to very large or very small companies. Huws also noted that those in secretarial, writing and education based telework tended to be women, whereas consultants and computer professionals who teleworked tended to be men.

Reasons for implementing telework

There are a variety of different reasons for adopting teleworking, many of which are listed below, but overall the drivers for increased teleworking fall into four main categories:

- **improved competitiveness** – large companies can keep down costs and overheads in comparison to non-teleworking competitors. Small companies that are growing fast can expand without major capital investments.

- **better lifestyles for workers** – more flexibility, less commuting stress, better balance between home and work lives.

- **environmental considerations** – reduced commuting means less pollution, better use of office space, less traffic congestion.

- **improved technologies** – developments in the use of ISDN (videoconferencing, fast file transfer), the Internet (email and World Wide Web) as well as increased compatibility between IT systems make teleworking a practical alternative.

The Small World Connections/*Flexible Working* magazine 1997 corporate teleworking survey found that 35% of companies say they introduced teleworking at the request of staff. Around 30% do so to reduce office costs, and another 30% to ease travel or commuting problems. Maternity, illness, office relocation and overcrowding are all cited by about 10% of companies. Very few companies reported productivity or efficiency as the initial reason for adopting teleworking, although 56% listed productivity increases as a benefit. Office cost reductions were identified by 46% of respondents as a major advantage while 45% (rising to 60% of respondents already using teleworking) felt that staff effectiveness was a major advantage.

Teleworkers work in a wide range of fields. As a general guide, all jobs that do not involve physical production, extensive face-to-face customer contact or expensive specialist equipment can be teleworked. Other tasks suitable for teleworkers include those where the work can be easily measured, those that involve mental rather than physical effort, and those that do not require extensive hands-on management or a large degree of team work.

Typical teleworker categories listed in John and Celia Stanworth's *Telework: The Human Resource Implications* include:

■ **professionals and management specialists:** architects, accountants, management, marketing, public relations, human resources, finance, financial analysts and brokers.

■ **professional support workers:** book-keepers, translators, proofreaders, indexers, researchers.

■ **'itinerant' field workers:** company representatives, surveyors, inspectors, property negotiators, auditors, journalists, insurance brokers.

■ **information technology specialists:** systems analysts, software programmers and engineers.

■ **clerical support workers:** data entry staff, word processor operators, directory enquiry staff, telesales staff.

Other categories who often telework include technical support staff, quality managers and software localisation experts.

Teleworking advantages

(with thanks to *A Manager's Guide to Teleworking* and *TeleFutures*)

Employer teleworking advantages

■ **obtaining greater productivity**

Productivity gains quoted in published research due to teleworking range from 10–60%. The improvements can be attributed to a number of different factors:

- **reduction of distractions**: office gossip, interruptions of colleagues, noise in open plan offices etc.

- **reduced commuting** means that staff can be available for work at a given time irrespective of traffic conditions, weather, breakdowns etc.

- better coverage during **severe weather**: BT's Inverness Directory Enquiries experiment which included 12 people working from home found that the teleworkers were able to provide a service even when their office based colleagues were unable to come to the office in bad weather.

- **reduced sickness** – studies have shown that teleworkers have lower absenteeism. Lombard North Central bank found their average sick leave halved from 6 days to 3 days per annum. Travelling to work puts

WWF practises what it preaches

The environmental charity World Wide Fund for Nature (WWF) has used teleworking, email and videoconferencing to save thousands of pounds on airfares while preparing its submission to CITES, the convention on endangered species.

WWF activist Stuart White explains that the organisation has 15 regional organisers covering 4–5 countries each. "Part of the job is providing PR, managing volunteers and creating a local profile. All the regional officers are home-based teleworkers and have been for at least 10–12 years", says Stuart, who also says the organisation has an "email culture".

"Being an environmental organisation we use telephone conferencing a lot and have video conferencing facilities which are mainly used to link to our other offices. I even interviewed someone for a job over the video link – they were in Switzerland so they came into the Swiss WWF office and used the link."

up a barrier which may encourage the decision to stay away, anticipating a worsening condition. Removing the effort of strain and commuting means teleworkers may consider themselves fit to work. An improvement in their condition during the day may also mean they put in half a day's telework, but would not have turned up for work if commuting was involved. Fewer people to mingle with means fewer bugs to spread, and no central office means no sick building syndrome

– **increased flexibility:** staff working from home show greater flexibility. Teleworking may assist a company to provide a service out of hours – a rota of teleworkers could more easily provide this than getting people into a centre at times when travel might be considered unsociable or even dangerous.

■ **retaining valued staff**
Individual staff training costs can sometimes amount to tens of thousands of pounds per annum, and skills updates are estimated to take up 10–20% of managerial time, so losing valued and skilled staff is a drain on resources. If staff need to move in order to fit in with a partner's career, teleworking may provide a solution whereby the employee could continue to work for the company.

■ **accessing a wider pool of skills, or skills only needed on occasion**
A teleworking policy allows Helensburgh-based publishers Crossaig to trawl more widely for staff – quite simply the number of people they need with medical and specific technical knowledge do not live within commuting distance of their office. Without a teleworking policy the company might have to relocate, be restricted in its growth or provide

extensive staff training. Employees live up to 80 miles away and may visit the office only once or twice per year.

Brian Goggin of Wordwrights designs and develops courses for large organisations ranging from Aer Lingus to IMI – mostly Dublin based – from a spare bedroom in his home. "If you are good at what you do, most companies don't care how or where you do it," he says. Goggin believes companies will streamline their organisations further and make more use of services like his. "Companies know they can hire us for a particular project without having to commit to taking us on forever."

■ **reducing office overheads or avoiding moves to larger premises**

Research by Digital's Stockholm office in 1993 indicated that the average overhead costs for a European office worker amount to £6,000 per head per annum. The average office space used per employee is 11 square metres. It has been independently estimated by Noel Hodson of SW2000 that, taking into account holidays, weekends, and daytime-only use, office premises are unused for 86% of the time. A flexible working policy introduced by Digital and supported by computer integrated telephony allows staff to occupy any desk space and have calls routed to them whatever their location. The new approach has enabled 650 people to work from one building in Stockholm which previously accommodated 450. This allowed two other buildings to be closed at an annual saving of £2 million.

In the year to November 1995, IBM Ireland added 100 people to its workforce thanks to the ability of many of its workers to telework from home. Personnel manager Anne Keenan says: "Of our 350 full-time staff, at least 150 have the necessary equipment to work from home. We also have a number of staff who do a lot of work abroad, and for them we have created what we call a "smart office" – work space that different people use at different times. The company has made definite savings in this area because we are fitting 80 people into a space where we previously fitted 40."

However, some companies, including other European units of Digital, report that costs savings are negligible unless whole buildings or offices can be freed up, as there is a tendency to "double up" on equipment, and maintain a desk in the office for the teleworker.

■ **reducing the time mobile workers have to spend "in the office"**

Salespeople working for IBM in the US have cut out trips to the office between calls. Using laptops and wireless modems they can interrogate stock and price databases from the customer's office and print out quotations immediately. (BBC Radio 4 *In Business*, October 1995)

Field staff are an obvious occupational category to consider teleworking. Teleworking allows staff more time to complete the work and allows more time between jobs, hence reducing stress.

■ **maintaining competitiveness – faster services and lower costs**

At Instant Search, a small teleworking business based in Lancashire, customers phone in their requests for information on companies held at

> **Conclusions to the confused state of teleworking research**
>
> Perhaps only three clear points emerge:
>
> - teleworking is spreading as a trend;
> - most people who telework like it;
> - almost all pieces of academic research into telework should be treated with suspicion unless you have access to details of the questions asked and survey samples used.
>
> The best survey of teleworking research (and its shortcomings) in the UK has been carried out by Ursula Huws of Analytica for five government departments: *Teleworking: an overview of the research* 1996.

Britain's Companies House. Staff take down details and credit card numbers and then perform expert online searches of the Companies House databases. The information is swiftly faxed or emailed to the customer, providing savings in time and money over paper or in-person searches made directly by the customer.

■ **facilitating the management of a regionally-based service**

Burger King introduced teleworking for 600 of its regional managers. The company invested $5m in IT infrastructure and reported savings of $20m a year in reduced office costs. They shut down 12 out of 13 regional offices in the US and 50% of their office space outside the US. Managers reported preferring the freedom to choose when and where they worked and said they could manage their time better, but one said the downside was "You are never offline."

■ **taking advantage of labour in a different locality or timezone**

Cigna Benefits Processing, based in Loughrea, Co. Galway, handles health insurance claims for the American market. The claims are posted to a PO box at JFK airport in New York and sent by courier to Loughrea, where the Irish workforce is in constant contact with Cigna computers in the US via a leased line telephone link. The results of the claims are logged on the American computers for printout and dispatch of cheques by mail. The Loughrea location allows the US company to operate extra processing "overnight" and has the advantage of far lower staff turnover and training overheads compared to the American operation.

In Silicon Valley, the computer workers nod off after a hard day's work while the day is just beginning at the rain-spattered KITE telecottage near Enniskillen, Co. Fermanagh, run by Sheila McCaffrey. Handwritten CVs for that day's Silicon Valley job vacancies arrive by fax from San Francisco, are formatted neatly and sent back ready for immediate dispatch to clients of a job placement agency. Another recent KITE contract involves filing and preparing medical reports for a hospital in Boston. "They sometimes need us to do reports when it is the middle of the night over there and it would be hard to get anybody to do the job. We get a spoken report, put it into the computer and send it back down the line," explains Managing Director Sheila McCaffrey.

■ facilitating relocation or disaster recovery

When Digital's office in Basingstoke, UK, burned down, the company decided to restructure the 110 workers based there. All except 11 now telework. The remaining 11 are the core staff operating a virtual office with "hotdesking" facilities for the other workers when they need to use the office. When in the office, teleworkers pick an empty "hotdesk", plug in their laptops and notify the receptionist which telephone extension they are using. The company is said to be saving round £330,000 a year on premises costs.

Employee/self-employed teleworking advantages

■ job satisfaction

Teleworkers are actually more satisfied with their work than non-teleworkers according to a study by M.H. Olson (1989). In 1990 Ursula Huws and others surveyed 118 teleworkers and found that they were rarely dissatisfied with their tasks, their place of work, or life as a whole. They were mildly dissatisfied with their financial situation, relations with friends and neighbours, equipment and leisure time available.

A European research study (PATRA, 1993) suggested that teleworkers can in fact suffer more stress than office based workers, but they are happier with their lot, and the stress symptoms decline the longer a person

has been teleworking. The PATRA report also noted that teleworkers suffer fewer problems, such as repetitive strain injury, probably due to their freedom to take breaks and move around when they wish. Teleworking can allow time spent in traffic jams and on crowded suburban trains to be exchanged for more leisure, greater involvement in the local community, and a better family life. Teleworking can also satisfy the desire for autonomy and escape from office politics that a number of workers express.

■ freeing up commuting time and expense related to office work

According to the 1994 UK Department of Transport National Travel Survey, commuters take an average of 27 minutes to complete their journey to work (in London this rises to 57 minutes). The average weekly journey time therefore accounts for five hours per week – over half a working day simply to get to work and back. The time and the cost is usually borne by the employee.

Aside from costs of cars or public transport season tickets, there are a number of costs which, taken together, mount up for the employee. These include: clothing (the need to maintain a business outfit including several changes of suits, shirts and shoes and the associated cleaning bills), lunch and drink costs. Those who commute often do not realise that for perhaps a 13 hour day out of the house, they are being paid for a little over half of their hours.

■ retaining work after relocation

Nicola Sheridan teleworks for Ireland's semi-state Voluntary Health Insurance (VHI) company from her home in Castlebar, Co. Mayo on the west coast. Nicola had 11 years experience as a systems analyst with VHI in Dublin when she married and moved to the west. "I was lucky to have a progressive boss, who figured I could still do the job from home, put forward the idea of an "Electronic Cottage", as he called it, and arranged the whole set up." Nicola converted some space over her garage and VHI supplied the office equipment. She visits Head Office on average once per month and her boss visits her at least once a year.

■ balancing work and caring for families

Deirdre Talbot of Canada Life is an experienced underwriter who formerly worked from the company's Dublin office, but found that she was unable to spend the time she needed with her five year old son. Six months ago she decided it had to stop and planned to move back to her hometown of Nenagh, commuting 25 miles into Canada Life's Limerick office. Her boss had a better idea: "Deirdre was a very valued member of staff and we didn't want to lose her. We banged a few heads together and decided that there was absolutely no reason why we couldn't set up an office and have her continue to work from home."

Although some jobs require the teleworker's presence during a core of hours in order to communicate with colleagues, many tasks may not require this core presence, giving the teleworker the opportunity to work at times convenient to them – which can sometimes be early in the morning or late at night. Teleworking does not solve the issues of child care, but the additional flexibility and lack of wasted commuting time make it easier to deal with the problems raised. In emergencies it is possible to work with children around, particularly very young children who spend most of the time asleep. Teleworking can help women returners to combine work with child-rearing, and allow fathers greater involvement with their children.

■ **providing jobs in remote areas**

The former Grampian Regional Council joined forces with IT experts Hoskyns to create a telework centre in the remote Forres region near Aberdeen in Scotland. Here 80 jobs have been created. The centre uses document image processing and workflow management to process council tax forms and parking tickets quickly and economically. Each form is scanned into the computer system; once scanned, different parts of the form can be processed by different operators, speeding the entire process. The Forres centre works not only for local councils but also for a number of councils based in the south-east of England where wage rates are substantially higher than in Scotland.

■ **providing jobs for staff with disabilities**

Cathy Cumberbeach is a trilingual PA with 20 years experience. Five years ago a car crash and subsequent stroke left her with reduced use of one arm and a number of other health problems that preclude full-time office work. Through a scheme organised by the Disabled Drivers Association as part of the EU funded HYPIT project, Cathy has worked processing claims from her home office for an insurance company based in Dublin, which leaves her some time free to freelance her secretarial skills to other local businesses. Even if she were able to work full-time, insurance rules in Ireland which impose heavy premiums to cover workers with impaired mobility, would probably preclude an employer taking her on for a conventional office job.

Teleworking disadvantages

Employer teleworking disadvantages

■ **management resistance to the change**

In many surveys the main barrier to teleworking appears to be management attitudes. The Small World Connections/*Flexible Working* magazine 1997 corporate teleworking survey indicated that the attitude of senior managers was considered a negative factor in 60% of teleworking schemes. Other drawbacks to teleworking noted by the same survey were loss of feedback (60%), isolation (53%) and loss of control (47%). On the isolation issue, there was a split between those who were using teleworkers and those who were not. A majority of non-teleworking companies (56%) cited isolation as a problem, whereas only 35% of those using home-based teleworkers felt it was a problem, possibly indicating that the fears are more supposed than actual. Similarly, over half of non-teleworking users were worried about loss of control, compared to a quarter of those using home-based teleworkers.

BT's 1993 study of 115 senior personnel managers also found many personnel managers resistant to teleworking:

Corporate obstacles to teleworking	(%)
Corporate structure and identity threatened	35.3
Face-to-face customer interface needed	21.0
Difficulty in managing teleworkers (adapting from eyeball management to management by results)	12.5
Access to communications equipment	14.2
Cost of setting up teleworking	11.7
Isolation of teleworkers	2.5
Security (data, confidentiality)	0.9
Selection of teleworkers	0.9

BT itself, when it experimented with its teleworking directory enquiries operators in Inverness, found that middle management resistance to change was a far greater obstacle than the technical issues which had to be overcome. Interestingly, the Small World Connections/*Flexible Working* magazine survey indicates that those companies without teleworkers were likely to place much greater emphasis on the potential disadvantages than those who had already tried teleworking. The authors note: "Have the attitudes of managers changed in the light of their experience of teleworking, or have organisations with favourable managers implemented teleworking earlier [than others]?"

■ monitoring teleworkers' productivity

Some work tasks, such as answering directory enquiries calls, are very easily measured and unlikely to create much of an issue. Others, where work measurement is less easy, need to be piloted on a longer term basis until comparative statistics reveal whether value for money is being achieved. In all approaches a degree of trust is involved, and managers need to bear in mind that even in the existing office-based situation where they can "see" if someone is working, there is actually no guarantee that the work is being done, or being done efficiently. Conversely, not being able to see the employee does not alter this reality. This involves a change from "eyeball" management to management by results to see whether the work done represents good value to the employer, is completed to the correct quality and is delivered on time.

■ motivation of teleworkers

Contrary to expectations, research shows that motivation may not be a major issue. However, the results need to be treated with caution because many teleworking pilot studies have involved volunteers, anxious to make the system work, who may well have regarded working from home as a privilege that they were keen to retain. Implementing teleworking on a trial basis is advised (see Chapter 2, *Implementing Teleworking*). In the case of long-term teleworking employees, research by ICL/CPS specifies motivation and loyalty as two of the corporate benefits of their teleworking scheme since staff appreciate the flexibility afforded by teleworking.

■ isolation and consequent damage to corporate culture

The BT directory enquiries project found that although they had designed voluntary opportunities for team members to socialise, some preferred to use the time for hobbies or home activities. Some of the distractions that make up "normal" office life also provide an important informal communications system which is not available to teleworkers. However, where teleworkers are linked by the corporate email system, it is often used for social contact and informal communication as well as to send and deliver work. The necessity for a team to be in the same place in order to work effectively may also be overstated, as many group projects are in effect broken up into different modules carried out by individual team members. New software tools such as custom developments of Lotus Notes can enable a design team to remotely input alterations to one object viewed by all the group at their own locations.

■ security

Security is often perceived as a risk because it is assumed that the existing arrangement is automatically more secure than a distributed working

method. While there may indeed be security risks, usually the process of trialling telework will allow risks to be identified, and appropriate measures taken depending on the value and sensitivity of the information concerned (see Chapter 2, *Implementing Teleworking*). An increasing number of companies are adopting teleworking but maintain that trust and confidentiality are key issues. Therefore teleworking trials often involve existing company employees of long standing, rather than new recruits.

Employee/self-employed teleworker disadvantages

■ keeping 'office' and family separate

The opposite side of the coin from management concerns about motivation is the need for teleworkers to be able to "switch off". Despite the rosy picture, working from home can cause family stress, particularly if the teleworker does not have a separate room or office for work. Typical strategies include ensuring there is a separate "home office", use of answerphones on the work telephone line to buffer after-hours calls, and clear understandings about work duties between the teleworker and their family on issues such as interruptions and working hours.

Children often find it difficult to understand that a parent can be physically present in the home, but inaccessible to them while teleworking. Partners may find irregular working hours in the evening and weekends difficult to cope with, and computers don't take kindly to pet hair.

Teleworkers sometimes find that their work is not taken seriously by family, neighbours and colleagues when they first start working at home. However, the initial scepticism usually wears off. Fletcher (1992) found that 27% of teleworkers thought that others perceived them not to be working when at home, but the same report noted that 57% of teleworkers thought that friends and neigbours looked upon their work situation favourably.

■ reduced career prospects

"Out of sight, out of mind" is a real fear for many teleworkers. Employed teleworkers may worry that they will receive less pay than office employees for the same work, or that they will not get the same opportunities for promotion because they may not be informed when vacancies occur (Murray, 1992). They may feel that they have to continually remind their employer that they are there, what work they are performing, that they are serious about their career and that teleworking is not a soft option. In particular, teleworkers need to ensure that their skills are kept up to date and that they are not left out of training opportunities. Some managers can interpret a desire to work from home as a lack of commitment to corporate culture.

■ isolation

The disadvantage most frequently reported by teleworkers is isolation from the companionship of the workplace. A 1992 survey by the National Computing Centre found that 75% of respondents cited loss of face-to-face contact as a significant problem. Solutions include ensuring regular managerial contact, supplemented with face-to-face meetings for the work team on a regular basis, and the use of available communications technologies. These range from collaborative software tools such as Lotus Notes and email to videoconferencing and audioconferencing, involving the teleworkers in decisions and developments.

Isolation worries have been a major issue in the attitude of the trade union movement to teleworking (see Chapter 3). Telecottages, or telecentres (see Chapter 6) can also help to overcome isolation by providing a place for teleworkers to meet and discuss common problems. Some telecottages operate a jobs or skills agency and act as a source of work. Telecottages can also supply equipment which can be used on a bureau basis, or hired, but which cannot be justified for home purchase on grounds of high cost and low usage levels. Examples are colour photocopiers, the provision of meeting rooms and access to videoconferencing units.

■ **personal security**

Nomadic teleworkers (such as salesmen operating from car and home) can be vulnerable to attack, burglary and car crime due to the high value of the IT equipment and samples which they may carry with them.

■ **moving to self-employment**

Sometimes a move to teleworking is accompanied by a move to self-employment. These teleworkers take on the usual risks of self-employment – they need to earn adequate income for their needs, insure themselves against sickness and incapacity, contribute to a pension fund, and buy new equipment periodically. A teleworking 'veneer' will not prop up a business idea that is fundamentally unsound, and those moving to self employment must satisfy themselves on the viability of their service. Potential self-employed teleworkers should seriously consider the risks involved in giving up a conventional job, such as loss of social welfare benefits, as well as examining the many opportunities that teleworking can offer.

Environmental considerations

Teleworking is good for the environment because it reduces traffic pollution, uses less energy than conventional office work and encourages rural development. In the US, clean air legislation, particularly in California, has led a number of large companies to introduce telecommuting programmes in order to reduce environmental damage caused by their employees commuting to work. While there has been no major attempt as yet to reduce commuting into city centres in Europe, concern for public health issues related to car use is increasing. City-by-city transport legislation may result in the creation of toll fees for those who drive in to metropolitan areas, as has been established in Norway. Increasing use of toll roads (road pricing) is planned by the Department of Transport in the UK, where studies indicate that two thirds of commuters use a private car to travel to work.

Conventional employees with company cars and petrol benefits often use them mainly to get to work and back and may also have their parking costs paid for. While a teleworker may still need the company car, the use and associated costs are usually greatly reduced. In some cases the need for the company car may disappear and an alternative arrangement may be to the benefit of employer, employee and environment. In two-income households, where one person works from home, it is likely that the need for a second car will be reduced.

A 1993 study of transport/telecommunications substitution by Horace Mitchell and Eric Trodd examined Department of Transport statistics and found that 30 miles is the average travel-to-work distance avoided by teleworking. The national average figure of seven or eight miles is true if applied to all car journeys to work, but only because large numbers of people travel just three or four miles to work by car – these people are unlikely to look at the teleworking option. Only 4% of all car users travel over 50 miles to work, but they account for 22% of the total mileage of car commuters. Mitchell's argument is that the further the distance travelled, the more likely telecommuting is to become an attractive option. According to his analysis, if the top 15% of car commuters travelling the most miles switched to telework, it would halve the UK's total car commuting miles, petrol use and congestion.

Mitchell summarises that more miles on the data highway as opposed to the physical road means:

■ fossil fuels conserved;

■ emissions reduced and thus damage to the ozone layer reduced;

■ revitalisation of rural areas.

A more methodical approach has been taken by the Norwegian Institute for Transport Economics, which has assessed the possible impact of teleworking on the cities of Oslo and Bergen. Two scenarios have been developed: the "supplement", where little is done to stimulate teleworking and the "substitute", where teleworking is actively promoted. The former is predicted to lead to 10% of the population homeworking for more than one day a week, while the latter will lead to around a 20% takeup. The report also analyses the potential of teleworking on the reduction of travel and of travel based pollution and estimates a 3–6% reduction in car travel (both cities already have good public transport systems). This reduction is considered to be significant for peak hour traffic. A 1997 study commissioned by the UK Department of Transport in Cambridge, focusing on an employer with over 4,000 staff, indicated that if all employers in the city, known for its traffic problems, adopted an enlightened approach to flexible working, overall time and distances travelled in the city would reduce by 4–8%.

The EU SAVE project, operated by EA Technology in Sheffield, has estimated that working at home consumes up to 80% less energy than working in an office. Similar reductions in carbon dioxide emissions are also achieved. The project surveyed 106 Sheffield officer workers and 22 homeworkers. Andrew Wright of EA Technology comments: "The average energy consumption for offices is much greater than for domestic use because it's a lot less controlled – corridors need heating, lights are left on for cleaners, PCs are left on in the evening and so on. A shift to teleworking would also create a much flatter electricity load profile – currently domestic and office supplies impose peaks on the system in their different areas, requiring additional system capacity and the starting up of less efficient generators at peak times." Home offices are also occupied full-time, in contrast to wasted office space. Cornell University estimated that over 40% of all desks are unoccupied on any given work day, the equivalent of 3 million empty desks in the UK.

In rural areas, where the decline of agriculture, let alone recent food scares, continue to cause growing unemployment, teleworking allows job creation without sacrificing greenfield sites to manufacturing industry. Geographically isolated areas which suffer disadvantages through increased transport costs can also benefit from teleworking jobs.

Technology trends and telework

Technology developments such as the growth of the World Wide Web and widely available, affordable PCs have made teleworking feasible. The current spread of teleworking could be described as a "limited contagion". Almost everyone has heard of it, and at conferences the questions have moved on from the naive to the detailed "how to" and "what if". The cost of telecommunications services is likely to reduce drastically over the next few years as a result of the February 1997 World Trade Organisation agreement on the liberalisation of telecommunications markets, which will provide better economic justifications for teleworking. The WTO agreement will also provide trade challenges for European companies as the export of telework to locations such as Malaysia and India becomes technically and economically feasible. A number of other developments are likely to enhance teleworking possibilities over the next two years.

PCs spread into the home

According to market research specialists IDC, there were nearly 7 million PCs in 5.6 million households around the UK during 1996. This is in line with a similar survey carried out by Romtec at the beginning of 1996, which listed the installed UK PC home user base as 26% (based on a total of 23 million households). Intel and Mac platforms make up 19% according to ROMTEC (the remaining 7% include games machines, minority architectures such as Atari, and semi-obsolete machines such as the Amstrad PCW). The IDC survey indicates that 19% of the installed home PCs are Amstrads, 10% are IBMs and 9% are Commodores. Of those planning to buy a replacement PC over the next 12 months, the majority are looking at Compaq, Apple and IBM brands.

Romtec predicts that computers in the home are on an upward trend: :

Year	Estimated home PCs as a percentage of total PC sales
1993	15%
1994	18%
1995	34%
1996 forecast	36%
1997 forecast	42%

In fact, the 1996 survey by IDC indicated about 26% had home PCs, while the IT for All survey (also 1996), gave a result of 34%. The growth trend is partly due to the increased numbers of outlets on the high street and mail order chains, including Dixons, Dell Direct and Gateway. Home buyers tend to buy higher specification machines (Pentium Pros and multimedia machines), going for safer purchases and looking at the longer term usefulness of the machine – performance is more important than price in their choice of PC. IDC notes that home PC owners tend to be married, with children, younger and better educated than non-home PC owners, and estimates the average income of home PC owners at £31,762 or around 67% more than the overall average.

But how many of these computers are used for working at home? IDC estimates that there were 2.8 million work-at-home households in Britain in 1996, of which 1.5 million (54%) are PC owners. Of these 1.5 million, 40% bring work back from the office while the rest are involved in home-based office work, or are full-time telecommuters, or do contract work.

Separately, the British government's IT for All campaign surveyed 3,043 adults in August 1996 and discovered:

%	Item
34%	Have a PC at home
13%	Have a CD-ROM in their home PC
6%	Have a modem
4%	Have Internet access
10%	Say they use their PC for Internet or Email
25%	Work from home
54%	Bring work home and do it on the computer

ISDN

ISDN lines provide teleworkers with fast file transfer and access to collaborative working tools such as videoconferencing. To date only a few teleworkers have been able to justify the cost of ISDN lines, but tariffs are falling fast, and developments seem to be following the States, where telecom companies offer cheap ISDN access to teleworkers who "pre-purchase" blocks of usage. Widespread uptake of ISDN will lead to much more teamwork among teleworkers, as tasks which would normally require a physical meeting become possible at a distance through collaborative working software, speedy transfer of large files and videoconferencing. However, due to the poor penetration of ISDN to date, and the development of 56k speed modems which are nearly as fast as ISDN lines, there is a possibility that the ISDN technology may be sidelined due to its requirement for the installation of expensive fibre optic cables. ADSL (asynchronous digital subscriber line providing up to 6 Mb/s rates over existing copper twisted pair lines) and satellite technology, both of which are being developed for fast Internet access, may impinge on the ISDN market. Recent announcements by Nortel and Norweb Communications of a pilot system to provide Internet access via power lines in north-west England will also increase competitive pressures.

Internet phones

Video and voice compression techniques have made the infamous Internet phones possible by compressing voice data into digital signals which can be transmitted across the Internet. Although the quality is not as good as that from standard lines, it is acceptable and substantially cheaper. Major telephone companies such as AT&T are trying to persuade the US authorities to ban Internet phones, but it appears they are unlikely to succeed. The European regulatory attitude so far is to encourage competition and reductions in price through these new technologies. Many browser packages are now being bundled with Internet phone packages as standard.

Taking email and the Web to the limits

There is a great deal of uncertainty about how Internet technologies will develop in relation to teleworking. There are well-regarded IT pundits who believe that we will all shortly be using NetPCs, which will be very basic computers where all software as well as data is provided to the PC over the network. Others believe that interactive browser-type approaches to broadcast TV will lead to a convergence between TV and web technologies. In all cases, ease of use and price are predicted to improve but there seems to be little agreement on what we will use the new technologies for.

Dynamic links within email messages are changing the nature of information that is transmitted over the Internet. A number of software companies have converged email reading software with Web browsers so that instead of attaching a file to an email, the sender simply includes its URL (uniform resource locater). The reader then clicks on the URL and is immediately switched across the Internet to the source of the document, which he or she can read or download as they please.

"Java applets" are small application programmes which can be downloaded across the Internet, and carry out tasks for the person browsing the site on demand. One future scenario sees conventional software being overtaken by "on demand" access to Java applets – each time you need to spellcheck, the spellcheck applet is downloaded across the Internet to your word processor. The advantage is that your software is never obsolete, and that the software manufacturers can distribute at lower cost. Related to this is the idea that much desktop computing power is redundant, and that as the Internet develops we may end up with very simple, inexpensive NetPCs on our desks which get their functionality through their Internet connections.

Electronic commerce is growing steadily as confidence in security mechanisms increases, with many telebanking and "electronic cash" trials under way. It does seem likely that intermediary service providers, who can provide more security than standard Internet TCP/IP protocols but operate through the same interface as far as customers are concerned, will be needed to drive the e-commerce market forward. Companies such as Dell Computer are already allowing customers to select the computer configuration they want on a website, find out the price and pay over the Internet – the information is sent from the website to the manufacturing plant, where the customised computer is built to order, and then delivered.

The latest versions of the two industry standard web browsers, Internet Explorer and Netscape, take advantage of technology which "pushes" customised information directly on to the desktop in a manner which begins to resemble broadcasting. Internet Explorer now uses the idea of "active channels" to send material to the user whenever they connect.

Electronic publishing has taken a leap forward with the widespread adoption of Adobe's portable document format (PDF). This format allows a document to be transmitted electronically and read remotely, including all formatting, typefaces, graphics *etc.* without any problems of compatibility. The reader does not have to have the same software, computer system or fonts as the sender. In conjunction with the introduction of digital printing, where it becomes possible to print just a few copies of a full colour document to professional standards without incurring huge costs, remote printing (as opposed to the existing physical transport of printed documents around the world) is likely to increase.

The area of greatest change over the next few years may well be mobile services. Full mobile offices are already available, with portable faxes and two-way text messaging systems. The Nokia Communicator, a mobile phone which can also send and receive fax and emails, is the first of a new generation of more sophisticated handheld devices. According to Alan Cane writing in the Financial Times in August 1997, if the existing European manufacturers agreement on the UMTS (Universal Mobile Telephone Services) standard can be expanded, we may soon see mobile phones with miniature TV screens, as well as the ability to use the mobile phone for fast Internet connections, teleshopping and to play high quality sound. The development of low earth orbit satellite telephony systems such as Globalstar should also provide access to a full range of data services from almost anywhere on earth by the end of 1998 though costs may be high.

Providing the right support for teleworkers

A service that many experienced teleworkers require is remote technical support. The complexity of computer systems and the plethora of add-on devices which often accompany the basic PC multiply the likelihood of problems. Until recently, most people either relied on their company IT department or local computer dealer for help – very frustrating when your system has crashed and a deadline is imminent. Now a number of computer dealers and specialists are offering premium rate telephone helplines, or remote diagnosis assistance using modems. In the Far East, one company is offering a 24-hour helpline to business people staying in hotels who may have a problem with their PCs. However, technical support services have an inherent problem – you usually have to pay for them before you can find out whether the quality of support is sufficient for your needs.

Training: reducing the overheads

Internet-based distance learning courses are now available from a number of suppliers, including the Open University. Both the range and the availability of these courses are likely to improve as course materials are developed for new teletechnologies such as the World Wide Web. As telework practices spread, and the need for constant updating of software and other work skills increases, the days of conventional courses involving travel to a training centre may be numbered on cost and convenience grounds alone. However, face to face classwork will remain an important element of many training courses. Many established distance learning providers are concerned about the cost and access implications of these new technologies (it costs about 1.5–4 times more in tutorial time than conventional classroom support and is only accessible if you already have an Internet connection). It may turn out that conventional providers are not yet willing to exploit these opportunities, and that it will be the commercial computer training sector which makes the first moves of relevance to teleworkers.

Social trends and telework

Telework is maturing as a profession – though many might argue it is not a profession but just a way of working that covers a number of different disciplines. The problems and advantages remain remarkably consistent, whatever the area of work, and reveal a series of paradoxes.

Many of the initial technical problems, such as compatibility of software, reliability of electronic mail, credibility of homeworkers with clients and measurement of increased productivity have been solved, but a new set of problems are appearing. These include the difficulties self-employed teleworkers find in getting training to maintain their skills, and anomalies of social welfare systems that disadvantage teleworkers who become ill or otherwise unemployed, when compared to traditional, office-based PAYE employees.

Research has been carried out to look at whether teleworkers become casualised, or suffer from low pay and poor conditions due to their isolation from processes of collective bargaining. In particular, some reports have claimed teleworking is bad for women, causing problems with the boundary between home and work, exploitation, interference with housekeeping duties, often assuming a domestic role for women as the status quo. These reports conflict with the strong enthusiasm of female workers for teleworking because it provides increased flexibility to combine home and work duties.

To examine whether this problem is widespread DGV, the Social Affairs directorate of the EU, commissioned Ursula Huws of Analytica to carry out a survey using a properly controlled sample across Europe (*Teleworking and Gender*, 1996). Some previous research studies had compared high-level professional male teleworkers against low-level clerical female workers, leading to the predictable conclusion that the women fare worse than the men. Female teleworkers have tended to be concentrated in areas such as data entry, telesales or routine computer programming, whereas male teleworkers have tended to be professionals or executives involved in systems design, sales management or engineering. To avoid this distortion Huws selected her sample of 188 freelancers through a translation agency with workers in all European countries and discovered that gender differences in conditions, problems experienced and other factors were much smaller than had been previously reported.

In fact, although previously women teleworkers had been reported to have greater difficulty with interruptions from family, Huws found that they tended to opt for clearer boundaries and working hours than their male counterparts, suggesting that they prefer and instigate a more rigid work structure.

Huws also found quite a few of the male teleworkers were "new men" who had chosen to telework in order to be with their children or partners, and to adopt a less stressful rural lifestyle. Men who made these choices were "feminised" in labour market terms, often adopting less secure and lower paid work in exchange for their lifestyle choice. Overall, both men and women suffered from high levels of stress and insecurity. Twenty per cent worked more than 50 hours a week; 12% worked over 60 hours and 9% over 70. Huws comments: "Although the most common reason given for preferring to work from home was the desire for autonomy or 'to be my own boss', these self-employed teleworkers had little or no control over the flow of work... Periods without work could not be enjoyed as 'leisure' but were times of hardship and anxiety about where the next job might come from."

Overall, current changes in patterns of employment seem likely to lead to more teleworking, with trends to more part-time workers, more service and IT-based jobs, and more women at work, who require flexible employment patterns. A separate survey of female professionals found that

80% are in favour of teleworking, preferring to work at home one to three days a week where possible.

In Britain, the DTI has launched a four year £35 million 'Information Society Initiative' designed to encourage British business 'take up tools' in the emerging information-based economy. There is also a European information society programme, and several other countries, including Ireland and Denmark, have Information Society Commissions.

The comprehensive package of DTI measures includes a help line, research programmes, local support centres, case study information, and a number of awards and competitions to stimulate innovation. Companies are also encouraged to run their own technology awareness campaigns in the communities in which they are employers.

European governments also seem to be convinced that a move to flexible working practices is crucial to maintaining competitiveness in comparison to other world regions. This trend implies a greater number of self-employed people and has perhaps moved too fast for existing member state structures, since in many European countries workers have a vested interest in not becoming self-employed, as they then lose many health and welfare benefits. There is also a general consensus that those who work from home need protection from what Bill Walsh of MSF Union describes as the "long and discreditable history of exploitation of home workers".

In 1996, the International Labour Organisation issued an international convention on homeworking, providing minimum levels of protection. The convention covers employees and the "pseudo self-employed", but not the genuinely self-employed, which the convention describes as those with "the degree of autonomy and of economic independence to be considered an independent worker under national laws, regulations or court decisions". The convention specifies the following rights:

■ the homeworkers' right to establish or join organisations of their own choosing and to participate in the activities of such organisations

■ protection against discrimination in employment and occupation

■ protection in the field of occupational safety and health

■ remuneration

■ statutory social security protection

■ access to training

■ maternity protection

The European Commission has agreed in principle that it will encourage EU member states to adopt the ILO convention. The adoption of the EU's Working Time Directive may also lead to an increase in teleworking. This legislation limits the hours worked per week by employees to 48, and therefore could be expected to lead to more outsourcing of peak flow work to teleworkers. However, it may have a negative effect on some teleworker's conditions because, like the ILO homeworking convention, it does not apply to the genuinely self-employed. Therefore more and more peak flow work requiring intermittent long working hours may go to self-employed teleworkers because they fall outside the scope of the Working Time Directive. In addition, the burden of labour legislation makes it more and more difficult for the self-employed to become employers themselves – if they employ others, as opposed to networking or subcontracting other self-employed people, then they make themselves extremely vulnerable since their employees will have more rights over them than they have over their customers. This problem may be exacerbated by recent legislation giving part-time workers the same employment rights as full time workers as the self-employed previously often started to employ by taking on part-time staff. Therefore the overall effect could be to increase the number of self-employed people with fewer employment rights, leading eventually to a two tier employment rights structure.

There is also the problem of the "pensions gap". On the one hand, ageing populations in many countries are putting severe stress on state-run pension schemes. On the other, many people are being encouraged to become self-employed, thus moving outside the state system. Few of the new self-employed workers take out suitable personal pensions, exacerbating the pensions "time bomb". Pension contributions may well have to become compulsory for the self-employed in a number of European countries, and social welfare provision may also need revision. More information on teleworking and the European Union is given in Chapter 14.

In general welfare systems have not moved with the changes in work patterns. In the UK if you have been self-employed for more than a year, you are only entitled to minimal, means-tested welfare benefits (unemployment assistance) should you become unemployed or suffer disability or illness. Although self-employed people in Britain pay national insurance, their contributions only cover the National Health Service and Old Age Pension, not the wider range of benefits available to PAYE employees.

Some trade unions have opposed the introduction of teleworking and flexible work on the grounds that it leads to casualisation, low pay and loss of employment rights, while others see it as a way forward and an opportunity to increase their membership and services to the new breed of workers. Teleworking was initially held up as a job creation tool which would allow long-term unemployed, and those in rural areas, to access work formerly restricted to cities. However, the technologies developed to allow teleworking, such as call centre software, are reaching levels of sophistication that require fewer, more highly skilled operatives, and major employment creation through teleworking seems unlikely – where jobs are created, they also tend to be in urban areas with larger labour pools. More information on teleworking agreements and trade unions is given in Chapter 3, *Agreements and unions.*

A further split seems to be appearing between those trained as low skilled teleworkers equipped to handle clerical work (who may have difficulty in finding work unless a former employer wants to take them on, and whose jobs are often threatened by technology developments), and the professionals who telework. The professionals by contrast are complaining of excessive demand for their services, overwork and stress, and the difficulties of keeping up their skills in an ever-changing work environment.

Motorola commissioned a poll of over one thousand adults and 100 board directors by MORI in July/August 1996 which highlighted the increasing separation between the information 'haves" and "have-nots" (*Prepared for the future? The British and Technology*). Nearly 43% of people have no access to items such as PCs, mobile phones, computer games and faxes. The "haves" tend to be in the ABC1 social classes, aged 16–44 , with higher levels of education, and children. The "have-nots" are aged over 45 and in the lower social classes. Those who are missing out include 48% of women and 56% of people in the 45–64 age group. Although 85% of people in Britain had heard of the Internet, only 17% had used it, and of the executives polled, 52% had no interest in the Internet. Overall, one third of men and 42% of women have no interest in the Internet. Yet of those in work, over 30% had taken computer courses in the past year, and a surprising 22% had paid for the courses themselves.

Add to this welfare benefits systems which, because they take into account the earnings of spouses or cohabitees, encourage either double income households with no leisure, or no income households with no work, and it becomes clear that we may be heading for increased social division as a result of increased use of IT and the move to flexible working.

Although telework undoubtedly offers opportunities to rural dwellers, it appears that it is the city dwellers who are gaining the advantage because of their greater skills and higher levels of telecoms infrastructure and physical communications available in urban areas. The Rural Development Commission's study on *Teleworking and Rural Development* (1996) found that current statistics were unreliable, but that in the main professional teleworking was concentrated in London and south-east England, while home-based work for a single employer tended to be carried out by low paid women in peripheral areas. The report was also pessimistic about back office functions being relocated to rural areas, suggesting that these tend to locate in industrial urban areas with large labour pools. Areas of opportunity identified included Internet marketing of specialist rural products, tourism teleworking, information services and services aimed at rural communities. The report recommends universal access to high capacity telecommunication networks, and the promotion of telework training for the self-employed in rural areas, plus support for networks of freelances or small businesses to support rural teleworking.

Statistics taken from censuses show relatively low levels of teleworkers in cities, yet most urban dwellers will be able to think of a couple of teleworkers in their street – architects, designers, financial advisors – the attraction of doing without office overheads is luring increasing numbers to work from home. Conversely, the number of successful rural telework businesses appears to be lower than the census statistics suggest – Ursula Huws suggested that this may be due to retired professionals in rural areas putting down a homeworking profession on census returns and surveys when in fact they are not active in business.

The global village is also some way away despite the handful of high profile examples of rural dwellers working for European and American clients featured in newspaper articles. The 1996 *TeleFutures* survey in Ireland confirmed that although 26% of the sampled companies allow their employees to telework, and 28% want to outsource certain tasks to teleworkers within a year, 81% would prefer to use a teleworker within a radius of 25 miles who would be available for face-to-face meetings.

So what's the conclusion?

A number of the often-quoted pieces of research have been extrapolated from tiny, statistically insignificant samples of as few as 20 actual teleworkers, or have selected their teleworkers in ways which bias their results. Others have asked confusing or ambiguous questions of their sample which lead to inaccurate conclusions. A large number of the research projects have been funded, designed or driven by companies which sell teleworking technology and have a vested interest in presenting teleworking in a postitive light, or from academic disciplines which have an axe to grind (such as women's studies PhD students looking into conflicts between telework and housework). No-one knows yet exactly how many people are teleworking; how, where and when they telework; or whether it is better for them than traditional office work. Base your actions on your own research, trials and experiences – it's your life, your family and your money.

Bibliography

Each chapter has a separate bibliography and contacts list. Because of the fast-changing nature of teleworking, the bibliographies are arranged in reverse date order, and subordered by alphabetical title. Prices are omitted due to the difficulty of maintaining accurate price information updates.

Periodicals

Flexibility
Editors: Edna Murphy, Andy Lake
Source: Home Office Partnership (HOP), Jeffreys Building, St John's Innovation Park, Cambridge
Comment: Periodical available on website

Flexible Working
Source: The Eclipse Group, 18-20 Highbury Place, London, N5 1QP
Tel: 0171 354 5858 Ref: ISSN 1360-9505.
Comment: Periodical

European Journal of Teleworking
Source: Addico Cornix Publications, 64 Morrab Road, Penzance, TR18 2QT.

Telecommuting Review
Editor: Gil Gordon
Source: Gil Gordon Associates, 11 Donner Crt, Monmouth Jn, New Jersey, USA Tel:
+001 8852 732 329 2266, Email: 74375.1667@compuserve.com
Comment: US periodical publication

Teletravail
Editor: Alain Maurice
Source: Sarl Teletravail,14 Rue Yvonne le Tac, 75081 Paris
Fax: +33 142522501 Email: 101572.527@compuserve.com
Comment: French teleworking magazine

Telewerken
Editor: Th Snijders
Source: Kommunikatie Service Nederland Tel: +31 4853 18008 Fax: +31 4853 13234
Comment: Dutch teleworking magazine

Teleworker Magazine
Editor: Alan Denbigh Tel: 01453 834874 Fax: 01453 836174
Email: teleworker@compuserve.com
Source: TCA Tel: 0800 616008 or 01203 696986 Fax: 01203 696538
Comment: Bi-monthly magazine for TCA members

Teleworx Magazin
Editor: Ulrich Pesch Email: logo-press@compuserve.com Web:
http://www.iwtnet.de/teleworx
Comment: German teleworking magazine

XIII Magazine
Author: CEC DGXIIIF
Source: Commission of the EC DGXIIIF,TR61 2/1, Rue de la Loi 200, B-1049 Brussels,
Belgium
Comment: Magazine of Directorate General XIII – concerned with European
Community policy for IT industries and telecommunications. Includes strong interest
in teleworking.

Publications

Corporate Telework Survey   *Date:* 1997
Authors: Small World Connections
Source: PO Box 162, South District Office, Manchester M20 3BB Tel: 0161 445 0630
Fax: 0161 445 1403 Email: small_world@compuserve.com

Portfolio People   *Date:* 1997
Author: Max Comfort
Source: Random House, 20 Vauxhall Bridge Road London SW1BV 2SA
ISBN 0–7126–7727–5

Teleworking: Guidelines for Good Practice   *Date:* 1997
Author: Ursula Huws
Source: Institute for Employment Studies, Mantell Building, University of Sussex,
Brighton BN1 9RF Tel: 01273 686751 Fax: 01273 690430

Teleworking and Potential Reduction in Work Travel   *Date:* 1997
Authors: Institute for Transport Economics, Norway
Source: Tel: +47 22 573800

Teleworking: an Overview of the Research   *Date:* 1997
Author: Ursula Huws
Source: Department of Trade and Industry Information Society Initiative

Tel: ISI info line 0345 15 2000 Email: info@isi.gov.uk
Comment: authoritative survey of existing research into teleworking

IT for All *Date:* 1996
Author: H.M. Government
Source: Department of Trade and Industry Tel: ISI Info line 0345 15 2000 Email:
info@isi.gov.uk

Prepared for the future? The British and Technology *Date:* 1996
Author: Motorola
Source: Tel: 01753 575555
Web: http://www.mot.com/General/Reports/British-Tech/future.html

TeleFutures – a study on teleworking in Ireland *Date:* 1996
Authors: Imogen Bertin and Gerard O'Neill
Source: International Services, Forbairt, Wilton Park House, Wilton Place, Dublin 2
Tel: +353 1 660 2244 Contact: International Services – Declan Murphy
Web: http://www.forbairt.ie/telefutures

Teleworking – A Director's Guide *Date:* 1996
Authors: Various
Source: BT, IoD, Tel: Director Publications, 0171 730 6060

Teleworking and Gender *Date:* 1996
Author: Ursula Huws Web: http://www.dialspace.dial.pipex.com/town/parade/hg54
Source: Institute for Employment Studies, Mantell Building, University of Sussex,
Brighton BN1 9RF Tel: 01273 686751 Fax: 01273 690430.

Teleworking and Rural Development (report 27) *Date:* 1996
Author: Rural Development Commission
Source: RDC, 141 Castle Street, Salisbury, Wilts SP1 3TP Fax: 01722 432773
ISBN 1 869964 53 5

Teleworking: an overview of the research *Date:* 1996
Author: Ursula Huws
Source: Analytica, 46 Ferntower Road, London N5 2JH Tel: 0171 226 8411
Fax: 0171 226 0813

Teleworking: Thirteen Journeys to the Future of Work *Date:* 1996
Author: Andrew Bibby
Contact: Turnaround Distribution, 27 Horsell Road, London N5 1X2
Tel: 0181 829 3000

The Social Implications of Teleworking *Date:* 1996
Source: The European Foundation for the Improvement of Living and Working
Conditions, Loughlinstown House, Shankill, Co. Dublin Tel: +353 1 282 6888
Comment: A series of three informative papers covering the legal situation in a
number of European countries: 1) The legal and contractual situation of teleworkers
2) The social security position of teleworkers 3) Teleworking health and safety issues

UK Home Report Series *Date:* 1996
Author: IDC/Link
Source: Tel: 0181 987 7100
Comment: Heavyweight market research reports on the usage of PCs in the home.

Being Digital *Date:* 1995
Author: Nicholas Negroponte
Source: Coronet Books ISBN 0–340–64930–5
Comment: Negroponte works at MIT; this book is thoughtful and widely read
futurology about the Internet age.

Communicating Britain's Future *Date:* 1995
Source: Labour Party HQ Tel: 0171 277 3389
Comment: A Labour Party pre-policy document advocating greater employment
protection for teleworkers

How Vehicle Pollution Affects our Health *Date:* 1995
Source: Ashden Trust, 9 Red Lion Court, London EC4A 3EB

Review of Telework in Britain: Implications for Public Policy *Date:* 1995
Authors: Andrew Gillespie, Ronald Richardson & James Cornford
Source: University of Newcastle upon Tyne, NE1 7RU

Rural England: A Nation Committed to a Living Countryside *Date:* 1995
Authors: Dept. of Environment, Ministry of Agriculture, Fisheries & Food
Source: HMSO Publications Centre, PO Box 276, London, SW8 5DT Ref: White Paper,
ISBN 0-10-130162-6

Silicon Snake Oil *Date:* 1995
Author: Clifford Stoll
Source: Pan/Macmillan, 25 Eccleston Place, London SW1W 9NF
ISBN 0–330–34442–0
Comment: By the author of *One Flew Over the Cuckoo's Nest* – musings on life in the
digital age.

Teleworking in Ireland conference proceedings *Date:* 1995
Authors: Imogen Bertin and Brian Goggin
Source: Telework Ireland, Reagrove, Minane Bridge, Co. Cork Tel: +353 21 887300

Transport Statistics Report *Date:* 1995
Source: Department of Transport, HMSO, Publications Centre, PO Box 276, London,
SW8 5DT

Working at a Distance – UK Teleworking and its Implications *Date:* 1995
Source: Parliamentary Office of Science & Technology, Houses of Parliament,
Millbank, London Ref: ISBN 1 897941 85 4

Work at Home: Estimates from the 1991 Census *Date:* 1995
Authors: Alan Felstead and Nick Jewson
Source: Employment Gazette, Department of Employment

1994 Survey of Rural Services *Date:* 1994
Authors: BMRB Int Ltd
Source: Rural Development Commisssion (RDC), Communications Dept., 141 Castle
Street, Salisbury, Wiltshire Ref: ISBN 1 869964 44 6

Teleworking: Right for your Business, Right for your People *Date:* 1994
Author: BT
Source: BT, Tel: 0800 800 060

DTI Teleworking Study 1992–1993 *Date:* 1993
Author: Horace Mitchell
Source: Brameur Ltd, 237 High Street, Aldershot, Hants GU11 1TJ

Flexible Work in Europe 1993: Survey and Analysis *Date:* 1993
Author: Home Office Partnership
Source: HOP, The Jeffreys Building, St John's Innovation Park, Cambridge CB4 4WS

Psychological Aspects of Teleworking in Rural Areas *Date:* 1993
Author: PATRA deliverable report
Source: Available from Professor David Oborne, Psychology Department, University
of Swansea.
Comment: This report is a literature review. Other reports from the PATRA project
may also be available from Professor Oborne.

Teleworking - BT's Inverness Experience *Date: 1993*
Author: BT
Source: BT, Tel: 0800 800 060
Comment: Much of the information from all pre-1994 BT booklets is summarised in the Teleworking Explained book, listed below.

Teleworking Explained *Date: 1993*
Authors: Mike Gray, Noel Hodson, Gil Gordon
Source: John Wiley & Sons, Baffins Lane, Chichester Ref: ISBN 0 471 93975 7
Comment: Extremely comprehensive teleworking guide.

Teleworking in Britain – A report to the Employment Dept *Date: 1993*
Author: Ursula Huws
Source: Research Strategy Branch, Employment Dept, Moorfoot, Sheffield, S1 4PQ, or Tel: 0171 273 6969 ISBN PP51 16304 494 52
Comment: Thorough national survey. Ref: Research Series No. 18

Transport/Telecommunications Substitution *Date: 1993*
Authors: Horace Mitchell and Eric Trodd, Brameur Consultancy
Source: Horace Mitchell Email: 100142.31@compuserve.com

Analysis of a Major (UK) Teleworking Survey *Date: 1992*
Author: W. Murray
Source: The National Computing Centre, Oxford Road, Manchester M1 7ED

Telework – The Human Resource Implications *Date: 1992*
Author: John and Celia Stanworth
Source: Institute of Personnel Management, IPM House, Camp Rd, Wimbledon, London, SW19 4UX ISBN 085292 465 8
Comment: Very clear and comprehensive guide to issues affecting employed teleworkers and personnel management

The Economics of Teleworking *Date: 1992*
Author: Noel Hodson, SW 2000, for BT
Source: BT, Tel: 0800 800 600
Comment: A shorter version of this report is available free as part of the BT Teleworking Programme

Marketing Telecottages and Teleworking *Date: 1992*
Author: Various
Source: TCA/ACRE, Somerford Court, Somerford Road, Cirencester, Glos GL7 1TW

Telecottages: the UK Experience *Date: 1992*
Author: Various
Source: TCA/ACRE, Somerford Court, Somerford Road, Cirencester Glos GL7 1TW

Contacts and URLs

The Telework Special Interest Group was set up by a group of volunteers at the request of the DTI. It does not provide services to teleworkers but runs events such as seminars and workshops. 212 Piccadilly, London W1V 9LD Tel: 0171 917 2920 Fax: 0171 917 2836 Email: telework-request@mailbase.ac.uk

The UK Telework Platform is an association of the leading UK telework organisations and exists to promote teleworking. It runs a promotion programme funded by commercial sponsorship and organises seminars and conferences to spread understanding of telework, focussing on employers. It coordinates national activities and is the focus for European Telework Week in the UK. Warbrook Mead, Warbrook Lane, Eversley, Hants RG27 0PL Tel: 0118 962 2123 Email: optima@cix.compulink.co.uk

DTI Information Society Initiative Tel: ISI info line 0345 15 2000 Email: info@isi.gov.uk Web: http://www.isi.gov.uk

Labour Market enquiry line, Office for National Statistics, 1 Drummond Gate, London SW1V 2QQ Tel: 0171 533 6176

Management Technology Associates, Clark House, King's Road, Fleet, Hampshire GU13 9AD Tel: 01252 812 252 Fax: 01252 815 702, Email: 100142.31@compuserve.com. Some of MTA's teleworking reports are available at http://mtanet.co.uk

http://www.labour.org.uk/views/info-highway/social.html Labour party policy document on the Information Superhighway

http://www.open.gov.uk/oftel/oftelhm.htm is a report on proposed changes to the obligation for voice telephony providers to supply universal service.

EA Technology (EU SAVE programme). Contact Andrew Wright, tel 0151 347 2364

http://www.att.com/Telecommute_America is Telecommute America!

Former *Teleworker* editor Barnaby Page has a series of articles on teleworking available at http://www.compulink.co.uk/~ludlow/ including topics such as environmental impacts, urban planning and the developing world, and the impact of flexible working on equal opportunities issues.

http://www.dnai.com/~isdw The Institute for the Study of Distributed Work has a number of academic resources available.

http://www.eclipse.co.uk/pens/bibby/telework.html is journalist Andrew Bibby's home pages which contain a number of articles on telework.

http://www.fedworld.gov - Telecommuting evaluation information also available by telnetting to fedworld.gov (IP address 192.239.92.203)

The Telefutures report is available online at http://www.forbairt.ie/telefutures

http://www.gilgordon.com Gil Gordon's website is a mine of useful information.

http://www.ghbg.org.uk gives pointers on how to take advantage of the ISI initiative.

http://www.icbl.hw.ac.uk:80/bill/telework/conts.html - A useful site from Heriott Watt University in Scotland including http://www.icbl.hw.ac.uk Community Teleservices International

http://www.isi.gov.uk is the address for the UK's Dept of Trade and Industry's new "Information Society Initiative", targeted at raising business awareness and use of Internet, open electronic networking etc.

European Telework Development project, which maintains the European Telework Online (ETO) pages at http://www.eto.org.uk.

ETO list server for journalists providing press releases from IT companies: http://www.newsdesk.com Tel: 0115 945 7000 Fax: 0115 984 6526 Contact: Catriona Riddler, Newsdesk International

http://ourworld.compuserve.com/homepages/Teleworker is some information from the Teleworker magazine

http://www.tca.org.uk is the location for the TCA web pages.

The International Flexwork Forum in Tokyo is accessible at iff-info@apic.or.jp

The Source – IT media information service which invites information on forthcoming teleworking events http://www.thesource.dwpub.com

Ursula Huws website: http://www.dialspace.dial.pipex.com/town/parade/hg54

Implementing teleworking

There are four main routes by which teleworking is implemented, which depend on the existing organisation structure. Your organisation may be a "hybrid" suitable for more than one route which you should identify.

1. In conventional organisations, **planned introduction of teleworking** usually involves three identifiable stages – the idea, the trial and the "contagion" by which the practice spreads out from the trial to widespread usage within the organisation. In this scenario, teleworking is no different from other changes that are introduced within organisations – it has to be justified, planned, and carried out with the consent of the people it will affect.

2. **Tacit teleworking** describes another method by which teleworking spreads in conventional organisations, usually through the practices of a management elite (who perhaps insist on being given laptops and modems so they can telework after hours or on the road). The elite may consist of individuals or groups who have high visibility and influence in the organisation. Elites sometimes include external figures such as consultants, academics or interest groups. They may not have formal authority, but they do have the attention of those in authority.

3. In flexible organisations, such as practices of professionals and some academic organisations, **teleworking is often endemic**. For example, at the Open University, which as its core business deals with remotely located students using teletechnology, there is an established tradition of email use and flexible work arrangements which has grown up on an ad hoc basis. Small virtual organisations sometimes begin from a distributed, flexible working basis. In these types of organisations, a review of the implementation of "endemic" telework arrangements covering issues such as software standardisation and training can be very productive.

Gil Gordon's US-based *Telecommuting Review* is one of the best known periodicals for teleworkers. His upbeat resolutions for 1996 were:

- **stop dabbling, start doing** – all the evidence from telework trials is that they work, so don't be tentative and feed the fears or the sceptics but "just do it".

- **stop trying, start testing** – teleworking isn't technology dependent, but whatever technology you do use, test it properly for suitability – don't just try it out tentatively

- **stop grovelling, start grabbing** – stop scraping and bowing for permission to give teleworking a trial – be assertive.

4. For some, the introduction of teleworking may accompany a **move to self-employment,** or be a method of reducing overheads and improving productivity for an existing small business.

This chapter looks at the steps involved in introducing teleworking to a conventional organisation, but many of the points made are relevant to flexible or virtual organisations, and to the self-employed.

Stages of implementation

Feasibility studies

It is worthwhile to assess the existing level of tacit teleworking at the beginning of any attempt to trial teleworking. Many personnel and human resource departments have no idea of the extent of tacit teleworking going on in their organisations – a celebrated exercise at the World Bank indicated that there were no teleworkers according to the human resources department, but a different story was told by the IT department – over 1,000 telecoms links being used for around 240,000 man days per year.

The feasibility study should outline the business case – including the operational, strategic, cost or employee advantages to be gained. If there are no gains to be made, don't proceed! The study should give an implementation plan covering the stages given above, and identify the main problems likely to be encountered and suggest solutions. This handbook does not cover cost benefit evaluations and methods in detail because they are admirably handled in BT's manual *Teleworking Explained* – the one book every manager implementing teleworking should buy.

Identifying suitable teleworking jobs

In order to select appropriate departments, some consideration needs to be given to the jobs that are encompassed. Some categories were listed in the previous chapter on page 5.

The stages involved in assessing a change to teleworking are:

- *feasibility study*
- *identifying suitable jobs for teleworking*
- *setting up a pilot project*
- *selecting suitable staff members*
- *drafting and agreeing changes to contracts and agreements*
- *arranging training*
- *installing the home office, mobile office or hotdesking system*
- *providing continuing support to teleworkers*
- *monitoring and evaluating the pilot*

11,000 into 3,000 won't go... except in Stoke

Stoke City Council is looking at teleworking to solve a major problem: the transfer of 8,000 staff from the county to the city council. Kevin Taylor, management consultant for the council explains: "Our initial interest in teleworking came from the need to provide extra office accommodation and parking for education and social services staff – we needed to look at the alternatives." Seven staff from the MIS department made up the pilot project, but Kevin believes issuing them with mobile phones was an error.

"There were excessive call costs incurred by the mobile phones and we want to use our own virtual private telephone network in future. This would also allow calls to be passed straight to the teleworkers," Kevin commented. Feedback from the teleworkers was largely positive with six out of the seven hoping to continue to telework. Their worries were mainly to do with career development and training opportunities, plus the "teleshirking" syndrome. "The teleworkers' colleagues saw the advantages as being home comforts and spending time with the family, while the teleworkers themselves cited increased productivity and better motivation. Nevertheless, those who came up with the negative aspects said they would like to do it if given a chance."

The main problem for customers was communication. One-third said they found it more difficult to get hold of the teleworkers due to calls being routed around the office instead of direct to the teleworker. Some customers, used to programmers nipping up the stairs to help them out in person, also found adapting to teleworking more problematical than others.

A classic example where teleworking has been practised for a number of years is journalism. Many journalists work remotely from their employer processing information from one form to another. The output is easily measured (pay rates for freelances are per thousand words) and the work is delivered by electronic means (fax, email or telephone). Technology has made it increasingly easy for journalists to deliver both text and images from remote locations, and many journalists prefer the peace of a home office to the hectic clatter of a newsroom, though most also like to visit the publication offices for social contact, feedback and ideas. In its extreme form the editorial office can simply be an administrative centre co-ordinating the various journalistic inputs.

In the long term, introducing teleworking may give the company access to the skills of former staff members who have left due to early retirement, family reasons, travel difficulties and so on, increasing the available skill pool and helping companies to maintain the latest buzz word, "corporate memory".

Setting up a pilot project

The first step is to establish a team for the teleworking pilot. You will need a project manager, clear responsibilities and reporting arrangements, and links to a sponsoring board member. The person driving the pilot project should have a neutral outlook on teleworking – neither a champion for teleworking nor a total sceptic – to ensure a measured and reasoned approach to the study. A number of organisations offer consultancy in telework trials and feasibility studies. You may not need to use a consultancy at all, but it is worthwhile talking to consultants to get an idea of the areas they cover – you may find you go back to them at a later stage for specialist help with a particular area of the project.

The second step is to identify the parameters that will be used to assess the success of the pilot – without a clear measure of success or failure it will be hard to spread teleworking beyond the pilot study to other areas. In looking at how to evaluate the pilot project, the team needs to bear in mind whether the function chosen for the project is limited to that unit, or whether it is representative of the wider activities of the company. A common error is to attempt the pilot project too quickly – a realistic timetable allows time for problems to develop and be resolved without constant "firefighting", and anxieties among those involved. The project should build in opportunities for individual and group meetings to review progress in order to quickly identify and resolve teething problems.

Teleworking implementation costs

These costs, based on a trial in an information systems department were presented at the TCA's 1996 conference. The costs are per annum with most costs averaged over three years.

PC hardware and software support	£1400
Office dial-in facilities (LAN access)	£126
ISDN telephone installation	£133
ISDN telephone line rental and usage	£937
Furniture	£110
Sundry setup and support expenses	£2901
TOTAL	**£5607**

Payback

Two additional hours per week	£4000
Two sick days a year saved	£700
10% productivity improvement	£2800
Staff recruitment and training savings	£1000
Two days a year travel disruption saved	£700
TOTAL	**£9,200**

The 1997 Small World Connections/*Flexible Working* magazine corporate teleworking survey reported average setup costs for a home based teleworker of £3,500 with annual running costs of about £1,500. Average setup costs for a nomadic teleworker were £3,700, with maintenance costs of £2,250.

Scottish Widows recruits full-time teleworkers

Pensions company Scottish Widows has been recruiting teleworkers for over four years. According to Duncan McKechnie, head of direct sales, the effect on costs of using homeworkers, and of operating a call centre, have been considerable. Turnover and efficiency are both up. "Productivity is far greater than when we had office-based staff. We have people with exceptional abilities and self-discipline and the quality of work is the highest I have ever experienced. Let's face it, the social aspects of work can waste time as well as cause mistakes to happen."

Scottish Widows used to have a network of ten branches in the UK, which have gradually been closed as the teleworking thrust increased. Team manager Gill Price stresses that the recruitment process is extremely competitive. Over 150 applications were made to Scottish Widows as a result of an advert placed in *The Teleworker* magazine. The homeworkers provide the Edinburgh call centre with secretarial support. Formal supervisions take place once a month, either by telephone or face to face. Day to day work scheduling is handled remotely through the computer system.

Gill Price explains: "Many good quality people sent CVs to us, but our work is very specialised. To date we have recruited just two from the 150 who applied. Our interview processes are every bit as stringent as if we were recruiting for office-based staff. We need the chemistry to be just right to ensure that the employer/employee relationship has the best possible chance of success." Gill herself is a teleworker who is now responsible for a team of over two dozen home-based staff. "We can employ a lot of high quality individuals who would otherwise be unable to work due to family commitments", she confirms.

The problem most widely encountered in teleworking trials is "middle management syndrome", which describes the difficulties encountered in management cultures where status depends on the number of people reporting to a manager. These managers like to see staff sitting at their desks and find it hard to make the change from eyeball management to managing by results. They can become a major obstacle to an effective trial.

Staff selection

It may be that teleworking is being offered to staff with caring responsibilities or with a particular reason to want to work from home – in which case the staff will be self-selecting. In more broadly based selections, experience has shown that some people are unsuited to the demands that teleworking may place on them. Those who think they are suited and wish to volunteer may not be. In particular, introverted people who are poor communicators are unlikely to adapt easily but may be attracted by the solitary workstyle. On occasion, personnel problems may arise if someone who is keen on teleworking is denied the chance to participate in a trial due to unfavourable personality traits. Managers must try to foresee such difficulties and develop workarounds if the trial is to run smoothly.

Some companies have used psychometric tests and counselling to ensure that applicants are likely to make a success of the change. The crucial personality traits are good decision making, effective problem solving and skills in self and time management – these are the people who will take the teleworking opportunity and run with it.

Kevin Curran and Geoff Williams in their *Manual of Remote Working* (1997) emphasise that although there are no personality inventories on the market which specifically measure suitability for working at home, several provide information about traits essential for remote working such as level of need for contact with others, self discipline and preference for certain kinds of work. These inventories include the Work Environment Scale, the Myers-Briggs Type Indicator and the Work Style Reference Inventory. However, use of psychometric testing is considered controversial and unfair by many HR professionals and trade unions.

Some employers may consider that established mature staff are more likely to want to telework and more likely to be successful at it. Staff selection, as with inspection of home premises for health and safety reasons, is a sensitive issue that needs to be handled carefully.

The physical situation in a staff member's home is also important to selection – a visit by a manager prior to beginning a telework trial to assess any problems is recommended, and investigations into the local telecoms infrastructure are vital. Some areas may have old fashioned exchanges which are unsuitable for high speed modem traffic, or else line quality to a

---

Nationwide saves on training and recruiting costs

The Nationwide Building Society has joined a growing group of financial services companies taking advantage of teleworking to retain skilled staff. Employee Relations manager Denise Walker explains: "We employ teleworkers because we want to try and access people with experience who prefer to work from home – such as mothers with small children."

Nationwide has had a policy of allowing employees to request the option of homeworking from their managers for several years. There are now around 300 teleworkers out of a total workforce of 12,000. Some of the teleworkers are involved in helping to shortlist recruitment candidates for retail sales positions through telephone interviews. Teleworking is also being considered in the estates department, responsible for buildings administration.

Walker stresses "Teleworking needs a different type of manager who can manage people they can't see, remembering for instance to include all teleworking employees in messages which are automatically circulated." The company is actively looking for opportunities to develop the teleworking option further.

Some organisations using teleworkers in Britain (August 1997)

Company	Type of work	Numbers
Local Authorities		
Aberdeen City Council	n/a	n/a
Birmingham City Council	Housing Department consultants	100
Cambridgeshire County Council	Social services, education and building standards	n/a
Dorset County Council	Chief Exec's office and personnel	20
Hertfordshire County Council	Oasis telecentres	n/a
Horsham District Council	Councillor's pilot scheme	9
Kent County Council	Social services, occupational therapists, educational psychologists, consultants	67
Leicester City Council	Computing and telecoms	3
London Borough of Brent	Various	40+
London Borough of Enfield	Various	52
London Borough of Sutton	Environmental services, planners, architects	15
North Wiltshire District Council	Pilot scheme for councillors also used by staff	10–20
Oxfordshire County Council	Social Services	250
Richmond on Thames B.C.	Pilot later this year	5–10
South Hams District Council	All departments	50
Stoke-on-Trent City Council	Analyst programmers pilot	7
Suffolk County Council	Social services, trading standards, technical and professional workers	30
Surrey County Council	Telecentre-based teachers, personnel officers, social services, environmental health, planners and business support	236
Wiltshire County Council	n/a	n/a
Financial Services		
Allied Dunbar	Various	1%
Barclays Bank	Personnel, policy development	n/a
Britannia Building Society	Word processing	5
Co-operative Bank	Debt collection and others	40
Ellis and Buckle Claims Mgt	Telephone researchers	n/a
Lloyds TSB	Systems developers	180
Lombard North Central	n/a	n/a
National Westminster Bank	n/a	n/a
Royal Bank of Scotland	Research consultants	34
Royal Sun Alliance	n/a	n/a
Scottish Widows	Financial Advisers, secretarial and admin staff	70+
Skandia Life	Programmers, sales, managers	25+

Company	Type of work	Numbers
Publishing and media		
Aldershot News	Sub-editor	1
BBC Southampton	Journalists	8
Classic FM	Disc jockey	1
Crossaig Huw Baynham	Editors	60
EMAP	Sub-editors, layout, production	n/a
OUP	Publishing work	50
Computers and IT		
3M	Marketing	1
BT	Various	825
Cable & Wireless	Various	2,000
Canon UK	HR, training, sales, eng., support	1,100
Cisco	Sales	360
Compaq	n/a	n/a
DEC	Various	1500
Evonet Telecoms	Consultants	n/a
Hewlett Packard	Sales, training, engineers, managers, professionals	100
ICL	Systems support, development documentation	300
Integral Solutions	Consultant	1
Tektronix UK	n/a	n/a
Unisys	n/a	500
Others		
Asda	Surveyors	n/a
Bailey Postner	Secretarial	n/a
British Airways	Information management	12
British Gas	Fitters, training, info. specialists	7,000
Business Space	Executive coordinators, secretaries	30
Coca Cola/Schweppes	Sales, merchandising mgrs, account execs, sales field reps	250
Davis & Co. Solicitors	Solicitors	20
Drake Beam Morin	Support	3
GlaxoWellcome	n/a	n/a
Glenigan (business info)	Telephone researchers	3
ICI	Sales staff	n/a
Jupiter Tyndall Merlin	Head, environmental research	1
Lily Industries	Sales Force	n/a
Manchester TEC	Business advisers	9
Open University	Sales force and academics	50
Rank Xerox	n/a	n/a
Royal Mail Consulting	Middle and senior mgrs	100
SmithKline Beecham	IT staff	n/a
University of Wolverhampton	Lecturers	40
WWF	Regional organisers	15

teleworker's home can be poor due to long runs of overhead poles. Availability of ISDN services should also be checked (see p. 47). It is also important that any disruption to the home caused by installation of equipment be kept to a minimum and negotiated with the staff member and their family in advance. Issues which need to be borne in mind in designing the home office are covered in Chapter 8, *Staying safe and legal* and in the Fittings and Furniture section of Chapter 12, *Teleworking equipment.*

Agreements and contracts

Issues related to agreements, contracts and trade unions are covered in Chapter 3, *Agreements and unions.* Where teleworking schemes involve a degree of part-time work or the use of sub-contractors apparently operating under self-employed working arrangements, it is important to clarify the arrangements with the relevant authorities in order to ensure that the employer does not incur liability for the contractor's tax and national insurance payments. This is also covered in Chapter 8, *Staying safe and legal.*

Training

Both management and staff will need training in order to adapt to the new circumstances. Much of this will focus on effective communication. Management in particular may need to adapt to a new culture – managing by results – which requires skills in the areas of delegation, co-ordination and orchestration. The common thread to the new management skills is improving interpersonal skills for a work environment involving less authority and more trust.

Specific management training material may be needed to cover:

- specifying aims and criteria clearly
- agreeing and negotiating work tasks
- relating pay to performance (where appropriate)
- conflict resolution skills for remotely based teams

Colleagues will also need to be informed of the teleworking initiative, including the company reasons for introducing it, who is managing the project and what the outcomes are likely to be, as well as how they will be measured. Open information should dampen speculation about the long term teleworking intentions of the company and also assist the teleworkers in their communications with non-teleworking colleagues.

Other training strategies may include a programme of workshops for new teleworkers, allowing new teleworkers to shadow more experienced teleworkers, and allocating mentors to the teleworkers. Specific IT training modules will probably be required, such as the use of dial-up email via a modem, which will be new to those used to using office Local Area Networks (LANs).

It is also important to look at the context of any other organisational changes which may be occurring at the same time. Often teleworking is introduced as part of a series of changes, and may occasionally be seen as taking things a step too far – one corporate which has pioneered teleworking reported that during its introduction of teleworking, there were 14 different change programmes going on within the company, and the teleworking trial suffered from the level of confusion introduced by the number of simultaneous changes occurring. The same experienced company also reported that when broadening a trial to other areas of the company, it is important to keep assessing different needs. Commuting pressures in London may not be quite the same sort of driver to teleworking in a comfortable regional office located on the outskirts of town.

Providing continuing support

Those who have been teleworking for some years report that lack of positive feedback becomes an increasing problem. Often teleworkers only receive feedback when there is a problem to be solved or a deadline to be met – they can get left out of team back-slapping when a contract is won or a customer's letter of satisfaction is posted on the office noticeboard. Rank Xerox, veteran of long term widescale use of teleworkers, takes the view that communications are also important to team building. Teleworkers are kept on circulation lists, listed in the company directory, invited to departmental meetings and invited to social functions.

The teleworking organisation is devoid of much of the informal communication that comes from people working in close proximity and needs to find a way of replacing the useful parts of this. However, the introduction of teleworking for part of a department can lead to a "them and us" situation. Management may need to think of measures to discourage this split (one employer encouraged a lottery syndicate to encompass all team members rather than just those "in the office").

Experienced telework managers have also reported the need to develop a "sixth sense" about detecting when teleworkers have a personal problem during telephone conversations. Don't forget that teleworking does not necessarily mean working at home in isolation 5 days per week, 20 days per month. A sensible teleworking programme should include regular face-to-face management meetings as well as opportunities for colleagues to mix at the office.

The pilot project team needs to create a support function which will deal with both technical and managerial issues arising from the project. In the main, these issues will be provision of technical support for computer and other equipment usage, and continuing management contact covering the following areas:

- reviewing performance
- determining pay and bonuses
- agreeing goals and improvements in performance
- individual development – counselling and training
- training (both giving and receiving)
- general gossip and banter that forms part of all working life
- providing space for "brainstorming", feedback and general discussion on the operation of the department.

The fact that the teleworker is now responsible for everything that goes on in the home office, including all supplies, can easily be overlooked. Hence it may also be wise to create a small budget for teleworkers to compensate for the extra burden – this could include paying for office cleaning, taking post, getting office supplies *etc*. Another solution is to arrange for a local supply of stationery, paid for from the central office. Review arrangements for petty cash expenses.

Keeping in touch

Careful choice has to be made to ensure that the most appropriate communications means are used for the different types of information. The communication needs to be clear and unambiguous and should provide a record of any agreements for action. The overall system should also ensure teleworkers are kept informed, to reduce any feelings of isolation.

A set of communications guidelines could be established to take into account the cost, convenience and practicality of different communication methods, their merits and recommended uses for different applications. The excellent guide *Teleworking Explained* contains a sample table listing types of office communication and how they should be achieved, which can be adapted as the basis of the policy.

County Council telecentre improves productivity and motivation

Surrey County Council opened its Epsom neighbourhood telecentre in September 1997. An evaluation six months later showed two thirds of those using the £88,000 centre felt it improved their productivity and motivation. The other third felt positively about the centre but had not used it enough to comment further.

Benefits listed by users of the centre included a reduction in travel to work time, an increase of time which could be spent with the family, removal of stressful commuter journeys and improved concentration. Drawbacks included "knowing how to contact staff... staff unavailable when needed urgently". Users of the centre included teachers, personnel officers, social workers, environmental health officers, planning officers and business support officers. The evaluation report states: "flexible working and property rationalisation are mutually compatible and together can produce substantial benefits in increased productivity, improved service delivery and substantial cost savings.

The telecentre facilities include: free car park; open plan area for 9 people (7 desks with PCs, 2 desks free for laptop use); a quiet room for 2 people (2 desks with PCs); a very quiet room for 1 person (1 desk with PC); telephones on all desks; meeting/interview room; conference room for ten people; reception/waiting area; kitchen facilities; telecentre support officers to help and suport users; photocopier, printer, virus checker, fax machine. Use of the centre is free until March 1998, when its role will be reviewed. http://www.surreycc.gov.uk/telecentre

For example, an urgent request for administrative work may well be best faxed, including details of when the task needs completing and so on. The fax can be annotated and returned, easily confirming the receipt of the request and highlighting any ambiguities. An electronic mail message in contrast may well go unnoticed for some time, unless there are guidelines for frequency of collecting email.

Telephone

The telephone is a vital way of reinforcing other communications – for example details passed through by fax and email can be followed up with a phone call to talk through and develop a greater comprehension, or to negotiate a problem. But at the end of a phone call, without some kind of written backup it is possible for two different interpretations of the topic to persist. The telephone is a useful way of informally airing problems where fax or electronic mail are too constraining, formal, or unambiguous. The disadvantage of the telephone is that it requires the simultaneous presence of both callers, and the syndrome of "telephone tag" between busy people is all too familiar. Teleworkers may also find continuous calling from the employer causes interruption to their work and is irritating.

Fax

Fax provides a good method of getting short, sometimes urgent, instructions across and delivering copies of documents that may be held in one location but not the other. Because faxes physically appear in the teleworker's office, they are good for urgent documents – in contrast to email which requires the teleworker to actively log on and check whether any mail is waiting. However, fax limits the subsequent processing of the information as it is not delivered in a computer-readable form (even if you use a fax modem, the fax transmitted to the computer is a graphical image, not editable text). Fax also provides a way of transmitting information quickly and more reliably to countries with a slow or unreliable postal service.

There can be a temptation to fax everything to save taking it to the post office. But faxing large documents is wasteful and if the recipient does not have a plain paper fax, then the document needs recopying from easily-damaged thermal paper in order to preserve it.

Post

Teleworkers usually need to move physical documents around by post. The organisation should instigate a method of ensuring that company mail is regularly delivered to the teleworker – for example pigeon holes can be allocated and regularly swept by the internal system. It will probably also be necessary to make arrangements for urgent deliveries via courier on occasion. The Royal Mail quotes that 92% of first class deliveries arrive next day, but it is reasonable to assume that the 8% that don't are to locations off the beaten track – such as to rurally-based teleworkers. Post in rural areas may arrive late and leave early, so specific information on the limits to local postal services is important and may vary for the range of locations where the company's teleworkers are based.

Email

Email is a good way of transmitting information that needs to be reworked by the recipient, and of keeping tabs on documents involved in a large number of projects, since most email readers provide an electronic filing system for messages. All commonly used email networks are "store and forward" systems which means the person at the other end doesn't have to be online at the same time to receive the message – it is stored on the system until the recipient logs on to collect it. Other applications include documents which need collaborative work, details of progress against a plan, circulating general memos to a large group and maintaining regular background contact. It is also a good way of providing quick technical fixes for software – these can be "zipped" (compacted) and sent to the user very quickly. Most systems can provide receipts which return a message to confirm the original document has been picked up by the recipient, which can prove a useful project management tool.

Email is excellent for developing documents and technical specs through the use of different fonts or colours or annotations in a mutually used word

Case study: Digital

Digital Equipment Corporation (DEC) has long been seen as a teleworking pioneer. According to DEC's former teleworking consultant Stephen Jupp: "we have saved £16m per annum in costs worldwide through teleworking and we have seen a 20–40% growth in productivity". DEC currently has 9,000 out of a worldwide workforce of 65,000 teleworking, and the UK operation has over one-third teleworkers, with 1,500 out of 3,500 home working.

There is no particular selection process, staff just ask if they want to telework, but the company has been keen to encourage teleworking where lease breaks occurred so that by teleworking a workforce they could dispose of a building. Once individuals decide to telework, DEC provides two courses, one to help them understand the differences between homeworking and office working, thinking through what work is all about. The other covers the practical side, such as accessing mail from home, handling client calls to home, and recording telephone usage.

processing package. The annotations show the additions and developments in a document passing through a team evaluation. Email is also a highly cost effective communications medium to international locations – a conversation of sorts can be held across thousands of miles and several time zones. Ironically a conversation with, say Australia, works better by email than a local one would, as the time phase difference means that email communications are less likely to cross.

Email generally makes a poor discussion medium and with the absence of intonation can sometimes be misinterpreted when opinions and views are conveyed. This has led to an etiquette around its use with various symbols and abbreviations, covered in Chapter 9, *Email and online Services.*

Many companies now have their own World Wide Web servers and password protected ftp file transfer servers. These can be used to supply teleworkers with a "library" of corporate information and documents which can be browsed from the teleworker's remote site when needed and downloaded onto the teleworker's computer. Web servers are also useful for providing software tools, a general noticeboard, news and other functions to staff. Internally focused web servers are usually called intranets, and can also be used to link workers at a number of sites. Where Web servers are not available, widespread distribution of corporate notices can take place by email, and these communications have largely replaced the traditional office memo in a number of organisations.

Equipment requirements

More detailed information on teleworker equipment and home offices is given in chapters 8 and 12, including issues of business rates, changes to MIRAS relief for the employee, and selection of hardware. This section specifically covers issues affecting organisations setting up a home office for an employee or telecommuters.

General considerations

In principle all equipment required should be supplied by, and remain the property of, the employer. As a ballpark guide to costs, a recent survey by Bill Murray reported in *Flexible Working* magazine gave an estimated average setup cost per teleworker of £2,250–£3,500, with annual costs (heat, lighting, use of home as office) ranging from around £1,000 to £1,500 per employee.

Equipment should be ergonomically sound especially where repetitive movements are likely to occur. Furniture should provide adjustment for correct working heights – a good quality, comfortable, adjustable chair is especially important. Lighting should also be reviewed as home lighting is unlikely on its own to be adequate for office work. As part of the health and safety requirements, the employer should consider inspecting all home office equipment for ergonomics and safety and should organise regular inspections to test for electrical safety as with all other company equipment.

Veteran teleworkers tend to favour a separate building for the home office to give a work environment away from the potential distraction of the home, to assist with "switching off" at the end of the day and to prevent work material becoming distributed around the house. Failing a separate office, the space for the home office should be carefully chosen to take it out of the main family thoroughfare – ideally it should be lockable.

Often home spaces are characterised by lack of space, so good use of available room needs to be made. Both office and home furniture manufacturers are beginning to recognise the home office as a new market and produce special ranges. Typical features incorporated are lock-away desks and cabinets where computers can be kept, space saving furniture (*eg* wall beds, high level shelving) and home-friendly office furniture (for example made of pine to match home decor).

Case study: Lombard North Central

Lombard undertook a two year teleworking trial for 10 professionals. All changes in working conditions were drafted into existing employment contracts. Managers visited worker's homes to advise on health, safety and security issues. The final results initially showed 20% productivity gains, which settled down to 10% above normal, but the quality of work also improved. Sick leave reduced by 50%, from the company's average of six days a year to three days.

Telephone equipment

A separate line is recommended in order to ensure that personal and work calls are distinguishable. This is desirable for both professional and psychological reasons. The phone costs should be paid for directly by the employer so that there is no perceived tax benefit. Additional services now available for standard telephone lines include call diversion, divert on busy, and conference calling, all of which are available at minimal cost and assist the teleworker in handling calls. Where much time is spent on the phone, hands free operation should be available and in some work situations such as technical support, a headset allowing more comfortable operation and less risk of strain injuries can be a boon. A cordless phone may also be useful to allow the teleworker the freedom of the house without missing calls.

Where a fax machine is required, an additional line rather than a line shared between telephone and fax is recommended. This has the advantage of allowing the teleworker to receive and send faxes whilst using the telephone and avoids annoying busy lines due to fax traffic. If significant online work is being performed a separate line for the modem should also be installed. If the use is not significant, sharing with the fax line should be adequate.

Increasingly, transferable personal numbers are being used. A permanent or personal number is rented by the company which can be linked to the teleworker's existing line. This means that if the teleworker relocates or moves back into the central office the number remains the same. When employees leave the company the number is effectively assigned to a company position and can simply be reassigned to the next person taking up that position.

Message taking

Corporate voice mail systems are often used to take messages for teleworkers, but a conventional answering machine is flexible and easily controlled and may well be a simpler solution. Users should be encouraged to provide a message which is dated, states when the teleworker will be next available, and if an alternative number can be called. A number of companies offer message taking services, which use call diversion from the teleworker's home and caller line identification tools to create a customised response.

ISDN (Integrated Services Digital Network) lines

With more sophisticated requirements, and larger amounts of data transfer, a high speed digital ISDN line may be appropriate. This type of line allows faster transfer of data, high quality voice communication and videoconferencing. A number of devices can share the same ISDN line, so only one is likely to be required per teleworker. ISDN is not available on some older exchanges, and enquiries will need to be made with your telephone supplier for specific locations, especially in rural areas.

ISDN lines are increasingly used for personal videoconferencing equipment. The equipment is fast reducing in cost and can be installed on a PC. It consists of a camera which is attached to the PC monitor or stands on a separate stalk, an ISDN connector, cards which fit into the PC, and software. The videophone, in addition to providing visual images, can transmit files and allow application sharing between remote users.

Another benefit of ISDN is that it can be used to provide an apparent continuous link to a remote computer whilst in fact disconnecting the line and saving call charges when there is no activity. This enables the line costs for remote staff accessing central databases to be substantially reduced, particularly if the access is intermittent. The technique is known as spoofing (this is also available on standard phone lines but is not as "transparent" in its operation owing to the lower speeds available). Spoofing is so called because it convinces the linked computers that a connection still exists even though the line may well have been "timed out". Algorithms controlling the disconnection point will take into account the tariff system – allowing, for example, for minimum call charges.

ACD (Automated Call Distribution systems)

The technology employed for the well-publicised BT Directory Enquiries project included the ability to distribute calls from a central location with an Automated Call Distribution system as well as links to a central database, electronic mail and videophone support. ACD systems allow incoming calls to be distributed to homebased teleworkers, giving an even loading amongst operators and equalising the caller response time. The degree of technology employed for clerical and administrative staff carrying out "call centre" type duties is quite likely to be greater than that for professional teleworkers.

The BT system used the two channels available through the ISDN2 digital phone line connection – on one channel voice and data were combined for transmission using a multiplexor. The other channel was used for videophone transmission. A further BT trial underway in Southampton has dispensed with the video link, but maintained the other equipment.

PCs and technical support

The computer, and in particular the software to be used, should be compatible with that available at the head office allowing greater flexibility, compatibility and support. This also eases the teleworkers transition to the home office and, where necessary, back to using the head office base. Technical support mechanisms should prioritise the teleworker who may well be isolated and unable to work without a functioning PC – in contrast to central office-based colleagues. For companies without their own means of nationwide equipment support, it may be worth looking at subscribing to a technical support service which can ensure speedy repair, assistance or replacement of equipment at teleworkers' homes.

Software for helping teams of people to work together is often known as

Case study: Oxfordshire County Council

Oxfordshire County Council employs 16,000 people, 80% of them female, and 57% part-timers, many of whom work flexitime. Recently, the Council introduced a flexiplace scheme, as part of a bottom-up, grass roots initiative to allow working from home where appropriate. Homeworking is always voluntary, and employees can return to conventional arrangements if they wish.

The prime consideration is that there should be no effects on the level and quality of the service provided. To date the scheme has been largely "budget neutral" – costs have to be met from the normal operating budget of the relevant department, and there have been no major workspace savings. The Council is now looking at establishing neighbourhood work centres around the county for employees who, for example, need to send the occasional fax but whose work does not justify purchase of an individual fax machine.

A survey of travel costs showed that the Council was spending around £3 million on car allowances and other costs. Journeys ranged from 290 miles a month for a social worker to 1,135 miles a month for an engineering works manager – teleworking is helping to reduce these costs and their associated environmental burdens.

Personnel officer Hilary Simpson stresses that giving employees flexibility about where they work is "an efficiency issue, an environmental issue and an equal opportunities issue", and the Council has won a Working Mothers Association Employer of the Year award for its activities. Equipment used includes faxes, mobile phones, answerphones, pagers and laptop computers.

Example 1

Gordon Copping, animal health inspector, can now drive straight from home to markets in North Oxfordshire without reporting to the head office in South Oxfordshire first. The Council is making major savings on the cost of journeys back to base, freeing the inspectors to devote more of their time to looking after animal welfare.

Example 2

Pam Block is a management accountant in the department of leisure and arts, and works a 30 hour week contract, of which 10 hours are now home-based. "I tend to work in the office between the hours when my children are at school. Then at home I usually work in the evenings when I can really get my head down."

Example 3

Debbie Dent is head of the trading standards information unit and works 25 hours a week. Normally she spends mornings in the Oxford office, and then does the rest of her work from home.

groupware. The most common application of groupware is customer tracking. For example, where a customer rings up a bank to enquire about a loan, a customer tracking form is automatically created. From that point forward, every telephone call, meeting, piece of correspondence and so on can be documented on the tracking form – gone are the problems of an employee being out sick with crucial documents locked away in their office. Groupware can also allow several people to work on the same document – all the team download the document and make their changes. The groupware software recognises which parts of the document have been changed and copies only those parts back to the central computer, indicating the author of the changes in each instance.

An example of groupware in action is the use of Lotus Notes by the Henley Management College in its global classroom project to overcome the geographical barriers to distance learning. Henley has adopted groupware technology to support its 7,000 distance learning students worldwide, providing interaction with peers, tutors, staff and other information sources. Electronic support for students using PCs and modems started in 1988. This interaction complements the written course materials, workshops, telephone helpline and newsletters also supplied. Henley adopted Lotus Notes in early 1994.

The key objectives were to provide students interaction with a peer group of students, a sense of community and the lasting networking opportunities that those offer, interaction with tutors and access to the Henley library. Students are provided with a remote version of Lotus Notes on their PC so that they can work on databases off-line – when convenient, they use a modem to "replicate" their databases with those on Henley's server. Students can send electronic mail, search databases and retrieve and send files, as well as being able to participate in electronic discussions led by Henley faculty. They can read profiles of other Notes users, and network with those with similar interests. The electronic booking of workshops and ordering of papers is in place; electronic submission and marking of assignments and course works was launched in 1996.

A tutor from New Zealand explains: "When I receive a query from a student on Notes, I have time to give a full answer with accurate references, indeed I can give the student a mini tutorial, and it will also be available to other students. The student raising the query gets the benefit of one to one tuition but other students can get involved if they wish."

Security

Physical security and insurance issues are covered in detail in Chapter 8, *Staying safe and legal.* Many commercial insurers have developed specific home office policies to reflect the move to teleworking, and the lower risk involved in insuring home offices. Domestic insurance policies will not normally cover home office equipment including PCs, and employees should be instructed to notify their home contents insurers of their intention to work from home.

The risk to data security will depend on the value and sensitivity of the data being handled. The solution is to develop procedures appropriate to these levels of importance. Start by reviewing existing procedures and identify processes which introduce an additional hazard by virtue of being remote. Procedures should cover a series of security layers applied to use of personal computers, access to central computing facilities (using for example dial-back facilities to ensure that an authorised number is linking in, also password control) and data transmission. It may be advisable to retain certain tasks for central processing rather than sending them out to the teleworkers, involving reallocation of some duties. Bear in mind that hacking is still a relatively rare phenomenon, and consult specialists in techniques such as firewalling Internet servers where necessary.

Security surveys show that the most likely causes of problems are not viruses or hacking, but more basic issues such as power cuts, hard disk crashes or fire damage, all of which can be minimised as risks by appropriate procedures. An important preventive step is therefore to ensure the integrity of data – having procedures and tools to cover backup procedures and the introduction of viruses. There are companies which offer remote backup facilities, allowing automatic dial up and uploading of data to a central repository by teleworkers.

It may be necessary to make specific instructions concerning the storage of important or sensitive papers – both by locking storage to prevent unauthorised access, and by using secure storage such as fire safes for certain crucial papers.

Self-employed contractors

The number of self-employed teleworkers, part-time arrangements, and flexible agreements is continually increasing. Employers need to ensure that they are not, through the nature of their arrangement with the contractor,

Flexible working at the sign of the Black Horse

Systems developers at Lloyds Bank/TSB Group have jumped at the chance to join a teleworking programme. The stampede has been so great that Nick Benjamin, flexible working programme manager, no longer needs to advertise the scheme to staff.

The pilot scheme started in 1992, involving 24 volunteers from the information systems department of the bank's retail financial services division. Now 180 people out of a total workforce of 560 are teleworking for an average of two to three days a week. Nick Benjamin reports:"The scheme has been promoting itself. It has taken us by surprise – we thought there would be a tailing off but it's going the other way, and we expect to reach 240 teleworkers by the end of 1996".

Once the decision to go ahead with the pilot had been made, the bank drew on internal expertise from other departments on issues such as health and safety, personnel and telecoms. Anyone who wants to take up teleworking is first assessed to gauge their suitability. According to Nick Benjamin: "The person must be an experienced self starter who knows their work well and is able to work unsupervised. They must also be highly motivated, organised and excellent time managers."

The work done from home is varied, ranging from programming, business analysis and design to report writing. "Really, anything to do with systems development can be done from home, with the exceptions of some types of system testing that have to be done in the office," says Benjamin. Staff from all levels of the department have taken up the option, and the decision on how many days a week to telework is a team decision. Performance is measured on results: "It is based on trust. It's down to the individual and their line manager to decide what is going to work for them".

Once an employee is accepted on the teleworking programme, health and safety checks are made to ensure their home environment is safe and conducive to work. Lloyds provides the phone, ISDN links, furniture, fax, filing cabinets, computer hardware and software, and staff sign an agreement to ensure the equipment is only used for bank business. The phone bill is picked up by the company, but there is no allowance for extra heating and lighting. Instead, staff get to keep their daily travel allowance even for days when they work at home. Benjamin comments: "No-one has complained. It is a fair exchange and most people realise that in return for the benefits they get from teleworking, it's a small price to pay."

A recent internal survey showed the advantages of teleworking outweighed the disadvantages, and because the scheme is open to all, there was no resentment. Staff turnover among the teleworkers is lower than for other workers, and Nick Benjamin is now helping other departments of the bank to learn from his experience.

establishing an employee-employer relationship. Simply creating an agreement which absolves the employer of any responsibility for the contractor's tax and national insurance payments is unlikely to be valid if the conditions are not agreed by the relevant authorities. Further guidance is given in Chapter 8, *Staying safe and legal*.

In the area of computer contracting it has become established practice for the contractor to set up a limited company – the client will engage the company to work and hence is responsible for payment of the company invoices and is not liable for tax or national insurance. This contract model may emerge as a better solution for the regular teleworker and helps remove the uncertainty created by having to assess each new contract on its detailed conditions.

Acknowledgements

Thanks to Croner Publications for allowing us to refer to text from *Flexible Working Practices* – a comprehensive guide for employers. Tel: 0181 547 3333 Fax: 0181 547 2637.

The TCA is also indebted to the following people for their guidance in preparing this section:

Maurice Parry-Wingfield of Touche Ross Tel: 0171 936 3000;

Mathew Brown of Independent Accountancy Services Tel: 0171 375 1001 Email: mail@iasltd.co.uk

Contributions Agency and Inland Revenue local offices and press office;

Stephen Jupp, Home Office Partnership.

Bibliography

Telecommuting Review   Periodical
Editor: Gil Gordon
Source: Gil Gordon Associates, 11 Donner Crt, Monmouth Jn, New Jersey, USA Tel: +001 8852 732 329 2266, Email: 74375.1667@compuserve.com
Comment: US periodical publication

Manual of remote working   *Date:* 1997
Authors: Kevin Curran and Geoff Williams
Source: Gower Publishing Ltd, Gower House, Croft Road, Aldershot, Hampshire GU11 3HR

Changing Places – A Manager's Guide to Working from Home   *Date:* 1996
Source: New Ways to Work, 309 Upper Street, London N1 2TY Tel: 0171 226 4026

Flexible Working   *Date:* 1996
Author: Steve Simmons
Source: Kogan Page, 120 Pentonville Road, London N1 9JN
Ref: ISBN 0–7494–1713–7
Comment: practical guide to flexible working including tick-box express implementation guide for the project manager in a hurry

Working at Home – A Study of Homeworking and Teleworking   *Date:* 1996
Author: Celia Stanworth
Source: Institute of Employment Rights Tel: 0171 738 9511 Fax: 0171 738 9577.

A Manager's Guide to Teleworking *Date:* 1995
Author: Ursula Huws on behalf of Department of Employment
Source: Dept of Employment, Cambertown Ltd., Unit 8 Goldthorpe Ind. Estate,
Rotherham, S. Yorks Tel: 0171 273 6969

Guide to Remote Working – A Practical Manual *Date:* 1995
Authors: Tynedale Network
Source: Tynedale Network, 362 Durham Road, Low Fell, Gateshead, NE9 5AP
Tel: 0191 420 0280

Flexiplace Scheme *Date:* 1994
Author: Oxfordshire County Council
Source: Commercial Services Print Unit, Oxfordshire County Council
Tel: 01865 815672 Ref. C21-17

Homeworking Strategy *Date:* 1993
Authors: Borough of Blackburn, Economic Development Department
Source: Shaheen Sameja, City Challenge Access Point, Brook House Business Centre,
Whalley Range, Blackburn, Lancashire, BB1 6BB Tel: 01254 676796

**Self-Employment and Labour Market Restructuring –
The Case of Freelance Teleworkers in Book Publishing** *Date:* 1993
Authors: Celia Stanworth, John Stanworth, David Purdy
Source: Future of Work Research Group, University of Westminster, 35 Marylebone
Road, London NW1 5LS Tel: 0171 911 5000

Teleworking Explained *Date:* 1993
Authors: Mike Gray, Noel Hodson, Gil Gordon
Source: John Wiley & Sons, Baffins Lane, Chichester Ref: ISBN 0 471 93975 7
Comments: Extremely comprehensive teleworking guide

Teleworking *Date:* 1992
Source: National Communications Union (NCU), Research Dept, Greystoke House,
150 Brunswick Rd, London, W5 1AW
Comments: Includes section on conditions of service

Contacts and URLs

Blackburn Borough Council Homeworking Liaison Office, City Challenge Access
Point, Brookhouse Park, Whalley Range, Blackburn BB1 6BB Tel: 01254 676796.

Coventry City Council Homeworking Officer, Economic Development and Planning,
Tower Block, Much Park Street, Coventry CV1 2PY Tel: 01203 831285.

Leicester Outwork Campaign, 116 St Peter's Road, Leicester LE2 1DE Tel: 01162
470940.

Liverpool Homeworking Project c/o MTUCURC, 24 Hardman Street Liverpool L1 9AX
Tel: 0151 707 2376.

Nottinghamshire Outworkers Support Group, c/o REC, 67 Lower Parliament Street,
Nottingham, NG1 3BB Tel: 01159 586515.

Rochdale Borough Council Homeworking Office, PO Box 15, Town Hall, Rochdale,
OL16 1AB Tel: 01706 864377.

National Group on Homeworking, Office 26, 30-38 Dock Street, Leeds LS10 1JF

YHLPU, 102 Commercial Street, Batley WF17 5DP Tel: 01924 443853.

http://www.collaborate.com is the address for Collaborate Inc., a CSCW consultancy
that maintains a useful site with info on Workflow and Groupware/Teleworking
systems. They also produce a commercial newsletter.

Eurostar employees do it on the train

Train operator Eurostar has installed a remote access system which allows up to 1,000 employees to work either from home or whilst travelling. The employees can log on to Eurostar's Novell based network using one of two hosting packages: Carbon Copy or Reach Out. Access is either via local area network or by telephone. Technical support staff can view the network status by dialling in or through an Internet Protocol connection. *(Computing 10/4/97).*

http://www.eema.org is the site for the European electronic message association, a professional group for users of electronic messaging.

http://www.isi.gov.uk is the address for the UK's Dept of Trade and Industry's new "Information Society Initiative", targeted at raising business awareness and use of internet, open electronic networking *etc*

http://mtanet.co.uk is a site with information about UK management consultants MTA's teleworking reports

http://www.labourtel.org.uk is the Labour Telematics Centre and its site has guidelines from trades unions for teleworkers.

http://www.RACE.analysys.co.uk is the excellent server operated by the British telecoms consultancy Analysys. It contains information on the EU's RACE and ACTS programmes. Do not miss the SONAH section which gives succinct, practical useful summaries of the equipment and software recommendations of several EU projects.

http://www.sisu.se/projects gives information about the CoopWWW programme which aims to provide a set of interworking tools for group collaboration using WWW.

http://www.tagish.co.uk/ethos/ is the website of the EU ETHOS project which gives information on the EU's TAP programme.

http://www.voffice.com is a site for 'virtual' offices for hire in London.

http://www.volksware.com/mobilis is the address for Mobilis – the mobile computing lifestyle magazine.

The following are groupware sites taken from the Collabra hotlist:

http://www.bittco.com/ Bittco Solutions – provides real-time Internet teleconferencing and decision support.

http://cu-seeme.cornell.edu/ CU-See Me is a Low cost/low bandwidth Internet videoconferencing tool from Cornell University.

http://www.lotus.com/ is Lotus Notes, the best known groupware environment and application development tool.

http://netwire.novell.com/ServSupp/groupware/nwgindx.htm is the site for Novell Groupware including GroupWise, InForms and SoftSolutions.

http://www.teamw.com/ is for TeamWARE Office E-mail, conferencing, scheduling, document management and task routing.

http://www.crew.umich.edu/~brinck/cscw.html is Tom Brink's Groupware/CSCW page and has various links on Computer Supported Collaborative Work.

http://www.ora.com contains information and free 60-day demo system on WebBoard from O'Reilly. It runs on Windows NT in conjunction with any CGI 1.1 compliant HTTP server.

http://www.softwords.bc.ca contains information on CoSy 4.2 which implements a full email and conferencing system with fully threaded messaging and a full HTML interface. Runs on any VMS or Unix platform. Ports allegedly underway to NT.

http://www.cbs.state.or.us/external/ooe has information produced by the Oregon Office of Energy about telework and telecommuting.

Agreements and unions

A number of teleworking agreements have been prepared by organisations as diverse as county councils, trade unions, telecoms companies and finance companies. This chapter extracts common issues which need to be addressed in teleworking agreements for PAYE employees, drawing on work carried out by Cathy Murray of the Small World Connections consultancy which was published in *Flexible Working* magazine in January 1997. It does not cover arrangements for contracts with self-employed teleworkers. Where the teleworker is becoming self-employed, advice to the teleworker on provision of sick pay, health insurance and pensions will be needed (see Chapter 8, *Staying safe and legal*).

Suitable jobs and teleworker selection

The corporate teleworking survey carried out for *Flexible Working* magazine in 1997 showed that only 25% of home-based teleworkers have special employment contracts covering the arrangement, making both employers and employees vulnerable to misunderstanding and often failing to provide any outlet for contentment or dissatisfaction on either side with teleworking.

Jobs which are suitable for teleworking are essentially those with an easily measurable output, and where minimum face-to-face contact or direct supervision is required. Where a teleworking trial is being carried out, often those involved will select themselves through volunteers or through the nature of their job description. Employers should be aware that once teleworking goes beyond a trial activity, there may be difficulties if a worker believes they have been unfairly excluded from the teleworking option. Therefore a policy statement on those jobs considered suitable for teleworking should be considered, and a clear route for approval of a teleworking arrangement (*eg* by a line manager and the human resources department) should be outlined.

Some employers have made selections on the grounds of the results of psychometric tests of employees, looking for qualities such as ability to manage time, independence and so on. The use of psychometric tests in this way is likely to meet resistance from any unions involved. Another sensitive issue is that of whether the teleworker will have a suitable home office or other space to work from as many people do not have a "spare" bedroom in their house. Issues of planning permission and business rates are covered in Chapter 8, *Staying safe and legal.*

The effect of teleworking on colleagues remaining in the office, and on customers should also be considered. Oxfordshire County Council stipulates that there should be no adverse effects on the level and quality of service, or increases in the workload of non-teleworking colleagues.

The procedure for ending a period of teleworking should be laid out in any agreement – usually this involves specifying a period of notice by either side, which is often one month. Other issues such as the return of company-owned home office equipment will also need to be specified.

Working hours and overtime

It is usual for teleworking agreements to specify a number of core hours when the teleworker is available for contact by telephone by colleagues. Outside these hours, it is up to the teleworker to decide their pattern of work in order to achieve the tasks they have been set. Otherwise working hours are not usually changed by teleworking, although there may need to be variations to the procedure by which overtime and sick pay are agreed, claimed and monitored by the employer. A procedure for the teleworker to report for meetings at the office as required should also be included.

The home office

In general, employers provide all relevant IT equipment (computers, faxes, scanners, photocopiers, modems *etc*) and supply and pay for a separate telephone line, often with an answerphone or voicemail to buffer "after hours" calls without disturbing the employee. In large organisations it is usual for there to be an inventory system for the equipment provided to the home office, including labelling, a procedure for returning the equipment if the teleworking arrangement is ended, procedures for replacement if the equipment is lost, stolen or damaged, and for repair when necessary. If an arrangement is made for the teleworker to use their own equipment rather than the company's, then it is important that the teleworker checks their home insurance policy to ensure the equipment is covered for such usage.

With regard to furniture, some employers expect the teleworker to supply their own furniture (such as GlaxoWellcome) whereas others, particularly those whose employees may be involved in long hours at the computer, choose to supply suitable ergonomic office furniture so that they are certain they are carrying out their health and safety responsibilities. The scenario of a persistent back problem caused by using a computer on the kitchen table rears its ugly head. Another solution is to provide an allowance for the purchase of suitable furniture (Shell UK provides this as an option for teleworking employees – the amount granted is £300).

Stationery and other office consumables will also be needed in the home office. In some companies these are provided from central stores, in others a stationery/postage allowance is paid, or expenses are reclaimed.

Because of the employer's health and safety responsibilities, some companies insist on initial and periodic inspection visits to the home office. This is an issue which must be handled with some sensitivity due to the difficult border between home and work – family members may resent being "on parade" for the boss' visit, while workers may feel stressed by the need to present their entire home and family, not just the home office, in as

The boss in the bedroom?

The former HR manager of a financial services company who wishes to remain anonymous supplied the following warning:

Full-time employed, home-based teleworkers present special HR issues due to the necessity for the employer to have access to the home in order to check on issues such as health and safety of the home office, security and confidentiality of data and so on for which the employer is responsible.

Where the teleworker's premises are separate to the home (in an annex or a telecottage) the problems are minimal, but if the teleworker is using, say a spare bedroom in the home, special care is required. Many people may feel uncomfortable about the blurring of the distinction between work and home.

On a large housing estate, the arrival of a "stranger" who disappears up to the bedroom with the lone teleworker for a couple of hours can raise eyebrows and start tongues wagging. Some family members may be unhappy about an "inspection" of their home, and some partners may be uneasy about home visits.

The possibility of sexual harrassment is an issue in every office, but the possibilities for misunderstandings to arise between two people in a home environment are much greater than in an office. Terms for home inspections should be agreed at the start of a teleworking trial or agreement, and it is prudent to ensure that two company staff are present at any visit.

good a light as possible to their employer. Usually a period of notice before a home visit is specified in writing. Oxfordshire County Council recognises the right of its employees to keep their home telephone numbers and addresses confidential – something which is not difficult if a separate telephone line paid for by the employer is used, and if the postal address remains in the main office. Surrey County Council advises its teleworkers not to hold meetings with clients in their homes for reasons of personal security but to use council premises instead.

Another area which may be problematic is that of childcare. Some agreements specify that the teleworker must have adequate childcare during working hours – teleworking is no substitute for childcare, despite the usual media stereotypes of the toddler cuddled on mummy's knee while she taps at the keyboard. But all parents will be familiar with the problems of the suddenly sick or distressed child, and since one of the aims of a teleworking agreement is to provide flexible work practices which allow better balance between home and working life, agreements which are draconian in this area may be self-negating. A statement to the effect that employees must complete their assignments on time, and that the company expects children to be cared for while working, particularly during school holidays, is probably sufficient.

Some agreements also specify the duty of the teleworker to maintain their home office area safely for themselves, and for others, including family members or work colleagues who may enter it.

With regard to insurance, the company is normally responsible for the worker while they are using the home office. Some employers, such as AT&T, specify that they are not liable for accidents involving third parties or family members, and that the teleworker should take out their own insurance to cover such eventualities.

There are many examples of insurers providing cover for employees working at home, but in some cases such as that of Stoke City Council, it has been necessary to agree with the insurance company a "cordon" around the working area which is clearly specified. For employer liability purposes, the insurer/employer is responsible for this work area and so should take steps to check that, for instance, the electrical wiring is safe in the home office room. Outside this area the employer is not liable (eg if the worker falls down the stairs and suffers injury).

Health and safety

Shell UK provides its teleworkers with detailed guidance on teleworker health and safety, covering the following issues:

- Equipment layout
- Positioning of cables
- Lighting
- Ventilation
- Handling and carrying equipment
- Suitable chairs
- Lighting levels
- Noise levels
- Ventilation and humidity
- Fire safety issues such as the fitting of smoke detectors and access to an extinguisher.
- Inadvisability of allowing children to play with company PC.

This level of detail may not be required in some situations. It is important that employers specify how they will check and monitor the health and safety of the employee's working environment. Oxfordshire County Council issues a health and safety checklist to employees for completion, while Glaxo Group Research includes in its teleworking contract that "the individual must provide a working environment which satisfies Company security and health and safety requirements". The Health and Safety Executive produces a leaflet on best practice for home offices.

Communication procedures

Different communication methods and their advantages and disadvantages are spelled out in Chapter 2, *Implementing telework*. It can be useful to clarify how the teleworker is expected to use different methods (phone, fax, email) to avoid misunderstandings and communication difficulties.

If the company already has detailed reporting procedures or communications guidelines between colleagues or between managers and subordinates, these may need some revision to incorporate teleworking.

It is also important to specify how the teleworker will receive technical support for any problems with company owned equipment, or perhaps with remote connection to an office network. Often this will simply consist of a telephone helpdesk during normal hours, but in some situations, giving priority to teleworkers (who may be unable to continue work unless they can resolve their IT problem) can be worthwhile and reduce feelings of isolation.

In addition, few agreements seem to take account of the support that teleworkers and managers may need to get started – access to sources of advice through association membership may be an area which more companies should consider writing into their agreements.

Security

Security procedures are usually similar to the Company's existing security procedures, but may require slight adjustment. For example, if secure document waste is normally shredded, but the teleworker has no access to a shredder, it may be necessary for documents to be returned to the office for shredding.

The main area of concern is likely to be computer security, and encompasses issues such as the use of keyboard locks, the importance of complying with software licences (non-duplication of software) and the application of suitable virus-checking procedures. In addition, the teleworker may be requested to secure all company documents and network connections before leaving the home office. See Chapter 8, *Staying safe and legal* for further security guidelines, and Chapter 12, *Teleworking equipment.*

Career development and training

A major worry for many potential teleworkers is that they may miss out on opportunities for promotion or training, and become isolated from the company. Many agreements contain a clause stipulating that entitlements and arrangements for career development, training and performance appraisals will be unchanged by a teleworking arrangement.

Pay, taxation and expenses

The introduction of teleworking involves a degree of readjustment in pay and conditions which can have financial implications for both sides. In general, most companies pay allowances to teleworkers to cover their home office costs. For smaller organisations, a system of reimbursing receipted expenses, plus payments covering increased energy usage and so on are the norm. For larger organisations with many teleworkers, the administrative burden of handling individual receipts may be uneconomic, in which case an annual or monthly agreed allowance will be preferable.

A fixed amount payable to the employee revisable on a yearly basis is perhaps the neatest way of proceeding. The sums involved may be based on before and after usage or on an apportionment in relation to space used for work within the home. In the latter case, the basis of the allowance should be an analysis of the running costs of the house (heat, light, cleaning repairs, insurance, council tax) divided by the proportion of the house used for business. These amounts should be declared on the annual P11D form returned by the employer. Alternatively, dispensation for the amounts should be agreed with both the Inspector of Taxes and the Contributions Agency. Employees could be liable for tax if the employer pays more than can be shown to be a justifiable amount.

Shell UK pays an allowance of between £1,040 and £1,860 depending on the number of days spent working at home to its teleworkers. Oxfordshire County Council pays £50/month for wear and tear on the home office plus increased energy usage. At the other end of the scale, GlaxoWellcome Research Group believes that added expenses for teleworkers are balanced out by savings on travel and does not make any payment. This was also the position of Britannia Building Society when it trialled teleworking – heating costs would be balanced out by travel savings.

The payment of allowances has tax implications. All non-cash benefits and expenses provided to employees in the course of their employment are taxed. Once the equipment is available in a home context the employee could be liable to tax on the benefit from personal use of the equipment. The amount involved is not large – *eg* equipment valued at £3,000, annual depreciation at 20%, and used for business for 95% of the time gives tax payable on private use of £30 per annum. However, for this reason many employers include statements in teleworking agreements forbidding personal use of the computer, or advising the teleworker that it is their responsibility to seek advice on the tax implications of personal use. Surrey County Council requires its teleworkers to declare that no private use will be made of the equipment provided for business purposes.

Advice should be sought before making any one-off payment to compensate for a change in working practices since these can also be deemed a taxable benefit. More information about taxation isues is given in Chapter 8, *Staying safe and legal.*

It is difficult to be definitive about types of expenses in isolation so it is wise to verify the detail of compensation arrangements with the Inspector of Taxes and the Contributions Agency before paying the expense. One of our advisers said: "You could line up ten tax inspectors and get ten different answers" – and suggested agreement should be sought in writing. The problem is not confined to inspectors as different tax advisers also give conflicting advice, reflecting the complexity of interpreting tax law and its changing nature as new types of teleworking develop. Gradually the authorities are beginning to accommodate the new ways of working, however. In 1995, the Inland Revenue acknowledged that, in relation to tax relief on mortgage payments (MIRAS), "it is becoming increasingly common for properties to be used both for residential and business purposes."

Recompense can be made for proportions of heat, light, cleaning and council tax according to some sources. Small World Connections, in its 1997 corporate teleworking survey for *Flexible Working* magazine reports that 85% of companies using teleworkers pay for business calls, while 75% supply office stationery. Around 25% pay for insurance, while 5% pay for heating, lighting and a contribution towards rent.

Travel

The good news is that an employee working at home can argue that the home is the real place of work and hence travel to the office is business travel and reimbursable tax free. Maurice Parry-Wingfield of Touche Ross however advises caution in this area: "It is essential that the employee is formally instructed by the employer to work at home rather than at the employer's workplace and to use the equipment at home. If teleworking is purely a matter of personal choice the employee will not be able to claim deductions for domestic or travel expenses provided."

The situation is clearer for mobile teleworkers such as sales force staff who use home as a base – in most situations, all their travel costs will be reimbursable.

Trade unions and consultation

For a teleworking agreement to be successful, it must be widely supported and agreed by both management and workers. Practical experience indicates three key points:

- **Consultation** – often happens through a trade union.
- **Voluntary** nature of the agreement – anyone who becomes dissatisfied with the arrangement must have a clear route back to the main office available to them.
- **Timescale** – all involved will need time to consider the issues and for discussion before any decisions are made or agreements signed.

A recent Labour party document on the Information Society notes the increased scope for teleworking, but is concerned about reduced opportunities for social interaction, suggesting that office-based training schemes, regular employee feedback meetings and the maintenance of central recreational facilities might all be included in a code of practice to be employed by government agencies, employer's federations, trade unions and voluntary organisations.

Some trade unions have strong reservations about teleworking which were summed up in a 1991 TUC report: "Overall the relevance of the union to the membership would almost certainly suffer as they (teleworkers) become one step removed from direct contact with the union through its representatives. The likelihood is that there will be a diminution in meetings and less contact with union representatives. Members will also be less likely to participate in any of the activities of the union which may become so distant the teleworkers will see union membership as an irrelevance." Teleworking may be seen as part of a destabilisation and casualisation of the labour market, particularly because of the way in which it is often associated with part-time work, short term contracts and outsourcing.

The 1997 TUC report *New Information and Communications Technologies at Work* points out that the Autumn 1996 Labour Force Survey in Britain shows 69% of those working at home, and 67% of those working in different places and using home as a base are self-employed. This figure also includes non-teleworking homeworkers, but gives some idea of the relationship between a move towards homeworking and a move towards self-employment. The report highlights trade union concern that: "Teleworking can lead to the development of a two-tier employment structure, with full-time, permanent, office-based workers at the core and part-time, temporary, home-based workers at the periphery." These

concerns are also tied to a more general phenomenon of "pseudo self-employment" where companies encourage workers to become self-employed in order to reduce their responsibilities (the example of Rank Xerox consultants in Britain who were given the option to become self-employed rather than being made redundant in the 1980s is often given).

The document states: "It is clear that while teleworking suits some workers well, for others it creates problems. These may vary from person to person and will also vary in different workplaces, depending on the particular teleworking arrangements. Trade unions need to be able to respond to the issues affecting a particular worker or group of workers in different situations. It is clearly vital that trade unions are able to represent the interests of those who wish to telework and those who do not." Examples of imposed teleworking leading to unhappiness in the workforce quoted in the report include Manweb, the Manchester electricity board which imposed teleworking on account managers in 1992, and the Ministry of Agriculture, which forced a number of civil servants from regional offices which were closing to work from home.

The TUC report highlights the equal opportunities issues which may be raised by teleworking. "25% of telework managers in Ursula Huws' 1993 survey listed 'maturity' as a criteria for recruiting teleworkers and over 45% listed self sufficiency. There is a danger of bias if managers make largely subjective judgements over [such] factors... as with all recruitment situations, selection of teleworkers should be based on criteria that can be objectively measured... some may be barred from teleworking because they do not have access to a quiet space which could be used for work during the day... it would be highly discriminatory for such factors to mitigate against employment and this creates a strong equal opportunities argument for not designating certain jobs as teleworking jobs." One of the case studies listed in Small World Connection's 1997 corporate teleworking survey (published in connection with *Flexible Working* magazine), an NHS trust, specifically mentioned that in future they will be assessing staff suitability for teleworking as part of a pre-recruitment exercise using a structured questionnaire format. It is not clear whether this procedure would also apply to those joining the trust as new employees.

Another case study in the same document, Skandia Life, gives details of the reasons why three out of seven teleworkers dropped out of a teleworking trial instigated to cover a skills shortage by utilising women returners over a period of years. One of the teleworkers is described as "playing games" and not putting in the time and effort to get the work done. Another had "a short history of domestic crises interfering with work which eventually resulted in the individual leaving of her own accord". The third showed "no apparent problem for some time and it seemed that the individual concerned was enjoying the work and getting on well, until out of the blue it seemed that she was no longer able to carry on teleworking. It seems likely that pressure from the family contributed in this case."

Skandia Life had discussed the special demands of teleworking with all the teleworkers before the project began, and suggests that other companies might like to learn from their experience and in future get feedback from other family members before recruiting teleworkers. This sentiment is understandable, but again shows the "territorial" and borderline difficulties which can arise between equal opportunities, business objectives and employment rights when home and work overlap.

Issues of union concern related to teleworker health and safety which are outlined in the TUC report include:

- less likely to have the correct work equipment – commonly, teleworkers use domestic tables and chairs rather than adjustable furniture;

- they are subject to the commonest domestic hazards – faulty wiring leading to electrocution or fires, inadequate fire prevention or escape facilities, badly carpeted stairs and so on;

- they are often distracted from the hazards they are facing by the domestic surroundings – and sometimes by dependent children whose safety they are likely to put above their own;

- they are likely to be isolated from fellow workers, which can cause stress and make it more difficult to resist unsafe working arrangements;

- mobile teleworking can cause muscular and skeletal problems due to the weight of equipment carried;

- mobile teleworkers may be vulnerable to the threat of violent attack because they often work and travel alone, carrying valuable equipment.

The isolation from co-workers inherent in teleworking certainly can restrict negotiations for appropriate rates of pay, as shown in the University of Westminster's 1993 Work Research Group survey of self-employed teleworkers in the UK publishing industry. Over 100 respondents indicated that loneliness, isolation and lack of contact with clients and colleagues caused problems. Over half of the interviewees did not receive a "living income" due to insufficient workload and low rates of pay. The report noted that "neither the National Union of Journalists or the Society of Freelance Editors and Proofreaders has been able to foster sufficient solidarity amongst freelancers to maintain any generally observed rates of pay." Many unions are concerned that teleworking can mask an attempt by employers to push employees towards self-employed status.

However, Bill Walsh of MSF (Manufacturing, Science and Finance) Union sees it this way: "The alternative to taking a positive stance on these potential developments is to try to sustain the unsatisfactory and unpopular employment status-quo for many people who want to opt for change... For these reasons, MSF is campaigning to ensure that home-based working is a genuine extension of freedom for people at work... The union wants to see a wide range of employment opportunities being made available to the home-based worker."

MSF has produced guidelines, and a code of practice for employees:

- Teleworkers should be employees of an enterprise and not deemed self-employed.

- To avoid isolation, contracts of employment should require home workers to periodically attend the office.

- There should be a separate room available at home for teleworking, a separate telephone and payment for additional costs such as heating and lighting.

- There should be regular meetings between teleworkers and the provision of electronic mail and telephone links with other teleworkers, all to be provided at the employer's expense.

- There should be regular weekly liaison discussions between a teleworker and his or her supervisor/manager.

- Teleworkers should enjoy the same rates of pay and employment benefits as office-based workers including childcare provision and family leave. There should be a defined number of working hours. They should be included in career development and appraisal schemes including training opportunities.

- All computer equipment should be provided, paid for and serviced by the employer who will be responsible for the installation, maintenance, insurance and compliance with health and safety requirements. The employer should also accept legal responsibility for any accident or injury.

- Teleworkers should have access to trade union representation and be able to attend meetings within working hours. Health and safety advisors and trade union representatives should be able to visit teleworkers.

- Teleworking should be voluntary with a right to return to working from the office.

Source: Peter Skyte, MSF Union

MSF has also set up a Teleworking Interest Group to examine how it can meet the needs of teleworker members and those running their own businesses, covering ideas such as help and advice on cashflow, health and safety, taxation, legal issues and other small business problems, as well as partnerships with suppliers to supply discounted business equipment, travel and insurance.

In addition, the banking trade union BIFU notes the following points for negotiators:

- desk, chair, paper, pens to be supplied by the company;
- no 'spy in the home' cameras or key depression monitoring to be fitted to a homeworker's VDU;

- management should ensure that each homeworker has the opportunity to meet and discuss issues appertaining to their work at least once a week;
- teleworking should never be used as an alternative to adequate workplace or state childcare;
- all homeworkers' contracts should be collectively agreed between management and the union, thereby ensuring that individuals do not find their terms and conditions worsened in comparision with other staff.

The public service union UNISON also has guidelines which include the following points (as well as several which are similar to the MSF guidelines):

- a particular manager should be assigned to ensure regular contact;
- homeworkers should enjoy the same rights as other workers to join trade unions and have their own representatives;
- all teleworkers should be entitled to an annual review of their working arrangements.

The Society of Telecoms Executives made the point in their agreement with BT that: "Teleworkers can expect a career in BT. Their managers must give them feedback on their performance, including an annual appraisal, and must identify development needs. Teleworkers have access to all appropriate training packages and courses. They should also be notified of current vacancies within BT, via the same channels as office-based workers." A poll of teleworkers in BT found this issue was not always dealt with satisfactorily because many teleworkers did not receive information about vacancies. Those who did receive the information felt they could not really apply to move jobs in case they had to return to an office. However, in general they reported few feelings of isolation, and had access to training, assisted by BT's general promotion of distance learning packages.

The National Union of Journalists provides members with subsidised email and online information services, and is moving into providing relevant training in software skills for members. Over 25% of NUJ members are self-employed.

The Communications Workers Union has also created a model agreement in relation to BT's teleworking arrangements where it requested that it should also have access to the technology linking teleworkers to management (such as email) in order to provide member services on an equal basis. The CWU in America has requested a message be displayed from the union when telecommuters enter the company computer network, as well as an assurance from employers that telecommuters will be given time regularly to consult with their union representatives. The CWU in Ireland is involved in representing teleworkers and developing teleworking through the European Telework Development Project. Such a development is also in line with the move by a number of European white collar unions to begin representing the self-employed as well as PAYE workers, although as writer Andrew Bibby points out: "There will remain a core philosophical area which will separate unions from simple commercial information and advice services. There is still the concept of solidarity – the idea that individuals who join a union do so not just to help themselves but also to help each other."

The TUC report recommends the creation of "cyberspace safety reps", a sort of virtual branch officer, available over the Internet or by phone to union members to provide answers to information requests, advice on safety rights and responsibilities, and to help develop policies on risk assessments.

Celia Stanworth's *Working at Home – A Study of Homeworking and Teleworking* picks out some of the problems of insecurity and exploitation encountered by employees where there is no formal agreement, particularly in relation to call centre work.

Andrew Bibby's *Trade Unions and Telework* report for the international white collar union federation Euro-Fiet also makes clear recommendations on teleworking agreements and outlines some of the problems of relocation of work overseas which may result from teleworking. In relation to call centres, Bibby writes: "Call centre staff are under the control of [ACD] technology in a way which is normally unfamiliar in white collar working. The similarity rather is with Fordism, the assembly-line method of working which has long existed in manufacturing... ACD technology enables employers to automatically monitor employees' work performance, such as the time taken in dealing with callers. In many countries, a feature of call centre life is the random secret monitoring of calls for supervisory purposes." However, he also notes that because staff must be motivated to work in this environment, employers tend to rely on modern, participative and informal management styles which encourage team working.

Overall, Bibby recommends that unions should "fight fire with fire" and start to use the new technologies to attract new members, including self-employed teleworkers. He quotes the example of the UK banking union BIFU, whose members in the telephone banking service First Direct used the company's tried and trusted "roadshow" method to recruit their colleagues. According to BIFU: "It is a norm of First Direct that when a department formulates a new product or campaign, it holds a roadshow to explain it to the rest of First Direct's staff. To do this they set up a conference room with posters, games, competitions, videos, literature and even balloons. So that's what we did: we set up a conference room with a video, info on the union, a quiz, free gifts – biros, balloons, rulers *etc* – and a group of talkative union representatives." (Leif Mills, BIFU, 1995).

When it comes to the crunch, some companies formally draft a variation to the contract of employment of the teleworker (which can be a fairly simple, one-page affair outlining the main issues). Others have been advised by their lawyers to avoid making a specific agreement, particularly if the teleworking arrangement is purely a trial. Both approaches – contractual and informal – have merit and should be considered as part of the consultation. Other issues which might be considered in the consultation process before drawing up any teleworking agreement include:

- equal opportunity rights
- job security (retainer/guarantee of minimum work *etc*)
- use of cars
- holidays
- benefits (replacing central benefits such as canteens)
- low interest loans and advice services
- provision of cheap IT equipment.

Bibliography

Flexible Working Magazine
Source: The Eclipse Group, 18-20 Highbury Place, London, N5 1QP,
Tel: 0171 354 5858 Ref: ISSN 1360-9505.
Comment: Periodical

New Information and Communications Technologies at Work   *Date:* 1997
Source: Trade Union Congress Publications, Congress House,
Great Russell St, London WC1B 3LS

Guide to Teleworking   *Date:* 1996
Source: Surrey County Council, County Hall, Penrhyn Road,
Kingston upon Thames, Surrey KT1 2DN

**Homeworking: Guidance for employers and employees
on health and safety**   *Date:* 1996
Author: Health and Safety Executive
Source: HSE Books, PO Box 199, Sudbury, Suffolk CO10 6FS
Tel: 01787 881165 Fax: 017187 313995.

Teleworking and Gender   *Date:* 1996
Author: Ursula Huws
Source: European Commission DGV, Brussels

Trade Unions and Telework   *Date:* 1996
Author: Andrew Bibby
Source: Fiet, Avenue de Balexert 15, CH-1219 Chatelaine-Geneva, Switzerland
Web: http://www.eclipse.co.uk/pens/bibby/fietrpt

Working at Home – A Study of Homeworking and Teleworking   *Date:* 1996
Author: Celia Stanworth
Source: Institute of Employment Rights Tel: 0171 738 9511 Fax: 0171 738 9577.

Employment of Homeworkers: Examples of Good Practice   *Date:* 1995
Authors: Ursula Huws and Sarah Podro
Source: International Labour Organisation

Teleworking and the Labour Movement   *Date:* 1995
Author: Labour Telematics Centre
Source: 3Com Europe Ltd, Eaton Court, Maylands Avenue, Hemel
Hempstead, Herts HP2 7DF

Self-employment and Labour Market Restructuring –
the Case of Freelance Teleworkers in Book Publishing   *Date:* 1993
Authors: Celia Stanworth, John Stanworth, David Purdy
Source: Future of Work Research Group, University of Westminster, 35 Marylebone
Road London NW1 5LS Tel: 0171 911 5000

Contacts and URLs

Labour Telematics Centre, GMB National College, College Road, Whalley Range,
Manchester M16 8PB Tel: 0161 860 4364 Fax: 0161 881 1853
Email: labourteladmin@mcr1.poptel.org.uk
Web: http://www.labourtel.org.uk

Trade Union Congress Congress House, 23-28 Great Russell Street, London
WC1B 3LS Tel: 0171 636 4030 x1305 Fax: 0171 467 1317 Contact: Janet Williamson

European Foundation for the Improvement of Living and Working
Conditions, Wyattville Road, Loughlinstown, Dublin, Ireland.
Tel: +353 1 204 3100 Fax: +353 1 282 6456
Contact: Eberhard Köhler, Research Co-ordinator
Email: eberhard.kohler@eurofound.ie

MSF Union Contact Peter Skyte at MSF, 50 Southwark Street London SE1 1UN
Tel: 0171 717 4000 Fax: 0171 717 4040 Email: peter.skyte@geo2.poptel.org.uk

Communications Workers' Union of Ireland 575 North Circular Road, Dublin 1
Tel: +353 1 836 6388 Fax: +353 1 836 5582 Contact: Chris Hudson Email: chris@cwu.ie

Ursula Huws Web: http://www.dialspace.dial.pipex.com/town/parade/hg54

http://www.eclipse.co.uk/pens/bibby/telework.html is journalist **Andrew Bibby**'s
home pages which contain a number of articles on teleworking including the FIET
report.

Survival guide

This chapter is based on the experiences of members of several teleworking associations and users of the Telework Europa forum on Compuserve. It represents advice from the "horse's mouth" on how to take advantage of the flexibility of teleworking and avoid the pitfalls.

Getting the job done

In interviews and media discussions about teleworking, journalists often ask teleworkers: "How do you make yourself sit down at the computer and start work in the morning? Why don't you just stay in bed?" Any self-employed teleworker can give them the reason: no work – no pay. You need to pay the rent or mortgage, buy food, buy paper and so on. One contributor said: "I add up how much I owe my creditors or how much I still owe on the mortgage. This does wonders for my motivation". Another commented: "My main incentive to work is the arrival of the childminder so I know I've got to get stuck in while I've got peace and quiet!"

This teleworker takes things to extremes: "The central heating in my large and drafty house is off until the evening. I keep the room I use as an office heated with a calor gas stove. As well as being more economical, it effectively puts the rest of the house out of bounds during the day unless I put my thermals on, which does wonders for the motivation". The voice of experience shines through the next contribution: "Try and plan your work so that the first thing you have to do in the morning is not difficult or unpleasant. Break off in the evening at a point which leaves you an easy start first thing the next day. This means that if you do run into a problem the following day you will already be in full swing."

So behind the simplistic journalist's query is a real dilemma: organising your work when there is no-one physically hammering on your office door to ask where that report/memo/piece of software has got to. To avoid upsetting clients or employers, teleworkers need to get good at managing their time and the projects assigned to them very quickly.

One invaluable aid is to buy a personal organiser package which runs on your computer. Not everyone gets on with these (and it has to be said that a well-maintained handwritten list can do the job equally well), but the best of these packages, such as Microsoft Outlook, will keep track of your tasks as well as holding information like contact addresses.

Typical teleworker tasks that need to be covered by any personal organiser software you purchase include:

■ urgent deadline based tasks

■ major projects which may contain a number of sub-tasks

■ routine work such as monthly reports

- regular tasks such as backing up computer data or preparing VAT returns
- calls to be made
- appointments and meetings

To carry out this range of tasks you will need:

- a diary function (with meeting alarms and planners)
- a contacts database (addresses, phone, fax and email numbers)
- a "to do" list which is prioritised and which allows automatic prompting of regularly scheduled tasks.

It's also a big help if the time manager has a function that allows you to record what time you spent working on which project for billing or cost centre purposes. Perhaps the most important piece of advice in this chapter is to ensure that you log every hour that you spend working, whether or not you can claim for it. Do it on the same day, or in the morning of the next day, before you forget what you were doing.

Start your day by collecting your email, post, and any messages, and working through your "to do" list in the light of the new messages, prioritising tasks. It is well worth taking the time to eradicate junk mail from the post you have to open by subscribing to the Mailing Preference Service, and its companion the Telephone Preference Service, so that your name is removed from mailing lists. For information on preventing junk email see Chapter 9, *Email and online services*. Log your incoming post in a book, or better, on a spreadsheet so you have a record of what came in. Stamp it with the date it was received and file it immediately before it clutters up your work surfaces. Your filing system does not have to be complex – it could be just the classic in, out and pending, or action now, action later and information – but if you have one you'll be able to find what you need without having to excavate the piles of paper taking over your home office.

Beating deadlines

"If you're working to a serious deadline, put the answerphone on. You can always interrupt it if an important call comes in, otherwise you can call back after the deadline work's completed."

Be realistic about your time estimates. If it's obvious something isn't going to get done by the deadline, inform the customer or client. Often a deadline can be stretched, or the customer or client can rearrange their workload – it is much better to let people know what is happening than to let them down at the last moment.

"Make sure you know all the last posting times and courier pickup times. There's nothing worse than panting into the post office after a day racing a deadline and then finding that you've missed the van because they changed the pickup routes."

When agreeing deadlines with clients, don't forget to take account of

Voices of experience...

"I find that it's important to juggle workload according to mood. Some days I am good for nothing but administrative tasks such as catching up on the bills. When I'm working on something involving major writing or creative input, there is always a stage of displacement activities I have to go through before I can start. This is quite stressful at the time because you are ticking yourself off for cleaning out the fridge when you should be in front of the computer racing a looming deadline, but over the years I have realised it is a necessary part of the creative process – whilst I clean the fridge, some sort of composting process takes place in the brain and then the structure, idea or phrase will come that allows me to face the blank screen and get going."

"I used to complete and deliver jobs well ahead of the deadline. Now, I may well finish the job ahead of time but I've learnt not to deliver it until close to the deadline. That way, people think I'm busy and leave me alone! It's not a matter of planning your work but of planning your life, setting yourself targets for both the personal and professional spheres and aim for the proper balance."

regular tasks that have to be fitted in to the working day, such as filing, backing up data, accounts and so on, otherwise you will find that these tasks always get pushed into evenings and weekends to make room for deadline work, and you end up overworking.

It's good to talk...

Teleworkers need to make maximum use of all the tools available to them to keep in touch with the people who pay them. Because you are not physically in the same office, it is vital to respond quickly and effectively so that your client or employer feels secure that you are on top of your work for them and they can rely on you to complete the task. It's good to talk, as the advert goes, but for teleworkers the secret of success is to pick the right communication tool for the job. Telecommuters, or employed teleworkers, may well have a corporate policy laid down about when email should be used, when face-to-face meetings are needed and so on, but the self-employed usually have to learn by their mistakes. Teleworkers don't have the luxury (or nuisance, depending on your view) of constant face-to-face meetings, with all the nuances of body language and time for discussion, or of informal chats in the corridor. It is very easy to pick up the wrong end of the stick and make an expensive mistake, or develop a grudge or irritation with a colleague which would never happen in the conventional office environment. Learning to be a teleworker requires good attention to communications tools and skills. On the other hand, face-to-face meetings for teleworkers often take on new and more interesting roles – they may become about team-building, training, developing relationships and discussing possibilities rather than about imparting routine information.

Telephones

Communicating is about imparting and receiving information, and the most widely used method of communication for teleworkers is the telephone. To make sure there has been no breakdown in telephone communications, take written notes of telephone calls. Where possible restate any information received before finishing the call to check you have understood correctly. When imparting information, it often helps to write down the points you plan to make before starting the call, ticking them off as each one is discussed. Check the following:

■ are you talking to the right person?

■ do they understand who you are? Did you introduce yourself and your work context?

■ are your communications accurate and complete (have they received the fax you are supposed to be discussing?)

■ is your communication timely? (have you missed the deadline for applications already? If so there's no point in going further with the call).

When communicating with your manager or client:

■ have the relevant documents to hand

■ ensure your message is clear and unambiguous

■ keep it short – the manager's time is precious

■ check if people have time to talk and if not, make an appointment for a long call at another time

■ don't use excessively costly communication methods such as videoconferencing unless they are necessary

■ always try to imagine yourself in the other person's place – empathy.

Often calls made by telephone are discussions or negotiations, or the development of an idea. Be concrete – use examples of what you mean wherever possible to reduce the possibilities for confusion.

A number of other techniques are important in the effective use of the telephone.

"When working alone, it is important to establish trust in your answering machine. Clients must feel confident that leaving a message on the answering machine is as good as a direct contact. This confidence may be established by acknowledging messages quickly, even when it is not necessary to do so and explaining to clients that the presence of the answering machine may only indicate an absence of a few minutes. I, for example, may simply be sitting in the garden with the laptop and will check the machine frequently." Equally, when leaving messages, always state your name, the time and date of your message, your telephone number and leave a clear, brief message.

It is well worthwhile to keep a duplicate message book by the phone, for writing brief notes of telephone calls, who from, time and date. This

Telephone communication skills

If you are **imparting information:**

- don't assume the receiver sees the conversation the same way you do or hears exactly what you wished to say
- don't use irritating words and repetitive phrases
- don't use inappropriate language (swearwords, sexism, jargon) which the other person doesn't understand or feel comfortable with
- don't mumble, fidget, or use distracting mannerisms – speak clearly
- don't interrogate the receiver aggressively
- avoid jargon
- ask one question at a time
- listen carefuly to the answer
- be concise.

If you are **receiving information** try to avoid:

- jumping to conclusions and interrupting
- changing the subject
- talking too much
- thinking about what the receiver is going to say next rather than listening to what they are saying now
- switching off or ignoring what is being said
- seeking to score over the other person
- competing rather than cooperating
- pretending to understand when you don't to avoid embarrassment
- being judgmental
- being defensive rather than open to the information you are receiving.

Active listeners, or receivers of information try to:

- signal their interest
- listen between lines
- ask questions for clarification
- avoid criticism
- summarise the message before the end of the call.

gives you a record of information from the telephone call, and also provides a method for other people in the house to take messages and leave them for you in an agreed format and place. Using message books in conjunction with listening to your answerphone messages can also be useful – otherwise if you get interrupted by another call while listening to the answerphone, you may forget the content of the message.

More and more teleworkers also have mobile phones, and here the difficulty is not receiving the information, but recording the salient details of the message while pulled over at the side of the road, or walking along a railway platform. Some phones now have a message taking utility but if yours does not, it can be useful to invest in a pocket memo recorder such as the Philips Voicetrack, or a Walkman with a good recording device to carry with you when you are out of the office. You can record the details of the mobile call straight away, and play back the recording when you return to the office for action. Of course, pen and paper also work well for this task, but small tape machines are also useful for that brilliant idea, or task you've forgotten, which strikes you while sitting in a traffic jam. Another technique is to use your mobile phone to dial your home answerphone and leave details of the message or idea there for collection and action later.

The wide range of telephone features now available to assist teleworkers, including detailed billing and call waiting, are described in Chapter 12, *Teleworking equipment*. It is worth noting here that considerable development work is being put into making CTI technology (computer telephony integration) more widely available. CTI has until recently only been available on mainframe installations in call centres. It uses features such as caller line identification to allow your PC to produce relevant information from your database about a caller, and to record and make calls without having to physically dial. It is particularly useful for people involved in the areas of sales and support. On a smaller scale, the introduction of tools like Microsoft Exchange, part of the Windows 95 software, as a single "send, receive and file" point for your faxes, emails and contacts database has encouraged many more teleworkers to make and record their communications on their PC.

One telephone communication method which is often overlooked is the audio or telephone conference. Audioconferences can be arranged through telecoms companies or, if you are working in the voluntary sector, through Community Network (0171 359 4594). Theoretically up to 20 people can join in an audioconference, but from the point of view of running an effective meeting, audioconferences work best with up to 10 people. An effective "chair" who works round the participants collecting views, resolving conflicts and summing up the meeting decisions is vital. Audioconferences are extremely cost effective for a group of people who need to discuss a topic but don't want the time and expense of a face to face meeting.

Fax

Faxes are great for urgent written communications, but it's important to use them only as appropriate. For example, if the document is one the recipient will have to work on or edit, it would be better sent by email so they don't have to type it all in again – even if they are receiving the fax on a computer, what they are receiving is an uneditable graphical image, not a piece of editable, computer-readable text. There's also the long-running problem of decomposition of thermal fax paper. If your fax is not plain-paper or computer-based, be sure to copy important documents received onto ordinary paper, otherwise when the client tries to sue you a year later and you go to look in the file, all you may find is a blank piece of paper.

Many people now use fax switches (where the fax shares the voice line) or computer-based faxes, but teleworkers disagree on the best practice on these two issues. Fax switches have the disadvantage that some don't work very well, and that you may severely annoy an important client who has to listen to a tinny voice asking him or her to wait, followed by some clunky electronic music, before they can press the button to send you the fax. Also if you only have one line, and are sending or receiving a long fax, then voice calls can't get through. On the other hand, modern fax switches are much more effective and almost transparent in use, and there is the cost saving on the second telephone line to consider.

Computer-based faxes allow you to save the cost of a fax machine, but have the disadvantage of often slowing your computer considerably when a

The transatlantic bank manager

Liz Codling spent 25 years working for the Bank of Montreal's Institute for Learning in Canada before deciding to return to her roots in Britain in 1994. Liz had been involved in the creation of the bank's Learning for Success scheme since 1991, and led a team of eight people: her employers were loathe to lose her.

Now she is a transatlantic telecommuter, working from her home near Dorchester, and has to cope with a five hour time difference from her colleagues. "I attend to my correspondence between 6 am and 8 am. I then have the mornings with my husband and start my working day at 12 noon, or rather, 7 am Toronto time. My colleagues know to book meetings in the morning if they need to include me."

"I miss out on the 'water cooler' conversations but colleagues are good at remembering to let me know about changes. I also found it particularly hard after tough meetings or conversations, because after I hang up I am on my own – I am unable to grab a coffee with a colleague to discuss the outcomes. I've accepted that my decision to become a permanent international telecommuter may well limit career opportunities but I am not complacent. I am always looking at how I can make sure that my job continutes to be of value to the organisation."

fax is being received. As the computer fax modem is also often used for email, if you handle a lot of messages you may find the fax is occupying the line when you want to send email and vice versa. Also, you will need to leave your computer on all the time so that faxes can be received on a 24 hour basis. If your computer crashes it will affect faxes being received. Most experienced teleworkers have a separate line and machine for faxes because of congestion problems.

When you receive a fax, do check that all the pages have arrived before filing it, especially if it is not something you are going to take action on straight away.

Email

Email is pretty much addictive. Once you have started using it for work communications, the ability to record messages by filing them on computer, plus the fact that the other person doesn't have to be there to receive the message at the time you send it (as with a phone call), makes it the most convenient form of teleworker communication. It is not without its problems, however. Some people are notoriously bad at reading and dealing with their email, whereas they will handle a fax or telephone call with no problem – you need to be sure that the person at the other end of the communication is happy with using email. Many people are quite able to send short plain text messages, but aren't clear on the ins and outs of sending files over the Internet (see Chapter 9, *Email and online services*), which is crucial for effective teleworking.

It's also frighteningly easy to take the wrong "tone" in an email and end up with an unintended dispute on your hands (hence all the "flame wars" on the Internet). Email requires a high level of facility with written communications, yet it is an informal method – abbreviations and cyberslang abound – and therefore is often used for communications which might better be handled face-to-face or by telephone. These tensions have led to the development of "emoticons", collections of characters intended to express tone, such as smiley faces. It is interesting to note that these are more widely used in North America than in Europe, and that they tend to be dispensed with by experienced teleworkers. There are three keys to successful use of email:

- use a mail reader which allows filing of messages by project, and which will allow you to sort or search messages by sender, subject and date. This allows easy retrieval of information or instructions relating to a project

- use a mail reader with an easy-to-use address book function, which allows you to quickly "lift" an email address to put into the book from an incoming message

- keep a pad by the computer when you are reading your email to write down information on instructions received which you need to act on, email contact numbers and URLs for websites. Of course you can print out the whole message, but usually it's only a couple of words that you actually need. Either way, do something to put the information on your action list, or you will forget the contents immediately after reading the email.

Videoconferencing

Videoconferencing can allow effective meetings while avoiding travel costs. If you are fortunate enough to have access to videoconferencing, you will find that although the technical standard of affordable systems today is no replacement for face-to-face meetings, it offers a big improvement over the audioconference, especially for delicate meetings or negotiations where a face-to-face meeting is not possible. However, most ISDN PC-based systems are still a bit jerky and this means you need to learn to moderate your body language. Also, on many systems only one person can "speak" at one time (rather like a VHF radio system). This means it helps the flow of the conversation if you can indicate clearly by your voice tone or other gesture when you have finished making a point. Otherwise conversations can either degenerate into a staccato cutting from one participant to another as you accidentally interrupt each other, or to a Quaker-like silence at the end of each point while the person at the other end tries to work out if you've finished talking. Videoconferencing facilities are covered in Chapter 12, *Teleworking equipment*. Although they are still beyond the pocket of many teleworkers, a number of telecottages and other bureau services are providing videoconferencing on a local basis.

Post and couriers

In many situations work still needs to be sent by post – even if it's on disk! Unless you have access to ISDN file transfer, the practical limit in cost and time terms for moving files around by email is about 2–3 megabytes. The postal service (or courier where extra speed is required) provides a largely reliable and fast door-to-door service. It is important to be clear on issues such as the last posting time at your local box or office, the time at which your post arrives (in some rural areas this can be as late as 3 pm, causing problems for teleworkers who need to turn work round fast) and the different services available, such as Swiftair, registered post and Mailsort. Equally, courier companies will have last pickup times for your area, and different delivery times for areas of the world. You don't know when you'll need them, so make sure you have up to date pricelists and contact numbers for all your delivery services.

Do log all incoming and outgoing post so that if anything goes missing, you can show when and how it left you. When disks arrive by post, check that they are readable immediately, even if you don't plan to work on that project for a few days. That way if there is a problem, you can request a replacement disk without disturbing your schedule, and the client won't know that you "sat on it" for a few days – it can be difficult to explain phoning up to request a new disk the day before the deadline...

The housekeeping

There are four chores you must find time for regularly if you are to survive as a teleworker:

- **keeping timesheets** should be done daily and the hours added up at least monthly. If you don't know what hours you worked on what project, how can you tell whether you are achieving sufficient reward for your work? And why should your employer or client pay you?

- **preparing bills** regularly and chasing payments (at least monthly). Usually regular phone calls will ensure prompt payment (bother the accounts department, not your client within the company, who probably has no control whatsoever on when your invoice will be paid). The next step for non-payers is usually a stiff solicitor's letter, which may have to be followed by use of the small claims court (see box below).

- **backing up your computer data** (at least weekly). Backup tools are covered in Chapter 12, *Teleworking equipment.* Most backup programmes can run unattended and automatically, perhaps in the evening after you have finished work for the day. Do not ignore this chore or you will regret it. The average time between failures for computer hard disks is just over two years. Sooner or later it will happen to you – you will lose all your data – so make sure you have backups, that some are kept offsite to avoid fire risk, and that you test and update backups regularly.

The maximum amount that you can recover through the Small Claims Court is £3,000. The Small Claims Court offers a simpler court procedure which is swifter, less formal and less intimidating. The registrar's decision is binding. Normally the only cost incurred is in issuing a small claims summons which costs 10% of the claim up to a £500 claim, £60 up to a £1000 claim and £80 for up to £3000. If you choose to use a solicitor you should be aware that solicitor's fees are not recoverable by either party, though costs for an expert report of up to £200 can be recovered.

Amanda Walker of home-based publishing company Phoenix 2 has used the service successfully. "The system is cheap and it's efficient – people are usually scared into paying at the point where they get the summons. They don't want to go on record as not paying their bills." The best source of advice on the Small Claims Court is probably the Citizen's Advice Bureau (local offices listed in the telephone directory) or from legal advice centres. Amanda Walker also found that County Courts provide practical assistance: "County courts are not allowed to give you advice but they are very helpful with filling in the form – it's up to you to ask the right questions. The only problem I've had is that sometimes people will send the amount directly to us without the cost of the summons added, in which case it may be best to cut your losses and accept this."

- **marketing or researching new opportunities** If you are self-employed you should be devoting somewhere between a quarter and a third of your time to marketing; for the PAYE teleworker, substantial time should be devoted to keeping in touch with the office, knowing what is going on, and ensuring that people remember you and what you do.

If you are unwell or on holiday, let your most active clients and contacts know in advance or leave a message to this effect, but try not to invite burglars through a detailed answerphone message. However, if you normally use a business name, an answerphone message may be OK – how is the burglar to know you work from home, as opposed to a busy office block? While you are away, Royal Mail Keepsafe service can hold your mail at a cost of £5 for a fortnight or £15 for two months. One week's notice is required – ask at your local post office or telephone 01345 740740.

Balancing "home" and "work"

While a formal family agreement may be excessive, prospective teleworkers should discuss and suggest ground rules as to how the family can best help and least hinder the process of working from home. For example, children's voices in the background of telephone calls create a bad impression to customers and put strain on the teleworker intent on creating a professional image. On the positive side, the teleworker is much more available (by virtue of being there in emergencies and no longer spending time commuting). Over time, a greater appreciation by the teleworker's family of what they do usually develops. Here are some starting points for discussion:

- where is the office?

- is it out of bounds to partners, children or pets? All the time or just at certain times? (Final reports have been decorated by older children with pictures of elephants… two children discovered playing frisbee with backup disks while a third is feeding the disks into the CD player "because they fit, Mummy"; pet hair tends to disagree with computer disk drives but cats in particular love to sleep on a nice warm photocopier or laser printer)

- who tidies the office? (Desk is tidied and important paper filed in bin; computer dies during crucial email of final report as it has been unplugged to make room for the vacuum cleaner)

- is company equipment available to the family? (If not, how can you explain the disappointment to games-mad children whose greatest pleasure in life is saving all those lemmings from certain death?)

- is the teleworker available for domestic chores? Which ones and when? Who does the school/childminder runs? ("What are you doing here? You're supposed to be picking the kids up from swimming!")

- who pays for the extra food needed for the teleworker's lunches and snacks? Who makes sure the food is available? ("But darling, I *always* have Boaster biscuits with my tea…")

- can the teleworker expect help from the family *eg.* with mailings? What's the "quid pro quo" for help? A family treat or money?

- how are business calls and visitors to be handled by members of the family? If the teleworker is out, do they let the answerphone go off, or do they answer the phone?

When planning the home office it may be a good idea to draw up a sketch plan, with paper templates representing the various items to be fitted into the room, and get the family to help in designing what should go where. Bear in mind the realities – a loft office may have steep steps where children just love to leave toys to trip up the teleworker, whereas a room which is a pathway to others will always cause the teleworker to suffer interruption. And remember: "There is never enough room. The paperless office – the biggest joke of all time!"

It's also worth discussing how you see the teleworking routine working. Some teleworkers report that they need to keep to a strict schedule in order to maintain their work discipline. Others find that it helps their motivation to continue to put on "work" clothes. For some it is the boundaries that are important – quite a few report that they go for a walk before and after work time to divide work from home life. Some teleworkers go to the other extreme and may work late into the night. All of these changes and routines can cause strains if they are not talked through, leading to interruption problems such as the "ogre in the spare room" syndrome, with children creeping round the house unnaturally quietly because "Daddy is working".

THIS IS THE SPARE ROOM WHERE YOU'LL BE SLEEPING – NOW – IF THE FAX GOES OFF IGNORE IT, EXCEPT IF IT BLEEPS THEN YOU'LL HAVE TO CHANGE THE FAX ROLL… THE ANSWERING MACHINE IS ON AUTOMATIC, BUT IF IT'S BILL FROM BRISBANE, COME AND WAKE ME UP…DON'T WORRY IF THE COMPUTER BACKUP TAPE STARTS………

Hints for homeworkers

Homeworking has its good points –
Forget about that bus
And the rush-hour crowds and tube strikes
Have no effect on us.

The downside is the effort
It takes to fill each day
When all you've got ahead of you
Is work to earn your pay.

The routine I've developed
Is big on washing up.
Take each item separately,
Wash, rinse and dry each cup.

Another thing I'd mention
That really helps time pass is
Tightening up those little screws
On specs, if you wear glasses.

Some people check their cheque stubs
Other clean their shoes
Displacement chores are plentiful:
It's up to you to choose.

You'll find your own distractions,
(And don't forget the phone).
There's nothing like a day to fill
When you are on your own.

Simon Rae
(first published in Guardian Weekend section)

Most parents find that they need to either arrange for the children to be out of the house at school or a childminder's, or arrange for a childminder to be present in the home if they are to telework successfully. Stresses can arise if the burden of childcare shifts from one parent to the other and everyone is living and working in the same space. "I found I couldn't concentrate because I didn't believe my husband was looking after our daughter properly while I was working. She was at a demanding, toddler stage and he would just watch the telly in the same room instead of attending to her. If I heard her crying it was almost impossible for me to stay in the office. Things did improve when we changed the glass door of the office to a solid one so that she couldn't see me when I was working, but it was still stressful for me." To add to the stress, childcare costs are not tax deductible and must be paid in full.

The support organisation Parents at Work publishes a guide on *Balancing Home and Work* – contact 0171 700 5771 or fax 0171 700 1105.

Housework duties may also change as a result of one or both adults teleworking. Ursula Huws, in her study *Teleworking and Gender*, 1996, found that in households with more than one adult, only 11% of men had taken on primary responsibility for housework, whereas only one-third of the sample contributed more than three-quarters of the household income. Around 45% of the men contributed less than half the household income, so overall it appears that men are doing less income earning but are not replacing this with housework responsibilities to any great extent. The women in Huws' sample were more likely than men to work standard office hours, and women were also three times as likely as men to be interrupted by children when working. Men, on the other hand, were three times as likely to be interrupted by friends when working...

On the bright side, once teething troubles have been resolved, teleworking allows far more opportunity to integrate home and work: "It can be hell when they're small, and friends tell me boys are worse than girls. Always say goodbye and greet them back from school – never be too busy – put the answering machine on instead. Do the taxi runs such as guides, music lessons *etc* Make them feel that there are times when they can use the equipment (under supervision when tiny) and that there are things they must not do (such as "format c:"); but they must also understand there are times when you are not to be disturbed." It's also a good idea to decide on a review of the situation after an agreed initial period so everyone in the family can have their say about whether teleworking works for them.

"Plan your day around the family. There is no point in getting frustrated with the children coming home from school and interrupting you. Plan breaks at times such as these and enjoy them rather than try to battle on irritably. One of the joys of teleworking is surely that you can have more time for the family when it needs your time."

"I enjoy teleworking because it means I have more time with the family through not having to commute. Also a lovely rural setting and a roomy office make working from home very attractive. The downside is that work is always there, lurking in the corner of your mind and you feel yourself inexorably drawn to it. However, in any conflict with the housework, work wins hands down. I'm often glad of the excuse it gives me to ignore the dust for a bit longer!"

"Not everyone may agree, but interruptions from family members need not necessarily be unwelcome if you organise your work properly and establish ground rules."

"It is very important when working at home to keep your business and family phones separate. Nothing is as frustrating as continually answering calls for your teenage daughter or discovering that an important caller could not get through because the phone was engaged by family members all afternoon."

Maintaining the worker

A number of physiological complaints can result from long-term use of computers and include eye strain, blurred vision, burning eyes, back pain, sore shoulders and RSI (repetitive strain injury). Teleworker home offices need to be designed with appropriate desks and chairs to minimise these problems, and teleworkers need to be aware of their existence (see Chapter 8, *Staying safe and legal*). It usually helps to arrange the work place to face outwards towards stimulating views, and to take sensible breaks at regular intervals.

"The BT directory enquiries experiment in Inverness found that although teleworkers suffer less stress than their office-based counterparts, they suffer more snack attacks. I can relate to this totally. The only way I cope is by banning biscuits for the house, and allowing myself one chocolate bar when I take the post to the shop at 4 pm."

Surprisingly, many comments were received about the problem of overworking.

"An important problem I find – and it may seem a curious one – is a tendency to overwork. Your work is always there and it is easy to be tempted to do it rather than something else. I think it important, therefore, to have a clear idea of why you are teleworking in the first place (living in the country, more time for the family, *etc*) and carry out periodic audits to see if you are effectively achieving your aims. Resist the temptation to overwork. Make your breaks real breaks away from the computer. Stop and eat; don't nibble and keep going. Plan your social and family life and make your leisure commitments as binding as your professional ones. Comfort yourself with the quantity of work completed rather than worry about the work remaining to be done. Take that walk in the morning if the sun is shining. You can always catch up in the evening when it may well be raining. Set yourself reasonable targets (daily, weekly, monthly) and learn to relax when you have reached them."

These comments are backed up by a Joseph Rowntree Trust report which found that over a quarter of working fathers in Britain already work more than the 48 hours maximum prescribed by the recent European Working Time directive. The report looked at a series of domestic tasks, who did what and how often families socialised together. For men who worked over 50 hours a week these activities dropped right down. The report also identified a minority of mothers whose partners provided little help in the home. These women were discontented and vulnerable to depression – a possible indication of the future for workaholic teleworkers.

"The one thing a teleworker should strive not to be is what I have become. I am addicted to personal computers much as someone could be said to be addicted to crack cocaine. I have two PCs in my home office and they are on from 0700 to 2000 six days a week. The day off is my wife's idea but you should see me get the jitters at 1700 on a Saturday. Holidays away

A BOON to the remote worker

BOON (Business On Open Network), is headquartered in the Duchy of Cornwall's industrial development at Poundbury in Dorset and runs a number of schemes which Manager Drew Llewellyn is keen to offer at a distance, or else to develop similar franchised services in other regions. BOON received some initial funding from Dorset councils, the RDC and Barclays Bank, but has been a freestanding commercial enterprise for two years.

The **Mouse to Mouse Resuscitation**™ scheme offers a complete service to local businesses, specifying equipment for them, purchasing, optimising and installing it. "Mouse to Mouse ensures that the system works really well and gives the customer an instant start – a computer that can be used usefully and productively the moment it arrives in the office. We make sure they don't spend money they don't need to on hardware, but that they have the system that they need – and we throw in a free fax modem. Usually the charge is about 25–30% of the equipment cost, but often we are advising a substantially cheaper computer than the one they originally intended to buy, so that cost can often be "invisible" to the small business." Drew believes 80% of computer problems can be solved over the phone, with the other 20% requiring either a visit to the customer, or the customer bringing the computer in to BOON for checking.

The **Countrywork** scheme provides computers to small businesses to try out for a couple of months. BOON has around 24 laptops and desktops for hire, and the costs vary from about £30 plus VAT per month to over £100 per month depending on the machines. "Hiring computers works very well for a lot of startup businesses. The cost of the computer hardware is insignificant these days compared to the cost of getting it set up correctly and learning to use it properly", says Drew.

Six people also work on contracts to **install and upgrade software** for larger businesses in Dorset and surrounding counties. Recently they completed a project to reconfigure 220 PCs for their local NHS trust, and they take on database publication work as well as supplying IT support to the council's economic development team. A project to enter details of all operations carried out in Dorset hospitals provided work for four BOON people for a period of several months.

Finally, BOON also acts as a **drop-in centre** for people to use computers, print out their work and network their skills. One of BOON's associate teleworkers records translations from Japanese to English on tape. BOON transcribes the tapes and emails the results to the teleworker's clients worldwide. Drew's advice to prospective telecworkers is: "Forget everything except two things – what you're going to do and who you're going to do it to. If you focus on that you won't go wrong because you'll be fitting the technology to your own circumstances. Otherwise you can easily spend £5,000 on luxury electronics that you don't really need."

from home and the office can get hairy. Whatever you do, make sure you can walk away from your work without thinking about it."

At least this teleworker has insight into his condition – others become tedious workaholics, unable to see that what should be a method of introducing freedom and balance into life has become an excuse for self-imposed slavery. An old hand recommends: "Set yourself a limit on the number of hours a week you will normally work except in exceptional circumstances."

"Make sure that you don't push yourself too hard and that you "leave" work at a regular time. Don't forget how lucky you are to have escaped the commuter lifestyle. But don't forget the bumper sticker that says: 'Even if you win the rat race, you are still a rat!'"

"Take advantage of the flexibility of teleworking by arranging at least one exercise session a week during "normal" working hours – it breaks up the routine and makes you feel privileged to be a teleworker – you get empty pools, cheap horseriding and so on."

"If you're working alone, put the answerphone on or take the phone off the hook when you go for a toilet break."

Another area where "maintenance" is required is the updating of skills through appropriate training. Teleworkers have to adapt to three new areas of skill

- ■ communication
- ■ handling customers and clients
- ■ networking to find work and opportunities.

These areas represent significant challenges to the new teleworker and formal training can ease the transition considerably. However, after a period of years teleworking, it is likely to be core skills such as software packages and professional qualifications which will need updating. For the self-employed, this means planning budget and time to take courses. For those in PAYE employment, training is an issue which needs regular discussion with your manager to ensure you don't end up in a skills backwater.

Loneliness of the long distance teleworker

Teleworkers, particularly those who are disabled or based in rural areas, can suffer from isolation if they work from home for long periods. There are a number of online services which provide "coffee shops" for teleworkers, including Internet listservs and the Telework Europa forum on CompuServe. Professional associations such as the TCA that provide helplines and conferences can also assist in reducing isolation. Telecottages and telecentres also provide an alternative workspace where contact with peers can be maintained.

Some teleworkers choose to share an office with a neighbour or colleague who is teleworking for companionship and because they find that being "observed" makes them work, even though their companion is not their boss and may well work in a completely different field.

"Based on my experience as a freelance translator, I found that one of the key aspects was the relative lack of praise and positive feedback when working alone. Customers call when there is a panic to sort out, or when they want an urgent piece of work, or when they get a bill and want to whinge. Creative work requires constant positive feedback if it is to maintain its spark. I think most lone workers suffer from a definite lack of professional backslapping. I don't know how to solve this other than by establishing a kind of mutual admiration society for lone workers which sounds dreadful."

"I make a point of getting out to see someone in a business capacity at least once a week face-to-face. It doesn't really matter who they are – client, suspect, prospect, supplier – but it meets the need for face-to-face networking and avoids teleworking cabin fever, especially during the early spring. It may even lead to some business!"

"There was one occasion when I was tempted to use the Samaritan's online service. I was owed a lot of money, the work was piling up and my concentration was just shot to pieces. I found I was just reading and rereading my email messages instead of getting anything done and things were geting out of control. In the end I went to my GP and that solved the problem, but the Samaritan's email address is jo@samaritans.org for anyone else who gets that way."

"Translation is a lonely business at the best of times – you do not really need much contact with your clients and don't want it from anyone else while you are working – so that it is necessary to get the balance right. I find it useful to visit my clients, circumstances permitting, even when it is not really necessary. This puts phone contact onto a human basis afterwards and you get the feeling of belonging to a group of real people."

"I've been a teleworker for more than a decade and have prided myself on being able to keep customers and have a good working relationship with them from a distance. But this spring a grant from an enterprise group allowed me to bring over two people from one of my export customers and I was amazed what a difference it made to work with them face-to-face for a day and then go out and relax with them over a good meal. It's surprising how much you can get the wrong impression of people over email and the phone – now our calls are much more relaxed and chatty."

Other activities that can help to reduce isolation include attending workshops, exhibitions and seminars (these also help to keep your skills and contacts up), joining professional associations, and seeking out discussion groups on the Internet.

On the other side of the isolation equation, city-based teleworkers report plagues of neighbours dropping in to borrow envelopes, stamps, use photocopiers, browse the web and so on. A quiet word, or the imposition of a nominal fee for the facility often solves this problem.

Technical support is an area of isolation which directly affects all teleworkers at some time or other. There must be a law about why software problems always develop after office hours. PAYE teleworkers will often have access to company IT specialists to solve their problems (and may have priority over their onsite colleagues in use of these services). But self-employed teleworkers are usually dependent on their computer supplier: "The main reason for using a reliable small local computer dealer rather than buying mail order." A number of computer manufacturers operate premium phonelines for support which do cover evenings and weekends, but often these give limited help for the first 60 days after a purchase. There is definitely a gap in the market for competent IT support personnel to provide premium rate support services to teleworkers. The problem is that teleworkers often have high specification systems with many add-ons which can make it difficult to diagnose the difficulty even where a modem is available for the engineer to use for dialling in.

Some companies are now offering telephone-based technical support advice. Steve Argent of Computer Troubleshooters asks an annual fee of £29.99 for access to unlimited telephone support from 9 am to 9 pm during the week, and 9 am to 6 pm at weekends. He says: "If there is a software issue, we are nearly always able to sort it out. If there is a hardware problem, we have to stop if it is a fault but we try to identify the problem. Most people don't know where the problems lies because of the complexity of software packages." However, because Computer Troubleshooters uses a BT One Number (07071) system, your call will cost you about 35p per minute in the daytime, about 25p in the evenings and 12.5p at weekends. This is not a premium line service – CT make no additional income from this feature, but if your call isn't urgent you may wish to time the call to take advantage of lower rates.

Perhaps the most fitting piece of advice to novice teleworkers received is this one: "Learn to juggle. It also helps with the invoicing, customer, marketing, and those mountains of backup floppies. I'm still hopeless after 12 years."

Associations

The obvious place for teleworkers to get support is from a telework association. A number exist in Britain and Ireland, and were reviewed by Bill Murray of Small World Connections in the May 1997 edition of *Flexible Working* Magazine. Bill recommends that in deciding which group to join you should:

- Talk to the group's administrator and find out how many existing members come from organisations with similar profiles to your own
- Find out how often you will have a chance to share experiences with other group members

- Request samples of the group's published material;
- Ask for the names of one or two members you could approach for an opinion on how useful or not they find the group.

TSIG and the Teleworking Platform

The Teleworking Special Interest Group was set up by the Department of Trade and Industry in 1992 to pull together a number of initiatives, some of which were recently passed to the Telework Platform, which has no formal members but acts as an umbrella organisation to lobby government and sponsor the annual Telework UK conference. TSIG remains as a channel for exchange of information about teleworking. Membership is free. Contact is through email: telework-request@mailbase.ac.uk or telework.platform@awsf.cix.co.uk

The Corporate Telework Forum

Established in 1997, the forum has a founding group of 16 members, including three of the "big four" banks. It costs £850 a year for membership, and is aimed at large companies – "the opportunity for peers from different companies to meet and work together". Membership provides subscriptions to *Flexible Working*, the *Teleworking Handbook*, and the *Teleworker*, a quarterly newsletter, access to a closed user group, access to results of working group reports and discounts on quarterly seminars.
http://Teleworking.MadeEasy.com

Telework Ireland

Telework Ireland membership is for teleworkers, telecottages, corporates and those with an interest in teleworking. Established in 1993, the association membership has reached 250. Individual membership costs £30 p.a. Members receive a bimonthly newsletter, the Teleworking Handbook, and the Teleworker. There is a web database of member skills. TWI is allied to the Small Firms Association providing access to its events, seminars, discount schemes and magazine. A development officer has been apointed to promote teleworking as a business method for individuals and corporats and to assist in community development of teleworker support centres. TWI is developing a training programme and hosts an annual conference. Tel: +353 47 720069 Web: http://www.telework.ie

CWU Ireland

The Communications Workers Union in Ireland has a special "virtual membership" for teleworkers launched in 1997 which costs £99. Members get the *Teleworking Handbook*, an advice line including legal assistance, access to union sickness benefits and insurance schemes, and a free web advertisement for their services. There are plans for a virtual work agency for teleworkers and training programmes. CWU also acts as a lobbying group for teleworkers and has close contacts with the Irish government's Information Society Commission, as well as being the Irish national coordinator for the European Telework Development Project. There is an annual conference. Tel: +353 21 887403 Web: http://www.cwu.ie

Telework Scotland

A Scottish Teleworking Association was establsihed in 1995 which worked together with the TCA in delivering information to members. Two groups are planning to take this forward – contact Roy Guthrie Tel: 01324 664164 Email: Roy_Guthrie@compuserve.com and Linda Robertson Tel: 01967 411209 Email: lrobertson@cix.compulink.co.uk for further details.

Telecottages Wales

Established in 1991, Telecottages Wales has around 102 members, mainly individuals and telecottages. Membership benefits are as for TCA, plus a Welsh newsletter and meetings in Wales, and a well organised forums section on its website. TCW is also involved in the Telemart work agency for teleworkers project. Membership is free while the association develops its range of services, which will include advice on teleworking issues and telecentres and keeping members in touch with "teleopportunities". http://www.telecottages.org Tel: 01938 556822

The Telework, Telecottage and Telecentre Association (TCA)

Established in 1993, the TCA has around 2,500 members, mainly individuals. and telecottages and costs £30 a year. It provides members with the *Teleworking Handbook*, and the bimonthly colour magazine *Teleworker,* plus an online newsletter, information on work opportunities, an advice line, local groups, an annual conference, access to its teleworker training vocational qualifications and group discounts on some products. Tel: 0800 616008 Web: http://www.tca.org.uk

The Future Work Forum

Established in 1992, the Future Work Forum is run by Henley Management College and costs around £2,000 a year. It provides quarterly seminars, workshops, visits, an annual dinner, published proceedings, research reports and an information service. Aimed at corporates, it specialises in providing expert speakers and thinkers in the area of flexible working.

National Association of Telework

Established in 1992, the NAT has mainly individual members and membership is £100 a year. Members get subscriptions to the *European Journal of Telework* and the *Teleworking UK* newsletter, both of which are quarterly, plus access to a quality assurance programme and listing on a database of members. However, co-ordinator Steve Simmons says that the association plans to move to servicing companies rather than individuals. Tel: 01404 47467 Email: srs@cornix.co.uk

NB: European support groups are listed in Chapter 14, *The European perspective.*

Bibliography

Home Run
Author: Sophie Chalmers
Source: Active Information, Cribau Mill, Llanvair Discoed, Chepstow, Gwent, UK NP6 6RD Tel: 01291 641222 Fax: 01291 641777 Email: info@homerun.co.uk
Comments: Periodical on running businesses from home published 10 times per year

Teleworker Magazine
Editor: Alan Denbigh Tel: 01453 834874 Fax: 01453 836174
Email:teleworker@compuserve.com
Source: TCA Tel: 0800 616008 or 01203 696986 Fax: 01203 696538
Comment: Bi-monthly magazine for TCA members

30 Minutes... to boost your communication skills *Date:* 1997
Author: Elizabeth Tierney
Source: Kogan Page, 120 Pentonville Rd, London N1 9JN ISBN 0–7494–23676

Corporate Telework Survey *Date:* 1997
Authors: Small World Connections
Source: PO Box 162, South District Office, Manchester M20 3BB Tel: 0161 445 0630
Fax: 0161 445 1403 Email: small_world@compuserve.com

Get Yourself Organised! (60 minutes Success Skills Series) *Date:* 1997
Author: Mike Levy
Source: David Grant Publishing, 80 Ridgeway, Kent TN2 4EZ ISBN 1–901306–00–3

Hebridean Teleworker *Date:* 1997
Source: Western Isles Project Office Tel: 01851 880225 Fax: 01851 880386
Email: itproject@sol.co.uk
Comment: Networking newsletter for teleworkers in the Western Isles with database
of 500 skilled people which has been built up by the Western Isles Project Office.

Maximise Your Time (60 minutes Success Skills Series) *Date:* 1997
Author: Ronald Bracey
Source: David Grant Publishing, 80 Ridgeway, Kent TN2 4EZ ISBN 1–901306–02–X

The PC Novice's Handbook *Date:* 1997
Author: Harshad Kotecha
Source: Computer Step, Southfield Rd, Southam, Warwickshire CV33 0FB
ISBN 1–874029–62–8

Teleworking and Gender *Date:* 1996
Author: Ursula Huws Web: http://www.dspace.dial.pipex.com/analytica
Source: Institute for Employment Studies, Mantell Building, University of Sussex,
Brighton BN1 9RF Tel: 01273 686751 Fax: 01273 690430.

Parenting in the 1990s *Date:* 1996
Authors: Elsa Ferri and Kate Smith
Source: Joseph Rowntree Foundation Tel: 0171 486 8211.

Lone Parents & Their Information & Communication Technologies *Date:* 1995
Authors: Leslie Haddon & Roger Silverstone
Source: Science Policy Research Unit, University of Sussex, SPRU, Mantell Building,
Falmer, Brighton BN1 9RF

Work with Passion: How to do what you Love for a Living *Date:*1995
Author: Nancy Anderson
Source: New World Library ISBN 1–880032–54–6

Contacts and URLs

BOON Ltd (Mouse to Mouse Resuscitation™) Burraton Yard, Poundsbury Village,
Dorchester, Dorset DT1 3GR Tel: 01305 257577 Fax: 01305 257588
Email: boon.ltd@dial.pipex.com

Parents at Work formerly the Working Mothers Association, 77 Holloway Rd,
London N7 8JZ Tel: 0171 628 3578

Trouble Shooters – pay an annual subscription for telephone technical support with
your PC problems. Tel: 0171 323 5757.

Getting work

Much of this chapter is concerned with a topic of huge interest to self-employed teleworkers: getting work. Some sections are therefore not relevant to telecommuters. For ideas on services which can be offered by teleworkers, see Chapter 7, *Ideas for teleservices*.

Marketing yourself as a teleworker

Many teleworkers have excellent skills in their areas of expertise, but know nothing about sales and marketing. Think about getting professional help with marketing and assertiveness training if the whole idea of selling makes you nervous. In the UK, your local Business Link, TEC or LEC would be a good place to look for help. In Ireland, talk to FÁS and your local County Enterprise Board. But perhaps the first thing to do is adjust your mindset.

From your customers' point of view, they probably aren't that interested in whether you are a teleworker, even though you may see teleworking as a central issue. So begin your marketing review with a simple resolution coined by Horace Mitchell of telework consultants MTA Associates:

"Don't mention the T-word (teleworker…)"

What your customers are probably looking for is higher quality and lower cost than they can get elsewhere. How are you going to convince them that you can achieve this? Here are some quotes from a TCA conference on marketing teleworking:

"If people are sending work out of their office they expect it to be done better than if it was done in their own office. Everything has to be slicker and more efficient. You have to have a control system that makes absolutely sure work doesn't get mixed up, that it's done in the right order, on time and accurately. You have to be more careful than if you were working for one particular business. One of the problems of our company name is that if you pick up the phone and call a potential client, you get the secretary who immediately thinks you are out to take her job away! Big disadvantage!" *Judith Verity, Office Ghosts*

"I looked at what the competition were charging for their reports and tried to get in at that sort of level. People tend not to take you seriously if you are not expensive enough. And when people ring to place an order, we answer the telephone in exactly the same way. To the customer it is a unified response although it may be a different voice. It is like a corporate image over the telephone line." *Anthony Capstick, Instant Search*

The second change in mindset you need to make concerns marketing. Marketing is not selling or public relations. Marketing is the process of adjusting what you are selling (your product) to best fit the demands of your customers. It can cover all kinds of strategies, including the timing and method of delivery of work, the pricing, the technical details of the work (such as the software packages used). Successful marketing is the key to a successful small business.

Establish your objectives

Objectives can be difficult to define for teleworkers. Some teleworkers want a way of working which allows them more time with their families. Others are concerned with improving profits through lowering overheads. Others may be motivated by the desire to avoid commuting to work. This chapter limits itself to looking at business objectives, but it is recommended that anyone considering starting up a teleworking small business should consult the small business guides listed in the bibliography, and spend some time with their family working out a set of objectives – which might cover profits needed to cover living expenses, number of hours to be worked each week, circumstances under which the teleworker can be disturbed in the home office – and which everyone in the family understands and agrees to.

You need a clear business idea and set of objectives before you start thinking about marketing. Equipping yourself with the computer and the telephone is not enough. You need to know:

■ what services will be offered? See Chapter 7, *Ideas for teleservices*

■ who is going to use the service?

■ how do people buy it? By phone and fax? Pay attention to answerphone messages and fax presentation – the "shop window" of a teleworked business

■ when do people buy it? Are there peak periods (such as thesis deadlines) that need to be covered in terms of staff levels?

■ where do people buy it from? Through the Yellow Pages, or through a personal recommendation, or perhaps through a Web page?

Location, location, location

There are plenty of case studies giving examples of people working far from their clients or employers such as programmers working from Australia, or Irish call centres servicing the North American market. Teleworking can allow work to be independent of distance. But all the evidence is that most companies prefer to use teleworkers who are located close enough to be able to pop in and discuss work face-to-face when needed. The *TeleFutures* study in Ireland (1996) found that over 80% of companies would prefer their teleworkers to be situated within 25 miles. The exception to this is people with rare skills or combinations of skills, who can usually lay down their own conditions on how they will work. Some people promote teleworking by having two different prices for their work – a lower price if the job can be teleworked without on-site client meetings. Overall, however, the lower your skill set (*eg* secretarial), the more likely it is that your clientele will be local, so build this factor into your business plan.

- do others already offer a similar product or service? Is your service an improvement on these competitors? Is there any evidence that customers want an improvement?

- how much is it going to cost? Are you going to be cheaper, on a par with, or more expensive than your competitors?

- what is the business going to be called (eg something that relates to your business, your own name, an abstract word, a telecottage, telecentre, telebureau, or teleservice)? The name will depend upon your target market. For example, community resource centres find the term telecottage well understood and reassuring. In contrast commercial organisations may prefer not to use the telecottage name at all, but talk of a business resource centre, or teleservice centre. People offering a teleworked professional service may prefer to use a version of their own name as the business name since the clients are essentially "hiring" that person.

- what happens if a contract goes badly wrong? Do you need professional indemnity insurance in case a customer sues you? (N.B. It is often a condition of professional indemnity policies that you do not tell your customers you are insured because that could make them more likely to sue.) Do you need to take legal advice to draw up a general contract for signature with clients?

Brian O'Kane's guide *Starting a Business in Ireland* suggests two exercises which help in clarifying your business idea.

1. **Write your own CV** for the position of managing director/administrator of your business. What are your skills and experience? Build on these. Look at your technical, personal and business skills.

2. **Write a short description** of the processes which must be completed before you have something for which you can invoice a customer (eg receive enquiry, discuss with client, give quotation, use software package on computer and so on). Throughout, keep a list of every item which will be required, from paper to printer right down to the chair you sit on.

Market research

Once you have your business idea clear you need to do some market research. If you are applying for any kind of outside assistance in starting up a small business, the questions which grant-giving bodies or banks will want answered include:

- what is the total market for this service and what are the overall trends in this market area (static, expanding, contracting)? Look for national surveys undertaken on market share and size – many are available from good reference libraries.

- how much of that total market is practically accessible to your service (*eg* if it is a geographically limited service, check out what percentage of the national market is in your "catchment area")? Research basic figures in your local library such as the population in your area, the percentage of people unemployed, the breakdown of types of employment into service, manufacturing, agriculture, and so on).

- how much of the accessible market could you reasonably hope to capture? This answer should take into account practical constraints (*eg* maximum number of productive hours in a year which you expect to work) and will look more convincing if you give a minimum and a maximum and then show that you are selecting a fairly conservative figure between the two.

- what competitors do you have? Their strengths and weaknesses? How much do they charge? To provide information on costs, there is little alternative to ringing round competitor companies to check out prices. This is a horrible job but vital. Make sure you have a "project" for them to quote on or they will quickly realise that you are not a bona fide customer. If you are competing only with other community organisations, you may not need to apply this cloak and dagger approach – just ask! Look through Yellow Pages to see how many companies are working in your area. Don't forget that your competitors may be listed in different sections of the telephone directory such as secretarial services, computer graphics, desktop publishing, computer training, computer consultancy and so on.

- ask existing customers, family, friends. Why do people use your services?

The information from your market research will be used to prepare your business plan.

Business planning

There are many books and guides available which will help you to put together a formal business plan (see bibliography). Many Business Links have advisers who can help with business plans, as do high street banks. The purpose of a business plan is to produce a document, probably only around 10 pages in length for a simple small business, which has four basic functions:

- to help you clarify your thinking – focusing your thoughts and making sure you have done the calculations needed to ensure your plan is realistic;

- to establish that your business idea is financially viable;

- to provide an accessible, clear document which contains all the relevant information about your business idea for outsiders including advisers such as accountants, and people you want to invest in your business such as bank managers;

■ to provide a baseline against which the progress of your business can be measured.

There are many different structures for business plans. Here is a simple one which covers the basics provided by Liam Kelly of Forbairt.

1. **Principals:** who are you? Why should anyone believe you can do this? Brief history and objective of your business. Past performance (if available).

2. **Product:** what will you sell and what processes are involved before you have something to sell to the customer? How is it different to other competing services? Is it ready to sell now or do you need to develop it in some way?

3. **Location:** where will you carry out the business? Why have you chosen that location and how does it fit in with how you need to carry out your business? Do you have specific premises in mind? Indicate the purchase cost or rental. If you are working from home, estimate the reduction in overheads compared to a conventional office.

4. **Machinery or equipment:** what is needed for your product or service? Give cost estimates and indicate if you already possess any of the relevant equipment.

5. Are any **raw materials** or parts needed?

6. **Employment:** who will be employed by the business? On what basis? Full-time, part-time, subcontracted? Don't forget all those boring administrative tasks vital to continued successful operation, such as chasing debts.

7. **Management:** what will the management structure be? Outline the qualifications and experience of the key personnel.

8. **Finance:** where will you get the money from? How much will be invested by the principals? How much will be borrowed and on what terms? How much are you looking for in terms of grants (if any)?

9. **Profitability:** the figures bit. Provide audited accounts for the last two years if you have them. Give projected profit and loss acounts and balance sheets for the first two years of the project.

10. **Marketing:** how will your products be sold? Do you have any firm contracts or orders? Market surveys? Competitors?

Setting prices and quoting

Preparing a business plan can seem to be a bit of a circular process – how can you know how much to charge until you know what the running costs are that you will have to cover? Or how successful your service will be? But in fact, a combination of estimating running costs and researching the prices charged by others for similar services will probably give you a fairly good guide to what you should be charging. This in turn may get you to refine your ideas about your start-up costs – what you will really need to get going.

So start by doing the cash flows and other business calculations to find out what you need to earn to cover your running costs. If you aren't sure of how to do this, refer to some of the small business guides in the bibliography or get professional help from an accountant or business adviser. Your selling price must be higher than this breakeven cost. Selling price in turn affects your choice of target market, means of communication, choice of name and so on.

Many teleworkers find quoting for jobs nervewracking initially. Applying common sense is the best advice. If you aren't sure, ask to prepare a small section of the work as a "free sample". Work out how long it takes you, and multiply up to the size of the whole job. Use the trial section of work to get the exact details of the job agreed with the customer. Novices tend to underquote so think about adding on 20% to the final amount you arrive at. Some customers find it reassuring to know the underlying cost per hour that you are calculating from. Others want you to quote a fixed price for the whole job. If you are on good terms with other teleworkers, ask them for advice on quotes.

Raising finance

The next step once you have a business plan is to raise the necessary finance for starting up. Double check your business plan figures with the checklist of items overleaf which you may need just to get started. Decide which are priority items, and which non-priority or unnecessary. Can you reduce costs by buying secondhand or borrowing? Remember to include VAT in the prices unless you are VAT registered, in which case you will be able to reclaim many VAT amounts.

One important item you will need to decide on with your accountant or financial adviser is whether to register for VAT. You are required to register for VAT if your business turns over more than £48,000 in the UK, or more than £20,000 in Ireland for service-based businesses (the manufacturing threshold is £40,000 but most teleworkers count as services). However, it may be worth your while registering even if you turnover is lower in some circumstances. For most teleworkers, the issues are:

- if you register then you can reclaim VAT on equipment you purchase

- if your customers are VAT registered, it will not inconvenience them that you charge VAT; but if they are mainly *not* registered, then it is actually going to cost them more to use you if you do register

- if you register, you will need to set up, learn and keep VAT accounts and make regular returns. In some ways this is a pain, in others it is a blessing in disguise because it forces you to keep your accounts up to date.

Checklist of items

Item	Priority	Cost new	Cost secondhand
Computer			
Software			
Modem			
Telephone			
Answerphone			
Printer			
Fax			
Photocopier			
Scanner			
Repair contract			
Tape drive for backup			
Surge supressed power sockets			
Consumables (paper, ink cartridges *etc*)			
Disks			
Disk storage			
Files and shelves			
Online subscriptions for email			
Desks			
Chairs			
Filing cabinets			
Suspension files			
Labels			
Postal scales			
Desk light			
Pinboard			
Reference books			
Stationery - paperclips and pens			
Envelopes			
Postage stamps			
Business cards			
Compliment slips			
Letterheads			
Brochures			
Professional fees (accountant, solicitor)			

Other sources of finance and advice

Business Links: Originally called 'one stop shops' the intention of Business Links is to provide one source of information and advice for small businesses rather than a huge range of enterprise agencies as had previously been the case. There are now around 250 Business Links covering the UK (called Business Shops in Scotland and Business Connect in Wales.) You can contact your local Business Link by ringing the Business Link Signpost line 0345 567765 – in some cases they can put you through directly.

Business Links are partnerships of a number of organisations which include TECs (Training and Enterprise Councils), Chambers of Commerce, local authorities, and enterprise agencies. They are a first point of call and their business advisers should have a good idea of the types of grants, funding, export support, venture capital and other schemes available. Some of the schemes they should be able to advise you about are:

Business Start up Allowance (formerly the Enterprise Allowance): This has recently been changed to a one-off payment of £250 with a requirement to attend 4 days of business training. In certain assisted areas the old style allowance which paid £40 per week for a start-up phase may still be available. There are a number of qualifying parameters which include submitting a business plan.

DTI Loan Guarantee Scheme: Provides a guarantee for established businesses which have been trading for two years for up to £250,000. There is also a Small Loans scheme for amounts up to £30,000. The DTI guarantees 85 per cent of the outstanding amount to the lender for which you pay a guarantee premium – though the lender should take this into account when making charges. Details of the scheme are available through your business bank.

Enterprise Investment Scheme: The tax incentive scheme to encourage business investment. Here a business creates an investment opportunity and at its own expense arranges for it to be approved by the tax authorities. The investors can then claim tax relief on their investments. You need good legal and financial advice if you are considering this option.

Career Development Loans: This scheme provides subsidised loans for training and retraining purposes.

Local advice: Development officers from local council economic departments will have information on the grant and funding schemes available within their areas. This will include advice on regional funding, European schemes as well as any local schemes such as discretionary rate relief, or business start-up assistance. Training and Enterprise Councils (LECs In Scotland) are also a good starting point. Details from your Business Link or the TEC National Council, Tel: 0171 735 0010.

Sources of finance and advice continued...

Enterprise Agencies: Many of these are being drawn into Business Link partnerships so you may be duplicating information but check your phone directory for local agencies.

You can also consider:

- *Selling unwanted items and equipment*

- *Borrowing against the value of your house*

- *Cashing in shares and stocks*

- *Using credit cards*

- *Borrowing from friends and relatives – when they can afford it and with clear arrangements about when they'll receive their money back, and what interest will be paid*

- *Buying the book Grants for Business (£39.50) which provides information on many sources of finance (Associated Management Services, Tel: 01793 480374)*

- *Contacting the Prince's Youth Business Trust if you are under 25.*

You are more likely to be successful if you take a conservative approach to start-up costs and "make do" rather than going for expensive items and incurring large financing charges, but beware: a common error is to underestimate start-up costs. Your financing will also need to include working capital – the money you need to start up and keep going until the first cheques come in. Bear in mind that unless you are doing basic secretarial work where people call in to collect their work, and you can extract money as you deliver work, you are unlikely to be paid less than 30 days from the date you invoice a customer. In many cases the delay between completion of the job and invoicing, and payment of the invoice, will be 45 or 60 days. Don't strangle your business at birth by failing to accommodate these delays with adequate finance. The most common cause of business failure is cash flow – so make sure that you invoice at the earliest possible instance, follow up with a statement to remind them, and then chase payment.

The options for raising finance are:

1. Your own equity

2. Other people's equity (shareholders)

3. Debt – fixed or floating, short or long term

4. Grants (almost without exception, grant-making bodies will require that you raise at least half the cost yourself).

Start by thinking about what finance you yourself can raise, and by taking a careful look at which of your assets you would need to retain if your business went under. You may not want to mortgage your house as collateral for a business bank loan, but other possible items might include:

- cash
- shares
- luxury items such as jewellery or paintings
- cars
- land/houses.

Now consider the possibility of investment (other people's equity). In general small businesses have difficulty raising equity capital or venture capital except from friends and relatives because the amount of money is too small (normally around £500,000 is the minimum investors want to look at because of the expense of checking and setting up the operation).

Whatever the source of your equity finance, be very clear on the following points outlined in Brian O'Kane's guide:

- are you prepared to allow other people to own (and therefore control) part of your business?
- what reward can they reasonably expect for their investment?
- can your business offer the kind of return that would attract outside investors?

The amount of debt finance you can raise will almost certainly be defined by what your bank manager is prepared to lend you and will be based on your business plan and available security. An old adage suggests that bank managers are looking for the three Cs – **character** (your track record), **collateral** (security against any inability to repay) and **cash flow** (evidence that your business is financially viable). Arnold S. Goldstein's American book *Starting on a Shoestring* suggests that unless you know the answer to the following points before you go to see your bank manager you may not get very far:

- why do you need the amount requested?
- what will you do with it?
- how do you know that it's enough?
- how much less can you live with?
- who else will you borrow from?
- how do you propose to repay it?
- how can you prove you can repay it?
- what collateral can you offer?

Don't overlook banks as a potential source of finance – most of the high street banks have overhauled their services to small businesses within the last few years and many produce packs of useful information.

Before you start

PR consultant Lindy Beveridge, who works with hi-tech companies in Cambridge, gives some general principles about what to think about before embarking on any public relations activity. If you have the budget, there is little doubt that using a PR consultant makes sense; sadly few start-ups include sufficient marketing and PR budgets in their business plans.

"First, you have to formulate some idea of who you need to address, breaking down the audience into distinct groups, if you can. Then you need to identify the issues for the whole group and sub-issues which may only be of interest to particular groups in your audience. For instance, everyone presumably needs to be convinced that the service your company will produce is reliable, timely, virus-free, affordable and really useful. But only some groups will be interested in certain features."

"The basic aim is to create the best possible climate of opinion in which to do business with anyone whose good opinion will affect the success of your company. That means explaining the whole system clearly and interestingly in the first instance and addressing obvious concerns and issues right from the start openly. So you need to formulate a very good and lucid explanation about how it will all work, be charged for, have its quality guaranteed, be delivered and so on. After the first package of information has gone out, you need to collect responses – some of these will be fears, some criticisms, some good ideas *etc.* They need to be analysed and responded to appropriately and promptly."

"You also need to tell everyone how to contact you and what kind of timescale to expect for responses. Don't undertake the impossible or fail to give yourself time to think things through. You don't know what problems may show up and to maintain integrity and trust that your word is good, you need to make considered and effective responses. These principles would apply to all the sectors of your audience but clearly you will develop a different style to respond to different groups – software developers will need more complexity in their reply than general enquirers and so on.

"You need to establish absolute honesty and integrity over financial and legal issues from the start and make sure that you don't depart from the standards you aim for. You also need to establish a style of communication which is consistent and appropriate and reflects openness – *ie* the intangible but very important qualities that are associated with integrity."

"If all this sounds daunting, it's not difficult but you do need to think things through before sending out messages to a very diverse and scattered group of contributors/customers. Teleworkers' clients are quite likely to be alone with their screens too, and you don't want preventable misunderstandings or to spend hours disentangling them by email if you can help it."

Antony Capstick of Instant Search gives the following advice: "With PR and journalism one has to think of a peg to hang the idea on when you are selling it to journalists. When Companies House opened up its service to people from the outside, I marketed the idea for my Instant Search business through that 'peg'. I sent faxes off to the newsdesk saying 'Companies House has opened their computer to the outside; however, you can get the service if you don't have a PC because Instant Search are offering it as a mail order instant access service. The best publicity I got from that was the Manchester Evening News. They quoted me and I was flooded with calls from Manchester, lots of orders – it was very good.

"It also helps in background credibility if your name is mentioned for example in the FT or a quality paper; somehow people think you are better. There may be direct sales as a result of editorial coverage, but it also helps when you approach people directly if they have already heard of you."

Your prospective customers may list a number of common anxieties about using teleworkers. Here we look at some organisational suggestions you could implement and use as selling points with your customers.

- computer viruses – can you guarantee that the disks you send to your customers are virus free?

- equipment backup – what would happen if your computer went down? Is alternative equipment available quickly? Do you have ample data backups of work in progress in case of disaster?

- people backup – if you are a small operation, how will you deal with the inevitable peaks and troughs in demand? You can deal with fluctuations in workload through a network of associated teleworkers, perhaps through online systems such as the TCA email broadcast list. Set the system up before you are in a crisis!

- confidentiality – what happens if another teleworker accesses commercially sensitive information? Could somebody unscrupulous get hold of the client company's stationery?

- make sure your computer system is secure. Use security features such as passwords and file locking to prevent unauthorised access of client's files. Make sure your office is secure. Lock away customers' stationery and files if they are sensitive

- delivery methods – can you help your customers to get used to teleworking, for example by offering to help them to set up modems and learn to use email? If they aren't on email, do you know everything you need to about collection and delivery services for finished work? (*eg* what is the cut-off time in your area to get a parcel to DHL for delivery next day in Brussels? How much does it cost to get a motorbike delivery to London?)

- presentation – look at your fax cover sheets, letterheads, business cards. Do they reflect a professional image? How does your office look if a customer drops in unexpectedly? Can customers hear radios in the background when they ring up? Are all staff trained in telephone answering? There are few more effective ways of annoying a prospective customer than putting him or her on hold or asking their name and company several times over before connecting them. Fax cover sheets are often the first impression a teleworker gives to a customer. Give them the attention they deserve.

These issues are related to quality control and are covered in Chapter 10. If your organisation is large enough to bear the time involved, look into achieving formal quality control to ISO 9000. Use project management software to track progress on all jobs undertaken. Measure your response time to enquiries.

Handling press and publicity

Properly handled, your relations with the local and business press can be one of the most cost-effective forms of marketing, but they need to be seen as part of your marketing strategy – just as with direct mail or advertising campaigns, identify the target and then look at the most effective means to reach it. Apart from reaching new customers, former *Teleworker* magazine editor Barnaby Page believes press coverage can assist with the following:

■ reminding existing customers of your existence

■ a morale booster for employees or subcontractors

■ improved service from suppliers if they think of you as an important customer

■ bank managers, planning officers (always useful to have them on your side).

To get to these audiences you have to convince an intermediary target – the journalist. The key to success is to treat press relations as a partnership in which both you and the journalist want to reach the same people – the journalist wants to give them an interesting, useful read. You want to make the audience aware of your product or service. Helping journalists to achieve their objective is the secret of success according to Page, who provides the following guide to obtaining press coverage.

Step 1: identify the publication. It could be a business to business title, or a specialist trade paper. Be careful not to confuse business and consumer counterparts – mountain bikers don't necessarily read Cycle Trader, and turkey farmers may not have much interest in BBC Good Food magazine. If you're unsure, the reference bible is the voluminous and expensive monthly BRAD (British Rates and Data) which gives information on almost every periodical in Great Britain and some in Northern Ireland and the Republic of Ireland. It may be worth using a PR consultant just to identify your market and for access to BRAD – it's rarely to be found in public libraries although the Willings Press Guide is usually there.

Step 2: draft your press release, always keeping in mind the famous acronym KISS – Keep It Simple, Stupid.

Sites for job hunters (many of these are mainly non-teleworking)

http://dial-space.dial.pipex.com/eurotechnique
http://dial-space.dial.pipex.com/town/estate/gb56
http://www.exp.ie/Ireland
http://www.indigo.ie/softskill
http://www.infolive.ie/jobfinder/jobs
http://www.job-hunt.org/jobs-all.shtml
http://www.jobserve.com/index.html
http://www.jobsite.co.uk
http://look.net/blacks/jobs.html
http://members.aol.com/telwebsite
http://www.monster.com
http://www.nerdworld.com/nw38.html
http://www.octacon.co.uk/proj/telemart
http://www.reed.co.uk
http://www.taps.com
http://www.tjobs.com/jobopps.htm
http://www.topjobs.ie
http://www.tks.co.uk
http://www.ukdirectory.co.uk/employ/it.htm
http://wynnsystems.com/framed.html
irish-jobs@mail-list.com is a mailing list of IT industry jobs. There is a related web site at http://www.exp.ie
http://www.yahoo.com/Business_and_Economy/Employment/Telecommuting–catalogue where you may find more recent sites

- try not to exceed one page of generously-spaced A4 on your business letterhead
- use a short, clear headline that sums up the story in a few words
- get all the main details into the first paragraph. Further down, include an interesting quote
- avoid journalese – you are writing to attract the journalist's attention, not to do their job for them. Expunge words like "revealed" or "shocked" and keep in mind the news angle – why might your story generate interest?
- avoid jargon and stick to clear, quantifiable facts such as "This is the third government contract Anytown Design has won in two months" not "this places Anytown Design as an industry market leader"
- if you enclose a photo, try to ensure it is a print, not a transparency,

label it clearly on the back with the name and job title of each person, and briefly describe what they are doing. Do not use felt pen or biro for this label – in a pile of photographs the ink may come off the back of your photograph and on to the front of the one below, and biros can cause indentations that damage the photograph. Use pencil or a typed label. Don't expect to see the photo again, whether or not it is published

■ date it and include your contact details and telephone number at the bottom.

Step 3: make sure you're sending it to the **right person.** A call to the paper to find out, for example, who covers local business may get you a name. If you don't have a name, send it to a relevant sounding job title such as Industrial Correspondent.

Step 4: if a journalist calls you for further details, remember they don't bite.

■ be courteous and don't patronise in explaining your story. Today's trainee journalist could be a valuable contact on a national paper in a few year's time

■ don't lie or exaggerate – journalists aren't particularly interested in the skeletons in your cupboard until you lie to conceal them

■ avoid going "off the record" *ie* giving information which you do not wish to be published. Although journalists rarely abuse this privilege, mistakes sometimes happen

■ understand that you have no veto over what is printed – there is little point in demanding to see an article before it's published

■ don't antagonise journalists by complaining. Errors are sometimes made – if they are trivial let it lie rather than be branded as a time-waster. For a major mistake, write a polite letter to the editor.

Step 5: If at first you don't succeed, try again. Keep your name in the eye of the public, and in the eye of other journalists. If there's a subject where you have expertise, you may gradually become established as what's unkindly known as a "rentaquote", so that whenever a feature in your area comes along, you're the first person who comes to mind.

Mailing lists

The mailing list is both a junk-mail curse and a vitally useful tool in the right hands. Today's software tools allow records of contacts to be easily held, and the production of vast quantities of marketing materials which can be personalised to the addressee. However, they can have a negative effect if they are not correctly written and targeted, or waste your resources if they are not well planned.

First, you need to know whom you are going to contact and why. Use your business plan and market research to build up a profile of the likely customer. If you are selling to businesses, your next step will probably be to purchase a mailing list from companies such as Kompass, which hold

regularly updated and indexed lists of companies. As you pay "per name" you will need to build up a brief for the mailing list company which may include parameters such as:

- number of employees
- market sector (most mailing list companies have a series of ID codes for different market sectors)
- person to contact within the company (*eg* finance director, human resources/personnel)
- service, manufacturing, export sector
- number of years established
- ownership (*eg* foreign owned or domestic)
- geographical location
- telephone number (vital for qualifying the list – see below).

Mailing list companies have an incentive to get you to buy as many names as possible, whereas you want the smallest number that will give you a good response rate. To avoid this poacher/gamekeeper conflict you may wish to use a mailing list broker. Bill Moss, an experienced broker, explains: "Mailing list brokers get a discount from suppliers such as Kompass because they buy in bulk. They also know the various mailing lists extremely well. So you can get professional advice from a mailing list broker to produce a well-defined list, get the broker to obtain the list for you, and pay the same amount as you would have done buying direct – the broker pockets the difference between the discount and the standard retail price as the fee for his or her advice."

The broker will also be able to help you ensure that you get the names in a format that you can use. The safest format to ask for is CSV (comma separated variable), which will work with most spreadsheet and word processing programmes. You will probably need to put the list into spreadsheet format whilst you qualify and sort it before using it with your word processing mail merge feature. Other commonly used formats are DBF and ASCII though some suppliers will provide lists in mail merge format for specified word processing packages. Bill also gives a checklist for those buying mailing lists, whether direct or through a broker:

- Does it matter where the client is located?
- What contact name (job function) is needed if any?
- Do you need telephone or fax numbers?
- How is the list you are buying compiled, and how old is it?
- Is the list owner registered for data protection?
- Is the list owner a member of the country's Direct Marketing Association. If not, think twice about employing them.

Before you even consider the logistics of sending out your mailing, you must qualify the list. This is a tedious process which consists of telephoning the company and checking that the person on your list is indeed still the managing director/human resources manager or whatever, that you have their correct title, and that they are responsible for the area of activity you are interested in. Be polite, patient and persistent with receptionists – they get many such calls each day and sometimes can be a bit short with the *nth* enquirer, whom they may well think is either a salesman or yet another jobseeker. If they offer to put you through to the person in question, grasp the opportunity. Briefly explain why you are contacting them and tell them you will be sending a mailing shortly. Don't get depressed if they express no interest – you've just saved yourself a wasted stamp and follow-up call.

The next step is to set up a sensible schedule for mailing and follow-up. Be realistic – most mail-outs have a very low response rate of less than 5% so build this into your workload projections. For business to business services it is highly unproductive to send out several thousand mailings at once, a large proportion of which will go straight in the bin. Instead, send out small batches in stages, and follow up by telephoning again a few days after the mailing to ask whether the mailing was received, and whether they are interested in your product or service. If they are not interested, ask whether they would mind explaining why, so that you can better target your marketing in future. This approach may elicit useful information about what's wrong with your service; however some respondents will treat this tactic as a hard sell technique and refuse to elucidate.

For consumer or retail services, it may be more effective to use geographical mailings to all houses in a district, usually organised through the Post Office on a cost per copy basis. Such campaigns are almost always more effective if press coverage or advertising is used at the same time.

In either case, before embarking on a mailshot be sure you have costed it properly and that you have put aside resources for the follow-up, and for capturing details of any prospective customers who contact you as a result. Amongst the costs are:

Measuring advertising response

Anthony Capstick of Instant Search comments: "The next area I went into was direct advertising in newspapers. I tried all the national newspapers, the *Sunday Times, Times, Telegraph* and the *Observer*, particularly the small ad section in the back."

"We run, for example, a six line ad in the *Sunday Times* advertising our services which costs something like £70 resulting in something like 10 or 15 orders per week, and it's generally busy Monday or Tuesday. You need to run the ad for a specific period of time. I went in and out a couple of times at the beginning because I didn't want to spend too much. But I did notice that when I left it in, I was getting a much better response. People often browse papers, and may see the same ad again and again. The fourth or fifth time they may ring you up. If they have just see the advert once they may think the company is not very reliable. Persistence pays."

"But the whole thing is wasted if you do not ask every single person who rings in where they saw your service advertised, where you got that enquiry. Otherwise you are just throwing money away. I constructed a spreadsheet with the cost of the advert, when it appeared, the number of enquiries and the number of conversions from that enquiry. When people call in and their orders are taken, a code is entered about where they saw Instant Search advertised. At the end of the month, when I'm booking the next level of advertising, I can see, for example, that a £200 ad in the *Sunday Times* brough in £500 of business, whereas the Daily Telegraph only cost me £80 but brought in only £60 of business. Stick to the Sunday papers if your business can go overseas – we have agents in Moscow picked up from a three line ad in the *Sunday Times*."

- mailing list purchase
- time and telephone costs for qualifying the mailing list
- design, editing and printing of the mailshot material
- envelopes, laser labels and postage
- responding to enquiries – as a rule of thumb, you should expect around a 10–15% response rate if you also follow up the mailshot by phone – have you planned for the expected increase in demand for your services?

As well as keeping track of your responses, you will need to have some method of estimating the overall conversion rate between the money you have spent on the mailing and the increased business which directly results from it.

To keep costs and postal rates down, think about printing one-coloured ink onto coloured paper for your mailing, and bear in mind that as long as

IWS: a telework job agency for Wales

Innovative Work Solutions is providing what it describes as a "high quality temp service" using teleworkers from west Wales. Director Siân Thomas explains: "Companies don't have to limit their activities to skills available locally. Teleworkers can take the strain of a direct mail campaign, or fill in for staff during peak holiday periods. Using our services also allows companies to expand output without increased premises costs."

Siân feels IWS understands the headaches faced by managers who contract work to be carried out remotely. The agency ensures that:

■ the teleworkers are qualified and trained

■ they have access to suitable hardware and software that matches the company's requirements

■ full in-house technical support is provided to the teleworkers

■ job specifications are checked and the job is completed to ISO 9000 quality standards.

Each job carried out by IWS has a worksheet which specifies the requirements for the job such as spacing, tabs, paragraph styles, preferred spellings, page layout, fonts and formats. Typical administrative services (eg word processing by someone with RSA II or III and a minimum of three years office experience) costs about £6.50/hour. Preparation of presentations using Powerpoint costs about £12.00 per hour plus consumables (eg overheads) costs. Work is returned by email, disk or as a hard copy printout according to the customer's specifications.

IWS also works on translations (especially Welsh) and provides a wide range of documentation services. Siân Thomas summarises: "Our services give companies freedom to concentrate on their business, not on their administration problems." But she is still encountering resistance to outsourcing in many companies: "Managers quite like to have their names associated with IT but, when it comes to the nitty gritty, they panic at the throught of releasing tasks to outside workers. Unfortunately we don't have the funds at present to cover the educative process required, and no one else is running evening classes for managers in how to manage "future work" yet." However, IWS is getting substantial work in the translation area from companies like S4C, who deliver and collect their work entirely by email. (http://www.telecottages.org/iws)

you have affixed a clear mailing address label and postage, it is quite legal not to use an envelope, but to fold the document neatly and secure with a small adhesive label easily broken open by the recipient. Mailing labels can be printed in sheets on most laser printers. To save licking all those stamps, most post offices can arrange to frank large mailings for you but normally you will have to prepare the mailings with all envelopes the right way round. For mailings of over 2,000 you can use the "Mailsort" service which considerably reduces postal costs, but is only available if the postcode is clearly included in the address labels. Some companies can act as bureau services for Mailsort.

In Ireland franked mailing is available at main sorting offices only and must be paid for in cash or by banker's draft.

Some companies are now using fax shots, although professional marketing people are divided about whether the level of negative reactions from people receiving unsolicited faxes outweighs the value of fax shots. Keep the message short and simple – one A4 page or less. Fax numbers can be found in the fax directory available from BT, and from local business directories. Many specialist business associations will sell their directories to non-members for a price, or have reasonable membership prices that give you access to the listing.

Advertising

You will probably want to advertise at first so that customers will be aware of your existence. Think carefully about which media (newspapers, local radio) will work best for you, and compare prices. The basic options are:

- newspapers
- trade magazines
- World Wide Web
- local radio
- TV.

Try to think about how you will measure response to your adverts so that you will know where to spend your money next time. Keep asking new customers where they heard about you and record their replies.

Directories and networks

An increasing number of businesses are making use of directories to market their services. The best known and most widely accessible publication is the telephone directory (Yellow Pages, or Golden Pages in Ireland). Before advertising in Yellow Pages take a good look at the entries for your area. A problem that many teleworking businesses come across is that there is no obvious place for their services in Yellow Pages at present – or rather too many. Teleworkers would often need to make entries in a number of categories to cover all their services, including office services, desktop publishing, graphic design, bookkeeping, secretarial services and so on. Yellow Pages may be a good option if your business fits into a niche – such as market research – but very expensive if you cover a range of categories. Remember that you are entitled to a free basic text entry in Yellow Pages if you pay the business, rather than residential, tariff on your telephone. Make sure you get that and that it is correctly worded – Yellow Pages entries for the whole country are becoming widely available on CD-ROM so this constitutes a useful form of advertising with nationwide coverage.

If you decide to pay for a more complex Yellow Pages ad, think through the different options and prices. Often a plain text advert in bold type will be more cost effective and practical than a graphic. In general companies are more concerned about reference clients than they are about the size of your Yellow Pages advert. Think of it in plumbing terms. If you are looking for a plumber, you may indeed use Yellow Pages to find the number of a particular plumber, but you are more likely to choose the plumber based on personal recommendation or reference from friends and neighbours than "cold" through any directory. So it's important to have your contact details accessible but it may not be so important to take a large ad.

Local business directories may also be worth buying entries for – your local chamber of commerce or library should be able to give you information on the directories operating in your area. Chambers of commerce and other business networking organisations also often publish local directories and encourage their members to use the services of other members.

Individual teleworkers may find it worthwhile to register with employment agencies as some are now taking on board the task of getting in work for teleworkers. A number of agencies advertise on the World Wide Web, although most of the requests are for permanent staff, not for temps or teleworkers.

Get out there and sell!

Many teleworkers have found conventional advertising or mailing too expensive in the long term, and insufficiently rewarding. Other suggestions include:

- prepare a brochure or prospectus of your services for selected mailings. If you want to give names of your existing clients to add weight to your material, don't forget to ask permission. Even better, see if you can get endorsed statements from your clients to use in your marketing material

- work out how much it will cost you to have your own page on the World Wide Web (See Chapter 9, *Email and online Services* for further information)

- telecottages can join forces to make joint approaches to larger companies

- teleworkers can form umbrella organisations to market their services co-operatively

- "piggy back" your mailings with those of local computer equipment suppliers by agreement, sharing costs

- speak to local business groups, chambers of commerce, women's institutes (ICA in Ireland), farming groups

- if you have suitable premises, think about organising occasional social get-togethers for your customers and workers so that people can put faces to names, and be aware of all the services you are offering. How about a working lunch involving a presentation?

■ personal visits. No-one likes cold calling, but if you can talk to businesses on a one-to-one basis you could get a trial piece of work that will get your foot in the door. Try writing to your prospective customer, then telephone to say you will be in the area, and could you call in? Arm yourself with some facts about the cost savings and convenience of using teleworkers

■ if you specialise in a particular area, is there a relevant software user group with a newsletter (*eg* Corel Ventura Users for DTP)? These newsletters are often cheap to advertise in and hit direct to your target market.

■ editorial copy is free but you need to do as much of the journalist's work for them as possible in order to get your story into a paper. Talk to all local journalists – press, freelancers, local radio, TV. Keep up the contact. Phone them, write to them, send them press releases and good photographs. Just keep your name in front of them too often for them to ignore. Invite them to visit your premises. Try holding an Open Day. Take photographs of all events – remember you need black and white photos for some newspapers, not colour.

■ follow up professional contacts such as former workmates where appropriate

■ the best of all advertising is word-of-mouth. Keep up the quality of your service and you will be repaid by personal recommendations. On the down side, it has been estimated that if a customer has a bad experience of your service, he or she will probably report this to 26 other people.

Acknowledgments

The TCA thanks Brian O'Kane for permission to use material from his guide *Starting Your Own Business in Ireland*, published by Oaktree Press, ISBN 1-872853-17-X.

Barnaby Page, former editor of *The Teleworker* magazine, contributed the sections on handling the press.

Bibliography

Tales to Knock Your Socks Off Service   *Date:* 1998
Authors: Kristin Anderson and Ron Zemke
Source: Amacom, 1601 Broadway, New York, NY 10019
ISBN 0–8144–7971–5

30 Minutes... to write a Business Plan   *Date:* 1997
Author: Brian Finch
Source: Kogan Page, 120 Pentonville Rd, London N1 9JN ISBN 0–7494–2364–1

30 Minutes... to write a Marketing Plan   *Date:* 1997
Author: John Westwood
Source: Kogan Page, 120 Pentonville Rd, London N1 9JN ISBN 0–7494–2363–3

The Complete Guide to Quick and Easy Marketing that Works *Date:* 1997
Source: Tel: 01252 317700

Lloyds Bank Small Business Guide *Date:* 1997
Source: Penguin ISBN 0–14–024898–6

Marketing your Consulting and Professional Services *Date:* 1997
Authors: Dick Connor and Jeff Davidson
Source: John Wiley & Sons ISBN 0–471–13392–2

The 24 Hour Business Plan *Date:* 1997
Author: Ron Johnson
Source: Random House, 20 Vauxhall Bridge Road London SW1V 25A
ISBN 0–7126–7779–8

The 4 Routes to Entrepreneurial Success *Date:* 1997
Author: John B Miner
Source: Berrett Koehler, 155 Montgomery Street, San Francisco, CA 94104–4109
ISBN 1–881052–82–6

The Complete Idiot's Guide to Starting a Home Based Business *Date:* 1997
Author: Barbara Weltman
Source: Alpha Books, 1633 Broadway, 7th Floor, New York, NY 10019–6785
ISBN 0–02–861539–5

**Stop Telling, Start Selling – How to use Customer focused
dialogue to close sales** *Date:* 1997
Author: Linda Robertson
Source: McGraw Hill ISBN 0–07–052558–7

Webonomics *Date:* 1997
Author: Evan I Schwartz
Source: Penguin, Harmondsworth, Middlesex. ISBN 0–14–026406–X

101 Ways to Promote Your Business
Authors: Godfrey Harris and Gregrey Harris
Source: Kogan Page, 120 Pentonville Road, London N1 9JN Ref: ISBN 0–7494–18443

**Starting a Successful Small Business/ How to Set up your Own Business/
Successful Marketing for the Small Business** (three publications)
Source: Kogan Page, 120 Pentonville Road, London N1 9JN

Running your own Word-Processing Service
Author: Doreen Huntley
Source: Kogan Page, 120 Pentonville Road, London N1 9JN Ref: ISBN 0-7494-0344-6.

**Work for Yourself – A Guide to Self-Employment and Setting up a Small
Business/ Earning Money at Home** (two publications)
Source: Consumers' Association, Castlemead, Gascoyne Way, Hertford

Daily Telegraph How to Set Up and Run Your Own Business *Date:* 1996
Source: Kogan Page 120 Pentonville Road, London N1 9JN 12th edn
Ref: ISBN 0–7494–1969–5

TeleFutures – a study on teleworking in Ireland *Date:* 1996
Authors: Imogen Bertin and Gerard O'Neill
Source: International Services, Forbairt, Wilton Park House, Wilton Place, Dublin 2
Tel: +353 1 660 2244 Contact: International Services – Declan Murphy
Web: http://www.forbairt.ie/telefutures

A Marketing Action Plan for the Growing Business *Date:* 1995
Authors: Shailendra Vyakarnam and John W. Leppard
Source: Kogan Page, 120 Pentonville Road, London N1 9JN Ref: ISBN 0–7494–1313–1

BBC Complete Small Business Guide *Date:* 1995
Author: Colin Barrow
Source: BBC, 4th edition Ref: ISBN 0–56337083–1

Management Pocketbooks: Balance Sheet/Managing Budgets/ *Date:* 1995
Managing Cashflow (three publications)
Authors: Anne Hawkins and Clive Turner
Source: 14 East St, Alresford, Hants SO24 9EE Tel: 01962 735573 Fax: 01962 733637

Endless Prospects: 301 Tactics to Reach Hard to Reach People *Date:* 1994
Author: C. Richard Weylman
Source: McGraw Hill ISBN 0–07–069630–6

Do Your Own Market Research *Date:* 1994
Authors: Paul Hague and Peter Jackson
Source: Kogan Page, 120 Pentonville Road, London N1 9JN Ref: ISBN 0–7494–1779–X

Running Your Own Business *Date:* 1994
Author: David Williams
Source: Allied Dunbar Personal Finance Guides (Nicholas Brealey Publishing)
Ref: ISBN 1–85788–092–7

Survive & Prosper – Rules for Business Success *Date:* 1994
Author: Tony Boffe
Source: Kogan Page Ref: 2nd edn ISBN 0–7494–1276–3

The Which? Guide to Earning Money at Home
Author: Lynn Underwood *Date:* 1994
Source: Which? Consumer Guides, 2 Marylebone Road, London, NW1 4DF Ref: ISBN
0 85202 507 6

Contacts and URLs

Enterprise Advisory Service PC-based database of grants. Details can be obtained
by ringing 0345 343434. TCA members should ring 01280 700 102 to contact EAS
directly in order to claim a discount on Explorer.

IWS: Tel: 01437 766441 Email: sian@iws.cymru.net
Web: http://www.telecottages.org/iws

Regional Development Agencies

For information on sources of funds allocated to specific areas of the UK
RDC – Rural Development Commission (areas of rural England) Tel: 01722 336255
DBRW – Development Board for Rural Wales Tel: 01686 627518
LEDU – Local Enterprise Development Unit (Northern Ireland) Tel: 01232 242582
IRTU – Industrial training Research and Technology Unit (Northern Ireland)
Tel: 01232 529475
WDA –Welsh Development Agency Tel: 0345 775566
HIE – Highlands and Island Enterprise Tel: 01463 713504
Scottish Enterprise Tel: 01412 482700
Northern Ireland Growth Challenge is a private sector initiative to promote
industry and development of the Northern Ireland economy. It has a "subcluster" to
examine growth and development opportunities for teleworking which plans to pilot
a teleworking project and work to develop call centres in Northern Ireland.
Tel: 01232 468362 Fax: 01232 468361 Contact: Tom Douglas

Local funding

Some funding can be very localised – for example, enquiries to Gloucester Business Link yielded information on:

Gloucestershire Business Angel Scheme (linking potential investors and small businesses) Tel: 0800 135235

Royal British Legion small business advisory service (close army contacts) The Cottage, Ordnance Road, Tidworth, Wilts SP9 7QD

Midland Bank Enterprise Fund for the South West has an investment fund of up to £150,000 for application to businesses in the south-west. Contact Gloucester TEC Tel: 01452 524488.

Funding aimed at Youth :

Prince's Youth Business Trust Age range 18-29, loans up to £5,000 and grants up to £1,500. To qualify must have a viable business idea, be disadvantaged in some way and be unable to otherwise raise finance Tel: 0171 321 6500

LIVEWIRE Grants and support aimed at young people aged 16-25 are available Tel: 0191 261 5584

Teleworker magazine regularly provides information about initiatives relevant to teleworking and telematics projects, small business and rural areas.

General

Management Technology Associates, Clark House, King's Road, Fleet, Hampshire GU13 9AD Tel: 01252 812 252 Fax: 01252 815 702 Email: 100142.31@compuserve.com.

http://www.tjobs.com/ is a telecommuting jobs web page for people to find telecommuting employment. Works two ways, either enter the job-line to check out jobs available, or enter job-seeker area to provide info on type of work sought together with work experience.

Thomson Directories CD-ROM which can help you identify possible customers in your area: Tel: 0645 636261 Web: http://www.inbusiness.co.uk

Yellow pages Web: http://www.yell.co.uk

Teleworking Associations

National Association of Teleworkers Glebe House, Henford Square, Chew Magna, Bristol BS40 8RA Tel: 01275 332612 Fax: 01275 333515 Email: group_practice@underwood-lamb.demon.co.uk Web: www.underwood-lamb.demon.co.uk

Scottish Teleworking Association, Roy Guthrie, GCS, Tel: 01324 664164 Fax: 01324 664154, Email: royguthrie@compuserve.com

TCA Tel: 0800 616008 or 01203 696986 Fax: 01203 696538 Email: 100272.3137@compuserve.com

Telecottages Wales, Paddy Moindrot Tel: 01691 648887 Email: 74431.1372@compuserve.com

Communications Workers Union Ireland and the Irish contact point for the European Telework Development project Reagrove, Minane Bridge, Co. Cork, Ireland Tel: +353 21 887403 Fax: +353 21 887402 Freefone 1800 225070 Email: imogen@ctc.ie

Telework Ireland (also covers Northern Ireland) KITE, Cornagun, Kinawley, Enniskillen, BT94 2FR Tel: 01365 348943 Fax: 01365 348944 Email: 100073.1111@compuserve.com.

Telecottages and Telecentres

A telecottage provides the local community with low cost access to computer and telecommunications equipment, which in turn give access to information services and work. Telecottages also support teleworkers and small businesses. Other terms used in addition to telecottage include telecentre, teleservice centre and electronic village hall.

The first centre claiming the title telecottage in the UK, the Moorlands Telecottage, was set up in 1989, but like many good ideas, it appears that telecottages were being independently "invented" in a number of places. A recent TCA survey turned up examples which predate the first Swedish telecottages in 1985, such as Daily Information in Oxford. Since the early 1990s, numbers of telecottages have grown rapidly to a total of 165 in the UK and Ireland in July 1997. The growth in numbers is set to continue with a number of initiatives planning networks of telecottages, such as the RATIO project for 40 telecentres in Devon and Cornwall, and the inclusion of telecottage facilities in the ACRE village hall improvements project which has Millennium Fund backing.

Many different forms of telecottage have been set up. Some are community orientated and offer training and use of resources for community groups. Others are highly equipped commercial enterprises. Experience from Sweden, where there are around 23 telecottages, and from the more mature UK telecottages, suggests that centres need to adopt a commercial attitude if they are to survive beyond an initial grant-funded start up. A key to success appears to be creation of a core business, often software training, around which other complementary services are offered. In Newfoundland, the concept was extended to cover local enterprise support centres where access to a wide range of online resources is also available. The Newfoundland experience showed the effectiveness of combining a network of online resources which people can access from their homes in conjunction with local centres.

The practice of using telecottages as bases for groups of teleworkers (often referred to in the US as neighbourhood work centres) has been slow to get going. Some centres have housed a variety of individual positions such as rural field officers, but there have been few larger scale projects such as the group of 25 county council workers who used the Antur Teifi telematics centre. Recently a number of other county councils have taken up the idea, including Surrey, Notts, Kent and Oxford, as part of their flexible working strategies.

Because rural areas are often short of resources, telecottages can become a focus of community and commercial activity, providing a centre where the isolation of working from home can be broken down. Teleworkers can network through the telecottage, using each other's services to provide backup on larger contracts.

Services

Telecottages usually offer both formal and informal training, computer hire (some offer "take-away" computers too) and access to photocopiers, laser printers and faxes. Other facilities include use of workspace, and meeting rooms. A more complete listing of teleservices which could be provided through telecottages is given in Chapter 7, *Ideas for Teleservices*. Trained staff are often available to provide secretarial assistance, word processing and desktop publishing, which can be invaluable to teleworkers who need additional help. Ideas followed up by some telecottages include:

Product demonstration rooms

Telecottages represent a potential network of centres where product demonstrations can be made to local small businesses. With the level of computer equipment already available in centres, plus ISDN lines in some cases and the office support available, telecottages have been used in this way on a number of occasions.

Sales force support centres

National sales forces often have a far flung group of people who may need to meet up with regional managers, hold small conferences or drop in and use the facilities. Telecottages have been approached to offer these facilities and can network with other telecottages to offer coverage of an entire region.

Product agency agreements

Agency agreements on a number of product lines related to the telecottage business can be arranged such as computer sales, office supplies and printing.

Mere Telecottage

Our business is helping small businesses – outstanding range of services at small business prices

- *Photocopying (enlarging/two colour)*
- *Typing/printing (official documents)*
- *Telephone answering service*
- *Foreign language translation*
- *Total accounts package*
- *Computer training RSA/NVQ accreditation*
- *Desktop publishing*
- *Computer hire by the hour*

No job is too small – our reasonable rates will surprise you!

Homework club

Some telecottages have offered access to computers for children for homework or games usage. By adopting a fixed timetable, disruption to other telecottage users can be avoided.

Cybercafe internet access

A number of cybercafes have been set up, usually in town centres, where they have created a lot of interest in the Internet by offering access at £5 per hour. Telecottages could offer an Internet education package – a getting started course followed by a number of sessions at the telecottage.

Local council information centres

A number of county councils are keen to develop on-line information access points or satellite offices in rural towns and might welcome a site for an additional terminal which could be rented to them.

CD-ROM library

Some libraries offer a CD-ROM lending service – this can be expensive to set up (*eg* set of 200 CD-ROMS at £3,750) but shared between a number of organisations it could prove to be an income generator. Contact Ramesis Tel: 01274 737376

Job club

Telecottages can provide a site for job information, a noticeboard, latest job information faxed over or jobs information available on-line. Contact your local Job Centre for information.

Business adviser outpost

Business Link, your local TEC, council or regional development agency are all potential clients for use of the facilities to meet customers. Using grantfinder database software, the telecottage could also charge an access fee and assist small businesses to find information.

A detailed list of commercial service ideas is given in Chapter 7, *Ideas for Teleservices*, but a typical example from Mere Telecottage, a community-based enterprise in Wiltshire is given opposite.

Telecottage statistics

At the end of 1994, the TCA supported a survey of telecottage activities by Bill Murray of Small World Connections. The results give a snapshot of the "typical" telecottage which can be useful to those thinking about setting up. All the figures are averages or approximations.

- Centres have 40 regular users and 40 occasional users.
- 40% subcontract work to local teleworkers.
- One third see themselves as "telecottages"; other titles given include Community Resource Centre, Computer Resource Centre, Office Bureau, Teleworking Centre.

- Half are based in towns (the survey did not distinguish between small rural and large, urban towns), with a quarter in small villages and another quarter in remote rural settings.

- Most telecottages have 1.5 full-time staff, 2 part-timers, 2 volunteers and 1.5 subcontracted workers; in fact patterns are more complex with over half having no volunteer help, and fewer than 25% having subcontracted help. Nearly a quarter have no full-time staff at all and 10% have no employees – just volunteers and subcontractors.

- One fifth of telecottages are privately owned. Over a quarter are co-ops or charities or companies limited by guarantee. About half are supported by local councils, colleges or other public authorities.

- Half are "breaking even" financially, with one third making a loss (usually the most recently set up telecottages) and about one in seven making a profit. Incomes ranged from £6,000 to £180,000 with an average of £50,000.

- Facilities vary widely but almost all have IBM compatible PCs, laser printers and photocopiers. A large number have a flatbed scanner; over two thirds have modems, half have CD-ROM drives. Most have three to four telephone lines, 6.5 PCs, 2.5 portable PCs, two laser printers and an inkjet printer (often colour). Around 20% have at least one Apple Mac.

- Over half see one of their main functions as training, with provision of office facilities a close second. Almost one third see administrative facilities such as word processing as a main key service, but general awareness raising was also seen as an important function.

- Income comes from funded training for over a third of centres, with office services and secretarial services a close second. Niche businesses providing income included: accommodation addresses, message taking, membership subscriptions, online services, bookkeeping and accountancy, newsletter production, conference management, desktop publishing and graphic design.

Case studies

During the 1990s it has become increasingly apparent that successful telecottages fall into one of two models. Under the first model, they develop a core niche business which often creates the infrastructure (equipment and premises) that subsidises the economically priced services of the telecottage. Under the second model, they receive their support from various agencies in exchange for providing training services. Within these two models, there are some interesting variations, such as telecottages which also manage a number of startup business unit premises, telecottages attached to sub-post offices or tourist offices, and integrated telecottages, such as KITE, and WREN, which work to provide training, commercial work and childcare facilities on one site.

Antur Tanat Cain Telebureau

Antur Tanat Cain Telebureau developed out of a community development scheme to revamp Llangedwyn Mill in rural Wales into a number of units. The Antur also trained local people for new technology jobs, but found many were then having to travel long distances to work, or were relocating. The solution was to bring work into the area to follow the training courses, and the first contract was through a locally-based consultant who was working with ICL. The telecottage worked to capture historical data using a text scanner. The teleworkers then reformatted the scanned text for an information retrieval system, and this work turned into a number of major contracts providing work for several people. However, a couple of further contracts through Telecottages Wales failed to materialise, and then funding for the Training for Work programme (which the telecottage had been running) was cut further and further until it was not feasible to continue its operation. On top of the funding crisis, the Antur's computers – Amstrad PCWs and 1640s – badly needed upgrading, and local authority support was restricted because the Antur was about to be "moved" across a county border. In the end, the training scheme was discontinued and the staff, a trainer, an administrator and a part-time trainer, were found other jobs. The telecottage manager and two builders stayed on to keep the business units going. Now the new local authority, Powys, through its telecottage support

Rural Areas Videotelephone Access Network (RAVAN)

The RAVAN project is backed by the DTI's Multimedia Demonstrator Programme and organised by the TCA. It has installed PC-based videotelephone equipment in a group of UK telecottages and performs demonstrations to small business of how the equipment can be used to enhance business performance. In Lanarkshire, a local textile designer has shown scarves to Italian clients over the screen, a tour company has courted US clients, and steel workers relocating to Wales have held face to face interviews. Another local firm has secured a £100k deal to supply recycled laser cartridges to Italy, partly assisted by demonstrating products onscreen and sharing a costs spreadsheet showing pounds and lire. In Co. Fermanagh, videoconferencing has been used to enhance a contract where New York emergency room notes are processed. In Norfolk MPs can hold constituency 'surgeries' by videoconference from Westminster. In Durham a local photographic agency has got to know US clients without the expense of conventional business travel. In East Kent, the chamber of commerce has held video meetings with their opposite numbers in Lille, France. The RATIO project in Plymouth has used videoconferencing equipment to link telecentres for remote learning. WREN Telecottage in Warwickshire has developed a protocol for demonstrating videoconferencing, while in Cumbria the equipment is being used by one local business to save travel time on face to face meetings in Newcastle. Further details of the RAVAN network: http://www.tca.org.uk and in Teleworker magazine.

officer Joyce Morgan, has encouraged the telecottage to become a cyber-cafe, reopening the café formally operating from the Mill. An application has been made for European training funding to put 10 people through the Teleworking NVQ, and another contract from ICL is in the offing. Maureen Wilde, the telecottage manager, says she has been kept going by the supportive managing body, which includes councillors, local organisations, economic development officers and "anyone interested". She is convinced Antur Tanat Cain is back on its feet, and points to the continuing need for training: "What we need to do now is to retrain many of the people who worked on the original ICL contracts to use the latest software and really everyone is going to need constant retraining in their working life to keep up."

Informatica

Staffordshire-based Informatica has specialised in training for local farmers. Informatica was approached by agricultural information service provider Farming-Online to help out because the company's product helpline found that they were providing over-the-phone training in computer and on-line basics to farmers which they could not afford. They asked Informatica to design a basic introductory course. Storm Barratt of Informatica has developed a course that teaches farmers how to use Farming-Online for up to date prices, news and commentary as well as detailed weather forecasts and Internet connectivity. She began by doing some price research: "Farmers are prepared to pay around £60 for half a day's training and about £100 for this introductory course", she confirms. Informatica are currently developing a "train the trainers" course to assist Farming-Online in delivering training for other areas of the country.

Barnham Telecottage

Barnham Telecottage near Bognor Regis was set up as a private venture in June 1995 by husband and wife team Jane and Eric Pascal. Jane is a retired teacher, and Eric recently sold off his computer bureau business. The centre is run from a shop at the front of the Pascal's house and follows the pattern of some of the more recent telecottages which run the telecottage on the back of an existing core business. The computer systems and development work which Eric continues to offer provides an income of around £25,000. The telecottage income amounts to a further £6,000, which is expected to grow to £10,000. The telecottage makes use of the equipment amassed through Eric's business.

One of the largest income earners for the centre is training, and the majority of the trainees are women returners. Other services include photocopying, printing, Internet training, desktop publishing and business support. The telecottage is a boon to local home-based businesses as Jane Pascal explains: "There are lots of small business converts to the telecottage – people who work from home but probably wouldn't call themselves teleworkers. Also we get students in to type their work, or if they've left it too late, to get it typed by us!"

The value of the centre is also backed by an enthusiastic local user: "I think telecottages are an excellent concept – I have been setting up a business venture from the dining room table with no resources. The telecottage has been ideal – I don't think I would have been able to get this far without help from them. I use their email number on my letterhead which has added credibility. I intend to get computer trained in the future – they have put everything they do for me on a space on the computer – and I look forward to the point when I can get going on this myself."

Because they have a core business interleaving with the telecottage, the Pascals have been able to provide economically priced training to the community without any subsidy. Eric is keen to stress that the telecottage would not exist on its own, but it appears to work well with the existing business supplying the basic infrastructure of premises and equipment.

Cape Clear Telecottage

At the other end of the spectrum, a tiny telecottage on Cape Clear Island off County Cork in Ireland provides office services, photocopying, faxing and word processing from its North Harbour office. The same premises acts as a bookshop and tourist information centre, as well as helping the co-op that runs the island's ferry service. In addition, administrative services for the Electricity Supply Board operate from the telecottage, and the local turbot fish farm has its accounts and records provided by telecottage staff. The island has a population of 150, swelled by tourists and students attending courses in the Irish language to 1,000 during the summer. The telecottage received a small amount of startup funding from the economic development agency for Irish-speaking areas, Udarás na Gaeltachta. (ccteo@iol.ie)

Daily Information, Oxford City

On the commercial side, Daily Information in central Oxford began as an adjunct to a privately-run broadsheet listing of events, which was published daily in the university area of the city. Owner John Rose invested in three giant Philips word processors and a number of IBM electronic typewriters in 1979. "For the first six weeks, the Philips machines didn't work. For the next six months, we had no idea what they were really for. They cost £10,000 each, with annual maintenance costs of £1,000", recalls John. He offered free learning time to customers and soon found that demand was so great the computers had to be available 24 hours a day for thesis and book preparation. The Philips machines were retired in 1985, and Daily Information quickly built up a stock of 30 PCs for hire on site or to take away. Daily Information probably did more than the University's computer department to introduce PCs to the students. John now turns over £200,000 a year, selling PCs and laser printers, as well as disks, cartridges and paper, and offers access to sophisticated photocopiers and colour printers. "Now that the machines are small enough to take away, we don't have to open overnight. The biggest problem is that technology changes so fast that the business eats up capital just to keep it going", says John. In the past few years, business for printing out theses has fallen as more people have their

HM prisoners do it in Styal

Ten women in Styal prison are teleworking from the "comfort" of their own prison cells. The ten have studied for vocational certificates in teleworking, and have worked on a number of projects including a mailing list for a national charity, a database for a government department and Christmas card designs for prison service charity shops.

Prison governor Mike Goodwin said the women had gained experience of the world of work and gained self-confidence as well as supporting each other as a team. The project has been funded by Prison Enterprise and the European Commission, and was the brainchild of Manchester consultant Bill Murray of Small World Connections.

Call centre and fulfilment operations are planned for the future. Murray comments: "The programme provides women prisoners with much better prospects when they return to society – and we believe it means they could be less likely to re-offend."

own printers, but the sophisticated photocopiers and scanners at Daily Information are still proving a draw for customers. Access to the Internet is proving popular, and the broadsheet is now available on the World Wide Web, along with a computer exchange for secondhand equipment. His telecentre, which was operating long before the term was invented, has achieved the status of an Oxford institution. (http://www.dailyinfo.co.uk)

Resource Solutions

Based in Hulme, Manchester, Resource Solutions is backed by employment agency Reed plc and Manchester Metropolitan University. The centre employs four full-time staff and has six teleworkers. Equipment is top class with ISDN, videoconferencing and fast Internet connections, but the project has been set stiff financial deadlines – it must create 40 full-time jobs within two years and have a turnover of £1 million within five years. So far the centre's anchor work is for Reed, inputting CVs for the company's online recruitment service. Other clients include local companies which use an online proofreading service, and a virtual office answering service for local small businesses. Project director Julie Bagnoli hopes to recruit further teleworkers from the Women's Electronic Village Hall, and local residents who have completed the VQ level 2 qualification in teleworking.

Eccles House Telebusiness Centre

Eccles House is the brainchild of the Peak Park Trust and arose because Trust member Godfrey Claff had visited telecottages in Scandinavia. Blue Circle Cement donated a Grade II listed farmhouse with outbuildings to the Trust, which spent £400,000 and several years converting the buildings using monies from both the public (Rural Development Commission and European Social Fund) and private sectors. The site was opened in February 1992 and is managed by Collective Enterprises Limited, a commercial company based in Glossop.

The old barns and outbuildings now provide twelve individual offices and small workshop units, which vary in size from 179 sq ft to 880 sq ft. These units are used as accommodation for startup businesses or for professionals. The farmhouse provides the focal point for the Centre's services, housing the Centre staff, several meeting and training rooms which are for hire, and a coffee bar for site users. The administration and secretarial services offered on site include the usual word processing, desktop publishing, database and reception services, supplemented by other services from CEL's head office in Glossop, including training, consultancy, research and other telematic services.

Isles Telecroft, Shetland

At Unst in Shetland, Laura Baisley runs the Isles Telecroft, one of six telecottages set up in 1991 by the Highlands and Islands Enterprise (HIE) with funding from British Telecom under a three year project. Two of the telecottages were schools-based, the others were attached to existing community organisations. "One member of our community co-op was keen on IT, which was how we got involved initially", explains Laura. Isles Telecroft began by running two projects. On the first, four women who live on remote islands were trained in telework both through conventional courses, and by carrying out a telework project to put museum records onto a database. The four women had computing equipment provided by the project at home, along with modems for communicating with Unst and elsewhere. Funding for this project came from the local authority, Shetland Islands Council and from Shetland Enterpise. On the second project, seven people with disabilities who live in rural areas of Shetland were trained to achieve an IT qualification. The telecottage derives some income from telework services, but sources of income are limited, especially since the closure of the civilian airport which formerly serviced the oil industry on the island. "We do get pressure to increase the income from telework from the local enterprise company, but we have no budget or resources to do the marketing required at the moment, so it's not easy." The telecottage has recently prepared some World Wide Web pages for Unst, and hopes to expand this area of activity.

At the moment there are four training projects in progress, funded through the European Social Fund (ESF) and the local enterprise company. One caters for disabled people, the second provides training to unemployed and women returners in a socially deprived area, and the third is providing IT skills to members of the Shetland Tenant's Association. The fourth project provides IT training for 10 local women as part of an integrated training scheme for women returners. As ESF funding cannot be used for capital purchases, re-equipping as equipment becomes obsolete is a problem. However, depreciation charges and maintenance costs are allowed, so Laura does a bit of creative accounting and tries to upgrade the existing machines instead. Separate grants have also provided the telecottage with a colour printer and flatbed scanner. She would like to improve her own IT skills, which have been restricted to the level of the training she delivers, and sees the lack of training and development opportunities for staff as one of the pitfalls of operating on a shoestring.

Her advice to other community telecottages is not to worry about the technological aspects "People are much more important. You can buy technical expertise when you need it. Try to tack the telecottage on to an existing service such as a post office, and make sure there really is local support, and it's not just the brainchild of a couple of boffins. And do a good business plan. That's vital."

A report by the Arkleton Trust in 1993 offered hope and encouragement for telecottages such as the Isles Telecroft which have very small "catchment populations" of users in rural areas. The report studied the six telecottages in the Highlands and Islands, and concluded that three had established a basis for financial self-sustainability, with one already 75% self-sufficient. Even in small communities Arkleton found a demand for desktop publishing and office related services, which can often be more cost-effectively provided through a collective facility than through individual purchase of equipment. Arkleton agrees with Laura that the best telecottage managers are generalists, not technology boffins, with community skills and good local networks. The report also noted that 90% of the telecottage users lived within 10 miles of the site, and that 70% of the clients were aged between 25 and 44. Typically they were small-scale, irregular users with no previous computer training. Laura adds a footnote that lack of ISDN in Shetland is currently frustrating the telecottage's desire to join the RAVAN videoconferencing project.

KITE, Co. Fermanagh, Northern Ireland

Kinawley Integrated Teleworking Enterprise is located in West Fermanagh, close to the border between Northern Ireland and the Republic. It is a highly successful enterprise which sources 60% of its work from North America, and offers childcare facilities as well as training. The purpose-built telecottage is the brainchild of Sheila and Michael McCaffrey, both of whom have backgrounds in health service administration. Sheila identified the basic requirements to set up the enterprise – premises, childcare facilities, training, equipment and a market for their services. The search for funding was long and arduous. In the end, most of the funding came from Europe, including the European Social Fund, the Human Resources Initiative, and the European Regional Development Fund. Other grants came from the Community Business Programme of the Northern Ireland economic development agency LEDU, and the Department of Agriculture.

Because of the low level of infrastructure in the area, KITE had to build its own premises and fight hard to get an ISDN connection put into a rural location. The centre began operations in 1993, and eight women returners were put through a training programme which included the City & Guilds teleworking VQ, software training, personal development, communications skills and social interaction training as well as marketing skills and European awareness. From the beginning, Sheila and Michael felt that the telecottage needed a commercial input as well as its community aspect, and they worked hard to get contracts such as preparing eye records for Specsavers and handling enquiries for Sandpiper Holidays. But Sheila found that the conversion time for British and European business was too long – the delay between initial contact and the first paying job could be up to a year. So with assistance from the US State Department as part of the Peace Process funding, she tackled the North American market, travelling to the US for six weeks at a time to meet prospective clients. Now KITE has sixteen staff and prepares work for Boston hospitals and San Francisco recruitment agencies, receiving work by Internet, fax or tape and returning it over the ISDN lines. They now need funding to train more teleworkers in anticipation of increased business, but funding is just as hard to come by second time round as it was the first time.

Recently KITE has been piloting a project to transcribe notes from American hospital casualty staff. The notes are dictated to a voicebank, and downloaded as audio via KITE's ISDN link. Staff log on, download the messages and transcribe them. Some teleworkers have received training in anatomy and medical terms from retired nursing tutors, who also provide quality control by checking the notes before they are returned.

Sheila feels that funding bodies do not appreciate that training has to be carried out in advance of the jobs being available. "If I want to expand the business, I have to start training more people right now so they'll be ready when the new contracts come in." She also feels it is very important to select people through the training process, helping them to work out their own goals and motivations as they develop their skills. "The plan is to get 64 people trained in basic skills on the RSA/IBT II course. Of those, perhaps 12 will go on to the one year teleworker vocational training, and in the following year we would hope to employ 10 of those trainees."

The McCaffreys are working to expand the size of the existing telecottage building, with completion expected in December 1997 – another expense that needs funding, as will expanded childcare facilities such as an after school club and a holiday club.

SPEC: Standon Parish Electronic Centre

SPEC, set up in early 1995, is truly owned by its own community – the main financial support comes from an additional £4.50 on the council tax of local residents. The centre was set up with grants from Herts County and East Herts District Councils but running expenses were initially covered by the Parish Council grant. Telecottage manager Frank Wallder began on a Community Action programme which pays for 18 hours a week of his time – additional time is provided by volunteers.

Once it had established a local presence, the centre moved to more convenient premises, again funded through the council tax, that include rooms which can be let to the Parish Council and to other local service providers for field operations. The Citizen's Advice Bureau uses the centre once a week, and it is also used for Parish Council meetings, and for meetings with other local councilllors. There is a book order point for purchase and delivery, and the local library catalogue and county council information services can also be accessed through the centre.

SPEC has an ingenious arrangement with local web design business Moat Services which operates within the premises and provides local employment. In exchange for its workspace, Moat manages the SPEC services, including volunteer rotas, photocopiers, publicity and organisation of courses. The telecottage is providing courses in Word, Excel and the Internet and has participated in the BBC's Computers Don't Bite campaign. SPEC is working towards a separate company limited by guarantee which would enjoy close links with the Parish Council by having a number of councillors as directors. "By the end of year three we hope to break even in terms of operating costs", says Martin Dudley, project manager on behalf of the parish council.

Ottery St Mary – Project Cosmic

"What we are basically is an Internet café", explains Ian Clifford from Project Cosmic, located in an old railway station in the Devon village. Ian applied to the National Lottery for funds to start up the project, and received £85,000 over three years on condition that he found matching funding. The matching funding has come from the county, district and town councils, the local Lions club and the Rural Development Commission. Now the cybercafe, which has a fast Internet connection and uses Pentium 150s, brings young people and businesses together. There are two youth club sessions a week at Project Cosmic which have kids queuing up in advance – they get an hour's connection for £3 using a timer device and a software screening system is in use to ensure there is no access to pornographic sites. Ian is also running a telework agency called STAR, which recruits teleworkers from all over the country for Devon employers: "We're looking for HTML writers and database writers, graphic designers, specialists accountants and people of that ilk", says Ian, who charges a commission for contracts successfully negotiated.

21st century village halls

A bid for £10 million pounds of Millennium funding to refurbish English village halls and to include telecottage facilities has been approved. The bid, put together by rural communities charity ACRE and supported by a number of organisations including the TCA, will benefit 180 halls, ranging from extensions and major refurbishments of existing halls to 6 or 7 new flagship halls.

Project manager Bob Bradshaw began work in December 1996, and there will be three application rounds with short timeframes. The TCA has an advisory role in the project and has provided guidance notes for applicants who wish to establish telecottage facilities in their halls. Bids covering Scotland (SCVO) Wales (WCVA) and Northern Ireland (RCN) have been longlisted for the next round of funding.

Community resource centres – Herefordshire and Worcestershire

The Herefordshire and Worcestershire rural community council has created a network of 22 resource centres located in village halls, community centres, schools and libraries. The centres are provided for non-profit making organisations, the unemployed, small startup businesses and youth businesses. Each centre is run on a self help basis by a volunteer coordinator, often a retired person. The opening hours vary, but when open, the coordinator is available to help with use of the resource centre equipment, which usually consists of a computer, printer, photocopiers, scan printer, binding and stapling machine. Once users have been shown the equipment, they operate it themselves. Sometimes arrangements for trusted users to pick up a key to the centre outside normal opening hours can be made.

The network of centres is able to avail of group purchasing discounts, to learn from each other, to fundraise together and to adopt standard procedures. The council pays for the coordinator and supplies the equipment.

WREN Telecottage

Once established, a telecottage can act as a platform for various additional services. The WREN Telecottage was founded as Warwickshire's first telecottage in 1991. WREN "belongs" indirectly to the Royal Agricultural Society of England (RASE), and received startup grants from ARC, BT and Coventry and Warwickshire TEC. Through RASE, WREN has educational charity status and trading status.

WREN combines access to IT, training, open learning, and business services, and has also developed a social and networking function which it considers essential for micro business support, aiding the incubation of new small businesses. WREN works in partnership with a variety of local and European agencies, a role recognised by an EC Local Development Award. The telecottage is a DTI Local Support Centre, working with a BusinessLink partnership, and is also part of the DTI's IT for All initiative. It also carries out training for the Farming Online service.

WREN's early development was assisted by contracts to run EC-funded training projects, such as Rural Women Back to Business. This provided WREN with a funded core activity and helped train a pool of freelance workers who have become part of WREN's client and supplier network. In recent years, the commercial services side of the telecottage has been developed. Any profits the telecottage makes from such work are used to subsidise local services.

WREN's equipment includes the usual computers and office equipment, but in addition it has videoconferencing equipment, its own email and information service, and offers a nursery where telecottage users can "park" their children while they train or work. WREN has developed a national and international role as a demonstration telecottage, facilitated by its location at the National Agricultural Centre, Stoneleigh, and by its work in combining community and commercial functions. Recently the ISDN line installed by WREN for its videoconferencing unit was used by a number of local radio stations to provide an "outside broadcast" studio during the Royal Show which takes place at Stoneleigh.

Setting up a telecottage

Start by defining your aims. Telecottages can take many different forms and serve a variety of purposes, ranging from community education through economic development to purely commercial ventures. Telecottage services include training, equipment hire, services for teleworkers, and jobs agencies. Those who use telecottages include self-employed and employed teleworkers, unemployed people improving their skills and community groups. You need to decide the function of your telecottage and then keep checking that your activities are directed towards that purpose.

Interested parties

The first step is to gather together interested people into a management or steering group. This could be an informal group of like-minded people, or a more formal working group. Try your parish council, chamber of commerce, local politicians and community school. Discuss the services that could be offered, and the premises and equipment that will be needed for the services. Don't forget all the bureaucratic issues – planning, insurance, tax, financial structure. Check that you will have access to a digital telephone exchange, and preferably to ISDN services. Get expert help on the equipment issues.

Visiting a telecottage

Visit an established telecottage. Many hold occasional open days including:

■ WREN Telecottage: based at the National Agricultural Centre, Stoneleigh, Warwickshire. This centre is something of a showcase, and

is housed in an adapted exhibition building. Open Days are held about once a month, though special visits can be arranged where there is demand. The cost for the half day is £10 per person including VAT, refreshments, online demonstrations and an information pack. The maximum number is 15. Contact Jane Berry on 01203 696986.

- Moorlands Telecottage: based in school premises in the small village of Warslow, Staffordshire. Users come from a series of villages in the surrounding area, and the telecottage has specialised in developing training materials for teleworkers. Visits are by prior arrangement and cost £30 for up to 10 people. The visit lasts about 90 minutes, and covers what the telecottage does, how it was set up, its training courses and support for the local community and local enterprises. Visits by educational organisations and small community groups are free. Moorlands telecottage has branded itself the UK's first telecottage and was responsible for the development of the TCA Teleworking VQ. Contact Simon Brooks on 01298 84336 Email 100135.2516@compuserve.com

- KITE Telecottage near Enniskillen in Northern Ireland provides training, childcare and commercial work for around ten staff. KITE likes to have a detailed advance discussion with prospective visitors on what they want to see, which can cover childcare facilities, obtaining European funding, the teleworking operation (which works for US companies using ISDN links), and initiatives to promote US/Northern Ireland trade sponsored by the US State Department. Prior discussion allows the visit to be tailored to visitors' needs. The cost is £30 for up to 10 people, and the tour normally takes just over an hour. The price includes an information pack. Contact Michael McCaffrey 01365 348943 Email 100073.1111@compuserve.com

Try contacting a centre in your area using the list and map at the end of this chapter to see whether they would take visitors or offer consultancy on setting up a telecottage. As you are taking up valuable time, remember you may be charged for a visit.

Market survey

Next, assess the need for the centre by performing a market survey of the locality up to a radius of fifteen miles. Try a questionnaire targeted on individuals working from home, small business and community groups. Assess any similar services in the area. You could combine the market survey phase with an open evening to discuss the idea locally. Contact potential sponsors and relevant local authorities as early as you can. Then prepare a business plan (see Chapter 5, *Getting work* and the end of this chapter) and examine the available funding sources.

Funding sources and fundraising

Raising money to buy the telecottage equipment is bound to involve a search for innovative funding methods. Sponsorship can be highly productive for both donor and recipient. Many different sponsors, including

European funding will develop Manchester EVHs

The Manchester network of four electronic village halls (EVHs – community-based centres similar to telecottages) has received nearly £2 million in funding from the European Regional Development Fund for expansion. There will be an additional 8 centres and a 6 person development team based at the Manchester Multi-Media Centre to run the Manchester Telematics and Teleworking Partnership. There will be a telework agency linked to the EVHs and the network plans to capitalise on the city's reputation as a centre for music and the visual arts. The Women's EVH offers training, drop in computer and web access and plans to set up a new Women's Technology Centre providing training, workspace and support for women setting up in business. Contact clem.herman@mcr1.poptel.org.uk 0161 953 4049

equipment manufacturers, telecommunications companies and high street banks, have seen the potential of the telecottage idea. Think about linking up with a local bank to provide meeting rooms for their customers who run businesses from home, or charging local agencies for using the telecottage as their base in the local community. Offer to act as a local representative for an office supplies wholesaler such as Office Supplies Online, which has an online ordering system and recruits local agents.

Try to make sure that your sponsorship idea would create commercial value for the sponsoring company. An equipment dealer may consider a telecottage an excellent place to display equipment so that it can be seen and used by potential customers. A large company which is laying off staff may wish to balance this by helping to create a local service that can train former employees in new skills, and support new businesses. They may also have redundant equipment.

Because telecottages often use software for training, they may be entitled to educational discounts on software prices. Companies may also be prepared to offload equipment that is obsolete for their uses, and which has low secondhand value. Such equipment is often perfectly functional for telecottage use.

A subscription scheme can be designed to raise money for capital equipment. Once the money has been raised and the equipment bought, the subscription is redeemable against a number of hours of free use of the equipment.

Draws, raffles and lotteries are old stalwarts for the fundraiser. Try to add a twist to the prizes to gain interest – for example, games that children can play on the telecottage computers, business or personal stationery to be designed by the telecottage for the winner and so on.

If you have written a credible business plan and cashflow forecast, don't be frightened to approach your local high street bank. It may be prepared to offer cheaper banking services, or loans, or suggest other sources of funding. Keep in contact with government business support agencies.

Some telecottages think about using professional consultants to find funding for their startups. Before taking any such step, it is worth consulting a checklist produced by the Forum for Private Business which warns against consultancies which claim 100% accuracy or claim special relationships with government. Much of the information offered by consultants may be available free from various sources including economic development agencies. Contact FPB on 01565 634 467. There is a software package which can help in identifying grants available at a discounted price (for Lloyds bank customers and members of the TCA) from Enterprise Advisory Services 01280 700102.

A recent trend has been for telecottages to tie up with a local Internet provider to provide a cybercafe, or to advertise access to the Internet. However, this can be difficult to bill effectively so think through the charging mechanism.

The National Lottery

Any organisation set up for charitable, philanthropic or benevolent purposes is eligible to apply for national lottery funding. Grants cannot be given to individuals. Applications can be made for capital or revenue funding, and the minimum amount is £5000. However, a successful pilot scheme for small grants under £5,000 is shortly to be made available nationally, incorporating a simplified application form and reduced decision times, as well as different rules on the use of funds.

Currently, each round of grants has a specific theme which influences applications from organisations, but it is intended that a rolling programme of grants will be introduced – given the regional variations and changes, start by contacting your local office for information relevant to your region.

To get an application pack, phone 0345 919191 (line reopens in 1998). John Lakeman, a director of the TCA and recent assessor for lottery funding, points out that because bids exceed available funds, you must put in a high quality bid that satisfies strict criteria. Consider your application in the light of:

■ how well planned and financially sound a proposed project is;

■ the value for money it offers;

■ whether there is adequate management and staffing;

■ whether it includes an appropriate commitment to equal opportunities;

■ the level of user involvement and encouragement of community participation;

■ plans for the project's future survival, or an exit strategy once lottery funding expires if the funding is requested for more than one year.

A number of other funding sources are listed at the end of this chapter, and at the end of the *Getting Work* chapter.

State support

Local councils have been very supportive of teleworking in geographically isolated areas. A telecottage can be an ideal support centre for the council's economic development strategies. In Britain, the Training and Enterprise Councils (TECs or LECs in Scotland) which are responsible for training workers, have used telecottages as a platform to deliver TEC services to rural areas. FÁS and the VECs provide similar services in Ireland (the best example is North Tipperary VEC). Some telecottages have contracts to provide employment training on behalf of these authorities. The Consortium of Rural TECs (CORT) may be able to advise on TECs involved in telecottage projects.

There are a number of EU schemes which can provide funds to telecottages that deliver specific training services. Women returners are catered for by the NOW scheme. Rurally disadvantaged areas can get funds under the LEADER scheme. Obtaining EC funds requires specialist help – for example from County Council economic development departments. The EU is interested in many areas of teleworking and related technologies (usually grouped together under the term "telematics"), and research into this area is carried out under the ACTS and TAP programmes (See Chapter 14, *The European perspective*).

Rural Community Councils exist in England, with sister organisations in Wales, Scotland and Northern Ireland. RCCs work at parish council level to assist community development. Some RCCs have become involved in telecottage projects. For details of your local RCC, contact ACRE (the Association of RCCs). ACRE is also involved with the Countrywork scheme which has benefitted a number of local TCA groups. The Rural Development Commission in Britain has supported several telecottages. Highlands and Islands Enterprise, in conjunction with BT, has sponsored six telecottages. The Welsh Development Agency and the Development Board for Rural Wales have also supported telecottages.

The Department of National Heritage has two schemes that could be used by community groups wishing to find out about funding a telecottage – the Local Grants scheme, which helps groups to learn from each other through study visits, and the Support Grants Scheme, which helps large voluntary and community organisations to support smaller groups.

Lloyds TSB funds top £20m

Telecottage startups could do worse than to apply to Lloyds TSB Foundations. There are four foundations, covering England, Wales, Scotland and Northern Ireland. The Foundations receive 1% of Lloyds TSB group's pre-tax profits. Funds are projected to exceed £20m by 1999, making it one of the largest general award-giving organisations in the UK. Grants are to charitable organisations only, and the current focus includes employment training for disabled and disadvantaged people, volunteering, the elderly and parenting. Particular stress is laid on the needs of young people and rural areas. Foundation grants are typically in the range £2,500 to £5,000 and rarely exceed £100,000.
Tel: 0171 204 5276.

Telecottage cash flow: year 1

	Start	Jun	Jul	Aug	Sept	Oct	Nov	Dec	Jan	Feb	Mar	Apr	May	Total
INCOME														
Grant or Capital	10000													10000
Sales														
Copying/binding		72	96	108	120	144	144	72	168	192	240	240	240	1836
Fax/messaging		80	125	125	200	200	250	250	250	300	300	300	300	2680
Equipt/Hot Desk Hire		20	30	30	100	100	100	100	100	150	150	200	200	1280
Commercial training			350		525	700	875	175	875	1050	1225	1225	1225	8225
Community training		250	250	250	500	500	500		250	500	500	500	500	4500
Teleshopping		50	80	80	120	120	200	200	120	120	120	200	200	1610
Telework		0	0	750	750	750	750	750	750	750	750	750	750	7500
Publications		50	50	80	80	60	50	50	30	30	30	50	50	610
Room hire			150	150	300	375	375	300	375	375	375	375	375	3525
Business Services		100	100	200	400	400	600	400	400	600	700	800	800	5500
Retail sales		50	100	150	300	400	600	700	500	700	850	1000	1250	6600
Total	10000	672	1331	1923	3395	3749	4444	2997	3818	4767	5240	5640	5890	53866
EXPENDITURE														
Retail sales cost	1000	33	65	500	195	260	725	455	325	455	552.5	650	813	6027.5
Wages														
Manager/Trainer		1000	1000	1250	1250	1250	1250	1250	1250	1250	1250	1250	1250	14500
Assistant										400	400	400	400	1600
Teleworkers				600	600	600	600	600	600	600	600	600	600	6000
Freelance Trainer			100		200	400	500		500	600	650	650	650	4250
Support worker										100	100	100	100	400
Staff costs		200	200	250	250	250	250	250	250	350	350	350	350	3300
Overheads														
Rent/Rates		500	500	500	500	500	500	500	500	500	500	500	500	6000
Light/heat/power		100	100	100	100	100	100	100	100	100	100	100	100	1200
Insurance		75	75	75	75	75	75	75	75	75	75	75	75	900
Promotion	850	120			250		120			100	80	80	80	1760
Telephone	100		225			350				400			400	1475
Stationery	300			400				400				400		1500
Subscriptions		170												170
Postage	50	25	25	25	25	25	25	25	25	25	25	25	25	350
Copier/fax Lease		75	75	75	75	75	75	75	75	75	75	75	75	900
Consumables/software	700	30	30	30	45	45	45	45	50	50	50	80	80	1280
Repairs/servicing														0
Premises fitting	6000													6000
Equipment lease		260	260	260	260	260	260	260	260	260	260	260	260	3120
Bank charges/fees		20	50	50	50	50	50	50	50	50	50	50	50	570
														61303
TOTAL	9000	2608	2480	3940	4275	3890	4925	4085	4160	5370	5118	5645	5808	61303
Opening balance	0	1000	-936	-2085	-4102	-4982	-5123	-5604	-6692	-7034	-7637	-7514	-7519	
Plus/minus		-1936	-1149	-2017	-880	-141	-481	-1088	-342	-603	123	-5	83	
Closing balance	1000	-936	-2085	-4102	-4982	-5123	-5604	-6692	-7034	-7637	-7514	-7519	-7437	

Notes: This cashflow is for illustrative purposes only and should be adapted based on local conditions, service offered and market research. The Telecottage begins to break even by end of year one if sales targets are reached; overdraft should be cleared by end of year two — realistically this level of activity would need considerable pre-start promotion and contract development. In a self-employed situation the manager's wages would be drawings against profit and would be half that shown to avoid overdraft. For a community initiative the deficit shown might be carried by a sponsoring organisation. Lease payments are for fax/copier on 3 year lease. Service contract and repairs begin in year 2. Equipment leasing based on £8000 worth over 3 years. Rent/rates reflect a property big enough for multiple activities including room hire.

Telecottages and telecentres Sep 1997

To be included on this list, updated bimonthly in Teleworker magazine, a telecottage must offer public access to computers and other IT equipment, provide training facilities, and supply services to assist other businesses. The location information indicates the nearest post town to the telecottage. However, telecottages come in many different flavours, so to get exact details of services, please telephone the telecottage in question. To add to this listing or make a correction contact Alan Denbigh (Tel: 01453 834 874, Fax: 01453 836 174, Email: 100272.1472@compuserve.com).

1 START (Shetland)
2 Wirral Business Bureau
3 Antur Tanat Cain Llangedwyn
4 Welshpool Telecentre
5 Antur Teifi
6 BOON Ltd.
7 Dereham Digital Centre
8 Hunsbury Telecottage
9 Connemara West
10 Fakenham Technical Services
11 Daily Information
12 Telelink
13 Copyplus Telecottage
14 Durham Dales Centre
15 East Clare Telecottage
16 East Kent Telecottage
17 Eccles House Telebusiness Centre
18 Gittisham Village Press
19 Ileach Teleservices
20 Alford IT
21 Instant Search
22 Sheringham Telecottage
23 Mizen Telecottage
24 CITU Belfast
25 The Resource Centre
26 Pathfinder Open Access Centre
27 Wingrave Telecottage
28 Warsop Telecentre
29 Adur Resource Centre
30 Codford Telecottage
31 Colne Valley Trust
32 Comharchumann Chléire Teo.
33 Crickhowell Community Office
34 Knightley Telecottage
35 Wearhead Community Telecentre
36 Tarbert Community Teleservice Centre
37 Isles Telecroft
38 Kingsley Telecentre
39 Stornoway Telecentre
40 ORBIT Carrefour
41 Mere Telecottage
42 Moorlands Telecottage
43 PATCH, Dublin
44 North Tyne Telecottage
45 Odiham Telecottage (COLCO)
46 Rathcoole Business Centre
47 Cahersiveen Telecottage
48 SIMTRA Aberaeron
49 SIMTRA Crymych
50 SIMTRA Fishguard
51 SIMTRA Llandeilo
52 SIMTRA Narberth
53 SIMTRA Saundersfoot
54 SIMTRA St Davids
55 SIMTRA Tregaron

56 Stonesfield Telecottage
57 Tele Teach
58 Union Lane Centre Workshops
59 West Cumbria Telecottage
60 WREN Telecottage
61 Wolds Enterprise Bureau
62 Ness Telecottage
63 Boston Spa Training
64 Balvenie House Ltd
65 Llanfairfechan Business Centre
66 Chorlton Workshop EVH
67 Launceston Telecentre
68 Midhurst Resource Centre Ltd
69 CROW Ltd
70 Manchester Womens EVH
71 CEB Telecentre
72 Ilkley Telecottage
73 IT Works – Diss
74 Guthrie Creative Services
75 The Business Base
76 Goireas Business & Computing Centre
77 Kington Connected Community Co.
78 Daventry Tertiary College
79 Colwyn Telecottage
80 Menter Bro Ddyfi
81 Network Personnel Ltd
82 Rural Business Centre
83 Naver Teleservice Centre
84 Porthmadog Telecentre
85 Hindon Telecentre
86 Aberdeen Teleworking Centre
87 CATS 2000
88 Menter Bro Preseli
89 U-Compute
90 Reydon Infobase
91 Kinawley Integrated Teleworking Enterprise (K.I.T.E.)
92 Moira Telecottage
93 Goatacre Telecottage
94 Mevagissey Telecottage
95 Strathyre IT Centre
96 Hackney Resource Centre Telecentre
97 York Telecottage
98 W.C.E.I.R.D.
99 Brackley Telecottage
100 Declare Business Centre
101 Barra Telecottage
102 Worth Telecentre
103 Rhondda Enterprise
104 Honeybun Secretarial Services
105 RNIB Teleworkers
106 Informatica
107 Honeytree Services
108 York Word Processing Bureau

109 Varitech Telecentre
110 Castell-y-Dail Telecottage
111 Romney Resource Centre
112 Computer Advisory Services
113 Rutland Business Communications Centre
114 Ockment Centre
115 Llanwrtyd Wells Telecottage
116 Miracle Graphics
117 The Business Base
118 Support Shop
119 Premier Services Telecottage
120 Presteigne Community Resource Centre
121 Selsey Regeneration
122 Beara Community School
123 Business Focus
124 Commpact
125 SPEC
126 Cenin Ltd
127 IT Drop in Centre
128 Epsom Telecentre
129 Downham Telecottage
130 Project Cosmic
131 Barnham Telecottage
132 Slamannan IT Centre
133 Bramshall Telecottage
134 Basford Hall CFE
135 Soho Computing
136 Burford Telecottage
137 Lindum House Telecottage
138 A M Computer Services
139 Leek Telecentre
140 Highland Teleworking Centre
141 Sledmere BARN
142 Skills Station
143 Longton Telecottage
144 Nunsthorpe Telecottage
145 Yeovil College Telecentre
146 CTF Training
147 Newport Advanced Teleservices
148 Clydesdale Telecentre
149 Phoenix Telecentre
150 Skye Teleservice Centre
151 Flexit
152 IT Works – Loddon
153 IT Works – Acle
154 Time Travellers Telexbureaux
155 Berwick on Tweed Telecentre
156 Resource Solutions Telecentre
157 Webtel Telecentre
158 Castle Douglas Community IT Centre
159 JTA Business Services
160 East Rendlesham Telecottage

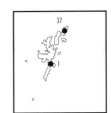

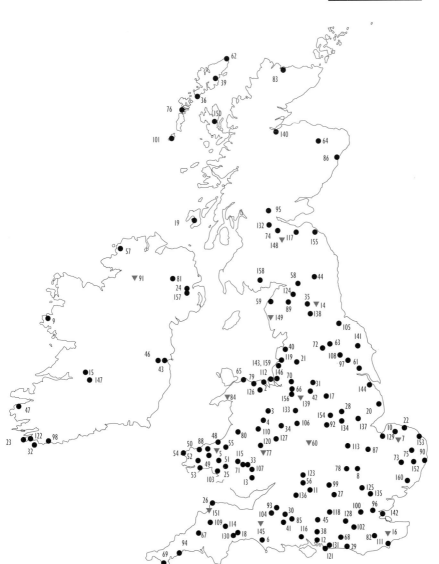

Bibliography

Why Teleworking? *Date:* 1996
Authors: Stoney Stanton Telecottage
Source: Stoney Stanton Telecottage, P.O. Box 7, Stoney Stanton, Leicester LE9 4ZW

British and Irish Telecottages *Date:* 1995
Author: Laura Burt, University of Edinburgh
Source: Laura Burt, 27/3 Blair Street, Edinburgh, EH1 1QR
Email: 9157561@lewis.sms.ed.ac.uk
Comment: Dissertation following 1994 large-scale survey of telecottages. Available in paper or disk format.

Community Economics *Date:* 1995
Source: The New Economics Foundation, Tel: 0171 377 5696

Survey of Telecottage Activity and Finance *Date:* 1995
Authors: Small World Connections with support from the Telecottage Association
Source: Bill Murray, Small World Connections, Tel: 0161 4456 0630.

Sussex Telecentre Network *Date:* 1995
Authors: Sussex Rural Community Council
Source: Sussex Rural Community Council, 212 High Street, Lewes, East Sussex BN7 2NH, Tel: 01273 473422 Ref: ISBN 1 873850 13 1

Telecottages: How the Usage of Information Technology can counter Rural Disadvantages *Date:* 1995
Author: Tatjana Gosau, MA in European Business Administration
Source: University of Northumbria

A Survey of the Users of Selected Telecottages in Britain *Date:* 1994
Author: Colin Cummings, University of Plymouth
Source: Seale-Hayne Faculty of Agriculture and Food, University of Plymouth

Golden Valley Information Project – Initial Report *Date:* 1993
Author: K A Webb
Source: County Libraries Service & BLCMP Ltd, Libraries Division, Shire Hall, Hereford, HR1 2HY

Telecommuting Centers and Related Concepts: A Review of Practice *Date:* 1994
Authors: Michael Bagley, Jill Mannering, Patricia Mokhtarian
Source: Institute of Transportation Studies, University of California, Davis, California 95616 Ref: ISBN UCD-ITS-RR-94-4

Telecottages, Teleworking and Telelearning *Date:* 1994
Author: Lilian Holloway
Source: Teldok, Sweden, Tel: +46-8-23 00 00 Fax +46-8-10 13 27

Final Report on the Evaluation of Community Teleservice Centres in the Highlands and Islands *Date:* 1993
Authors: John Bryden, Stuart Black, Frank Rennie
Source: The Arkleton Trust, Coulnakyle, Nethy Bridge, Inverness Tel: 01479 821 393, Fax: 01479 821 441 Ref: 0 90 6724 41 4

Marketing Telecottages and Teleworking Date: 1993
Author: ACRE/Telecottage Association
Source: ACRE, Somerford Court, Somerford Rd, Cirencester, GL7 1TW Ref: ISBN 1 871157 33 1

Best Practice in Developing Community Teleservice Centres *Date:* 1992
Author: Steve Graham

The Ratio programme

Ratio (Rural Area Training and Information Opportunities) is a programme to set up 40 local "drop in centres" in parts of Cornwall, the Isles of Scilly, Devon and Somerset which fall into the European Union's Objective 5b areas. Each centre will provide computers, email, digital satellite reception and videoconferencing, to be used by people seeking information, work and training.

Ratio is a collaborative venture bringing together education providers, local authorities, government departments and regional bodies, as well as businesses and the voluntary sector. Its main function is the provision of access to training and information (such as information on grants, local authority services, the EU, employment, education and welfare). Fourteen centres have already opened in low population areas such as Mevagissey and Dartmoor, and each has a facilitator. The facilitators have backgrounds in further education, and are chosen for their commitment to the aims of the project. They provide necessary skills to local people as part of the centre setup process. The centres are in council premises, libraries, village halls and some private enterprise sites.

The project also employs "roving" technical support workers and a website development worker. The website will provide FAQs and up to date information. There are also two centre development officers based at the University of Plymouth to help users get the best out of their local centres. Teleworker training will be provided through a vocational qualification administered by Truro College. The total cost of the project is around £5 million, including £2.3 million from the government's Regional Challenge prize, local authority funding and EU funding.

Source: CASR, Faculty of Economic and Social Studies, University of Manchester, M13 9PL

So You Want to Start a Telecottage　　　　　　　　*Date:* 1992
Author: Beverley Shelley
Source: Gloucestershire Community Council, 15 College Green, Gloucester, GL1 2LZ

Telecentres - Australian Experiences
Authors: Graham MacKay and Ian Reeve, University Of New England　　*Date:* 1992
Source: Dept. of Learning, Devt & Comm, RDC, University of New England, Armidale, Australia

Telecottages – The UK Experience　　　　　　　　*Date:* 1992
Author: ACRE
Source: ACRE, Somerford Court, Somerford Rd, Cirencester, GL7 1TW
Ref: ISBN 1 871157 31 5

Contacts

Partners in the Countryside is a non-profit making organisation established to promote a business approach to rural regeneration. The organisation provides information about rural intiatives and uses its sponsor's funds to support a range of rural projects. Contact Anne Harris Tel: 01273 695776.

Australian Rural Telecentres Association http://www.arta.org.au. In 1993, the

Australian government awarded AUS$2.7 million for the establishment of telecentres nationwide. The resulting network has produced a best practice guide released in 1997. Copies of the packs, which include seven booklets and a video, cost AUS$70, and can be obtained from the Western Australia Support Network Fax: +619 227 8393 Contact: Sandra Greenwell.

Resource Solutions Julie Bagnoli Tel: 0161 281 4050 Fax: 0161 226 8943 Web: http://www.reed.co.uk/rs

Informatica Storm Barratt Tel/fax: 01889 271266 Email: informatica@farmline.com

The Community Investment Fund created by English Partnerships is for projects from priority areas such as rural development blackspots, former coalfield areas, city challenge areas and so on. Grants of between £10,000 and £100,000 in value are possible and can be for capital works to buildings or for revenue projects that are expected to produce social and economic benefits. Contact Sukhvinder Stubbs on 0171 976 7070.

Small World Connections Tel: 0161 445 0603.

The Rural Development Commission publishes a guidebook to financial and other forms of assistance available to entrepreneurs in rural areas. Copies are available free of charge from the Information Section, RDC, FREEPOST, SA122 141 Castle Street, Salisbury SP1 3BR.

Community Development Organisations
There are a number of regional rural community organisations which may be potential sources of information and advice for organisations starting telecottages and telecentres.

ACRE – Action With Communities in Rural England. ACRE can put you in touch with your local rural community council who may know of other schemes or funding awards in the area. Tel: 01285 653477

WCVA – Wales Council for Voluntary Action Tel: 01222 855100

SCVO – Scottish Council for Voluntary Organisations Tel: 0131 556 3882

RCN – Rural Community Network - Northern Ireland Tel: 01684 766670

NCVO – National Council for Voluntary Organisations (UK wide) Tel: 0171 387 9898

British Coal Enterprise – a number of locations in the UK principally in ex-coalfield areas.

NIAA – Northern Informatics Application Agency – aims to improve communications and information access in the Northern area including Northumberland, Tyne & Wear, Cumbria, County Durham and Cleveland. Tel: 0191 549 6577 Fax: 0191 549 6578 Email: chris.drew@niaa.org.uk

Ratio programme Contact Helen Watson Tel: 01752 232390 Fax: 01752 232392

http://www.ronneby.se/ronneby/infoc/projekt/attach.html is the home page for the Telematics Applications project **ATTACH** (Advanced Transeuropean Telematics Applications for Community Help)

http://ctr.cstp.umkc.edu/nevada is the Website for the Nevada Telecommunities project.

For details of other regional funding bodies, also see the Bibliography to Chapter 5, *Getting work.*

Ideas for teleservices

This chapter lists ideas for services, some of which are already offered by other teleworkers. Some of the ideas are only suited to telecottages. For teleworkers, many forms of consultancy not listed here, ranging from quality management to market research can be teleworked, but you need to already have the relevant skills and industry contacts to make them work. General issues of how to sell your teleworking services are covered in Chapter 5, *Getting Work*. You should also find Chapter 12, *Teleworking Equipment* relevant, although it does not cover software in detail. When considering what services to offer, be careful to evaluate the cost of software that will be required, and avoid substantial investments in this area without thorough market research on the demand for the proposed service.

Abstracting, editing, proofreading and indexing

Many teleworkers have skills in the publishing area such as copy editing, proofreading and indexing. There is strong demand for these skills if they are combined with the ability to handle scientific subjects. A much-publicised example of a teleworking business based on these is skills is Crossaig in Scotland. Crossaig arranges abstracting and indexing of biomedical articles for Elsevier's EMBASE database. The printed journals are

---

Proto-type

Ann Collins runs Proto-type, a remote word processing business based in Essex which services businesses in the City of London. Their main client is a quantity surveying group. Work is received as audio tapes or handwritten faxes, typed in and returned by faxmodem. At the beginning of each week, the customer gets a list of all the teleworkers and their availability, with the possibility of extending the service beyond normal office hours if needed. "We are effectively providing the organisation and quality control behind the teleworked service", says Ann. "The people we use need to be technically very good at the word processing package so that there are no problems if the client later needs to correct or alter the document. I interview all the teleworkers before they are registered with the client and confidentiality declarations are signed. Some of our teleworkers also offer translation services. The going rate for temping in central London is £12–£15 an hour, so we are undercutting this rate at the moment, but we really sell on quality and the fact that clients only pay us for productive time. We have regular customers whose ways of working we know, and unlike temps, we don't need half a day's training to get into the swing of things." But Ann is realistic about the future as more and more managers do their own typing, and voice activated dictation systems become widespread. "I believe this solution only has an eight to ten year lifespan, but teleworking has tremendous potential and we will need to develop new services."

OCR-scanned into computer text files at the company's offices and then sent by ISDN file transfer to the teleworkers around Scotland. The teleworkers work on a piece rate, but many have specialist skills and PhDs in areas such as marine biology or pharmacology and can earn up to £17.50 per hour for their work. This arrangement gives Crossaig access to the skills it needs, and the teleworkers access to work from remote rural areas.

Audio typing, remote typing, document formatting

Work arrives by fax, or on audio cassettes, is transcribed onto computer and returned as disk, printout, email or all three. For audio typing you will need a transcribing machine. This is a tape recorder with a foot pedal for playing the tape, stopping it and rewinding where necessary while leaving the hands free. There are three main sizes of tape: standard audio (C-size), Philips mini cassette and Dictaphone mini cassette, so talk to your prospective customers about the sizes they use before buying. The work can range from correspondence to whole books or conference proceedings. Perhaps you could link up with conference organisers in your area? However, be aware that this market is under threat from advances in systems which allow direct dictation to computer. If you plan to go into this area you will need to specialise or add value to your transcription services, and consider areas such as proofreading, indexing, editing, and translation.

Bookkeeping and accountancy services

Accountants may be prepared to send out the more tedious areas of their work such as putting purchase receipts and invoices onto computer. You will need specialist accountancy skills to succeed in this area. Alternatively, self-employed accountants and bookkeepers might want to hire your computers and software to work on themselves. There is a multitude of software packages in this area, and every company has its personal favourite. Be careful to check this out before investing in expensive software. Accountants who plan to telework from home themselves need to take account of the likelihood of client visits, and provide suitable parking and insurance cover.

Computer programming/software support

Several telecottages have been started up by small computer dealers who offer tailor-made programming services to customers as well as software training and support. If you have specialist skills in this area it could be for you. Offering technical support over the telephone to new computer users could also be a winner. But beware – you should think about getting professional indemnity insurance to cover yourself in case your advice leads to a financial loss for one of your customers – what would happen if you recommended a backup procedure that led to the loss of vital data? This kind of insurance can be very expensive. Specialist areas for computer programming and software include CAD/CAM (Computer-aided design and manufacturing), computer design of PCBs (printed circuit boards), mathematical and financial modelling, stress calculations for engineers,

The Dyer Partnership

Mark and Bill Dyer have been profiled in publications about Britain's Information Society Initiative for the way in which they have used the World Wide Web to expand their accountancy partnership. Mark Dyer explains: "Our website has generated interest from all over the UK and the world. For example, we've had contacts from the British Consul in Messina, Italy, and quite a number from the US, Canada and even Australia. We're doing business with people through email, acting as their accountants."

The Internet also helps with client credibility closer to home: "Where clients use the technology themselves, the minute you say you have email it establishes a lot of credibility and provides a good way of conducting business – we can send data files attached to email." Setting up the website took around 150 hours of work, and a further 100 hours has been spent marketing and maintaining the site. "Of course we are not the only accountants on the Internet, but we have interpreted the information, giving people a taster of what we can do on items such as why companies should pay dividends rather than bonuses – rather than putting up a page of detailed corporate tax law on the web."

quantity surveying and project management. The Ability Enterprise group in Dorset offers a tachograph analysis service.

Conferencing

Conferencing services help with "telemeetings". Telecottages can offer videoconferencing and audioconferencing facilities. For videoconferencing, you must have an ISDN telephone line and a videophone. Audio conferencing for up to three people is available using standard digital telephone services. For larger numbers, you will need to use either BT's audioconferencing service, or if you are a charity or resource centre, Community Network. Organisations using conferencing regularly may want to invest in a high quality telephone loudspeaker unit.

Data conversion

Converting data from one disk format to another, or from one software package to another, is a commonly requested service in telecottages. Software format conversion does need some knowledge of the package involved, and it's important to quiz the customer on exactly what they want to do with the resulting file in order to provide an appropriate format.

Data input

Many of the first generation of telecottages financed themselves with contracts from companies and government institutions to put large volumes of data onto computers. The more basic end of this kind of work is less available now because most historical data needed by companies has already been entered. However, many companies need to continue to

process data on a regular basis and, if you can offer low cost and high quality, they might be interested in a teleworking arrangement. The KITE telecottage in Northern Ireland won a contract to put customer records held by the SpecSavers chain of opticians onto computer. Data input work is not generally well paid, and is usually quoted as piece-work. However, specialist areas such as the construction of mailing lists can be more remunerative and could be tied in with preparing mailshots or faxshots (mailings by fax). An experienced person can design the database while the less skilled enter data.

Call centres

Call centres, where staff handle large volumes of telephone traffic, have been highly successful in the commercial sector and are used to deliver a wide range of services which fall into two major categories – telemarketing and data processing.

Telemarketing

- central reservations services for hotels, airlines and car hire
- technical support centres for computer hardware and software
- outbound and inbound telesales
- order processing
- consumer information centres
- market research.

Data processing

- abstracting and indexing
- health claims processing

- banking administration
- financial analysis
- magazine subscription administration
- medical transcription
- VAT reclamation
- central order processing (*eg* stationery, computer hardware)

The development of computer-telephony integration (CTI) is now making it possible for call centres to become smaller and more specialised – previously the equipment required meant that large operations, usually with mainframe computers, were important for paybacks. CTI distributes calls to operatives, brings appropriate customer records up on screen, helps staff to fill in information correctly according to a pre-prepared script, and to enter appropriate data. CTI systems also provide statistical monitoring of call handling.

Call centres are a highly specialist area, both in terms of technology and marketing, and in the appropriate training of staff. Call centre projects are best approached through the services of a consultant.

A typical telesales operation could involve ringing retailers and getting their orders for a manufacturing company. You need a telephone headset to keep your hands free for computer data entry. Some companies with high pressure selling techniques like to ring round prospective companies and question them by phone. This work can easily be done on contract by teleworkers. See if you can tie in telesales to mailing list and mailshot work. It is vital to recruit people with a good telephone manner for this kind of work and to give training where necessary. Several London agencies use "resting" actors because of their persuasive skills and good voices.

Equipment rental

This is a major source of income for most telecottages. It can take several forms:

- hire of computers and software on site (*eg* for people who want to use word processing, either for private use or to offer a service)
- hire of computers for private study for those who want to start using computers on an informal basis, perhaps before attending a formal training course, or who want to use software-based tutorials
- hire of equipment to teleworkers such as high quality laser printers and colour printers
- hire of equipment to "take away" such as portable PCs, small inkjet printers, for occasional teleworkers or overload work. The BOON telecottage offers a "try before you buy" PC hire service.

Sometimes this kind of service can be tied in to an existing shop or business such as a printshop. In the case of U-compute in Keswick, computers and photocopiers are on hire in a back room attached to the post

The Virtual Office

Richard Nissen has been running the Virtual Office for nearly fifteen years in Piccadilly, London. His business provides serviced offices, meeting rooms, telephone answering, fax forwarding, a mailing address and secretarial backup. Charges are £150/month for call answering, and £50/month for use of the prestigious London mailing address. Office manager Rebecca Benbow explains: "We have a lot of customers who have left large corporations and are used to having a hundred people running after them. They are there to make money, and we do the menial things."

office and craft shop. There is also a Village Shops Scheme run by the Rural Development Commission which supports the introduction of technology to village shops – in the main this covers electronic point of sale technology such as scanners and computerised tills, but in some situations it may cover the introduction of PCs and printers.

Farm skills

Farmers need secretaries, bookkeepers and people who know how to fill in complex EU forms and maps. A teleworker with specialist knowledge in these areas could prove invaluable to a rural community, though many farmers are uncomfortable about using someone who also works for their neighbours and may know details of their cultivation plans. The WREN telecottage initiated a scheme whereby four farmers clubbed together to buy some crop management software and used it on a collaborative basis rather than each having to buy their own computer and software. It may be worth contacting suppliers of specialist products such as Farmplan and Optimix to discuss possibilities. See the Informatica case study in Chapter 6.

Faxing/photocopying services

Copying charges average about 10p/sheet for low volume. Fax varies at £1–£2.50 per sheet. Colour photocopying or high quality laser photocopying comes in at about £1/sheet. Think about your location before buying equipment for bureau services. If you are based half way up a remote valley, are people really going to drop in for a few photocopies? On the other hand, if you have the only decent photocopier on an island, you could be in business.

Information broking

Almost every business sector needs facts of some description. Information brokers are experts at accessing paper and online information sources and distilling the results into a product they can sell to clients. Stepping Stones, based in London, provides information on European tenders through its TED and BC-Net agencies. Alert Publications, also based in London, used to summarise online sources for telecoms news and provide the summaries to clients via daily fax bulletins – interestingly, this business idea was overtaken by the customers beginning to use the Internet directly to get their information, a timely warning on the need to keep up technologically with your customers. Most brokers are specialists who know the resources in a particular subject area intimately. Good personal contacts are also important. Charges are usually via an hourly or daily rate, or by subscription to a briefing document. (See information about Instant Search in Chapter 5, *Getting Work*).

Information services/booking agency/tourist information

Teleworkers can provide box office services for professional and amateur theatres. They can arrange bookings for coach services, village halls and sports facilities. Other related ideas include registers of business services and local organisations. These could be computerised if there is sufficient volume of information. Tourist information such as B&B lists, sites of interest and events diaries are provided by several telecottages in holiday areas. This seems to be a service that fits in well with other telecottage activities, and can attract funding or sponsorship from government agencies. A number of telecottages manage tourism web sites on behalf of local tourism development groups.

Internet-based services

Internet services offer a wide range of opportunities for the dedicated (and technically knowledgeable) pioneer. See page 230 for the example of Mark Francis-Jones and his jewellery-over-the-net service. Or page 112 for Siân Thomas and the IWS Internet-based organisation for teleworkers. Many consultants and workers in the publishing industry use the Internet to market their services. Others advertise and sell rare goods. See if you can find John Eagle, who sells his dramatic photographs, posters and postcards of Irish lighthouses over the Internet – he's based in a remote village where employment opportunities are few. The main problem with Internet-based services are charging mechanisms. More people are now prepared to send their credit card numbers to "secure" commercial Internet sites, but there is still concern about this area, so providing a scheme for alternative payment methods is vital.

LETS

The Local Enterprise Trading System (LETS) scheme can provide telecottages and teleworkers with additional resources. Under LETS, local services are exchanged in cashless trading, with different services attracting different rates of LETS. Each subscriber gets a cheque book for their LETS tokens, and abuse is discouraged by monthly statements showing the indebtedness (or otherwise) of each subscriber. The system is promoted as encouraging local trading, and re-enfranchisng people on low incomes by allowing them to exchange services and goods without money. Telecottages can operate as administrative centres for local LETS systems.

Office services

A number of virtual office services have grown up over the past five years providing an official "front" for businesses including telephone answering,

Neighbourhood work centre facilities at Antur Teifi

Antur Teifi, a combined business park and telematics centre in Wales, participated in the OFFNET EU project to provide services to workers that would reduce their commuting burden. The social services and trading standards departments of the now-disbanded Dyfed County Council began using the centre in March 1993 for field workers who spend over 50% of their time out of the office, travelling at last ten miles to return to the office between visits. The council workers can deal with their workload more effectively, and use their normal database and word processing facilities on the council mainframe over an X.25 link. Initial uptake was low, but after 5 months over 30 individuals were regularly booking in to the four reserved workspaces. Contact: Lynne Davies 01239 710238 or email 100141.2166@compuserve.com

accommodation addresses and meeting space. These services aim to fulfil all the functions of a traditional receptionist/secretary, without of course the expense.

Telecottages can also be used as accommodation addresses by very small businesses. As well as correspondence services, think about message taking – the advantage to the businessperson is that their customers do not have to leave a message on a machine, they can speak to a real person. The telecottage can help the small businessperson to present a more professional image. Local enterprise agencies can often help telecottages by handing out cards to those enquiring about starting their own businesses.

Publishing, design and multimedia

There are a number of areas where teleworkers can be involved in publishing, including preparing diagrams on computer, editing text, layout work, proofreading and graphic design. However, they all require specialist skills. It is not just a case of buying the desktop publishing software! Related areas include preparing overhead projections and 35 mm slides for presentations, as well as the growing market for computerised presentations incorporating sound, graphics and animation (multimedia).

Remote office services

A few corporations have created telecentres remote from their main offices where much routine correspondence and administration is done. Examples are GlaxoWellcome in Teesdale, and Rank Xerox. The advantages for the companies are that, rather than relying on disparate teleworkers with varied equipment, they can specify the equipment to be used and the procedures to be carried out, as well as controlling the teleworkers more closely. By locating these centres in rural areas, they can reduce labour and premises costs. The French company Telergos, which specialises in providing back office services recently opened a subsidiary on Tyneside to exploit these opportunities.

Scanning

Scanners are used for three purposes: to scan text, to scan line graphics and to scan photographs. For text scanning, you will need a flatbed scanner with an automatic feeder, and OCR (optical character reading) software. Text scanning works well on clean, typed manuscripts. It does not cope well with heavily edited typescripts, or with handwriting (yet). For scanning line graphics such as simple company logos, a cheap hand-held scanner will be sufficient. To scan photographs at high resolution you need a high quality scanner, and specialist knowledge of printing processes such as halftoning to get best results. For colour reproduction, expensive colour separation drum scanners are used. These are normally provided on a bureau basis by reprographics or typesetting companies. Standard desktop colour scanners do not provide sufficiently good quality for high volume colour printing, although they are excellent for adding interest to short print run documents such as internal report covers.

Skills register

Many telecottages now maintain a local skills register of individual teleworkers and can refer work to them. Sometimes the telecottage takes a percentage of the value of the work if a contract is arranged through the telecottage. In others, because the teleworkers are using telecottage equipment, no commission is taken. Some telecottages simply maintain a skills noticeboard that teleworkers can advertise on, whilst others hold social events such as lunches where teleworkers can exchange ideas and form business relationships. But beware – if you are acting as an employment agency you need a licence from the Department of Employment (see Chapter 8, *Staying safe and legal*).

Teleshopping services

Teleshopping services are in their infancy but are being developed in a number of rural areas. Some, such as the Cotswold Shopping Service or the Ross on Wye scheme assemble all the items which rural dwellers want and deliver to them for a commission fee, normally about 10% of the total bill. Others use electronic ordering to provide a greater variety of goods which could not all otherwise be stocked in local village shops. Ordering is usually by telephone but may increasingly be over the Internet in years to come. Some towns, such as Leominster, are operating "town loyalty" schemes where a card entitles the holder to access to discounted products at a number of participating shops within a town. A similar scheme is in operation in Richmond in North Yorkshire.

Training

Most telecottages offer a variety of training courses introducing people to information technology. Other areas you can consider include training in specific software packages (particularly word processing, spreadsheets and databases), training in business skills and special vocational qualifications for teleworkers. Much software training is now done by means of interactive tutorials or videos. These are usually based on CD-ROMs.

Funding is often available for these courses from Training and Enterprise Councils (TECs). Larger telecottages could think about becoming examination centres for qualifications such as the RSA word processing examinations, the City and Guilds diplomas and the Cambridge syllabus information technology modules, including teleworker training qualifications such as the VQ in teleworking.

Telecottages should also consider linking up with their local Further Education college as TCA member Su Pointer did, following up an article in *Teleworker* magazine: "I immediately contacted a senior member of one of the colleges in the area, some 30 miles away. He was more than willing to meet and discuss possible developments. Three months further on, and we have already run, and been paid for, three successful subsidised computer courses."

A number of colleges are starting to look at providing courses supported by remote means such as modem and videophone (*eg* Open University, Stroud College of Further Education). A telecottage can provide a learning base for students without these facilities.

A related area of opportunity is the production of training courses and materials. Such documents can run to hundreds of pages, and command high prices, especially where they are prepared for professional bodies or large corporate clients. The preparation of distance learning materials is a major growth area, but requires skills in editing, teaching, high level word processing and/or desktop publishing.

Translation services

Translation services are increasingly in demand, and translation work is often received and delivered via email these days. Translations can be tied in with word processing and desktop publishing services. By connecting together a number of language teleworkers, telecottages can provide a complete European service. Try contacting local chambers of commerce or enterprise agencies to sell this idea.

Word processing and desktop publishing

Word processing (typing) services can be offered to home workers, businesses, political parties and pressure groups, community newsletters and societies. If you are in a university area, see if you can get involved in typing theses and academic papers. Another area which is more within the skills range of most telecottages than full-blown publishing services is the use of desktop publishing to prepare brochures, newsletters, pricelists and instruction leaflets for local companies. One telecottage combines producing the local community newsletter with training exercises for word processing trainees. Another, Daily Information, arguably the first telecottage in the UK, began by combining word processing training and services with the production of the Daily Information free broadsheet covering activities in central Oxford. Think about making commission arrangements with a local printer to provide printing of documents as well

Call centres get smaller... and more frequent

More and more companies are dealing with their customers by phone. The first call centres were set up in the 1960s by airlines to deal with their reservations. But until recently they have tended to be large, office-based institutions which often required staff to carry out monotonous, repetitive work. Janette Menday of the Call Centre Focus magazine defines call centres by their use of ACD (automated call distribution), where incoming calls are distributed to operatives by computer. She comments: "The first stand-alone ACD was commissioned by Continental Airlines in 1973. The 1980s saw the introduction of ACDs for small centres, and 1989 marked a watershed in the UK when First Direct launched their telephone banking facility. The 1990s have seen the introduction of PC-based ACDs, making call centres viable for any business."

Dataquest suggested there were already over 3,000 call centres in the UK by 1994 – today there are thought to be 5,000. In Ireland, over 3,500 people are employed in about 50 centres. UK call centres average 33 agents, and account for 33% of European call centres. A survey by Call Centre Focus in 1996 found the following industry sectors using call centres: Finance and banking 23%; insurance/assurance 12%; marketing/advertising 14%; public services (government, health, military etc) 13.5%; manufacturing 11%; retail/mail order 10%; leisure/travel/airlines 9.5% and utilities 6.5%.

Horace Mitchell of the European Telework Development project divides call centres into two areas. Firstly there are those set up inhouse to deal with the customers and business of a single company. Secondly, there are multi client centres who take on work from other companies under contract.

Ewan Gowrie of the Call Centre Association sees customer carelines as a major growth area: "In the USA, more than 90% of packaged goods offer a careline number. In the UK, the proportion has risen from 8% in 1992 to an estimated 21% in 1995, so the absence of such a facility will soon be a competitive disadvantage... the predictions are that call centres will become the definitive structure on which organisations, in both the private and public sectors, will build sales, service and support operations."

Many commentators have predicted call centre work will migrate to low cost countries such as the Phillipines. Some foresee a split where basic response handling may well migrate away from Europe, whereas more complex calls will remain with centres of higher skill level. In Ireland, the call centre industry has become so successful that there are major skill shortage worries, and third level education courses are being cranked up to produce more suitable candidates, especially those with language skills. Another development is likely to be interconnection with the handling of web site enquiries. Dell Computer now makes over $2 million each day from web enquiries which are followed up by its call centres.

Lasair lights Lewis telework flame

Donnie Morrison is one of a number of recent returners to the Western Isles of Scotland. Formerly sales and marketing director of a computer company, Morrison has taken advantage of the Highlands and Islands Enterprise (HIE) board's skills register to set up Lasair (which means "red hot" or "flame" in Gaelic), providing editing services. Morrison now has 80–90 teleworkers, 50 of whom will be working on contracts for Oxford University Press editing manuscripts into formats which can be used to prepare books, web text or CD-ROMs.

Other Lasair clients include an American publisher and the Metropolitan Police Forensic Laboratory. The HIE activities have focused on bringing in work for people in outlying areas. Morrison claims that three companies contacted him on Christmas Eve looking for visual basic programmers, and that all three now plan to open offices in the Western Isles to take advantage of the talent pool. "At first we made the mistake of restricting the register to IT skills – it is now just a skills database – we look for example for people with language skills and then give them the IT skills". Morrison welcomes the newly launched University of the Highlands and Islands, which is to receive £35 million from the Millennium Commission, and is to have its initial courses validated by the Open University. The new university will use the Internet, audio and video conferencing and visiting lecturers to support its far-flung student body.

as typing and layout. You may also want to invest in cheap forms of binding such as a comb binding machine, or a lamination machine which provides a protective plastic surface for documents such as menus and price lists.

WWW pages

The production of World Wide Web pages is something that many teleworkers have tried their hands at. It is "flavour of the month", with many businesses requiring help to advertise their services on the Web. To produce Web pages, you need appropriate authoring software and a working knowledge of HTML, the programming language used. It is a big help if you have graphic design or information editing skills, as many client companies are not good at putting together clear information, or understanding how to structure it for use with hypertext. Some Web sites include forms and other areas for users to enter information. Programming skills in cgi scripting, and in Java, the programming language used to send small, self-running programmes over the Internet, are in high demand. Some telecottages already have their own Web sites and are letting space within their sites to local businesses.

Bibliography

How to series: Freelance Teaching and Tutoring   *Date:* 1997
Author: John T Wilson
Source: How To Books Ltd, 3 Newtec Place, Magdalen Rd, Oxford
ISBN 1–85703–407–4

30 Ways to Make Money at Home   *Date:* 1996
Author: Jennie Hawthorne
Source: Rushmere Wynne Group Plc, 4–5 Harmill, Grovebury Rd, Leighton Buzzard,
Beds LU7 8FF ISBN 0–948035–25–0

Online Business Information and Business Information Basics (2 publications)
Source: Bowker-Saur Tel: 01342 330100
Comment: Useful publications for those interested in information broking.

Online Notes
Source: ASLIB Tel: 0171 903 0000
Comment: Useful publication for those interested in information broking.

Contacts and URLs

The Institute of Information Scientists, 44-45 Museum Street, London WC1A 1LY,
Tel: 0171 831 8003, is a useful organisation for those interested in information
broking.

The Dyer Partnership, contact Mark Dyer Tel: 01420 473 473 Fax: 01420 487 695
Email: info@netaccountants.com Web: http://www.netaccountants.com

The Shopping Service, Freepost SWC1221, Cheltenham, GL50 1ZZ
Tel: 01242 243342 Fax: 01242 513883 Email: Mike@shopalog.demon.co.uk

Staying safe and legal

This section is intended for employers, employed teleworkers and self-employed teleworkers. If all the laws which could be applied to teleworking were enforced absolutely rigorously there would be very little telework. There is a great deal of anachronistic law because legal reform has not kept pace with the speed of change of work practices. In general, the advice has to be to inform yourself, use your common sense and not to worry unduly – few authorities want the headache of regulating home offices. Get yourself a good accountant and solicitor, and ask for advice about anything you're not sure of, either from your advisers or from the relevant authorities. If you encounter a problem that is not easily solved, let the TCA know about it so we can try to resolve the issue and warn others who may be affected.

Health and safety

Health and safety authorities have draconian powers of inspection and enforcement, and all HSE legislation includes workplaces in the home. However, in reality the HSE does not have any register of teleworkers, or the resources for a large number of inspections. There is nothing in health and safety law that prevents working alone at home providing it does not affect the worker's health and safety. Strictly speaking, all workplaces should have an approved safety statement.

Some may feel the 1974 Health and Safety at Work Act means that teleworker's employers have less onerous duties as they cannot be deemed responsible for the safety of an employee's home. However, any equipment used by the employee in the course of their employment should be deemed safe by the employer. In general it is advisable that the employer should provide the teleworker with all equipment and ensure that the equipment is inspected and checked on a regular basis, and in accordance with the company's on-site practice.

In order to reduce risk of RSI or other injuries due to poor work furniture, the employer is also advised to supply all working furniture. The main relevant law to teleworkers is the Display Screen Directive 90/270/EEC which requires:

- clear and stable screen, bright and free from glare, which should swivel and tilt easily
- adequate arrangement of keyboard characters, adjustable keyboard with sufficient space to support the hands and arms of the user
- sufficient user space to change positions and vary movements. Work desk sufficiently large, document holder adjustable and stable
- satisfactory lighting conditions

- minimised glare and reflection at the workstation, and minimisation of radiation levels
- work chair adjustable in height including the back rest
- a foot rest available if required
- environmental factors should be minimised including effects of reflection/glare, noise, heat and humidity.

Employers should put in place a system for their teleworkers to report accidents or hazards, as there would be in a conventional workplace. Practical experience within the TCA suggests the following are also often problems:

- insufficient power sockets leading to over-use of extension leads, trailing cables and adaptors
- shelves situated inconveniently so that heavy files are frequently placed and replaced causing stress on the spine and overbalancing
- inadequate office chairs and tables which are not the appropriate height or adjustability for long periods of work
- reading glasses not correct prescription for close work. Anyone working with computers should have their eyes tested, and the optician should be informed of the computer work
- lighting – spotlights and anglepoises are generally less tiring than fluorescents in small spaces. Light levels should be about 350 lm m^{-2}. Screens should be positioned at right angles to windows. Blinds to prevent sunlight making screens hard to read should be installed where needed.
- temperatures should be as near as possible to 18.5 degrees centigrade. Small home offices can easily overheat because IT equipment generates heat – temperatures may become uncomfortably hot in summer unless adequate ventilation can be provided
- adequate ventilation is also important where equipment such as laser printers may give off ozone or other fumes
- the use of IT equipment usually requires an additional 2 power outlets, and 1 or 2 telecoms sockets. Safely stowing cabling is important
- electrical equipment needs to be checked for safety (*eg* all cable grips in place, no burn marks on plugs or cracked sockets)
- psychologically, most teleworkers prefer to be situated so that they can see out of a window if possible, although it is important to avoid problems with glare and reflection on computer screens.

Prolonged computer work can also cause discomfort and fatigue to the back, shoulders, neck, head, eyes, buttocks, legs and wrists. Maintaining posture in a static position also causes blood flow to the muscles to be restricted. Ergonomics expert Éilis Duggan of Workright Consultants advises the following guidelines to maintaining a comfortable and efficient work posture:

- feet should be flat on the floor with knees bent at 90° or 100° angle
- the front edge of the chair seat should not be touching the back of the knee or press into the underside of the thigh as increased pressure on the back of the leg may lead to numbness, fatigue or knee swelling
- knees should be level with or slightly above hips
- the chair seat to chair back angle should be slightly backwards (10–20°)
- the document being typed should be placed by the screen at the same distance and height, and as close as possible
- change body position frequently, moving feet up and down, adjusting chair and/or keyboard height
- organise work so that you can take "mini-breaks" to stretch muscles
- exercise regularly and eat well.

Employers may wish to carry out a conventional health and safety risk assessment on teleworker's home offices. This involves:

1. Identifying hazards that may cause harm, however small (such as keeping potentially harmful substances out of children's reach).

2. Deciding who might be harmed and how (*eg* the homeworker, members of the household, visitors).

3. Assessing the risks and taking appropriate action (*eg* deciding what steps must be taken to eliminate or reduce the identified risks).

4. Record the findings – what steps have been taken to reduce or eliminate risks? Inform the homeworker or anyone else affected by the work of the findings.

5. Check the risks from time to time and take steps if needed, especially if there is a change in working procedures.

The Health and Safety Executive produces a booklet on safety for homeworkers.

Planning and building regulations

There is no question that setting up a home office does constitute a "change of use" in strict planning terms; however, as far as planning departments are concerned, the average teleworker is unlikely to require planning permission, particularly if they are not creating a nuisance to neighbours. Surrey County Council provides the following advice to its own teleworking staff: "Teleworking at or from home does not represent a significant change of use of a building likely to cause a nuisance or hazard to your neighbours. Unless you intend to make structural alterations to accommodate your working area, or extra noise, pollution *etc* is generated because you are

When teleworking upsets the neighbours... victims of success

Systems ReMarketing started off in 1990, when Michael Cahen, his wife Maggie and partner Chris Jones began a business from the study in Michael's house. The business involved sourcing repaired, second-hand or mildly obsolete computers, advertising the stock by email to a trade audience, and providing all ordering and other information over the Internet as well.

"Our biggest competitor at the time employed almost 200 people and couldn't provide the same level of service. By keeping the distribution costs to an absolute minimum, the business grew very rapidly. Before long, the team of three had grown to six. The atmosphere was great. The house overlooks a golf course, the alfresco lunches, the odd bottle of wine and a very civilised working environment suited almost everyone", Michael explains.

Except the neighbours. Althought the bulk of the warehousing and despatch was done from a different site, a few spares were kept at Michael's house for emergencies, and were collected by courier companies for delivery to customers. One of the neighbours in Michael's quiet, residential cul-de-sac complained to the council that a business was being run from a residential address. Following an unannounced visit from the council, SRM was threatened with an enforcement order unless the business moved or ceased trading. A planning application was made and rejected. Michael's wife Maggie was concerned about bad relations with the neighbours. If the planning application had succeeded, the cost of partial business rating would have been considerable. In the end, a small office was rented in Marlow, and the centre of the business moved there, with the Surrey office becoming a remote site.

working at/from home, there is no requirement for planning permission." Some other councils differ on whether home offices constitute a "material" or "ancillary" change of use (ie turning an outhouse into a garage and car repair workshop is rather more material than putting a computer into a spare bedroom). Material changes of use require permission; ancillary changes or temporary changes probably don't.

Decisions on whether the change of use is "material" are based on whether it will cause increased traffic, changes to the visible appearance of the property, nuisance such as noise or smells, or unsocial working hours. Unfortunately few local authorities have taken into account that teleworking is a form of homeworking which reduces traffic and generally involves no alterations other than provision of electrical sockets and telephone lines. Oldham Borough Council is an exception, recognising teleworking formally in its planning guidelines, and regarding home offices as ancillary changes of use. The Oldham document is available to other planning authorities, who can use it as a blueprint for their own guidelines if they wish.

The Department of Transport issued guidelines in 1994 which request local authorities to encourage teleworking. The document, *Planning Policy Guidance 13* (PPG13), contains recommendations for local authorities to "facilitate homeworking and the provision of facilities for small groups of employees to work together locally". In Ireland there is no overall guidance on teleworking, and policies vary between councils and corporations.

If the establishment of the home office involves any building work, such as conversion of a loft space, there are strict building regulations which much be adhered to, mainly relating to means of escape in case of fire. Loft ladders and space saver stairs are not favoured, according to Paul Kalbskopf, building control officer at Stroud District Council, because they require familiarity of use for safe passage. Roof lights should also act as a means of escape, so that you could get out or a fire officer could get in if necessary. You may also need to upgrade the floor between the loft and the rest of the house to give half an hour of fire resistance. Kalbskopf advises contacting an architect, and then approaching building control and planning departments for advice before starting work.

Another alternative to loft conversion which has been successfully used by a number of teleworkers is imported timber cabins from Scandinavia – if you have sufficient garden space to spare. These buildings are warm, well insulated and long-lasting – as a rough guide, a 12ft square cabin including electrical fittings and decoration, with a minimum of four inches of insulation will cost around £5,000.

MIRAS mortgage tax relief

Most taxpayers who have a mortgage in Britain can claim tax relief on their interest payments, known as MIRAS (Mortgage Interest Relief at Source). MIRAS is normally available for 15% of the payments on the first £30,000 of the loan. In 1995, the Inland Revenue made changes to its rules to acknowledge that many houses are now used partly for residential purposes and partly for business purposes. Under these rules, the house is notionally "split in two". The interest component on the work or office part of the building is fully deductible from your tax liability as a business expense. For the residential part, MIRAS can still be claimed.

At first sight this looks like a breakthrough for teleworkers – however, if you classify part of your house for business purposes, there are wider implications. The "work" part of the house is potentially liable for Capital Gains Tax, although as the first £6,000 of any capital gain is exempt, it is unlikely to be a major concern for most teleworkers. Perhaps more worrying is the possibility that your local authority may try to levy business rates on the "work" part of the house on top of normal Council Tax charges (see below). Other problems could include business rates being charged for gas and electricity, and the possibility of higher insurance charges. However, the Inland Revenue says it treats tax information as confidential

A big bill from the meter man

Roderick Prescott, a retired Edinburgh civil servant, was shocked to discover that he had to pay an extra £300 a year on his electricity bill because he runs a business from home. Roderick has a property business which he spends only an hour a day on. His problems started when he chased up a problem with Scottish Power on behalf of one of his tenants, but wrote the letter from his home address. "A man came from the electricity board saying he had come to read the meter. Afterwards he was having a chat with my wife who said we were retired but that I run a business in the spare room. The next thing I knew, a letter arrived which said we should be charged on an industrial tariff, which is intended for factory owners." This was later reduced to the "farm and combined premises tariff" which is aimed at people who use a lot of electricity for washing machines and baths such as B&B owners.

and does not pass on information to other public bodies, so these risks may appear more worrying than they actually are.

One home based salesman, Andrew Wood, found that his building society removed him from MIRAS after he informed them of his homeworking. The society told him he would have to reapply for inclusion through his tax office. Because the tax relief is automatically accounted in mortgage payments, building societies in effect administrate MIRAS. Fortunately the tax office disagreed and Mr Wood was allowed to stay in – otherwise he would have had to wait until the following April for reinclusion, followed by a further delay before receiving his missing MIRAS via an adjustment to his tax return and standard tax bill. In response to TCA enquiries, the Inland Revenue has said that building societies do not have the right to remove people from MIRAS simply because they work from home. If you find yourself in this situation, refer your building society to your local tax office, and if that doesn't work contact the TCA so we can try to help.

Anyone moving to self-employed teleworking will need to notify their mortgage provider if they have a mortgage. A few building societies do offer packages with a built in payment holiday or the option to reduce payments for a period of time. Those which don't would rather discuss the situation with you now than end up with a reposession on their hands...

One company, Legal and General, have recently launched a new mortgage package aimed at the self-employed which includes a variable rate guaranteed not to exceed 1.5% over base rate, the option for payment 'holidays' and additional payment and reborrowing facilities. The company stresses is it more interested in ability to make regular payments than in standard tax accounts required by most mortgage companies, but this mortgage is only available to existing mortgage holders.

Another, the Ecological Building Society, specialises in providing loans for environmentally-friendly premises. According to Chairman Gus Smith, "the question we ask is: Does it fulfill one or more of the following criteria for lending? Does it contribute to 1) the saving of energy and non-renewable resources 2) preservation of buildings and communities or 3) the promotion of self-sufficiency and the most ecological use of land." EBS looks favourably on environmentally friendly ways of working – however, if the business use of the building exceeds 40%, then semi-commercial rates rather than domestic ones are charged.

Restrictive covenants

Some properties, particularly estate houses and flats, may be subject to covenants which could in theory restrict working from home. The origin of these covenants is usually a condition put in place by a vendor selling land to prevent business rather than residential developments. A TCA member discovered his flat was affected by a covenant imposed by a local authority when selling land to a builder, and intended to prevent business use other than by a dentist or doctor. Another TCA member, Peter Fowler, a solicitor working on business-related legal matters and commercial property, fills in some background information on the two types of covenant, freehold and leasehold:

Freehold covenants

A typical restriction on a housing estate would be that no trade or business could be carried out on the property, and no use is permitted other than as a private dwelling house. The power of enforcement lies with the original estate owner or his successors, and in some cases owners of other properties on the estate who could be affected by physical damage or a fall in value of property. Most teleworkers are unlikely to cause damage as they are working entirely inside their home, although some problems could be envisaged (excessive parking obstruction from multiple visitors to a business). In general, it will be a case of common sense and keeping disturbance to neighbours to a minimum.

Sometimes old estates may flex their muscles and request payment for a licence to vary the original covenant, but often they have no direct right of enforcement and may no longer own any nearby property which could be affected. The threat of action is likely to be a bluff as the cost of enforcement could be prohibitive. They could also face a substantial claim from the teleworker if their claim failed, but in the interim the teleworker had been prevented from working by their injunction.

Leasehold covenants

Houses on very long leases such as 999 year leases will fall into the same category as freehold and the comments above apply. However, some small developments of houses or blocks of flats on long leases with ground rents pose a different problem. There will probably be an existing landlord or management company (possibly owned by the residents) who could enforce the covenants although, as before, they will have to prove that damage is being caused. Such proof is easier where covenants have been established for the common good. All that is needed to cause a problem is one resident who has been inconvenienced and an active resident's committee.

In general, if you are prudent and do not cause any nuisance from your business, even if you are in technical breach of an estate covenant, you will probably be safe enough to carry on teleworking. In many ways, the planning authorities are a bigger source of worry to potential and existing teleworkers.

Are you employed or self-employed?

The main criteria to be taken into account are listed in a free Inland Revenue bookled *Employed or Self-Employed?* which states that if you can answer yes to the following questions, it will "usually" mean you are self-employed.

- *Do you have the final say in how the business is run?*

- *Do you risk your own money in the business?*

- *Are you responsible for meeting the losses as well as taking profits?*

- *Do you provide the major items of equipment you need to do your job, not just the small tools which many employees provide for themselves?*

- *Are you free to hire other people on terms of your own choice, to do the work that you have taken on? Do you pay them out of your own pocket?*

- *Do you have to correct unsatisfactory work in your own time and at your own expense?*

Alternatively, if you answer "yes" to the following questions, then you are "probably" an employee:

- *Do you yourself have to do the work rather than hire someone else to do it for you?*

- *Can someone tell you at any time what to do or when and how to do it?*

- *Are you paid by the hour, week or month? Can you get overtime pay? (even if you are paid by commission or on a piecework basis you may still be an employee)*

- *Do you work set hours, or a given number of hours a week or month?*

- *Do you work at the premises of the person you are working for, or at a place or places that they decide?*

Proto-type's points for self-employment:

- The teleworkers provide their own equipment
- The client deals with the teleworker direct
- There is no guarantee about the amount of work the teleworker might expect to receive
- It is the responsibility of the teleworker to correct poor work at their own cost
- The teleworker's ability to take on other work is not restricted
- Separate invoices are issued from the teleworker to the main "work getter" (such as Proto-type) and from the work getter to the client

Business rates

If you do go through the process of receiving official planning permission for your home office, then you are liable for commercial rates or council tax on the portion of your house that you are using for work.

In the UK, as far as liability for business rates is concerned, a large grey area exists. The accepted advice is typified by internal Treasury guidelines issued for the management of its own homeworkers: "Generally when part of a home is used as a workplace where the non-domestic activity precludes the use at any time of that part of the property for living accommodation, the part will be non-domestic and therefore subject to the business rate. In practice where domestic use can take place after work has finished, it is unlikely that liability for the business rate will arise."

This view was confirmed by a local rating officer: "We apply what we call a six o'clock rule. If, after six, the room reverts back to domestic use, then it would not be subject to business rates. Generally as most home businesses wouldn't need planning permission we would only get to hear about this if a neighbour complained. It is highly unlikely that a home office business would require business rating." However, the same officer described an example of a publisher operating from home and using two rooms – one entirely for stock and the other as a computer room which resulted in an (amicably agreed) annual rate of around £300. TCA member Geoffrey Carter, who uses one room with a computer and a few files which the family have access to in the evenings, found himself with a bill for £450 for part use of the room after a visit by the valuation officer. After intervention by the TCA, the rating against Geoffrey was dropped. Another case, Fotheringham v. Wood ([1995] RA315, LT) found against an accountant working from home on the basis that the room was wholly or mainly used as an office – use of the room as living accommodation could not be envisaged.

More recent experiences suggest that "home businesses" are more of a target than employed teleworkers and if moving a business from a rated office-based premises to home, you may well be visited by a rating valuation officer as a matter of course.

Dublin chartered surveyors HPSG Hanson International give the following hypothetical case in Ireland – for a house in a rural area with a room of 15ft x 15ft in use as a home office, the General Valuation Office rateable value would be of the order of £5. Most councils levy a rate of around £45 so your annual rate bill would be around £225 per annum. Paul Kennedy of HPSG Hanson International points out that the process involves a surveyor being sent out from the General Valuation Office in Dublin, and that because of the expense of this in relation to the rates collected, some county managers may take a view that teleworking is a temporary arrangement not liable to commercial rating. Tongue-in-cheek, Paul suggests that perhaps in the future we may see the Belgian approach – in Brussels, instead of taxing property, they tax each computer in use.

"Business" charges by public utilities

Unfortunately for teleworkers, many power utility companies have a policy that to qualify for the minimum tariff, premises must be used wholly for domestic purposes. The practical situation is that they would have to know you are working from home before any change could be made, and that the exact conditions vary from company to company. Check with the relevant regulatory body such as OFFER or OFGAS, and contact the TCA if you have a problem.

For telephone service, BT does not compel people to use the business rate, but points out that the business service has the advantage of a Yellow Pages entry, and a Business Pages entry. BT also puts business users on a higher priority for fault correction than residential users. In both cases compensation is paid if the fault is not repaired within 24 hours.

VAT (4th schedule)

Another area of confusion concerns "4th-schedule" VAT. Where a teleworker is registered for VAT and performs data processing tasks for a VAT registered business located in another EU member state, no VAT is chargeable despite the transaction being for a service rather than goods. The existence of this rule is particularly important for Irish teleworkers because if they were forced to charge their export clients the high Irish VAT rate of 21% and oblige their clients to go through the cumbersome process of reclaiming the difference between this rate and that pertaining in their own country, they would be at a competitive disadvantage compared to teleworkers in other EU member states with lower VAT rates. Unfortunately, the existence of this VAT category is not widely known in regional revenue offices.

Employed or self-employed?

Many teleworkers and telecottages have reported confusions and difficulties when they wish to get help from other teleworkers to complete work. The difficulty comes over whether the other teleworkers are employed (PAYE) or self-employed. The definition used to distinguish between self-employment and PAYE employment is that of a contract **for** service against a contract **of** service:

- contracts for services are agreements for a specified piece of work to be completed. In teleworking terms these normally consist of the completion of a specified project by the teleworker for his or her client as a self-employed activity on which no PAYE (or PRSI in Ireland) is levied;

- contracts of service are standard employments – a teleworker operating on a payment by the hour for one single client is likely to be considered to have a contract of service, on which PAYE and National Insurance (PRSI in Ireland) are payable, regardless of the location of the teleworker in relation to the client/employer.

On occasion the tax authorities have taken a retrospective view that regular telework contracts which both teleworker and client thought were contracts for services were in fact employments (contracts of service), and have levied back tax and penalties. This confusion damages the willingness of businesses to use teleworkers, particularly as the "employer" can then be liable for both sets of taxes.

The erratic nature of telework contracts can also cause difficulties; two teleworkers may collaborate closely on a project for a third party for three months and then not work together for a further six months after that – are both self-employed, or is one employing the other during the three months, but not afterwards? The answer will depend on the extent to which one controlled the other's working patterns, how many other clients each had, whether one required the presence of the other at specific premises and times and other factors.

Richard Nissen of the Virtual Office took this issue up with his local tax inspector: "The fact is that you can employ people and have them working on a self-employed basis as long as they are not directed by you. The easiest way to do this is to send the terms and conditions for the worker you want to employ on a self-employed basis to your local PAYE office for confirmation that you can employ them in this way before you start paying them. However, even if you cross this hurdle, then there is another problem. If you ask a teleworker to do some typing for you that is then charged out and sold on to a third party, you fall slap bang into the scope of employment agency law (section 134 ICTCA 1988), so you would have to act like an agency and pay John or Jane PAYE and National Insurance. Yet if the person you employ is from another EU country then no PAYE is payable – it's actually easier to use a cross-border teleworker."

When is a phone line not a phone line?

A TCA member suffered problems with a phone line specifically ordered for modem use that would not allow the modem to operate at full speed. BT would not guarantee the line or test it for modem use.

Oftel advised that there is no requirement for BT to provide anything other than a voice service, but suggested asking BT to check their records to see if the line is short or long, or followed a mixed digital/analogue path which might cause problems. Further, Oftel advised paying for the line to be checked and asking BT to install resistors. BT commented that although their liability was limited to voice they encourage use of the phone for teleworking, fax services and so on. They recommended asking for the complaints review manager of the unit and requesting a thorough quality check.

Whatever the exact situation, where it is important that self-employed status is assured, get advice on formulating a contract and working conditions from your financial adviser and verify it with your local tax assessor.

The corresponding situation in Ireland is controlled by the Employment Agency section of the Department of Enterprise and Employment and is based on the 1971 Employment Agency Act. At first sight this act appears to cover someone obtaining work and distributing it among other teleworkers; however, in the case of the Telemart online work agency, the department ruled that as long as the other teleworkers are demonstrably self-employed, that they are not being charged for the service of obtaining the work, and that the client company pays Telemart, not the teleworkers themselves, then no agency licence is required. Due to the complex and confused status of Irish employment agency law at present, it is recommended that expert legal advice be taken for similar enterprises.

Ann Collins of Proto-type, a TCA member, has successfully established a situation where the four teleworkers she works with are classified as self-employed. Proto-type is a remote word processing service based in Essex and operating for city-based firms. The company's main client is a quantity surveying group. Handwritten documents and audio tapes are received by fax, typed and returned by modem. Ann explains: "We started off with just myself and we are still small, using four teleworkers, with very tight margins. The additional cost and the time in administering PAYE and National Insurance for employed status would have been sufficient deterrents to stop us from continuing the business. From the teleworkers' point of view, self-employment gives them greater flexibility. We had to argue the point with the local tax office, but a number of points eventually convinced them."

So what expenses can you claim for your home office? The best advice is to talk through the issues with your tax adviser, but you can claim expenses for heating, lighting, and telephone, depreciation of the fixtures and fittings, installation of extra power points, cleaning costs, business insurance, refurbishment, office equipment, postage and stationery. A previous loophole, where teleworkers who had their own limited company and "rented" the home office to that company, has now been closed by the Inland Revenue. The Inland Revenue's new statement of practice on this issue has not yet been tested in court. Claiming costs of acquisition of the property such as mortgage interest, building costs, solicitors fees *etc* could make you liable to Capital Gains Tax in future according to Mark Dyer, accountant and TCA member. "Although the domestic portion of a house is exempt, CGT could be due on the proportion of the gain related to the rooms used. If you used two rooms in a twelve room house, then one sixth of the gain would be due. But as the exempt band is £6,500 per person, and gains are inflation adjusted, realistically the problem will probably only occur when the gain happens in a year when other CGT gain items have been realised."

Tax changes – self-assessment

The tax system in Britain has been changed to "self-assessment". There are two main elements to the reform. Taxpayers now do their own calculations on how much income tax they are due to pay, while long established self-employed businesses have been moved to a "current year" rather than "previous year" basis for paying tax. For most existing self-employed teleworkers, this means that two year's profits (1995–1996 and 1996–1997) were taxed together for the year 1996–97, with the tax payable in January

and July 1997. In most cases, taxes will be levied on half the profits of the two years and tax-allowable business expenses currently being run up will only benefit from half the normal rate of tax relief. There is a cumbersome overlap accounting system for businesses whose trading year does not coincide with the tax year, involving tax credits being carried forward through the lifetime of the business. The services of a professional accountant will almost certainly be required by anyone who has not yet resolved their tax liabilities with the Inland Revenue due to the complexity of the transitional arrangements. A self-assessment enquiry line is available on 0345 161514.

In the Republic of Ireland, self-employed people have been taxed on the current year basis for some years so no equivalent change will take place.

Pensions

Those who begin teleworking are often entering self-employment for the first time and consequently losing the security of a former occupational pension. This area of financial services has been in turmoil for a number of years after the Maxwell scandal and investigations into sales advice about personal pensions given in the late 1980s. It can still be hard to get clear, unbiased advice because most pension advisers receive commissions on the pensions they sell. The best option is to look for an independent financial adviser (who should be a member of the regulatory authority FIMBRA) whom you can pay on an hourly rate (around £30–£100) to look at your situation and advise you – that way the adviser is paid by you to look after your interests, and not by the pension company to sell their policies.

The two types of pension – occupational and personal – differ widely in their tax breaks and regulatory regimes. In general, a well funded occupational pension scheme is likely to be preferable to a personal pension, but fewer and fewer people are eligible for occupational pensions, which were designed in the days of "jobs for life". Both types of pensions are paid on top of the state old age pension, which is a flat rate payment available to those who have paid into the state scheme for a sufficient number of years through their National Insurance contributions. Because of the increased number of older people in the population, and long term underfunding of the state scheme, it is likely that the value of the state pension will fall far below the present basic level as we move into the 21st century, and contributions to an occupational or personal pension scheme are strongly recommended where affordable.

An occupational pension scheme is normally run by an employer and provides a pension based on a percentage of your final salary rate at retirement, as well as on the number of years of membership of the scheme you have. Occupational pensions cannot exceed two thirds of final salary, and to achieve this maximum you will need at least 40 years membership of a pension scheme. Normally both the employee and the employer contribute to an occupational pension. Added benefits can include death in service grants and payments to widows or widowers.

When someone changes jobs they have two main options available for their pension – deferred pension or transfer value. If they become a deferred pensioner, they leave their contributions in the scheme untouched and quietly growing until they reach retirement, beginning a new occupational scheme with the new employer. If they opt for a transfer value, the pension scheme calculates the value of your pension based on existing contributions and arranges for its transfer into a new scheme. TCA officer Alan Denbigh found that when he became a teleworker, by taking out his new personal pension with the company that had operated his previous company pension, he was able to avoid the normal penalties of withdrawal – his pension was "converted" from an occupational to a personal pension with minimal pain.

Personal pension plans by contrast are based on how much pension you have "purchased" by your payments throughout your working life. What you receive depends on your contributions, and how successful the pension fund managers have been in selecting good investments. The big difference is that employers usually will not contribute to a personal fund, so the whole pension burden is borne by the teleworker.

However, contributors to personal pension schemes are entitled to tax breaks. As you get older, the amount of money you can put into a pension scheme tax free increases:

Up to 35	17.5%
36-45	20%
46-50	25%
51-55	30%
56-60	35%
61 plus	40% up to the earnings cap of £75,000

In the Republic of Ireland the tax free amount is 15% regardless of age until you reach 55 years, when it rises to 20%.

If you are starting a personal pension plan it pays to begin early – the rule of thumb used in calculating how much you should contribute is to halve your age and convert it to a percentage (so a 30-year old should begin contributing 15% of their income).

Many self-employed people wait until towards the end of the tax year, when they know what their total income is likely to be, and then buy single premium pension plans to allow them to use up all the available tax relief on the grounds that it is better to spend money on a pension than to give it to the government. The alternative is monthly regular premium policies, but these can be inflexible if your income varies – if you fail to make payments there are penalties. It is very inadvisable to stop payments in the first two years of a regular payments scheme. One company, Equitable Life, offers a regular scheme where there is no penalty if you cease contributing or vary your contributions. Equitable Life is also the only company which does not pay commission on its policies to salespeople.

To avoid a cashflow crunch at the end of the tax year when pension payments have to be made to qualify for tax relief, it can be worth looking at having two policies: one for small regular payments, and the other a single premium whose value depends on the maximum tax relief you can obtain. Single premium policies allow you to spread your investment over a number of different companies, reducing the risk that you might "pick" an underperformer, but regular premium policies are a lot less painful to the bank account.

In Ireland, proposed pension payments can be taken into account when calculating your preliminary tax liability in October. The payment must then be made by 31st January of the following year.

When selecting a personal pension plan, you are likely to be faced with a plethora of graphs and figures indicating how different companies have performed and many different options, such as with profits schemes and index linked bonds. The main points to watch for are:

- underlying trends of performance – the final value will depend partly on inflation and partly on the growth of the funds invested. Look at how your proposed pension company has fared compared to others over a period of years

- administration charge percentages (these can vary from 8% to 32% for regular premium policies, and from 13% to 39% for single premium over a 25 year period)

- commission charges, which can be more than half the first year's payments.

Within each company there are options on funds which carry risk and growth tags, such as investment in shares of companies trading in the Pacific Rim, or in property, or in index-linked bonds. A with profits policy is a calculation based on the bonuses of the company that reflects its overall level of profitability. Ethical funds are a recent development which invest only in companies conforming to certain standards, and avoiding areas such as arms production.

At retirement, currently you can take up to a quarter of your pension as a lump sum though this may change shortly. The remainder has to be used to buy an annuity, which provides a regular income for the rest of your life. You can choose which company to buy the annuity from, and it is a crucial decision for a comfortable old age.

Health insurance

In Britain everyone has access to the National Health Service for free medical care but you may need to think about extra health insurance if you are opting for self-employment. You will need access to welfare benefits or insurance payouts to replace your income should you become unable to work. Typical categories of insurance policy are:

- access to fast, private healthcare to reduce time out of work (private medical insurance)
- insurance against certain illnesses preventing you from working and earning that provides a lump sum (critical illness insurance)
- income protection insurance to provide a regular income if you are unable to work due to a serious injury or illness (permanent health insurance)
- insurance agains the consequences of accidents (personal accident insurance)

Private healthcare policies are available from a range of suppliers in the UK such as BUPA and PPP. These regular payment policies are not the same as the critical illness insurance policies currently being marketed which need very careful assessment, as many cover the basic unhappy events such as

Catch 22 – unemployable and uninsurable

Jane (not her real name) is a 35-year old teleworker who has been diagnosed with endometriosis, a condition affecting up to 10% of women of reproductive age where tissue from the lining of the womb migrates and grows in other parts of the body causing problems with fertility, the bladder and bowels. Symptoms vary but the disease is often accompanied by heavy periods, painful sex and depression. It's a chronic condition which cannot be cured but often can be controlled with drugs and surgery.

Jane comments: "It is impossible to know how the disease will progress. It has stopped me expanding my business because I can't take out a loan and risk not being able to pay it back. In many ways the worst problems are not the physical symptoms, but the fatigue and mental confusion that can be caused by changes in hormone levels, either from the disease or from the drugs taken to alleviate it. It's like suddenly being reduced to living your life by the light of a 40W bulb. I'm pretty much stabilised at the moment, but if I have to have a hysterectomy, the 10–12 weeks off work would be just about long enough for the business to go down the drain."

"Waiting lists make it hard to schedule an operation for a quiet part of the year, but going private would cost thousands. It would also be very hard now for me to get a permanent job because I could not pass a company medical. I looked into permanent health insurance, but it is a Catch-22 situation once you have been diagnosed. If you go to a company for income protection insurance you must declare the condition – and then they whack the premiums up so high you can't afford it. There is a massive change in your lifestyle if you have a chronic condition. It is vital people take out health insurance before they get sick. One in six people say they have a health condition which seriously affects their life – many are chronic diseases like arthritis or irritable bowel syndrome."

heart attack, stroke or cancer, but not chronic conditions such as arthritis or endometriosis which can prevent you from working just as effectively. The small print is well worth reading!

Self-employed people do pay National Insurance, but it only entitles them to the health service, disability benefits and the old age pension – not to unemployment benefit if their business goes under, although depending on circumstances other means-tested benefits may be available. The benefits system has become increasingly complex in the past few years, and it is worth consulting your local library or Citizen's Advice Bureau on your entitlements.

Any teleworker becoming self-employed should think seriously about taking out personal health insurance (PHI) to secure their income level should they become unable to work through ill-health. PHI does not pay your medical bills – instead, it replaces your lost income. Normally the policy provides around 75% of your usual salary (to give you an incentive to go back to work...). Premium levels depend on your medical history when you take out the policy, your deferral period, and any exemptions you select. The deferral period is normally around 13 weeks, and is a time delay between the onset of illness and the date when the policy begins to pay out. The longer the deferral, the lower the premium. Exemptions are usually created where you have a pre-existing problem (such as back trouble) which makes your premiums very high. If you agree not to claim with regard to back problems, you can get insurance for other conditions at more reasonable premiums. It is extremely important that you ensure your medical conditions are fully disclosed when taking out a permanent health insurance policy (check your doctor's report and make sure you let the insurer know if you think anything has been omitted). Otherwise, if you need to claim and have to undergo an independent examination, your claim may be denied. Permanent health insurance isn't a particularly remunerative sector for insurance companies, and many will only offer these policies if they are taken out in tandem with personal pensions. Friend's Provident does offer stand alone permanent insurance policies, however.

In Ireland membership of VHI or BUPA is to be recommended to ensure swift treatment of health problems for the self-employed. VHI premiums can be partially claimed against tax. Small businesses can also buy "key person" insurance for owner-managers so that the business receives a payout if the key person dies or becomes incapacitated.

Data Protection Act

The British Data Protection Act is over ten years old, but as many as 150,000 firms have still to register, risking fines of up to £5,000 plus costs. Many small companies complain that the data protection forms are overly complex and that registration is too expensive. Yet if you hold any personal data, including mailing lists, on your computer then you should be registered.

The Data Protection registrar will want details of the data you hold and control, the purposes for which it is used, where the data is obtained and to whom it is disclosed, both here and overseas. If your information handling practices are found to be negligent, you can be liable for civil action due to damage caused by inaccurate data, unauthorised data, loss of data or destruction of personal records, including liability for related distress caused.

Data subjects can request access to their personal data, and where appropriate, demand correction or deletion of a record. In return, data users can charge up to £10 for a copy of the data.

In general, if you are processing information on behalf of an employer, it is the employer's duty to register, not the employee's. The cost of registration is £75 and the forms are long and complex; however, you can have your forms "prefilled" as templates by expert staff before they are sent out to you if you ring 01625 545740. The information line number is 01625 545745.

The data protection laws in the Republic of Ireland by contrast are clear and unrestrictive. Only those directly involved as the main part of their business in processing or holding financial or personal data need to register. Teleworkers who keep their client's mailing lists on their computers do not normally fall into this category. For telecommuters, it is the responsibility of

Data protection principles and definitions

- *Obtain and process information fairly and lawfully*

- *Keep it only for one or more specified and lawful purposes*

- *Use and disclose it only in ways compatible with these purposes*

- *Keep it safe and secure from unauthorised or accidental disclosure or loss*

- *Keep it accurate and up to date*

- *Ensure that it is adequate, relevant and not excessive*

- *Retain it no longer than is necessary for the purpose or purposes*

- *Give a copy of his/her personal data to any individual on request.*

Personal data is any information relating to living, identifiable individuals processed by computer

Data users are any company or individual who controls the content and use of a collection of personal data

Data subjects are those to whom personal data relates

their employer to register. The forms are clear and easy to fill in, and the fee is £50. However, regardless of whether or not you are registered, you still have a duty to safeguard personal computer data that you hold and you must abide by the data protection principles.

Intellectual property and copyright

Although prosecutions for infringements of copyright and intellectual property rights (IPR) are rare, it is important to have a basic grasp of your rights and responsibilities, especially with regard to online material. In practical terms, most people don't necessarily want to be paid if you re-use something of theirs in your work. However, they almost certainly do want to be asked, and to have their IPR acknowledged in your document. Barry Mahon of information management association EUSIDIC comments: "Publishers would like you to believe that quotation is a cardinal sin, but that is because they make authors sign away their rights to allow quotation without payment. Equally, if you are an author, take advice before signing away all your rights to a publisher – it is possible only to grant limited rights." Many authors and agents distinguish rights for paper publication from those for online distribution these days.

Most countries in the world operate to the Berne convention, which means that even if a document does not have a copyright notice or use the © symbol, the work is copyright, even if it's merely a shopping list. Pictures are covered as well as text, and it is irrelevant whether or not you charge for your publication – even if you give it away free, if you include someone else's copyrighted material without permission it's an infringement of their IPR.

If you want to assert your own copyright on a document, add:

Copyright © [date] by [author].

With regard to information on the Internet, including newsgroups and listservs, nothing is "in the public domain" and therefore free to use unless it has an explicit statement granting it to the public domain attached. This particularly applies to material from online news services; you may be able to extract information, rephrase it and sell it on in some circumstances, where it could be regarded as "fair use", but in general beware of all but the most minimal quotation.

An excellent guide to copyright and IPR by Brad Templeton is available at http://www.clari.net, and includes this summary of "fair use":

"The "fair use" exemption to copyright law was created to allow things such as commentary, parody, news reporting, research and education about copyrighted works without the permission of the author. Intent, and damage to the commercial value of the work are important considerations. Are you reproducing an article from the *New York Times* because you needed to in order to criticise the quality of the *New York Times*, or because you couldn't find time to write your own story, or didn't want your readers to have to pay to log onto the online services with the story or buy a copy of the paper? The first is probably fair use, the others probably aren't.

Fair use is almost always a short excerpt and almost always attributed. (Do not use more of the work than is necessary to make the commentary.) It should not harm the commercial value of the work – in the sense of people no longer needing to buy it (which is another reason why reproduction of the entire work is generally forbidden)."

Training materials do not normally fall into the fair use category, a point of particular relevance to telecottages who may be copying training modules.

Another important area to consider is that of defamation, particularly when "flame wars" break out on the Internet. In general you should resist putting anything which could be considered defamatory in an email message, even one that is sent on a one-to-one basis. In ordinary written correspondence, a letter from one person to another in a closed envelope is considered to be "privileged" correspondence and it is unlikely that a defamation lawsuit could be made to stick in such circumstances. Email is not the same at all – it is not assumed to be private unless previously agreed between the parties. It's also very easy for a slip of the finger to send an email to entirely the wrong person. If in doubt, leave it out, particularly on public forums or newsgroups.

Security

Teleworkers need to address issues of data security as well as those of physical security (preventing theft and damage). Telecottages, which allow public access to premises, also need to look at the problems of supervision of visitors and casual users.

Issues of fire and theft head the likely list of incidents. Many home offices do not have fire extinguishers, smoke alarms, first aid kits or clear evacuation routes. If you are worried that an official safety inspection by the fire brigade might lead to your office being "banned", ask advice from a supplier of firefighting equipment on suitable measures.

No one is immune from crime, and in many ways a burglary has a much more drastic effect on a home office than on a conventional office. In an office, the employer takes responsibility for equipment, and can afford security measures such as closed circuit TV. At home, you will be dealing with the consequences of any burglary.

Computers have a high resale value and are likely to be the main target for a break-in. However, the advantage of most home offices is that they do not advertise "expensive kit in here". To all intents and purposes the risks of burglary are actually lower than for an ordinary house because working from home means there is someone on the premises for most of the day and night, but you might look at installing blinds if your office is on the ground floor so that the computers are not visible to passers-by. In general it is wise not to allow visitors into your home office unless necessary – the fewer

The security survey of telecentres carried out by the Telecottage Association in 1994 showed particular problems with user supervision:

- *One third felt people could get into their offices undetected during office hours*
- *Once inside the building, visitors were generally supervised by centre staff or clients, but less than half reported supervision "all the time"*
- *Over three quarters had no signing in or visitor's badge procedure*
- *Almost half allowed access to the office outside office hours by clients*
- *Only a quarter had an alarm system*
- *Almost half described their environment as "loosely controlled"*
- *Only 30% had any kind of disaster recovery plan*
- *Only 40% had plans for provision of alternative telephone lines*
- *Only 20% had plans to cope with power supply loss*
- *Less than half required users to employ passwords when accessing PCs*

53% of telecottages reported at least one security incident, at an average cost of £1300, although half of the cases were described as very low impact (one incident costing £10,000 substantially skewed the average cost). No incidents of hacking or computer fraud were reported, and the level of deliberate computer misuse was low compared to national surveys, although misuse incidents including loading of illegal (copyrighted) software, introduction of viruses and running up large unauthorised online charges were reported.

A series of security guidelines and policy suggestions entitled *Keep IT Safe and Secure* for telecottage managers is available from the association. Send an SAE with 47p stamp to KISS booklets, WREN Telecottage, Stoneleigh Park, Warwickshire CV8 2LZ.

people who know about your equipment the better. Check the credentials of utility company and local authority officials who call at the house.

Physical security advice will be available from your Crime Prevention Unit, contactable via your local police station, or from your insurers. Common sense measures include:

- five lever mortice locks on outside doors
- key operated window locks
- key operated bolts on back doors and patio doors
- ensure ladders or other tools that could be used to gain access are locked away

- a separate lock which allows the home office door to be secured against the rest of the house
- arrange for *eg* lights to be switched on and off by timer if away on holiday, and notify police
- leave a radio or light on in the house if popping out during the day
- lock all doors and windows before going out or retiring for the night
- photograph and keep a description of your IT equipment including serial numbers in case you have to report a crime or make an insurance claim

Specific deterrence devices for computers include:

- Trojan, an anti-tamper alarm that fits inside a computer
- Wobbler, an extremely loud alarm which goes off if the computer is moved
- PANDA Protected, a system of hard-to remove labels which contain a code held on a national register
- Retainaguard, a system of etching an ID number onto a piece of equipment such as a fax or mobile phone
- workstation cabinets that allow computers to be locked away out of sight when not in use
- cable security devices that lock computers to tables or other fixed items which cannot be removed such as the Tomco Secure-it lock.

Telephone and electricity supplies are often not considered when analyses of security risks are being made, but problems in these areas can effectively stop a business from trading. For most people the cost of providing an uninterruptable power supply, or generator backup for a whole office will be prohibitive, but systems are available which at least give you sufficient breathing space to close down the computer after a power cut without losing work in progress – check the Radio Spares (RS) catalogue which lists devices that will keep one computer powered for about 15 minutes costing around £130. It may be worthwhile to pre-arrange for the use of workspace elsewhere in the area should you suffer a loss of power for more than a day. The arrangement could be with a neighbouring teleworker or office services company, or with a telecottage.

Faster repair times are probably the main reason for paying business rather than residential rates for your telephone lines. However, if you have a residential line, and no need for the directory entries provided as part of business services, but still want fast repairs, you can pay BT £8.25 a quarter to get its Total Care service, which aims at a 4-hour repair time every day except Sunday.

Association member Stephen Thomas found that it is also possible to arrange with BT for an alternative number while your own is out of service, so that clients hear a message and can leave voicemail or speak to you, rather than getting a frustrating engaged tone or, more commonly, the phone appearing to ring out as though you were out. Dial 154 to ask for this service – but as it operates through call diversion, you need to have another, functioning number to which the calls can be diverted.

The most effective form of data security is to ensure that you take regular backups and that one set of your backups is held "offsite" in case of fire or other extensive damage to your computers and onsite backups. As well as physically swapping backup tapes or disks with a co-worker or local business, you could look into backing up your data remotely via modem or ISDN line – a number of specialist companies offer safe archiving services in this way. Remember that on average a computer hard disk will fail once every two to three years – and that the inconvenience hard disk crashes cause can be hugely reduced by even once-weekly backups.

Fire Safety

Fire officers advise that all home offices should be fitted with smoke detectors (costs in the range of £4–£14 each – those which are interlinked by cable so all go off if one goes off are better, and mains driven systems are preferable to battery operated). Bryan Bates of Gloucestershire Fire and Rescue Service said: "The main thing that we suggest is for people to get interlinked smoke detectors fitted. One in the hall, one in the landing, and one in the home office, particularly if it is a converted loft space. All new properties have to have them by law, but when people convert lofts they often forget to do it. It is the biggest life saver because a smoke detector goes off at the first whiffs of smoke, giving people time to walk out of the house, shut the doors and call the fire brigade. But systems must be maintained properly. Once a week – perhaps first thing on a Monday morning – it is important that they press the test button and get into a routine. Local fire brigades can supply a free brochure, *Fire Safety in the Home*, to give further advice.

Around 500 people a year die in home fires in Britain. Ted Savill of ES Safety Supplies points out that many insurance policies are invalid if you don't have fire extinguishers. The most suitable type of extinguisher for a home office is a CO_2 (carbon dioxide) extinguisher. Ted explains: "Dry powder can be used on anything, but it's very messy and will get into the works of your computer. CO_2 extinguishers are more expensive but better suited to electrical fires. A typical 2 kg model retails for around £65 plus delivery, while a dry powder model costs around £32." Whichever model you choose, check it is British Standard approved, and ensure that it is maintained according to the manufacturer's instructions (usually it will need servicing every 6 or 12 months).

Another issue for those with upstairs home offices is to look at escape routes if a fire were to make the stairs impassable. The most important point is that windows should be easy to open and large enough to climb out through. Steel ladders or stairs fixed to the outside of the house may be a possibility, but could be expensive, a security risk or unsightly. They may require planning permission. In some circumstances "rope ladders" which are bolted firmly inside the house and can be thrown down to provide access may be considered, but the ladder should have metal chains, and metal steps which hold the chains away from the wall in use so you do not scrape your knuckles. These ladders are not recommended by some fire safety experts because they require agility and familiarity for use. However, if you feel confident using such an escape route, and you alone are the usual occupant of the home office, it could be worth looking into.

Insurance

The insurance market is moving rapidly to catch up with the shift to home working. It is still the case that a standard home contents policy is unlikely to cover your home office equipment, but specific policies targetted at home offices are being produced to replace the plethora of computer, office and home policies previously designed to confuse the teleworker. These new policies also cover important business issues such as public liability, employee liability and loss of earnings which can affect teleworkers.

Standard domestic policies, even if you have remembered to inform your insurer that you are working from home, usually don't cover more than £5,000 worth of goods and may exclude single items worth more than £1,000 (which means many PCs won't be covered). Commercial office and computer policies will cover the computer equipment – but at a high price caused by the dramatic rise in computer theft. Home office policies generally cover equipment valued in the £5,000–£20,000 range and cost about 60% of the cost of an equivalent office policy. The higher the value of the equipment, the higher the premium. Whether your office is part of the house or a separate outbuilding may also affect the premium (in the house is considered more secure because it is constantly occupied). When adding up the cost of your equipment, don't forget add-ons and small items such as mice and tape drives which can easily turn a £1,000 basic PC into a £2,000 replacement cost. Be sure to make your calculations on a replacement, value not current value, particularly since computers depreciate in value so quickly. Also remember to inform your insurers about any changes, such as purchase of new computers, or a change in the number of visitors or employees, which affects the risk insured. Failure to inform can cause problems if you have to claim.

If you use an insurance broker who, on your behalf, moves your policy around different insurers to get the best deal, check that the material details (such as serial numbers of equipment) are properly recorded every time the policy is renewed.

Other items which affect the premium vary from insurer to insurer and include:

- client visits to your premises
- employees
- window locks

- mortice locks on doors
- presence of burglar alarm
- membership of neighbourhood watch (Community Alert in Ireland)
- age of policy holder.

Mobile phones, eminently portable and stealable, are often excluded from home office policies. Another area often omitted is stock held for resale such as paper, disks or publications. Other areas to consider (which are usually available at the cost of extra premium) are:

- loss of data (*eg* through virus or malicious attack)
- public liability or employer's liability insurance if people visit or work at your home office (this is a must for anyone operating in the Republic of Ireland). It is also important for employers to ensure that employees other than the teleworker visiting the home office are covered (*eg* managers or those involved in health and safety checks)
- business interruption insurance, which compensates you for your time spent putting your business back together and other costs incurred after an incident
- computer breakdown insurance – in some situations this can be cheaper than holding a maintenance contract and ensures that expensive part replacements are covered
- cover off the premises *eg* portable computers on business trips.

Because teleworker situations vary so much, it is well worth shopping around. Here are some example quotes from autumn 1997.

1. Professional teleworker

35-year old graphic designer working in a converted outbuilding in the garden of her house in postcode LE15 (small market town in Leicestershire) looking for insurance for £5,000 worth of PC equipment against fire, flood, theft, accidental damage and business interruption:

Insurer/broker	Policy	Cost per year	Excess	Notes
Burnett and Associates	Computer From Home	£200	£100	
Mathews Comfort	Computer/ Office insurance	£122.50	£50	Includes £10K business interruption
S-Tech	Homebase	£125	£250	Would need more info on outbuilding
Tolson Messenger	Home Business Insurance	£95	£100	

The variation is mainly due to some insurers not taking into account the location or business details which works against people in low risk areas of the country who do not see clients on their premises.

2. Office services

28-year old providing secretarial services from the spare bedroom of a semi-detached house in postcode SE26 (Sydenham, a medium-income outer London suburb). Clients frequently visit the premises. Wants to insure £2,000 of office equipment against fire, flood, theft and accidental damage:

Insurer/broker	Policy	Cost per year	Excess	Notes
Burnett and Associates	Working From Home	£250	£100	
Mathews Comfort	Computer/ Office insurance	£75.50	£50	recommend additional cover at £25.62
S-Tech	Homebase	£125	£100	
Tolson Messenger	Home Business Insurance	£120	£100	

Note: all premiums are subject to 4% insurance tax.

Several expressed concern about client visits – resolving doubts before taking out a policy is vital in case a claim has to be made. It is clear from these figures that variations in circumstances and requirements can mean a substantial difference in premiums. Look at all the risks your business may be exposed to and draw up a list of requirements before asking for quotations. Tolson Messenger also produce a free guide to insurance for people working from home; (Ian Jones, Freephone 0800 374 246), and have recently added professional liability and mobile equipment modules to their specialist policy. In Ireland, Hibernian Insurance operates a home office policy designed in conjunction with the Telework Ireland association.

Bibliography

Data Protection Advice on Homeworking and Computer Information   *Date:* 1997
Author: Data Protection Registrar
Source: Tel: 01625 545745 Web: http://www.open.gov.uk/dpr/dprhome.htm

Guide to Self Employed and Partnership Financial Security Insurance   *Date:* 1996
Source: Zurich Life Tel: 0345 581235 or 0171 702 4550

Homeworking: Guidance for employers and employees on health and safety   *Date:* 1996
Author: Health and Safety Executive
Source: HSE Books, PO Box 199, Sudbury, Suffolk CO10 6FS Tel: 01787 881165 Fax:

01787 313995.

Keep IT Safe and Secure (Security and Telecentres)   *Date:* 1995
Author: Bill Murray, Small World Connections
Source: Send SAE with 47p stamp to KISS Booklets, WREN Telecottage, Stonleigh
Park, Warwickshire CV8 2LZ
Comment: Part of 1994 security survey analysis, available free of charge to TCA
members, subject to availability.

IT Security Breaches Survey   *Date:* 1994
Source: National Computing Centre (NCC) Tel: 0161 228 6333 Fax: 0161 242 2400

Planning Policy Guideline 13   *Date:* 1994
Author: Department of the Environment
Source: The Stationery Office Ltd, National Publishing, 2nd Floor,
St Crispins, Duke Street Norwich NR3 1PD

Employed or Self-Employed?
Source: Inland Revenue Ref: Booklet no. IR56, free of charge

Contacts and URLs

Inland Revenue self-assessment enquiry line Tel: 0345 161514.

UK Health and Safety Executive, HSE, tel. 01422 892 345.

Data Protection Registrar Tel: 01625 545745.

Law Centres Federation Tel: 0171 387 8570 or 0114 278 7088

Oldham MBC have revised their **planning guidelines** to take account of
teleworkers. Their guidelines are available to other planning authorities. Contact
Dave Hashdi, Oldham Metropolitan Borough Council Tel: 01619 114 154.

Political parties websites:
http://www.conservative-party.org.uk
http://www.labour.org.uk
http://www.libdems.org.uk
http://www.snp.org.uk
http://www.uup.org
http://www.plaidcymru.org
http://www.gn.apc.org/greenparty (the Green Party)

Peter Fowler is a solicitor with a niche practice in businesss-related legal matters
and commercial property. Tel 01202 849 242 Email p-fowler@lds.co.uk
Web: http://www.lds.co.uk/pw.html.

IBM PC User Group Tel: 0181 863 1191 (runs computer insurance plan)

Tolson Messenger Tel: 0800 374 246 http://www.tolsonmessenger.demon.co.uk

Health and Safety issues: Eilis Duggan, Ergonomics consultant Tel: +353 45 861148

Information on trade union guidelines for teleworkers is available from
http://www.labourtel.org.uk – The Labour Telematics Centre website in Manchester

http://www.state.mn.us/ebranch/admin/ipo/giac/ is the site for a report on
Minnesota Government Use of Copyright and Intellectual Property.

http://www.imprimatur.alcs.co.uk contains information on the Imprimatur project on
copyright issues and you can register your interest in being involved in the Special
Interest Groups currently being organised.

Ecological Building Society Tel: 01535 635933.

Timber cabins for use as home offices – Tel: 01502 478794 Contact: Olof Ribenfors

Email and online services

The advances in electronic communications over the last ten years have opened up a vast range of possibilities for teleworkers and have even, in many areas of business, been the element that makes teleworking possible at all. Using email and online services, teleworkers can receive and send work to their employers or clients, get technical support or product information, and "network" socially with other teleworkers. They can also create "virtual companies" – teams of people who can be located anywhere, and who come together to work on a project, but may never meet physically. Instead, they pass around the elements of the project by sending messages and computer files by email. Online services – information sources accessed by computer and modem – also offer many opportunities for teleworkers to create service businesses by obtaining information, reprocessing it and adding value, and then selling it to customers. There's a world of work, friends and fascinating information awaiting the determined explorer – all that's needed to get started is common sense and a little help. The services that you can connect to fall into four categories:

Bulletin boards

Before the Internet became widely available, specialist bulletin boards (BBSs) provided online information and help with the ability to receive uploaded files from users. They were never able to provide general access, email exchange between users of other systems, or general-purpose information; these drawbacks mean that they have been large superseded by the World Wide Web and listservs, so they are not covered in this book. Some computer magazines still regularly give listings of BBSs, with details of their specialities, telephone numbers and the modem settings needed to access them.

Specialist information services: newswires and databases

To access a specialist online service such as the Dow Jones Newswires, or Dun & Bradstreet's credit ratings, you will usually need to contact the supplier and arrange contract details and payment methods. Then the service provider supplies you with an access telephone number or an Internet address, a user-id and a password. Some of these premium services offer free training on the basis that the more you know about the system, the more you will use it, and the more money you will spend.

Proprietary online services

Services such as CompuServe/America Online provide email, opportunities to "conference" with other users on topics of special interest, electronic shopping and often access to technical support for particular software packages on their own systems and using their own software. They also offer connection to the Internet and World Wide Web through their services.

The Internet and the World Wide Web

The Internet is a global network of computer networks. There are estimated to be 19 million computer "hosts" on the Internet, with somewhere around 70 million users (source: IDC via Nua Internet Surveys). The Internet was originally a US government funded academic network, but is rapidly becoming commercially minded with much research targeted at providing secure methods of payment for services and goods bought online.

Anyone with the right equipment and a subscription with an Internet service provider can "surf" the Web, or exchange email and files and take part in conferences via the Internet. Service providers may simply do just that, or they may also have some content of their own that can be accessed only by subscribers to that service – the biggest content providers are the proprietary online services, but many ordinary service providers provide services such as a showcase of their customers' web pages.

Most teleworkers link to the Internet via dial-up links such as those provided by Demon, Global Internet, Pipex and BT in Britain, or Ireland Online, TInet and Indigo in Ireland. Some use proprietary services such as CompuServe/AOL. Most national companies now allow you to connect for the price of a local telephone call wherever you are in the country. For these services you typically pay a joining fee and a monthly or yearly sum and are given a user-id and password on a computer connected to the Internet. This allows you to log in and send and receive email, and to browse the World Wide Web. Many experienced teleworkers have two or more email accounts to guard against one service being unavailable due to technical problems, or else to take advantage of particular facilities such as conferencing. Some recommendations about choosing a provider are given below.

If you want to have your own Web pages to market your services, you will normally pay a separate fee to "rent" space on a Web server for your pages, usually at a rate dependent on how much space your pages take up: see Publicising your business on the Web on page 196.

Email: cheaper, faster, better?

Why send a message by email rather than by fax or post?

- it's cheaper. If you are using the email system efficiently, the cost should be in the region of 10–15p per message

- it's more flexible. As well as text messages, you can also send complete computer files such as spreadsheets or desktop publishing layouts. If you are working collaboratively on a project it can be much more efficient to send a computer file that the person at the other end can use and edit themselves, than to send a fax which can only be read and annotated

- it's faster. Email is much faster than traditional post, and many teleworkers deliver their finished projects by this method

- it's convenient. Email can be sent at any time. The recipient does not have to be there to receive the message – it is stored until they are ready to receive it. It is also easy to send group communications, and many systems offer facilities for creating customer emailing lists.

Email has its disadvantages, but most are easily overcome. Peter Flynn of University College Cork explains: "Most email is restricted to the 96 printable characters of the ASCII character set (A-Z, a-z, 0-9 and punctuation). That means you cannot send binary files in their raw state. Binary files are those containing programs, accented characters, non-Latin alphabets, pictures or sounds. However, you can wrap, or encode the binary files, either using facilities provided in your email software, or by pre-processing the files with widely available programmes such as uuencode or binhex or MIME. The encoded file is converted to 7-bit ASCII, sent by email, and decoded back to binary format by the recipient. Many services can do this automatically. It is also important to remember that many email systems are not secure while in transit, so email is best regarded as an equivalent to a postcard, not a letter."

Many companies already use email for internal messaging over their local area networks (LANs). The most popular LAN-based packages are Lotus cc:Mail (and Lotus Notes) and Microsoft Mail. Internal email packages often flash up a message on the screen to announce newly-arrived mail so that the recipient can decide whether to read the message immediately or continue with their work and read their mail later. It is possible to create "gateways" from LAN-based internal messaging systems to access external sites and recipients over the Internet. But however you are using email within in an organisation, it will need managing. Peter Flynn comments: "Someone has to be responsible for setting up and maintaining the software, for keeping an eye on queue lengths and disk space, and for handling wrongly addressed messages." Security is also a major issue for larger companies, usually handled through a number of access restriction techniques."

To use email well, it is important to take advantage of productivity tools such as computerised address books that avoid the need to keep retyping the recipient's email address, and computer-based filing systems so that you read and reply to your mail in a structured fashion. Like traditional mail, email has its downsides. You will, in all probability, get some unsolicited messages from rather odd people, and you will also have a depressingly high stack of messages on your first day back from holiday.

Be properly addressed

Email addresses vary in format depending on the email system used by the person you are trying to send a message to. If the recipient is on the same system as you, normally you just address the message with their user-id. If you don't know their user-id, there is probably a command to help you find it. On CompuServe and many other proprietary systems, all you need to know is the person's name, and their location to find their user-id using the membership commands. On the Internet there is a "whois" command, but it can only find people who have chosen to register their identity on that particular server. Some commercial ventures are working to develop email directories. Fortunately, any message you receive by email will contain the sender's address, and normally you just "reply" to the message – your software will pick up the address from the original message automatically without you having to worry about formats. In any case, 90% of your correspondents are likely to be using a standard Internet format such as person@company.co.uk.

When it comes to sending messages to someone on another, linked system, you often have to give an Internet address format as the Internet frequently routes the message. This is why, if you are putting an email address on business communications, it is wise to use the Internet format. X.400 address formats are not dealt with in detail here for reasons of space. However, if you are having difficulties you can "convert" Internet to X.400 addresses and vice versa using the WEP (well-known entry programme) available via telnet at wep.ucd.ie and other Internet hosts if needed.

To message Internet user fbloggs on the Greennet Internet host (gn.apc.org) from elsewhere on the Internet:
fbloggs@gn.apc.org

To message Internet user fbloggs on the Greennet Internet host from CompuServe:
INTERNET:fbloggs@gn.apc.org

To message Fred Bloggs, CompuServe user-id 100001,1001 from the Internet:
100001.1001@compuserve.com

To message CIX user fbloggs from the Internet:
fbloggs@cix.compulink.com

To message CIX user fbloggs from CompuServe:
INTERNET:fbloggs@cix.compulink.com

To message Fred Bloggs on an IBM X.400 mail system in Ireland from the Internet:
C=IE;A=IBMX400;P=IBMMAIL;S=BLOGGS;G=FRED

Handling junk email

The following information was kindly provided by Gerald Abrahamson on the Compuserve Telework Europa forum. The obvious method of stopping junk email is to politely ask the sender to stop. Unfortunately, because junk email arouses such hatred on the Internet, usually the junk emailer will have given an invalid return address to prevent furious recipients "bombing" them back with a hailstorm of email insults. Another sneaky trick of the junk emailer is to force you to read their message in order to find out how to turn it off. If this happens to you, check the domain of the junk emailer (the bit of the address after the @ sign) and send a message to the postmaster (*eg* to postmaster@xxx.yyy to the effect that you cannot get hold of the the junk emailer and you would like their assistance in getting your name removed from their mailing list. Almost all Internet sites have a postmaster. However, this may also bounce, by which time steam will be coming out of your ears.

If the junk emailer has registered themself on the Internet X.500 directory, you may then be able to get the name, address, telephone number and so on of the company or person owning the domain name from the Internic site http://ds.internic.net. Most junk emailers are based in the US, in which case you can now get your revenge. Send a notice based on the following:

NOTICE REGARDING UNSOLICITED EMAIL

Please remove my personal email address from your mailing list. If your message was intended as advertising, it may be in violation of federal law (Telephone Consumer Protection Act of 1991), and collateral Code of Federal Regulations (47 CFR 64.1200)

Legal notice:

The Telephone Consumer Protection Act of 1991 (TCPA) and collateral Code of Federal Regulations (47 CFR 64.1200) define an unsolicited advertisement sent via fax as the equivalent same sent by email. To wit, if your computer has:
– a modem connected to a regular telephone line and
– a printer connected to that computer

unsolicited advertising sent via email to that equipment is considered (by definition of law) as sent to a fax. The TCPA allows a private right of action against the sender of such unsolicited advertising. The recipient can sue for $500, or actual damages, whichever is the greater.

However, in a recent US legal decision an Internet service provider (ISP) was forced to reconnect a company it had disconnected because of its "spamming" (sending junk email) activities. Although the company in question had a history of being disconnected by other ISPs for similar activities, the judge ruled that unfortunately spamming was not specifically barred in the ISP/client service contract in question. It's a good idea to check that your ISP's contracts ban clients from this antisocial and wasteful activity before signing up with them.

Transferring large amounts of data

If you are planning to use email to send large files, you will need to obtain a compacting utility such as PKZIP for the PC or Stuffit for the Mac. These programmes squash your files, commonly to about half their original size. You can then email the "stuffed" or "zipped" file in half the time, and with any luck save half the phone call costs. If you send your file in this form, the recipient needs to have the appropriate programme in order to unpack the file to its original size. Some compacting programmes, such as Compactor on the Mac and PKZIP for the PC, allow you to create "self-exploding" files – the recipient double clicks on the compacted file and it expands itself back to normal size. It's important to use the right version of the compacting utility for your system: for example, if you are using Windows 95 or Windows NT, you will need the latest version of WinZip that allows for long file names – assuming that your recipient can handle them too, of course. Zipped files are binary files, and therefore still need to be "uuencoded" or "MIMEd" before they can be sent over the Internet, but your browser or email programme should be able to handle that for you: see Information Exchange below.

There are a number of different messaging formats, and it may be worthwhile talking to your customers and suppliers about the systems they use to ensure that your email system can connect to theirs. The most widely used standard is Internet email with any binary files sent as MIME attachments. Some large corporates and government departments use systems based on the secure X.400 messaging standard. X.400 systems can exchange messages with the Internet, or CompuServe, but when X.400 messages are routed via North American gateway computers there can be problems as these gateways may not recognise European X.400 country codes reliably.

There are also some applications where a direct modem-to-modem link or an ISDN link is cheaper than using an email system. For example, dtp files for a four-colour magazine can easily exceed 10Mb in size. Many typesetting bureaux offer their own high-speed direct links to keep the cost of transferring such large amounts of data down, often using the widespread 4-sight ISDN file transfer software. There are also a number of PC packages to assist with direct dial-up access to office LANs, some of which use the technique of "spoofing" to disconnect the computer from the ISDN line when it is not active (see Chapter 12, *Teleworking equipment*). Increased availability of ISDN telephone lines, which allow extremely fast connections from remote computers (typically 1–2 seconds to log on), are likely to increase the use of links using what is called "client-server" architecture.

If you are involved in large scale file transfer, it is worth comparing prices between different modem speeds and ISDN lines to work out the cheapest methods for different file sizes. This will allow you to work out

whether the additional installation and rental costs of ISDN are justified in your situation. A recent report by the European Commission project FAIR predicts that by the year 2000 there will be about 133 million Internet users worldwide. Of these, around 18% will use ISDN to connect. Conventional modems will account for 65% of connections, while cable modems operating over cable networks will make up 5% of the total. A new technology, ADSL (asynchronous digital subscriber network) will provide 8% of connections, with various other routes making up the final 4%. ADSL is being trialled by a number of telecoms companies but is not yet generally available – it allows high speed access (around 1 Mb/s) over existing copper telephone wires.

Access to knowledge and information

Mailing lists and listservs

The Internet has a vast number of mailing lists on subjects of special interest. As with most Internet functions, the difficulty is finding what you want in the first place. A giant "list of lists" is maintained which you are unlikely to need to download yourself – your Internet host will probably have a copy that you can peruse. There's also a website which indexes listservs – http://www.clark.net/pub/listserv.html. Once you have the name of the list, and the address of the computer that administrates the list, you can subscribe automatically using the ingenious listserv command. You send an email to listserv@address.of.host containing one line:

subscribe name-of-list yourname

The listserv programme will add you to that mailing list and send you information about the different address where you can send your contributions to the mailing. From then on, you receive all messages that are sent to that mailing list – so check you also know how to "unsubscribe" and how to "nomail" while you are on holiday. Do remember that the address for subscription commands is different to that for contributions to the mailing list.

Usenet News – world's largest BBS

Mailing lists and newsgroups are easy to confuse at first, since newsgroups are really online discussion groups with very little news on them. Overall, listservs tend to be more specialist and have smaller subscriber lists than newsgroups. You also don't require any offical "approval" to create a listserv. Internet newsgroups, on the other hand, are a subset of Usenet News – a set of machines that exchange articles tagged with universally recognised newsgroup labels. There are over 20,000 groups and Usenet receives hundreds of megabytes of postings each day. Each machine collects all the newsgroups each day and allows you to download only those groups that interest you.

To get news, you must first subscribe to newsgroups using a newsreader utility, which is usually supplied by your Internet service provider. The

Newsgroup utilities (thanks to Computimes in the Irish Times)

FreeAgent for Windows (http://www.forteinc.com/agent/freagent.htm) organises and filters news messages offline

NewsWatcher for Mac (http://wuarchive.wustl.edu/systems/mac/info-mac/comm/inet/ya-newswatcher-216.hqx) does the same but only online

MacSlurp does what it says (http://wuarchive.wustl.edu/systems/mac/info-mac/comm/tcp/mac-slurp-15.hqx)

Finding newsgroups – searchable index at http://tile.net/news

same utility should allow you to browse through the groups to find the ones you want to subscribe to. Latest versions of the Internet Explorer and Netscape browsers have built in utilities to allow news and email to be read at the same time, without launching a separate newsreading application.

Any subscriber can contribute to a newsgroup, either by replying with mail to the author, or by "following up" to continue the newsgroup messages. As well as the publicly available newsgroups, there are others, such as Clarinet, which are commercial services; your host must have a contract with Clarinet before they will be available. The main newsgroup categories are:

comp   computer science, hardware, software

news   news networks and software

rec   recreational activities, arts, hobbies

sci   scientific research and applications, including some social sciences

soc   social issues

talk   discussion on controversial topics

misc   all the rest – including the useful misc.jobs and misc.forsale

alt   alternative ways of looking at things. Includes many bizarre topics. Unregulated

biz   discussions related to business. Allows advertising, unlike many other sections of the Internet

k12   teachers, students, topics related to the "kindergarten through twelve" age group.

Remember, before you jump in with your pearl of wisdom, that you are joining a conversation which may have been going on for years. Check out the FAQ (frequently asked questions) messages which are regularly posted on most newsgroups to find the information you want, or to discover whether the topic you are dying to message about has been done to death by the existing participants in the past.

Newsgroup postings "expire" after about three days. There are some sites which archive old postings (http://www.dejanews.com) but there is no central resource which "owns" newsgroups.

The World Wide Web

The World Wide Web (commonly abbreviated to WWW) is a distributed information source accessible from anywhere on the Internet via "HTML browsers" such as the ubiquitous Netscape Navigator and Microsoft Internet Explorer. It is much harder to describe than it is to use... It consists of files located on Internet hosts around the world. Each file looks like a page of text and graphics with certain words highlighted. These highlights are hypertext links – points which, if you click on them, jump you to another page of information. The links are often to pages located somewhere else entirely on another computer. The beauty of WWW is that it hides the confusing fundamentals of the Internet, providing a standard look so that all you need to worry about is where you want to go and what you want to find. You don't need to worry about where in the world the information is or about logging in and out from different Internet host computers – you just ask your Web browser to save the interesting file you've found on your computer, or to print it, and the software does all the rest. A good way to understand how the hypertext system works is to start your WWW browser and give the help command, which is usually held as hypertext.

For the technically minded, WWW files are written in HTML, a hypertext application of the ISO standard SGML text description language. Web browser software on the user's computer interprets the HTML commands to create a graphical display of the pages. Web pages can contain graphics in GIF or JPEG formats as well as text, and audio and video clips. The hypertext links are made by using URLs, or Uniform Resource Locators, which are a unique form of address for every page of WWW information on the Internet. You can recognise URLs, often seen at the end of press articles, by the initial characters http://.

Finding what you want on the Web

How do you find the information you want? A common criticism of the Internet used to be that it was like being dumped in the computer equivalent of the British Library, but without a catalogue. To find what you want on the vast, global network of Internet servers, you will need to use an online catalogue by browsing a catalogue site and entering a query. The most widely used catalogue is Digital's Altavista at http://www.altavista.digital.com, because it offers both simple and complex searching tools. An Altavista search will give a summary of pages and their URLs, plus sophisticated search functions including Boolean, proximity, wildcards and include/exclude tools. You can use Altavista to find the other major catalogues such as Excite (http://www.excite.com), Infoseek Guide (http://www.infoseek.com), Inktomi, Internet Search, Lycos (http://lycos.cs.cmu.edu), Open Text, WebCrawler, World Wide Web Worm and Yahoo (http://www.yahoo.com) – most people develop a "favourite" amongst these. You can also buy super-search programs such as

Symantec's FastFind, which searches the Web using all the major search engines in parallel, giving you the maximum chance of finding what you want with minimum effort.

Making the best of your time

If you always use the Web interactively, and whenever you feel the urge, you could end up spending a lot of money unnecessarily. One way to save time is use an offline reader where that is appropriate (more on this under What you need to get online on page 198). Another is to pick your time to 'surf the net'. While Web access is growing fast in Europe, it is already at very high levels in North America, and the busiest (and therefore slowest) times are those when America is awake. So you'll find things slowing down from early afternoon onwards, and experience snail-pace access in the evenings. Things don't improve at weekends, either, as so much American use is leisure-time access – the traffic in California on the afternoon of Christmas Day in 1996 brought the LA telephone system to its knees – 999 calls couldn't get through – so even the fastest modem won't help in those circumstances. The obvious lesson is to get up earlier...

Information exchange

In addition to receiving information, on-line services provide a method of exchanging information and interacting with other like-minded souls anywhere in the world. Much of this interaction began life as technical support for computer hardware and software, but has extended to the exchange of information on almost anything from arctic exploration to needlework to zoroastrianism. Information exchange is possible via either the proprietary services or the Internet.

CompuServe Forums

While all the proprietary systems offer some kind of conferencing, that provided by CompuServe is the longest-standing, the most comprehensive, and still the best. Forums cover special interest areas on topics ranging from rock music to the Apple PowerPC. Many are provided by manufacturers as a way of supporting their products, especially computer hardware and software, and thus provide an excellent way to get help "from the horse's mouth", and also from expert users. The interactivity of the forums makes for a real dialogue between suppliers and users – sometimes to the discomfort of the suppliers, and some have ceased to support users through forums in favour of providing Web sites instead, where there is less opportunity for users to show up the incompetence or arrogance of some suppliers. But forums still provide excellent value for money, especially when you are trying out new equipment or software or methods.

Each forum has a messaging area divided into a number of sections. Each section covers a topic of interest to the forum members, and contains a number of message "threads". Any forum member can start a thread by leaving a message in the appropriate section. Other forum members read the threads, and chip in with their comments or advice.

Threads can seem a little disjointed when you first start reading them, because they consist of a group of interconnected messages, and if you missed the beginning of the thread they can be confusing. Also, someone can read a thread that is a week old, and decide to reply to one of the first messages in the thread – threads are not time sequenced like a spoken conversation. Once you get used to them, they are a fascinating source of information and comment on many different subjects. To add your comment to the thread, just reply to a forum message – the software will notice that it is a forum message, not private email, and route it accordingly.

Each forum section has an associated library, where members of the forum leave files that can be retrieved by anyone who is interested. The files are checked by the forum sysops (system operators) before they are made publicly available, to ensure that they are virus-free, that they do not contain illegal or defamatory matter, and to check that the file matches its description (*eg* if it is described as a Microsoft Word file, that it can be read in Microsoft Word). Library files are usually zipped ASCII format, but can be in proprietary graphics formats – the library description will tell you the size of the file and its format before you choose to download it.

The forum that is likely to be of most interest to teleworkers is the Telework Europa Forum (GO TWEURO). This forum was started as part of an EU initiative to promote teleworking. It also contains a lot of information about the EU's ACTS and TAP programmes (see Chapter 14, *The European Perspective*).

You can "conference" or chat interactively with anyone else who is logged into the same forum at the same time. Telework Europa sysop Kevin Tea explains: "If you think of a forum as a town, the message section is where the townsfolk meet and greet each other daily. The library is like – well, a library, and the conference section is like the town hall where people meet formally to discuss a specific topic, although informal, non-agenda led conferences can be held. Conferences have not taken off much in Europe because of the high cost of access compared to the US, where local calls are often free."

The other cost factor is that, unlike email and other basic services, forums are subject to a CompuServe charge. But the benefits usually far outweigh the drawbacks. One less than obvious advantage is that, because of the time difference between Europe and North America, it is common to leave a query on a forum when you stop work in the early evening, and find an answer when you dial back in in the morning.

IRC – wild chatter on the Internet

Chatting on the Internet (similar to conferencing on CompuServe) is carried out using Internet Relay Chat. Once you are in IRC, commands begin with a / but everything else you type is broadcast. To join a chat, type /join channel name. Internet chats are unmoderated, and can be chaotic, but they are very useful for emergency technical support on a Sunday afternoon. The Finger command on the Internet tells you who else is logged in for chatting.

How to get and put files – worldwide

The simplest way to send and receive files is via your browser, if you have an up-to-date version such as Navigator 3 in which the mail system also handles any necessary encoding or decoding of your files. You just compress your file (as described above in Transferring large amounts of information) and Attach it to an email message. This method is usually slower than using a specialist FTP program, but not many people transfer so much information regularly for this to be a problem.

Alternatively, you can use ftp directly. "Anonymous ftp" allows Internet hosts to devote part of their disk space to public files in a way that doesn't require everyone who wants a file to have a user-id and password. You will need a piece of "ftp client software" to do this – many are available on the Internet, such as the public domain package winftp.exe or the DOS utility provided with many computers, ftp.exe. Normally you first connect to your ISP, then launch the ftp utility and log in to the host computer by issuing the command

ftp somewhere.domain

eg ftp gn.apc.org. When you are connected, an information line will appear, and then you can log in with the user-id anonymous. Netiquette requires that you give your email address as the password. Once connected, you use the dir and cd commands to move around the host computer. When you find the file you want, first be sure whether it is an ASCII or a binary file. Tell the ftp software the file type by giving the command binary, or ASCII as appropriate. Then:

get filename

Alternatively, if you are contributing a file to the host computer you "put filename". For multiple files, you "mput" the filenames.

The speed of file transfer depends on the speed of the links between the user and host, and on the number of people simultaneously ftp-ing. Netiquette suggests that you try to ftp outside normal business hours, to avoid slow speeds for other users.

Netiquette

The general etiquette of online services (network etiquette or netiquette for short) is one of consideration for other users. Most breaches of netiquette are due to ignorance, rather than any desire to offend. A simple example would be that typing in capital letters is the online equivalent of SHOUTING. Instead _underscore_ words or *asterisk* phrases. Because online communications do not allow body language such as ironic grins and shoulder shrugs, some people use symbols such as <bg> for big grin and "emoticons" such as the smiley face :-) (look at it sideways) or (%—)) (cross-eyed smiling man with hat and double chin) to embellish their messages. There are also a number of acronyms such as IMHO (in my humble opinion), AFAIK (as far as I know) and BTW (by the way) in common usage. Probably the most important piece of netiquette to understand is that blatant commercialism and marketing is disapproved of. Sales messages are likely to result in your being "flamed" – sent a hailstorm of rude replies. If you post sales material on CompuServe forums, you may be barred from that forum.

A less obvious form of netiquette stems from the world-wide nature of the Web. Words that have a quite innocent meaning in one country can mean something altogether more sinister or obscene in another. A UK group with a common interest in lace making found this out to their cost when they discovered that the term has a pornographic meaning in the USA. It's important to be aware that other people may have sensitivities of which you are unaware. It is also, unfortunately, true that many Web sites carry material that you might find at best distasteful, and that might be seriously injurious to children. It is possible to buy software (often from your ISP) that will screen sites for pornography ("net nannies"), and that will enable you to put out of bounds altogether sites that you do not want your children to see.

Publicising your business on the Web

Creating Web pages

Most people create Web pages either for personal "hobby" interest, or to market a service or product. The Web has been the focus of a great deal of marketing activity because it is cheaper than conventional print advertising or direct mail, and the content of the "advert" can be altered at any time, although it is still extremely hard to measure the response to Web advertising, or "cost per hit". Many Web sites are really PR activities rather than conventional marketing tools. However, Web users are likely to be young, affluent and educated, as well as being keen on "teletrading" over online systems, so they represent an excellent audience for certain products. But it is important not to get carried away by the hype – only a small proportion of the world's business customers are on the Internet at all, and of those many use email mainly and browse the Web rarely. Also many people using 14,400 baud modems find the Web so slow as to be almost unusable unless they choose not to see the complex graphics provided on many sites by turning off graphic viewing in their Web browser. Congestion is a problem at many popular sites.

Web pages are normally "hosted" by an Internet service provider – they have to be available 24 hours a day, so renting space on existing servers is usually cheaper than setting up your own. Many providers will also design pages for you if you don't want to learn to use HTML authoring tools or don't have graphic design and editing skills. HTML itself can look intimidating, but is actually a clear and well structured language. It does have strict rules, however, so most people use an authoring package which allows you to specify the structure of the document (heading levels, graphics and so on), and then inserts the correct codes to produce the

desired effect, checking for adherence to the rules as it goes along. Web authoring tools include:

Microsoft Frontpage (http://www.microsoft.com)
HTML Writer, available at ftp://lal.cs.byu.edu/pub/www/tools/hw9b4all.zip
HoTMetaL Pro, available at
http://gatekeeper.dec.com:/pub/net/infosys/NCSA/Web/html/hotmetal
HTML Assistant, available from http://cs.dal.ca/ftp/htm/asst/htmlafaq.html
Microsoft Word has an add-on called Internet Assistant, available from
http://www.microsoft.com for converting Word files to HTML
Hot Dog Pro is available at http://www.sausage.com
WebEdit by Ken Nesbitt is available at http://www.nesbitt.com

CompuServe users can download the Home Page Wizard from CompuServe to create their own pages, an approach now being taken up by a number of local Internet service providers in order to provide customers with very basic pages. This kind of software is not appropriate for creating complex sites with sophisticated graphic design, but it can be a way to get started and make your presence known.

For Mac users, Adobe has produced a set of commercially available packages including PageMill for Web authoring and ScreenSaver for converting existing Postscript graphics and photo scans to the correct formats for the Web.

When designing Web pages, it is important to keep information short and well structured, and not to go overboard with complex graphics which slow down browsing for the user. Graphics should be interlaced – a version of the GIF format which allows a browser to quickly sketch out the graphic on the page while it is waiting for the rest of the information from the host.

This is less frustrating for the user than watching a slow counter ticking off the bytes as a graphic is downloaded. Use the facility of hypertext – instead of creating very long pages, make small pages with logical links that users can select to get more information on a particular topic.

The Web also provides facilities to create online forms for collecting feedback from users. The information in these forms has to be processed on the computer where the Web pages are hosted, so if you want to use forms you will need to create what is known as a "cgi script" to process the form information. Because such scripts can cause havoc on the local server if they go wrong, most ISPs won't let you use this approach without some help from them in ensuring that the script is bug-free. There is an alternative – you can use "client side" forms instead which do not require any processing by the ISP server, but you will probably need to do some interpretation of the data received from the forms in either case.

Most people can learn quite easily to create simple web pages. But if you need to create an extensive web site with much interaction between pages, you may need a simple server of your own on which to test the system and each update. In those circumstances, especially if you do not have experience with graphics, information provision, cgi scripting and HTML, you should consider paying a consultant to prepare the pages for you.

Reaching your audience

Once you have created your pages, you need to signpost them so that people can find you. The cheap but time consuming way to do this involves visiting each catalogue site, such as Altavista and Yahoo, and filling in a request form. Or you can use a service called Exploit, which allows you to fill in the details of your site and submit it to ten search engines free; if you register the program, you get access to 500 search engines for £50 (http://ourworld.compuserve.com/homepages/exploit/sites.htm). Other commercial services which will post your details to a variety of sites include Postmaster and Owl's Eye Productions – the list is growing... Whichever service you select, before posting details of your site make sure that you have used the HTML Meta tag to (invisibly to the user) indicate the content and keywords of your site on your home page – this will help search engines to index your pages properly. Use of the meta tags should be explained in your HTML editing package.

What you need to get online

To get started, you have to have an appropriate computer system and the 'hard' software to enable you to make a physical connection over a telephone line. The basic elements are:

- computer
- modem
- software to control the modem
- telephone line

Computer and modem purchases are covered briefly in the Chapter 12, *Teleworking Equipment*. You need to check what ports (connections) your computer has free for attaching the modem. Modems usually attach to the serial ports on PCs, and to the port marked with a telephone icon on a Mac. The standard entry-level modem is now the 28.8 kbs or V.34 model. "Vfast" modems are also available which use software compression to achieve even higher transfer rates. However, local conditions such as the speed of the connection at the other end often restricts the practical speed at which Vfast modems can be used. Speed is measured in kilobits per second (kbs) or baud rates, which are not quite the same thing, but usually treated as identical and interchangeable units.

Modems are notoriously difficult to set up for beginners, and because of their low cost, computer sales operations are not keen on devoting time to modem technical support as the support costs erode profit margins. Some providers of online services also sell modems, and it is worth considering buying from this source because they have a vested interest in making sure your modem works properly so that you can spend money on their service. Do check that the modem has the correct connector for your telephone socket (British sockets differ from American, Irish and other European equipment). It is also illegal to connect a modem that is not BABT approved (green circular sticker) to British telephone networks.

Basic communications software to control the modem should be supplied with it. Alternatively it can often be obtained as shareware, such as Procomm for the PC, or RedRyder for the Macintosh. More sophisticated commercial software contains preset definitions for most modem models that ease setup problems, and may also have helpful scripting modules that allow users to automate their connection procedures. Increasingly, online service providers, like your local Internet service provider or systems such as CompuServe, provide their own Windows or Mac-based "client" software to control the modem and navigate the service, which you receive as part of your membership of their service. These software packages normally allow you to select from a list of modem types as part of the installation process, and may not cater for some more esoteric models; it's worth sticking to the well known names when buying a modem, or asking your online service provider to recommend a modem.

A separate class of software programmes are the "offline readers", packages that download your mail in bulk, minimising the time you spend connected to the online service, and so helping to keep your bills down.

If you encounter problems in getting connected and need to ask for technical support, make sure you have details of your modem make and model before you phone. You will also probably need to know five bits of jargon about the settings in your comms software if you can find them: the speed; whether it accepts 7 or 8 bit "data words"; how many "stop bits" are in use; whether the parity is set to none, even or odd, and whether error correction is in use. The middle three are often expressed as, for example,

N-8-1 (no parity, eight bits, 1 stop bit). The fifth piece of information is more complex. Most error correction tools (where the modems at either end keep checking on the data) confirms to the MNP standard, which has several levels such as "MNP5". A good rule of thumb if in trouble is to try turning error correction off, at least temporarily. Fortunately you do not usually have to worry about any of this if you are using dedicated "client" software, which handles these minor details for you. If you have difficulties with your client software, it's probably because you've misunderstood some of the information the package is asking for, such as "domain name server" or have mistyped your password (the upper and lower case characters are important). Check these thoroughly before calling technical support.

You do not need a dedicated telephone line for your modem unless you plan heavy usage. Many people switch over their fax line for the short time they spend online. Most telephone connections should allow you to connect at 9600 baud minimum, and in many cases up to 28,800 baud. If you are only achieving low speeds, and your modem is functioning correctly, get your line quality checked.

When you succeed in contacting the service you want, you will often be asked to identify yourself (your user-id) and to give a password – a process known as "logging in", although increasingly these details are held in the comms software you use so that the logging in process is automated. In some circumstances you are allotted these passwords by the service; in others you choose them. It is strongly recommended that whenever you have control over the choice of password, you choose a mixture of letters and numbers, upper and lower case, that are unlikely to be known to anyone else and impossible to guess. Do not use standard classics such as Fred, God, your middle name, your partner's name or a pet's name, but do use some ingenuity to think of passwords that, while impenetrable to others, are also unforgettable to you... Never reveal your password, and never write it down, but do give people your email address so that they can contact you.

Service Providers (ISPs)

Once you have the right hardware to make a physical link, you can, with some simple communications software, make a direct connection to a bureau or a customer to exchange files. To have full access to the knowledge, information and exchange described in earlier sections, you need a service provider.

Service providers come in two flavours: those who provide their own proprietary content and also access to the Internet, and those who are simply service providers with little or no content on their own servers. Some aspects of choosing a service provider apply to both types, and are covered next, followed by summary information about the major proprietary online services.

Choosing a service provider

Getting your priorities right is the first step to choosing a provider: if you don't, you may find it hard to choose, either because of the problems of finding a provider that meets all your needs perfectly, or through the lure into a painful complaint known as checklistitis, in which you try to get every bell and whistle you can think of even if you don't really need it. The main points to consider are:

■ Speed of access – apart from the speed of your own modem and line, your access speed will be faster if the provider has a low user–modem ratio, and a high band-width connection to the Internet. The best sources of information about this are the magazines that do regular benchmarks of all the major providers; Internet magazine provides monthly and six-monthly figures. Using the right search engine, and learning how to frame accurate searches, will also speed up access to the information you need.

■ Low cost of access – fast access is itself an element in this, of course, but you should also make sure that your provider allows you access at local-call telephone rates from your teleworking site. It's also important to go for a provider whose fee structure suits you. If you don't need to keep files on the provider's system, nor to use it to host your Web site, the free Web space offered by many providers is obviously no use to you. Those who offer unlimited access for your regular fee will almost certainly be the best value for using the Web, but may not provide everything you need, hence the advisability for many people of having two accounts.

■ Most providers offer annual contracts at a much reduced rate; this is fine if the provider turns out to be a good one for you, but expensive if things don't work out. Many providers give you a month's free trial, so it's often worth picking what looks like the best for you, trying it for a month, and then paying for a year after that if the trial is successful.

■ Exchanging mail and files may be done with the provider's own software, or with a separate browser that will often have more features. Many providers include Netscape Navigator or Microsoft Explorer as part of the service, and it's definitely a brownie point to look for. However, the email facilities provided as part of these browsers can be too rudimentary for serious teleworkers (no easy way of filing per project) so you may need a separate email reader.

■ Support for your system – not all providers allow true 32-bit access (for example with Windows 95 and NT Dial-up Networking) or from the Mac. Again, the magazine tables should tell you this.

■ Creating your own pages – some providers throw in free Web space on which to create your own site, but whether this is useful depends on what kind of site you want to build. It is possible to put together a simple site on your own (see Publicising your business on the Web on page 196), but for many applications you may need some help from your provider, which is unlikely to be free. You might be better off going to a provider who offers Web space at a sensible price including support, rather than one that offers you free space with no support for it.

- Support when up and running (or before) – almost all providers offer some free telephone support, so it's worth checking availability and quality before you sign up. If you are experienced enough to ask reasonably probing questions, ring up and ask some! Look at the provider's own pages, and see what help is given there; most have files of FAQs (frequently asked questions) which may not only contain useful information but also tell you something about the intelligibility of their answers.

- If you are likely to do more than just send a few email messages and do a bit of surfing, it's well worth seriously considering using two providers, to give you backup – once you have started to use electronic means of moving files to customers it can be highly frustrating to be unable to get online for a few hours at crucial times. Best of all is to use both a proprietary system and a standard Web provider – that way, you get the best of both worlds and backup. Most of the proprietary systems also regularly offer short-term free trials, usually by loading their software from a CD inserted in a computer magazine.

When is world-wide not world-wide?

All the proprietary service providers, and most of the major Internet-only companies, allow you to browse content pages and exchange email and files with other users of the same system. The proprietary systems allow you to send email to other systems, and to browse the Web, but some proprietary services do not allow you to exchange files with people who subscribe to an Internet-only service. If there is any likelihood that you will want to connect via a service provider other than the one you normally use, perhaps to check your email when you are on holiday, you should make sure that your provider offers a POP3 email service.

Proprietary online services

The AOL/Compuserve online service is the largest in the world, with approximately 11.6 million subscribers. Originally, there were two competing companies, AOL and Compuserve, and at the time of writing, details of how the two services will merge were not available.

CompuServe provides a worldwide network of access nodes for widespread local call access. The node network is of particular use to those who travel regularly (such as project managers) as it provides easy access from almost all parts of Europe. Internet users cannot browse CompuServe unless they have a CompuServe account.

Top ISPs in the UK from Internet Magazine

Internet magazine (available on the news stand on the 24th of each month) carries out monthly ISP tests based on the speed of accessing certain pages and the number of times they manage to get through to each ISP. The magazine points out that its ratings are based on a geographical mean, whereas day-to-day performance can vary substantially. We have only listed the first 20 providers published in the October 1997 issue, which means a number of regional operators have been omitted.

Rank	Name	Phone	URL
1.	SAQ Internet	0800 801514	www.saq.net
2.	Demon	0181 371 1234	www.demon.net
3.	Zoo	0345 326326	www.zoo.co.uk
4.	Onyx	0345 715715	www.onyxnet.co.uk
5.	I-Way	0118 958 0058	www.i-way.net.uk
6.	Pavilion	01273 607072	www.pavilion.co.uk
7.	Cable Internet	0500 541547	www.cablenet.co.uk
8.	UUNet Pipex	0500 474739	www.uk.uu.net
9.	Primex	070000 774639	www.primex.co.uk
10.	Poptel	0171 923 9465	www.poptel.co.uk
11.	Global Internet	0181 957 1008	www.globalnet.co.uk
12.	U-Net	01925 484444	www.u-net.net
13.	Dolphin	0181 932 5000	www.dolphinet.co.uk
14.	Technocom	01753 714 200	www.technocom.co.uk
15.	Internet Central	01270 611000	www.netcentral.co.uk
16.	Vossnet	01753 737800	www.vossnet.co.uk
17.	Easynet	0171 681444	www.easynet.co.uk
18.	Enterprise	01624 677666	www.enterprise.net
19.	Baynet	01222 256401	www.baynet.co.uk
20.	Rednet Online	01494 511640	www.rednet.co.uk

CompuServe forums cover areas of special interest from telework to vintage cars. Each forum has messaging sections where users can communicate and receive help from "sysops" (system operators), normally volunteers with expertise in the topic of the forum. There are file libraries related to each message section. The forums can also host online conferencing where several users type onscreen and view each other's comments. Average telework use (say around 20 messages per day plus some Internet browsing or forum usage) would incur bills of about £7 a month.

The German publishing conglomerate Bertelsmann joined forces with AOL in 1996 to provide online services in Europe, with a customer service centre located in Dublin. When AOL acquired Compuserve in autumn 1997, Bertelsmann took a 50% stake in Compuserve's European operations. Bertelsmann intends to make much of its content material from its magazines available electronically. In tone and content AOL has previously been fairly American oriented, and has a heavy concentration on consumer

WWW browser software

The latest version of Netscape is available at :

http://home.netscape.com

The original NCSA Mosaic software can be found at ftp.ncsa.uiuc.edu

Internet Explorer is at http://www.microsoft.com

IBM OS/2 Warp users can get Web Explorer from ftpq1.ny.us.ibm.net

Many ISPs also offer the option of downloading updated browser software from their homepages.

interests and home computing, in contrast to the 'professional' emphasis of CompuServe. One strong application is homebanking, already implemented by many German banks.

Microsoft Network (MSN): The initial launch of MSN, which took place through bundled Internet access supplied with copies of Windows 95, has so far not been the huge success predicted, particularly in Europe.

First Class is an email and workgroup software system combined, which operates on a number of different platforms including Mac, Windows and Unix. In many ways it is a hybrid between old-fashioned bulletin boards, with racks of modems for direct dial-in, and a fully fledged online system. As well as simple point-to-point messaging, First Class integrates group conferencing with cross-platform person-to-person messaging. Workgroup features include graphical "office memo" message forms, simple name-based addressing and file attachments, and online cross-platform graphic viewing. Other First Class features are drag-and-drop mail filing in custom folders, auto expiry of old mail and comprehensive built-in message tracking (showing who read your mail, when, whether they forwarded or replied or downloaded any attached files). First Class servers can be attached to the Internet via gateways. The First Class client software is available for different languages such as French Canadian, German, Portugese, Spanish, Japanese, Swedish and others.

First Class is a fast spreading technology, but does not offer the breadth of access that CompuServe or the Internet provide, due to the implementation of the Internet gateways. However, the rapidly growing popularity of First Class means it is a platform to be watched, particularly for the support of distance and open learning courses.

Other content-plus services

These include CIX, an inexpensive system much favoured by journalists in Britain, and the Manchester Host, an imaginative service that links education, community and commercial groups in the greater Manchester region.

Browsers

Most service providers include software to allow you to carry out all these tasks. The proprietary services oblige you to use their own software for browsing content pages within their own services, and usually for sending email and files, but generally allow you to choose another package for browsing the Internet if you wish. The most widely used browsers on the PC are Netscape Navigator and Microsoft Internet Explorer; up to now, Netscape has managed to keep one jump ahead of Microsoft with each new edition of its software, but Explorer is very popular with large companies because it provides an easy route for integration with Micorsoft's Office products. If you can, it is worth trying them both out, perhaps via the time-limited versions available on many magazine cover CDs, before making a final decision. There a good many objective arguments on either side, but for many people the final judgement is largely subjective.

If you use email a lot, you may find it worth buying a specialist package such as Eudora or Pegasus, which has better facilities for handling addresses and for managing the filing of quantities of email – a rarely mentioned but vital element, as, once you become a seasoned email user, you will find yourself accumulating many trivial messages but also some that you really will need to find six months later when you need to check some small 'and could you just' add-on to your customer's specification. It's a good idea to get into the habit of printing really important messages, and filing them in the good old-fashioned way, to avoid disasters.

Offline readers

Once you have done some initial exploring to orientate yourself to your on-line service, think about using an OLR or offline reader. Manually checking through forums or newsgroups for new messages or sendng and receiving your mail can be time-consuming and therefore expensive. An OLR is a programme that creates a customised, automatic script for all the actions you would take yourself, and performs them as quickly as possible. A typical script would check for waiting email, check for new forum/newsgroup messages in those areas you are interested in, and summarise any new library files. When you log on, the OLR zips through all the actions you have requested and logs off automatically – typically taking around two minutes for a simple script. You can then, at your leisure and without incurring further telephone charges, peruse the messages that have been downloaded onto your computer by the OLR. Once you have composed your replies and new messages, you send them as a batch using a second OLR script, again minimising connect time and keeping costs down.

Help and how to ask for it

Once you are on-line, help comes in various shapes and sizes on different systems. When you get stuck online in a proprietary system, typing ? or help will often provide you with a page of context-sensitive help. On the

Internet, most World Wide Web pages will contain an email address to which you can send messages with queries or problems. Almost all proprietary online services have sysops or system operators, who look after the technical and administrative issues – usually you send a message to the user-id "support". Another source of help are FAQ lists, or files of Frequently Asked Questions (and answers). On the Internet, an archive of FAQ files is held at rtfm.mit.edu. Large Internet sites also have postmasters who deal with message failures and wrong addresses, and moderators who check the contents of some news groups. Internet sites usually have a webmaster who can help with problems but there are no standard sysop arrangements. The Internet has two useful newsgroups – news.newusers.questions and news.announce.newusers which may also have the answer to your problem.

Acknowledgements

Kathy Lang, Mayflower Computing, Ro Dew, West Looe Hill, Cornwall PL13 2HH
Tel: 01503 263688 Email: kathy.lang@mayflower-cc.co.uk

Peter Flynn, Academic Computing Manager, University College Cork.
Email: pflynn@curia.ucc.ie

Kevin Tea, sysop on the Telework Europa forum. CompuServe 100136,1426.

Nua Internet Surveys Web: http://www.nua.ie

Bibliography

Internet Magazine (web site http:/www.emap.com/internet)   *monthly*
Publishers: emap Business Communications
Source: Subscriptions Hotline (+44) (0) 181 956 3015 Email: custserv@readerlink.emap.co.uk

30 Minutes… to Master the Internet   *Date:* 1997
Author: Neil Barrett
Source: Kogan Page, 120 Pentonville Road, London N1 9JN
ISBN 0–7494–2366–8

101 Essential Tips: Using the Internet   *Date:* 1997
Editor: Irene Lyford
Source: Dorling Kindersley, 9 Henrietta St, London WC2E 8PS
ISBN 0–7513–0419–0

How to series: Doing Business on the Internet   *Date:* 1997
Author: Graham Jones
Source: How to Books, Plymbridge House, Estover Road, Plymouth PL6 7PZ
ISBN 0–185703–364–7

The European Information Society at the Crossroads (FAIR project) *Date: 1997*
Source: European Commission DG13 Fax: +32 2 296 2981 Email: adb@postman.dg13.cec.be

The Rough Guide to the Internet and World Wide Webb   *Date:* 1997
Author: Angus J Kennedy
Source: Rough Guides Ltd, 1 Mercer St, London WC2H 9QJ
ISBN 1–85828–288–8

Web Marketing Cookbook   *Date:* 1997
Author: Janice M. King
Source: John Wiley and Sons ISBN 0–471–17911–6

Web Security Sourcebook   *Date:* 1997
Author: Ariel D Rubin, Daniel Geer, Marcus J Ranum
Source: John Wiley and Sons ISBN 0–471–18148–X

Digital Business: surviving and thriving in an online world   *Date:* 1996
Author: Ray Hammond
Source: Coronet/Hodder & Stoughton, 338 Euston Rd, London NW1 3BH
ISBN 0–340–66660–9

Digital Money – the New Era of Internet Commerce   *Date:* 1996
Authors: Daniel C. Lynch and Leslie Lundqvist
Source: John Wiley & sons Inc. Ref: ISBN 0–471–14178–X

The New Internet Business Book   *Date:* 1996
Authors: Jill H. Ellsworth and Matthew V. Ellsworth
Source: John Wiley & Sons Ref: ISBN 0–471–14160–7

Contacts and URLs

BT's Internet service, aimed at small businesses and home users: Tel: 0800 800 001

CompuServe Information Service (CIS) 1 Redcliff Street, PO Box 676 Bristol BS99 1YN
Tel: Freefone 0900 000200.

Demon Systems Limited (sales) 42 Hendon Lane, London N3 1TT. Tel: 0181 371 1234
Fax: 0181 371 1150.

Pipex (commercial Internet access) 216 Cambridge Science Park, Cambridge
CB4 4WA Tel: 0500 4-PIPEX (474739) Fax: 01438 311100 Email: sales@dial.pipex.com

Global Internet (commercial Internet access) 113-123 Upper Richmond Rd, London
SW15 2TL Tel: 0181 957 1041 Fax: 0181 957 1100 Email: info@global.net.uk

Ireland On-line (commercial Internet access) 87 Amiens Street, Dublin 1
Tel: 01 855 1739 Email: info@iol.ie

Internet Services Ireland (incorporating Ieunet) 35a Westland Square, Pearse St,
Dublin 2 Tel: +353 1 679 0832 Fax: +353 1 670 8118 Email: info@isi.ie

Teleworking Europa Forum: GO TWEURO on CompuServe. The Wizop for the forum
is TCA board member Paddy Moindrot. Tel and Fax: 01691 648887. CompuServe:
100145,3363. Also on the Internet at http://www.tweuro.com

European Electronic Messaging Association (association for large organizations
involved in messaging) Pastoral House, Inkberrow, Worcestershire WR7 4EL.
Tel: 0386 793 028 Email: info@eema.org
Web: http://www.eema.org

Greenet (Internet access specialising in community groups)74-77 White Lion St,
London N1 9PF. Tel: 0171 713 1941 Fax: 0171 837 5551 Email: support@gn.apc.org
Web: http://www.gn.apc.org

Dow Jones News Service, Winchmore House 12–15 Fetter Lane London EC4A 1BR
Tel: 071 832 9575 Fax: 071 832 9861

http://www.RACE.analysys.co.uk This excellent server is operated by Analysys
contains information on the EU's RACE and ACTS programmes. Do not miss the
SONAH section – succinct, useful summaries of the findings of several EU projects.

http://www.teleadapt.com is the address of a company which supplies adaptors and
kits for linking up to collect your email or browse the web anywhere in the world.

http://www.volksware.com/mobilis is the address for Mobilis: the mobile computing
lifestyle magazine.

http://www.netcreations.com/postmaster is a good, free way to register your Web
Pages at a dozen or more of the most popular search engines.

Quality for Teleworkers

Why do I need quality management?

Quality management, if implemented well, should make your company more efficient and also more responsive to customers, leading to greater customer satisfaction and increased sales. Many large companies will no longer deal with small suppliers who do not have a quality standard, so obtaining one can give you more sales opportunities.

However, teleworking companies should heed the words of Jacques McMillan, head of the European Commission department in charge of quality policy and certification for telematics networks and systems: "There are many enterprises going bust where the last flag as they go under is their [quality] certificate. I am trying to put it back in perspective so those companies that actually need it should go for it and those that don't shouldn't. It should not be thrust down the throats of small and medium-sized companies." Other critics say quality certification is expensive, bureaucratic and difficult to set up and maintain, and that companies mistakenly see certification as an end in itself, rather than as a step towards improving quality.

Poorly implemented quality systems can consist of documenting the existing procedures of a company, and then checking that those procedures are adhered to, or imposing stereotyped quality forms – a uniform process which can lead to uniformly awful products. Instead, the system should seek to identify and build on existing good practice.

Indeed, Stephen Simmons of consultancy Cornix believes that for small businesses, quality is simply a marketing issue – you need to demonstrate the will and ability to comply with customer requirements – a process that only rarely involves third party certification. Stephen also thinks quality consultancy is often "damagingly expensive". However, Lesley Carr of People, Processes and Systems disagrees: "If you work with a consultant who has the right attitude towards minimising bureaucracy, achieving certification does not have to be painful."

Either way, improving internal procedures should result in better efficiency, improved customer service and improved customer satisfaction. Using a documented quality system helps the different functions of your business to work together, and often results in considerable savings through preventing inadvertent mistakes. A good quality management system also provides a basis for monitoring and improving the company's performance. In contrast, an inappropriate system can become a bureaucratic overload that is particularly expensive for small businesses to maintain. Such systems stifle flexibility and innovation, so it is important to monitor the effectiveness of the system itself.

What is quality management?

Lesley Carr gives the following advice: "Quality management is consistently good business practice, and should be an integral part of working practices, not something 'bolted on'."

- a quality product or service is one that consistently satisfies the customer's requirements
- quality is right first time, on time, every time
- quality is achieving fitness for purpose at an economic cost.

While quality is a means of making sure your product or service is right for your customer, the term "total quality" describes a related management philosophy that harnesses everyone's efforts to achieve continuous improvement and cost reductions.

What are the quality standards?

Achieving a quality standard involves producing a documented quality system that provides a consistent way of controlling working procedures. The internationally accepted quality standards, known as the ISO9000 series, were issued in 1994 and replace the previous British Standard (BS) 5750. The ISO standards comprise a number of model quality systems together with guidance notes indicating which quality management system is applicable to what situation. Most teleworking businesses will fall under ISO9002 except for those involving design activities that will need to take note of the design control requirements of ISO 9001:1994.

Companies specialising in software development could also consider registering under the DTI's TickIT scheme for ISO9000–3, which provides guidance on applying ISO9001 requirements to the software design and development process. It is possible to apply for certification under ISO9001 and TickIT at the same time. A growing number of large companies who have business-critical or safety-related software requirements insist that their suppliers operate the TickIT scheme.

What's involved in registration?

Establishing a quality system

The steps needed to begin a quality system are fairly straight forward:

- decide that you have the motivation to improve your internal work procedures and customer service levels. Think about whether to involve a consultant now or later…
- obtain a copy of the standard (ISO9002 in most cases)
- analyse your current working procedures and document them
- identify which aspects of your service are most important to your customers (*eg* timeliness, accuracy, responsiveness)

- check the written procedures with all concerned for consistency
- get feedback and look at where improvements can be made
- work out ways of measuring how you are performing
- formulate improvement objectives and targets
- check that everyone is using the written procedures, and continue to ask for contributions towards improvement.

At this stage you will probably need some consultancy help or advice in interpreting the standard and producing a formal documented quality management system to meet the requirements, because the standards are complex, generalised and hard to interpret. Most consultants will also carry out a trial audit prior to the certifying body carrying out its audit in order to flag up any problems.

Obtaining registration

When the quality system is in place to your satisfaction and that of the consultant, and has been working for a month or two, contact the appropriate certification body. It is a good idea to approach two or three and compare their costs and registration processes. They will visit your business and assess your quality management system. Be aware that it is usually expected that you will operate the quality system for about four months before any certification is offered. If the certification body is satisfied both that the quality management system complies with the standard, and that it is being used comprehensively within your business, you will be awarded a certificate. You can then use the certificate and the registered company logo in marketing activities. After registration, the certification body returns periodically (usually once a year) to ensure the quality management system is up-to-date and in use. There is normally an annual fee to be paid for continued registration.

Is quality management different for teleworkers?

In a standard industrial quality system, a company controls its subcontractors or suppliers by insisting that they deliver in accordance with a documented specification defining the scope, timescale and standards applicable to the materials or service supplied. Teleworking is usually a much closer and more delicate relationship than that between an off-site supplier and purchaser, so the teleworker needs to put a lot more effort into integrating with the client company's quality management system.

Simon Burke of ISO9001-registered company Intermec Ireland agrees that ISO9000 is probably inapplicable to individual teleworkers or very small businesses of less than five people. "The effort involved and the corresponding documentation of the business processes could be enough to kill the business." Instead, Simon recommends making sure you can comply with your client's vendor assessment procedures. "A company like ours divides its purchases of goods and services into "primary" items that can affect the quality of our own products and services, such as software developments. Other purchases are "secondary", such as office stationery and consumables. All primary goods and services must be purchased from other companies that are listed on an internal "Qualified Vendor List". This list is compiled by the company, usually on the basis of a quality related questionnaire, sometimes called a "Vendor Appraisal Form". This must be completed prior to trade between the two companies. If the vendor is ISO9000 registered then there is no problem. If not, samples of goods or services will be tested, or they will be accepted through a reputable third party recommendation. A vendor is normally on the list only for a given product or service. If a vendor is qualified to supply one item, it does not qualify them to supply everything. So for small teleworking businesses, the best advice may be to be aware of your client's vendor assessment forms and make sure you can comply with their quality management system."

Teleworking consultancy Cornix has prepared a code of conduct for Devon & Cornwall TEC that gives a good starting point for teleworkers:

The Telnet code of conduct

(© Devon & Cornwall TEC)

1. To carry out the assignment which the teleworker has undertaken diligently, conscientiously and with proper regard for the client's interests.

2. To apply good management and quality assurance practices to all teleworking assignments.

3. To agree with the client a written statement which clearly defines the objectives and scope of the proposed work, the timescale and fee basis, and also where necessary to agree in writing any subsequent revision.

4. To respect all information concerning the client's business as strictly confidential and not to disclose or permit the disclosure of any such information without the client's specific prior permission.

5. To ensure that all property, data, text and other materials belonging to the client and held by the teleworker are stored in a secure location when not in use and handled appropriately when in use.

6. To only accept such assignments for which the teleworker is suitably qualified and/or experienced to carry out to a high standard.

7. To refrain from undertaking any assignment which would result in a conflict of interest and to disclose to the client any financial or personal interest which may influence the work carried out for the client in any way.

8. To ensure that all hardware and software used by the teleworker is used only in connection with the teleworker's professional activities, is properly maintained and that all reasonable care is taken to ensure that it is free from defects.

9. To ensure that the teleworker's knowledge and skills are kept up-to-date, where necessary through obtaining appropriate training and professional development.

What activities do the standards cover?

Contractual relationships

(© Devon & Cornwall TEC)

Agreed terms and conditions for sales should be implemented. There should be a process for defining the customer's requirements, and dealing with any conflicts or changes to the requirements. Ensure that your business can satisfy its contractual obligations for each sale. Cornix makes the following recommendations for a minimum teleworking contract:

1. Include identities and contact addresses of both purchaser and supplier, and if either is a corporate body, the names of the individuals concerned.

2. Describe in general terms the work to be carried out, its purpose and scope.

3. Specify the payment for the work, and whether VAT will be applicable.

4. Specify a timetable for both the work, and payment for the work.

5. Describe clearly the proposals for confidentiality and security of the work and its Data Protection Act status.

6. Define the ownership of any resulting copyright and intellectual property rights, if appropriate.

7. Arrangements for loan or supply of equipment, where applicable, including insurance arrangements, should be listed.

8. Specify arrangements in the event of illness, incapacity, holidays etc. and for any consequent subcontracting, if permitted.

9. If the workload exceeds 21 hours per week, and is an exclusive use of

the teleworker full-time, then arrangements for PAYE and NI deductions should be made as in these circumstances, the teleworker may be classified as an employee for the duration of the work.

10. Refer to the quality assurance system to be used, if any.

11. Where group working is involved, the identity of the individual responsible for quality within the group should be specified.

Lesley Carr lists other areas covered by quality standards:

Suppliers and purchases

All your suppliers should be vetted for the quality of the product or service which they supply to you. Suppliers with bad track records should be dropped. Purchase requirements need to be clearly laid out to avoid misunderstandings.

Production and process control

You will need a method of checking, inspecting and rectifying the product or service while it is being produced to ensure it meets customer requirements. At the end of the production, any goods or services that are not up to scratch must be identified and dealt with accordingly. The quality system should allow the status of individual products or jobs to be easily traced or identified.

Handling and storage

Any items handled by your business should be stored, packaged and delivered to the customer in a way which protects them from damage, deterioration, loss or misuse.

PR needs override quality results for cancer testers

Faulty cervical cancer test results have led to a hospital in Norfolk ending its homeworking scheme for testers although quality checks indicated the home-based workers often had better records than lab-based staff.

The James Paget Hospital had to repeat over 9,000 cervical smears after mistakes by one tester led to 357 minor and 19 serious errors. It takes two years to train a tester, most of whom are women. As some had left to start families, the hospital allowed a homeworking solution which also freed up lab space during a time of increasing demand for the smear tests. The report which investigated the errors recommended abolishing homeworking, and retesting all the homeworkers' samples.

The implication that the quality of the home-based workers was worse is not borne out by the evidence. According to Elayne Guest, director of corporate services, the quality assurance procedures in place indicated that mistakes by home-based testers are no higher than for lab workers. "Not all of our screeners live close to the hospital. They come in once a week and their work is supervised during the visit. Their slides are checked and a second opinion is sought when required."

Keeping records

The precise records needed for every business transaction or procedure should be specified. They should be identified, comprehensive, secure and accessible to all who need them. The records should be retained for an agreed time period and then archived or destroyed.

Financial affairs

There should be adequate control over aspects of finance that relate to the customer, such as invoice production.

Training and competency

Each member of staff should get the correct level of training, and should have the appropriate qualifications for the tasks they carry out. Records of training given should be kept.

Coping with complaints

A recognised procedure for dealing with complaints should be implemented to resolve problems.

Malcolm Lake of Effective Quality Management adds three more points:

Management reviews and audits

A regular and systematic review by the management of the business to check whether the quality management system is working well, and to monitor business performance, training needs *etc.*

Statements of responsibilities

A clearly defined statement of management/job responsibilities. Even if the business is operated very flexibly, the owner/manager will have different responsibilities from his or her assistants.

Corrective actions

A procedure for determining what to do when a problem occurs: ways of enabling the problem to be sorted out quickly and effectively, and of ensuring that it does not happen again.

Case studies

Antur Teifi – solving a quality problem

Mike Jones, Quality Officer for Antur Teifi, an organisation located on 6 sites with 30 staff that includes a well-equipped Telematics Centre, sums up the quality process: "It should be a bottom-up process – you need to keep your existing good practices. You have to ensure everybody owns the quality process – *ie* involve those who have to use it. Then write it down. I think anyone who is thinking about going for a quality standard needs to ask themselves the following questions:

1. Do we really need quality control?

2. Can we afford its costs?

3. Are we really committed to the work needed to maintain the system?

4. Do our customers expect us to operate to an ISO9000 standard?

If you decide to go ahead, the next step is to decide whether you are going to use a consultant, or whether you will try to "DIY" your quality system. Either way, the golden rules are:

1. Document what you do

2. Do what you have documented

3. Check that you are doing it

It took Antur Teifi 18 months to become certificated, but smaller organisations should be able to do it on a much shorter timescale. "During our certification, we encountered a problem with a contract we had taken on from the Employment Department. The contract involved training for long-term unemployed people that culminated in each participant having their CV typed by our Telematics Centre. Within 4 days of the end of the course, the Jobcentre should receive ten correct copies of each CV. For months there were problems, ranging from late delivery of CVs to incorrect CVs, and inconsistencies in the CV format. When I initially investigated the problem, everyone involved blamed everyone else for the errors. The tutors thought the typists were incapable of the work. The typists believed the tutors did not care about their work because of the poor quality of the manuscript CVs."

"We sat down and discussed the problem without apportioning blame, and the problem was tracked back to the lack of a procedure that everyone understood, that could be owned by everyone, checked independently, and where if anyone did not adhere to the procedure, non-conformance would be evident. The next step was to write down the problems and examine their causes rather than their symptoms. The tables and flow chart below show how we solved the problem and documented it for our quality system."

Quality on the move at Spektra Systems

Spektra Systems, a specialist software consultancy, has made its quality procedures and work practices available to staff who are teleworking or working on customer sites. The system uses Lotus Notes to provide online information, and also encompasses forms for expenses, timesheets and training records as well as for quality management. It is now being marketed to other companies as the PR1ME package. Euan Robertson, Spektra's Technical Director, sees several benefits:

■ *Quality becomes a banner for staff to rally around and is well received by clients*

■ *The quality system has helped introduce structure and a discipline approach*

■ *New staff can easily assimilate the company's methods and work practices*

Problem	Reason/cause	Answer
Late delivery of CVs	• Scripts not arriving at Telematics Centre on time for typing	Scripts to be posted 1st class to Telematics Centre on same evening as course is held
	• No-one available to do the typing	A minimum of 3 days notice to be given to the Telematics Centre of the arrival of scripts
	• Some scripts unreadable	CV details to be printed by trainees and checked by the tutor for accuracy
Incorrect CVs	• Scripts unreadable	All CVs to be checked by a second person after typing and only typists with good skills to be used
		Trainees to print rather than write details
		Tutor to check script prior to despatch to Telematics Centre
		All CVs to be checked by another person before leaving Telematics Centre
Inconsistencies in format	• No trainee or tutor had a format by which a standard could be set	Each trainee to fill a standard form with CV details

This analysis was used to draw up the following quality system documentation.

Using form 116 Jobsearch participant prints CV during the course, or presents a typed version if preferred. Form 116 is attached [not shown in this factsheet]

Completed form 116 or typed version checked by Jobsearch Course Leader by end of course and passed by end of Day 2 to Telematics Centre for typing

Information from form 116 to be typed in CV fashion and despatched by end of Day 4
(2 working days from receipt). Prior to despatch, typed CV to be checked for accuracy against original by person other than typist

Person who checks the accuracy signs and dates at item 5, page 6 of form 116 and passes copy and original through to the Training Department

In cases where complete form 116 is unreadable or obscure, the Course Leader is contacted by Telematics Centre staff. If the day 4 deadline cannot be met the relevant Job Centre is informed by Telematics Centre staff

Intermec Ireland – picking a teleworker

Margaret Burke, quality officer at Intermec Ireland, an ISO9001-registered company that specialises in barcode readers, printers and consumables, spells out what she is looking for in a teleworker:

"ISO9000 purchasing requirements list three questions that must be answered.

1. How can we control the quality of what we buy from subcontractors or suppliers such as teleworkers?

2. How should we assess our subcontractors/suppliers?

3. How do we control the quality of products given to us by subcontractors to include in our processes?

Let's look at how we might deal with this for two teleworking examples, one simple and one complex. First, Intermec have recently developed a new software package called 'Asset Tracking', which is a generic product for the barcoding market, and will be sold worldwide. We might need a teleworker to translate our user documentation into French or German. This is a specialised job, so just as though we were hiring a new employee, we would look carefully at the teleworker's qualifications and experience. We would hope to see a sample of work, but if we couldn't, perhaps because of confidentiality agreements, then we would ask for a referee, so we can assess the teleworker's basic ability to carry out the required work. We would then transmit our documentation electronically to the teleworker, who could retransmit the translated document. We might ask for the initial few pages of the document to review for quality of translation, correct use of terminology for the target industry *etc*. Our contract would contain confidentiality agreements if necessary.

The second example is more complex, and one where we intend to incorporate the product of the teleworking into our own products. Let's say we are overloaded in the software area and we need to contract out some development work on a once-off basis. As in the first case, we would look at qualification and experience, but we would also have to insist that the teleworker conform to our Development Standards Manual, which forms part of our quality system. The appropriate sections and samples would be provided to the teleworker, and we would also provide the teleworker with the functional specification from which the technical specification will be developed. From there on, the teleworker must conform to our standards. Development work would be reviewed by our team leaders at Intermec, beginning at the Technical Specification stage and progressing to testing of the software. Acceptance of the review could be authorised by electronic signatures, which can be used as a form of proof for an auditor. We would not accept a teleworker who did not wish to conform to these standards."

Somerset Computer Services – quality for microenterprises

Somerset Computer Services is a "1.5 man" operation run by Kieron McGrath and his wife. Kieron has three specialities – computer consultancy for small businesses, training for the local enterprise centre in the small business area, and a desktop publishing service. Kieron decided to go for a quality system with independent certification for two reasons. Firstly he felt that it would open doors in larger companies that he wanted to sell to by giving greater credibility. "Teleworkers already have a credibility problem because they tend to be microbusinesses, and because of the roses-round-the-door media image that has been promoted. Therefore it's actually more important to have a quality certificate than for other sectors", he comments. Secondly, he felt his business, like most small businesses was disorganised and too dependent on one person – himself. "After installing the quality system, when I went into hospital for a knee replacement, my wife was able to run the business quite happily for three weeks using the documented systems."

Kieron was fortunate in being able to join a subsidised quality course that was run at his local TEC, occupying one day a month for six months, which reduced his consultancy costs considerably. "I think that the standard

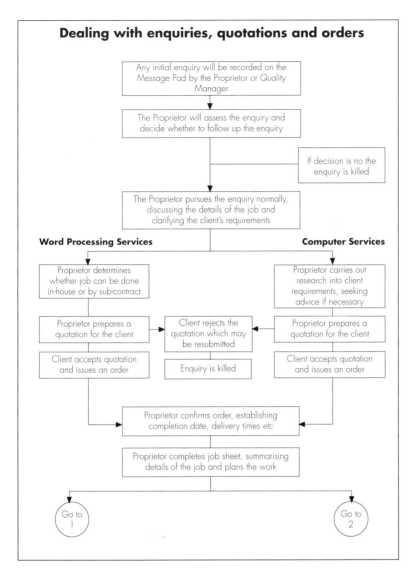

Dealing with enquiries, quotations and orders

Any initial enquiry will be recorded on the Message Pad by the Proprietor or Quality Manager

The Proprietor will assess the enquiry and decide whether to follow up the enquiry

If decision is no the enquiry is killed

The Proprietor pursues the enquiry normally, discussing the details of the job and clarifying the client's requirements

Word Processing Services

Computer Services

Proprietor determines whether job can be done in-house or by sub-contract

Proprietor carries out research into client requirements, seeking advice if necessary

Proprietor prepares a quotation for the client

Client rejects the quotation which may be resubmitted

Proprietor prepares a quotation for the client

Client accepts quotation and issues an order

Enquiry is killed

Client accepts quotation and issues an order

Proprietor confirms order, establishing completion date, delivery times *etc*

Proprietor completes job sheet, summarising details of the job and plans the work

Go to 1

Go to 2

is incomprehensible, and that means you can't write your own quality manual – you have to get a consultant to explain things and to look at how your existing system conforms to the standard."

Some requirements are straightforward and sensible practice for all businesses, such as the logging of all incoming and outgoing mail. But being such a small business has caused a few absurdities. Kieron has to hold monthly quality audits taking about 2 hours, and quarterly management review meetings, which are attended by himself and his wife.

Size had its advantages when it came to cost, however. Kieron was able to negotiate with an organisation offering certification. "I said £2,850 for three years just wasn't on for a two-person business that was going to take them half a day to assess, not one and a half days. I was about to go for a body specialising in small business certification instead, but then the original organisation came back and offered me £450 a year over three years." Another tip Kieron gives is to double check that your consultant and certifying organisation themselves have achieved quality standards. Kieron's advice on picking consultants and certifiers is to use word of mouth, and talk to other similar small businesses that have achieved quality standards. "It has definitely been worthwhile for us. Companies that wouldn't have looked at us are now letting us quote, and the business is run much more efficiently." The flow chart on the previous page gives an example of one of Kieron's quality procedures.

How much does it cost?

- staff time estimates are hard to make. However, if you contact a quality consultant at the beginning of your quality programme, they may be able to help you make an estimate before you embark on major expenditure. Stephen Simmons cautions that even the smallest group's scheme will involve at least 100 hours of effort: "The point is that the real cost is in own time expended, which is likely to be more expensive than the money cost."

- consultancy costs vary and you should obtain competing quotes. The NAT's scheme costs about £1,000 but does not lead to any third party certification. Kieron McGrath got his consultancy 50% paid for by his local TEC, reducing the cost to £1,250. Pat McCarthy of Quality Systems International recommends that companies in the same type of business should group together to save money on courses because the process is similar for each business. In Ireland, approved courses can qualify for grant aid under the FÁS training support scheme.

- certification costs (these are sometimes included in consultant's costs). Kieron McGrath got his certification at the bargain rate of £450/year for three years, but he was originally asked for £2850. Lesley Carr compiled the following information on total certification fees over three years. Check the details of each scheme – for example, some figures given here only apply to businesses with no design element to their work.

Certification body		Fees
National Quality Assurance	(1–10 employees)	
Lisa Kinnaird 01582 866766		£2,895
SGS Yarsley	(1–5 employees)	
Barry Holland 01342 305328		£2,620
BSI Quality Assurance (small business)		
01908 228008	('small business')	£3,120
Lloyds Register Quality Assurance	(1–30 employees)	
01203 882390		£3,400

*Note fees are based on a 3-year package *ie* application fee plus 3 annual surveillance fees

During the previous update of this list there was a considerable variation in the quality of enquiry handling between these bodies, which may or may not reflect on their efficiency at certification. Some gave comprehensive, clear and immediate information. Others necessitated up to 4 separate calls to different units to extract information. The only company which provided clear, fast answers suitable for very small businesses of 2–3 people was BSI Quality Assurance.

Margaret Burke gives an estimate of costs for Intermec's certification: "We have over forty employees. My salary is an obvious overhead, and I would guess that over the eighteen months we have been working on ISO, each employee has probably spent 15 days on quality issues – a significant hidden cost. But there were hidden benefits. We saved money because of the stringent procedures, and looked at all aspects of our business. We have 105 procedures in place, and three manuals – Development Standards, Quality and Procedures. I feel the other major problem with certification is the amount of paperwork created. Intermec was relatively paper-free, despite operating from four different sites. All main communication and documentation was completed on our IBM AS400. All ISO9000 proof of approval, acceptance *etc* requires sign-offs, which involve paper. I don't feel it's paperwork with a purpose – ISO does not support rainforests! " If you decide that certification is too expensive for your business, other options are:

- ■ use an independent scheme such as that operated by the National Association of Teleworkers (this will not entitle you to use ISO9000 in your literature)

- ■ discuss with your clients their vendor assessment and quality procedures. Make sure you are complying with their quality system, even if you don't have certification

- ■ develop a consistent quality system for your business that is compatible with ISO9000, but do not apply for certification and its extra costs.

One of Malcolm Lake's clients commented on quality: "I can now see that twelve months ago we merely "muddled along". Now we are well organised, we know where everything is, we all know what our jobs are and we have doubled our turnover with the same number of office staff. I do not need to go for external certification but I know that if I do I will easily obtain it." Malcolm Lake of Effective Quality Management provides a free telephone advice service to any teleworking organisation that would like to know more about ISO9000 and its organisational implications. "Previously it could have been argued that quality standards represented a heavy industry, top-down approach. Now the ISO9000 models allow each organisation to be free to operate top-down or bottom-up and to choose whether or not to see certification."

Acknowledgement

This chapter has been checked and updated by Brian Higton of Cygnet Solutions.

Contacts

Many local TECs (Training and Enterprise Councils) in Britain or FÁS in Ireland keep information on quality systems, and some run subsidised workshops for companies going for ISO9000. Local offices of the DTI can also provide UK information.

Copies of the ISO9000 standard are available from BSI Standards, Linford Wood, Milton Keynes MK14 6LE Tel: 01908 220022 Fax: 01908 320856

A list of quality certification bodies can be obtained from National Accreditation Council for Certification Bodies (NACCB) Audley House, 13 Palace Street, London SW1E 5HS. Tel: 0181 943 6311 Fax: 0181 943 7134.

Antur Teifi, Business Park, Aberad, Newcastle Emlyn, Dyfed SA38 9DB. Tel: 01239 710238 Fax: 01239 710358 Contact: Mike Jones

Cornix Teleworking Consultancy, 64 Morrab Road, Penzance, Cornwall TR18 2QT Tel: 01736 369477 Fax: 01736 369477 Email: 100021.2563@compuserve.com or srs@cornix.co.uk Contact: Stephen Simmons

Cygnet Solutions, Swan House, Darvel, Ayrshire KA17 0LP Tel: 01560 323444 Fax: 01560 323432 Email: sgf@cygnets.co.uk Contact: Suzanne Flynn. Cygnet helps companies to achieve ISO9001, ISO9002 and TickIT registration.

Effective Quality Management (EQM), Lake House, Wythop Mill, Cockermouth, Cumbria CA13 9YP. Tel: 01768 776687 Fax: 01768 77629 Contact: Malcolm Lake. This is the company that designed and developed Kieron McGrath's system.

Intermec Ireland, 19/20 York Road, Dun Laoghaire, Co. Dublin, Ireland. Tel: +353 1 280 0899 E-mail: iewfdprd@ibmmail.com. Contact Margaret Burke.

People, Process and Systems, 87 Waterloo Road, Wokingham, Berks RG11 2JG Tel/Fax: 01734 775892 E-mail lcarr@attmail.com Contact: Lesley Carr.

Quality Management for Teleworking, QMT Secretariat, Glebe House, Herford Square, Chew Magna, Bristol BS40 8RA (This is the uncertificated quality system recommended by the National Association of Teleworkers) Tel: 01275 332612 Fax: 01275 333515

Quality Services International Ltd, Shanballymore, Mallow, Co. Cork, Ireland. Tel/Fax: +353 22 25450 Contact: Pat McCarthy or Billy Nyhan, lead assessors.

Somerset Computer Services, South View, Runnington, Wellington, Somerset TA21 0QW Tel: 01823 661544 Fax: 01823 661544 Email: 100111.3412@Compuserve.com

Spektra Systems Ltd, Spektra House, 2 MacMillan Road, Alderstone Business Park, Livingston, EH54 7DF Tel: 01506 460234 Fax: 01506 460212 Email: euan.robertson@spektra.co.uk Contact: Euan Robertson This company is now selling its own Lotus Notes quality management system adapted for use by remote workers under the title PR1ME.

Disability and teleworking

Teleworking has the potential to offer some disabled people new employment opportunities. People with mobility, visual or hearing impairments can work from their own homes, or from a centre adapted for disabled teleworkers. The work carried out encompasses the whole range of teleworking, from word processing to software programming. However, some of the problems of teleworking can be more acute for those with disabilities – such as social isolation – while the implications for those receiving state benefits need careful consideration.

If you are disabled and seek employment through teleworking, be sure to get written advice from the Benefits Agency on how this may affect any benefits you receive. Additionally, some insurance settlements for the disabled are paid on the understanding that the recipient will never physically be able to take up employment again, whereas others have earnings thresholds which may not be exceeded. Peter Lisney of disabled training specialists Camrox advises: "Potential disabled teleworkers should first weigh up the possible penalties against the possible gains before investing in equipment and training."

Access to the technology

It is important to get a proper assessment of a disabled computer user's needs so that they can get the best access possible to the technology. The Computability Centre, based in Warwick, is a national charity that offers professional computer expertise to people with all kinds of disabilities. The Centre runs an advice and information service including a phone helpline, as well as an assessment service, training courses and consultancy.

In addition to helping those who are already disabled to get better access to computers, the Centre helps those who already use computers but suffer from progressive problems due to disability. In the case of British Gas payroll supervisor Eileen Knowles, who has Parkinson's Disease, Computability "saved her job". Eileen's hand tremors were affecting her keyboarding accuracy and she was having difficulty holding a pen. Computability provided Eileen with a keyguard (a template with holes for each key) and recommended moving the keyboard down to a tray below her desk. Eileen was amazed at the effectiveness of these simple adaptations.

For Jane Thurlow, a biologist at the Imperial Cancer Research Fund, severe back injury meant she could not sit down at all, and could stand for only 20 minutes in an hour. Writing and typing were causing her considerable pain. Computability helped Jane to experiment with different techniques for using the computer while lying down. Jane now has a computer with voice input, and the screen is tilted through 90 degrees so that she can read it lying down.

The Disabled Living Foundation holds information on 1,600 technical aids online. However, their database is only available on subscription so most people would access the information via Disabled Living Centres or local authorities who are subscribers. There is also a CD-ROM produced by the EU HANDYNET project which details 35,000 aids and adaptations available in Europe and can be accessed through the Disabled Living Foundation. In Ireland, the Central Remedial Clinic in Dublin can offer a similar service to that offered by Computability.

Technical aids for teleworkers

- latch keys allow users who can only press one key at once, or those who use a stick on the keyboard, to use modifier keys such as shift, alt and control on PCs, or command and option on the Macintosh

- for users with visual disabilities, brightly coloured keytops, or those with big or bold characters can help

- keyguards are rigid plates above keyboard keys that can take the weight of hands or arms, and have holes above each key for accurate key depression

- personalised keyboards can be very effective for people with hand/arm difficulties *eg* smaller size keyboards, programmable keypads, switches that can be used with keyboard emulation software, and keyboards for those who only have the use of one hand

- for anyone who has difficulty with data entry, word processors that predict word endings, and most likely next words (keystroke savers) are a boon

- computer mice alternatives include tracker balls, which are fixed in position but you roll a ball to move the pointer, touch-sensitive pads and joy sticks. Alternative shapes and sizes are available. Highly specialised devices such as the "twiddler" operate on delicate tilting movements of the hand, while others can be operated by the head, or operated by biometrics from vestigial movements. Mouse movements can also be emulated using the keyboard cursor keys in some situations

- help for the visually-impaired ranges from replacing old-fashioned poor quality screens, to altering colour combinations, and installing larger screens. Another approach is to enlarge the image, but when this is done the whole screen contents cannot be viewed at once. In some systems an enlarged image from part of the computer's main screen is displayed on a second screen (usually a closed circuit TV system that can also be used to enlarge printed material for reading)

- voice recognition software for blind and physically disabled users can act as a keyboard replacement and is available from a limited "command level" to "free text". The development of laptop computers in conjunction with speech synthesisers and voice recognition can now provide some disabled people with an easily portable communications tool. Another alternative is "screen reading" using braille output, where whole or half lines from the screen are produced on an electro mechanical strip close to the keyboard

- OCR (optical character reading) text scanning can be used to "read" text into a computer, producing text on the computer screen, or a synthesised voice, or both

- text telephones can help those with hearing disabilities to communicate by displaying conversations on a small screen connected to a normal telephone line. The most commonly used system is the Minicom. Text telephones are great for communications between the hearing-impaired, but need an interpretation service to aid communication with other telephone users. The RNID offers a "TypeTalk" service where an interpreter "translates" between the spoken word and the Minicom messages

- many items not related to computers can help disabled teleworkers, such as page turners for books and journals, lights to indicate ringing telephones, talking calculators and specially adapted work furniture

- BT has recently introduced a series of text payphones for the deaf and speech-impaired sited at UK airports. The phones can be used to link up to other textphone users, or to the BT funded Typetalk system, which provides operator mediated relay services between textphones and voice phone users. The text payphones look like standard payphones but have a drawer from which a keyboard slides out when callers using a special phonecard are connected.

- Cheshire Deaf Society has set up videophone terminals allowing users to link remotely to social services.

Certain items of equipment for disabled people are exempt from VAT, but rules vary according to local VAT offices. A campaign to ensure equipment for disabled people is free of VAT is run by Dolphin Systems.

Access to work

The Department for Education and Employment in Britain runs the PACT scheme which can help disabled teleworkers and their employers. The budget for this successful scheme has, after pressure from disability organisations, been increased from £12m to £19m, but the employer is expected to pay the first £300 of any new claim made by a disabled person who is already employed. There is still a question mark over support for self-employed disabled people because the government has yet to decide whether self-employed people must pay the normal employer's contribution. Each applicant can get help to a maximum value of £21,000 over a period of five years. To qualify, you must be registered disabled, or able to register but have chosen not to do so. Examples of acceptable uses include:

Milestone case laid down in San Francisco

A US citizen was awarded $90,000 damages in compensation for not being allowed to telework – with implications for future cases in Britain. Jack Nilles, the US telework guru was called as an expert witness for the plaintiff, Michael Faircloth, in his court case against his employer, the Bay Area Rapid Transit District (BART).

BART operates the light rail transit system for the San Francisco region. Michael Faircloth was a labour relations arbitrator for BART who is partially disabled by a neck injury which predated his employment with BART. The injury causes pain when sitting or standing for long periods. Faircloth was commuting 100 miles five days per week, causing him severe pain. He had been telecommuting informally for a number of weeks when he was refused the right to telecommute one day a week. Faircloth sued under the Americans with Disabilitites Act.

Nilles reviewed the records relating to the case and administered a teleworking screening questionnaire as well as interviewing Faircloth and concluded that he could easily telecommute at least one day per week.

The TCA consulted employment law expert Jeffery Shaw of Shaw Personnel services about the situation in Britain: "We now have the Disability Act 1995 in place which does not allow work to be refused simply because people are disabled." However, the full impact of this law will take some time to be felt since any case would take at least 18 months to come to court.

- a communicator for the hearing-impaired
- a part-time reader or assistance at work for someone who is blind
- equipment or adaptations to provide help at work
- transport or assistance with adaptations to cars.

Job Centres now have Disability Employment Advisers (DEAs), who can provide help with the Access to Work scheme, the Job Introduction Scheme (a chance to try out a job for an introductory period) and work preparation (such as job trials with an employer). The Disability Information and Advice Line (DIAL) is another good starting point for information about a range of services. There is also the Disability Information Database DissBASE, which is used by about 170 providers of disability information in the UK. You can telephone DissBASE and ask them to make an enquiry free of charge. The database contains information on over 4,000 national and regional organisations and services related to disability. It is also often useful to consult specialist groups who deal in particular disabilities, such as MS, as they may well have disability-specific relevant information.

> **"Access to work" cuts Lisa's risk of RSI**
>
> Lisa Lisney is an administration assistant with Telford-based computer training company Brain Train. Lisa was born without a left hand and forearm but used a standard keyboard and mouse and worked from home providing word processing services. Lisa's employer approached the local Disability Employment Adviser who arranged an interview and assessment for Lisa and her employer.
>
> The DEA recommended that Lisa should use a special Maltron one-handed keyboard, a trackerball mouse and an ergonomic flexible arm rest to reduce the risk of RSI. All these items were available from DEA stock, and Lisa was able to obtain the equipment at no cost to herself or her employer.

Access to training

The British government offers training through Training and Enterprise Councils (TECs). These organisations can offer information and support to people with disabilities who are thinking of starting their own business. The Training for Work scheme, which is run through TECs, is aimed at assisting long term unemployed people to improve their skills. Disabled people are exempt from the normal qualifying period, and are given priority for training places on this scheme. You can apply for this scheme through your local Job Centre.

For people who want to learn or update job skills, the Department for Education and Employment offers Career Development Loans which can provide 80% (and in some cases 100%) of training costs for up to two years. Loans are between £200 and £8,000 and the interest is paid by the Department for Education and Employment during training.

There are several schemes for training disabled people in their own homes, including the EDIT scheme (Employment for Disabled people using Information Technology) based in Derbyshire. EDIT provides courses in word processing, spreadsheets, databases and desktop publishing. Courses are provided on an individual basis to suit the learning capabilities and physical limitations of each trainee. The training is conducted in an employer's premises, in a sheltered workplace or in the person's own home. Assessments are made regularly and trainees are expected to reach the NVQ level 2 standard and be awarded certificates. The courses are free. Confusingly, there is another scheme also called EDIT which operates from the University of Wales in Swansea. This is a European project which provides disabled people with the ability to access training telematically – using email and computer conferencing – from their own locations. Tutorials can be arranged through videoconferencing. The courses are free to people living in Wales and the Borders, are 40 weeks long, and consist of

Speech bubble: POOR LITTLE BOY - HIS PARENTS ARE TELEWORKERS

Sign: SCHOOL PETS DAY

640 hours of theory and practical work. EDIT is also working to train human resources staff within companies that employ disabled people to assist them in introducing teleworking.

The national charity Outset works to develop technology related employment opportunities for disabled people. Outset is working to create a national network of training centres, and is co-operating with telecottages where appropriate.

Camrox Training, based in Telford, is currently developing a short course for people with disabilities who wish to use teleworking to further their careers, covering use of the Internet, employment opportuntities, hardware and software. However, you will have to raise funding to attend this course yourself...

Another option is to take a distance learning or open learning course. To find out about suitable courses that can be completed in your own time at home, contact your local education authority in the UK, or the National Distance Education Centre in Ireland. Another useful starting point is the *Open Learning Directory*, which lists many courses, some of which are available on floppy disc or CD-ROM, to help you learn while using the computer. The directory is stocked in many libraries. Some distance learning courses are now provided "online" – you obtain and return your exercises by email.

Teleworking networks for the disabled

Abilities Limited

Maiden Newton station in Dorset is the headquarters for Abilities Limited, which numbers among its major clients Excel Logistics, British Gas and P&O. Abilities carries out standard telecottage-type services such as data

Glittering success with Internet jewellery service

Mark Francis-Jones operates a service selling quality, British-made gold jewellery over the Internet. No stranger to self employment, Mark had previously operated 60 vending machines around Shropshire and the surrounding counties despite the limitations of his wheelchair.

Mark regards his wheelchair as the least of the disabilities imposed upon him by a road accident – other problems include pressure sores, dilation of the kidneys and migraines which can cause disturbed vision and vomiting.

Some years ago, Mark was one of the original teleworkers involved Antur Tanat Cain telecottage's contract to transcribe Weights and Measures documents for ICL. After completion of the project, he was at a loose end. He opted for an Open University course, but like a number of distance learning students, found that studying from home left him disillusioned and isolated, so he dropped out after completing one module. The vending machine venture was highly successful but the physical commitment has been huge and hard to handle. "Then I met an old school friend now employed in the jwellery trade, and identified the potential to marry his knowledge of the business with my knowledge of IT". Now, if situations dictate, Mark can operate his part of the business entirely from his bed. And he's on the expansion trail, looking for other teleworkers to earn commission by selling his jewellery.

http://www.francis-marrack.com

processing and accounts, but their specialist services include industrial market research and tachograph analysis. Most of the workers are disabled, and former director Henry Llewellyn comments: "I think that disabled people must form networks to telework successfully. There are two main problems to be overcome. The first is that many disabled people have a higher number of days sick in any given year, and they need to be able to pass on work to others if affected by health problems. The second is that it is very hard to get large firms to deal with individuals – a credible network hub like Abilities is vital." Henry also feels that a network can help those whose disability causes their work to be erratic: "Many organisations can cope with someone who can only manage 60% of the output. The big difficulty is when accuracy falls to 60%, and here you need an organisation that recognises the problems and can use some form of quality system to filter out inaccurate work." Henry also encounters problems with the wide range of software packages that customers use, and that their services must encompass. On benefits, he says: "I strongly advise any disabled person considering teleworking to consult a benefits adviser first – for example, you can't operate a trading business and claim invalidity benefit. It is crucial to take benefits rulings into account before launching into telework training." Henry would like to see funding bodies offering work contracts rather than cash grants.

Network Personnel

Ann McBride of Network Personnel in Northern Ireland is part of an organisation that provides training for 16 disabled people to learn computer skills in their own homes, and which subsequently tries to provide computer-based work for the trainees. Three of Ann's clients are now teleworking from home or at a local centre. She is very aware of the problems that people with disabilities face concerning their benefits when they wish to take up any form of employment, and suggests taking expert advice: "Earnings are deducted from income support, except for the first £15. Claiming the disabled working allowance can often mean that disabled people who work are no better off." But Ann believes teleworking opportunities are out there, and it is a matter of finding a niche in the market place both locally and further afield.

Ability Enterprises (Ireland)

Anne Dalkey (not her real name) suffered a car accident, and was left with little use of one hand and arm as well as problems with concentration. Previously Anne had worked as a bilingual executive secretary and personal assistant, and ran her own business supplying word processing services and temporary secretaries. One of Anne's customers, a pharmaceutical company, was extremely supportive and continued to send her secretarial work when she was well enough to start working from home, including correspondence, telephone dictation and production of bulk mailings. Anne also got help from the Irish organisation Ability (no relation to the Dorset-based Abilities), which keeps a register of disabled people who have teleworking skills. Anne has taken on several typing jobs for United Biscuits through Ability, but found that she could not get help with equipment or software from any organisation. She is critical of state rehabilitation services, which she feels did not assess her properly and sent her on an inappropriate high-level German course intended to train her as a translator. Another training course she was offered would have involved spending six weeks at the other end of the country which was impractical given her disability and personal situation. Instead, Anne borrowed money from her family to update her computer equipment and buy new software and a laser printer, which she is paying off. She has received some work for a Dublin insurance company through the HYPIT project, but technical difficulties with the remote access systems caused frustrating delays.

RNIB

Britain's Royal National Institute for the Blind has opened a telecottage in Darlington. Tom Boyd-Smith of the RNIB points out that 79% of visually impaired people of working age in the UK are unemployed, and says that the telecottage is part of the RNIB's interest in active job creation. He disagrees with Henry Llewellyn concerning sick days for disabled people, citing figures that show on average disabled people take less sick leave than the general population. The RNIB telecottage has two workstations, and a maximum of six are planned, though development has been restricted by a freeze on new job appointments caused by financial constraints. The telecottage has been founded with support from BT, the local TEC and the European Union. The Telecottage Manager is registered blind and uses a screen with enlarged characters and enhanced screen colouring. His computer monitor is on an arm so that he can swing it "to the end of his nose". Other modifications to the standard telecottage equipment include headset telephones, a talking calculator, large print dialling codes and liberal use of thick black felt pens. The telecottage also has a text scanner that can produce large characters on screen, or use a speech synthesiser to read out the scanned text. RNIB is also carrying out market research on opportunities for visually-impaired teleworkers, but recently the project has been held up by funding problems within RNIB.

Outset

Outset is a UK national charity which works to promote technology-based employment and training for disabled people, and is involved in two European funded projects, one to develop teletraining methodologies (ESPOIR), and the other to provide skills modules for people with disabilites to train for teleworking (INNOVA). The INNOVA project is also planned to provide work for teleworkers and will include a European database of employers of teleworkers, as well as of disabled teleworkers. The plan is to create an employment agency for disabled teleworkers.

ADP

The Association of Disabled Professionals focuses on employment, education and training issues relating to disabled people and actively encourages the principle of teleworking. ADP calls on the experience and connections of its members to help other disabled people to meet their employment potential.

Prison service uses teleworking to assist disabled employee

Paul Dixon had the misfortune to develop multiple schlerosis some 18 years ago, but due to the sympathetic nature of his employers, the Prison Service, he has been able to continue in his work until recently. "They were very good about my condition and I received support and various pieces of equipment which made my job easier", Paul recalls. The equipment included two closed circuit television sets – one black and white and one colour – as well as a text reading machine, since Paul is now registered blind. The government's PACT scheme also provided a computer, printer and modem. Four years ago, his condition deteriorated and he began to work from home. Paul had previously worked as a prison governor, but was assisted to become a supervisor for distance learning training, a job which could be carried out from home. He coordinated the training, dealt with any problems arising and attended a monthly meeting. After three years, civil servants are expected to move posts. This was impossible for Paul so he finally took retirement on medical grounds last year.

Employment opportunities

The Department for Education and Employment's employment service is the first port of call for disabled teleworkers. The employment service can assist with the funding of equipment, adaptations and transport. Normally you should call your local job centre and ask to speak to the local PACT (Placement, Assessment and Counselling Team) manager.

Opportunities is a leading national charity working to place disabled people in employment, and staffed by secondees from commerce and industry. The charity maintains a register of disabled people who want to work, and matches these with local employers looking for particular skills. Jobseekers get help in identifying and developing skills, preparing CVs and interview technique.

For those already in work, but coping with a new or increasing disability, the Employers' Forum on Disability is the national employers' organisation dealing with disability and employment. It is non profit-making, and funded by members. It provides good publications, a regular journal, and a range of introductory literature. The Disability Discrimination Act which is currently being implemented will have the following effects:

- it will be against the law for an employer to treat a disabled person less favourably, without good reason, because of their disability. It will also be against the law to refuse to serve someone who is disabled

- it will be against the law to run a service or provide goods or facilities in such a way that it is impossible or unreasonably difficult for a disabled person to use the service or goods.

The Prince's Youth Business Trust (PYBT) assists unemployed people including the disabled aged 18–30 to start their own business. The support comes in the form of loans averaging £2,500, grants of up to £1,500 and test marketing grants of up to £250. Additional support is given through the services of a Business Adviser. To qualify for PYBT funding, you must have failed to achieve funding through other sources. Examples of disabled people helped through the PYBT include graphic designers and disability access consultancy.

Electronic mail support groups

See Chapter 9, *Email and Online Services* for information on how to conduct searches on the Internet to find listservs, websites and newsgroups. CompuServe has several disabilities forums. The Internet has many mailing lists and newsgroups on disability issues. There is a listserv called the Able collaborative development group, run by the UK government's central computer and telecoms agency, which covers disability issues including telework. To subscribe send email to listserv@ccta.gov.uk with the message subscribe [your email address without these brackets] able. Once you are subscribed, send messages for discussion to able@ccta.gov.uk.

Contacts

Ability Enterprises, Ballindyne, Co. Mayo, Ireland Contact: Derek Farrell Tel: +353 94 65054.

Abilities, Station House, Maiden Newton, Dorchester, Dorset DT2 0AE Tel: 01300 321212 Fax: 01300 321270

ADP: Tel: 01924 283253 or Minicom: 01924 270335 Email: assdisprof@aol.com Contact: Sue Maynard Croft.

Camrox Training, Suite 203, Grosvenor House, Central Park, Telford, Shropshire, TF2 9TW Tel: 01952 277077 Fax: 01952 299510 Email: rollinson@msn.com

Central Remedial Clinic, Penny Ansley Building, Vernon Avenue, Clontarf, Dublin 3 Tel: +353 1 332206 Fax: +353 1 335496 Contact: Ger Craddock.

EDIT: University of Wales, Swansea Jean Hough Tel: 01792 295679 Email: 100321.1620

EDIT: Employment for Disabled people using Information Technology, Derbyshire Tel: 01629 826285

National Distance Education Centre, Dublin City University, Dublin 9, Ireland Tel: +353 1 704 5481 Fax: +353 1 704 5494.

Network Personnel, 80–82 Rainy Street, Magherafelt, Co. Derry, Northern Ireland Contact: Ann McBride Tel: 01648 31032 Fax: 01648 31033

Open Learning Directory 1995 published by Butterworth-Heinemann, Jan 1995 ISBN 0750623055

Opportunities for People with Disabilities, 1 Bank Buildings, Prices Street, London EC2R 8EU Tel: 0171 726 4961

RNIB, 224 Great Portland Street, London W1N 6AA Tel: 0171 388 1266. Specialist benefits advisors can be contacted on 0171 388 1266. There is a guid called Access Technology detailing available equipment for blind people and covering braille, large print and speech technology, available from 0181 968 8600

RNID, 105 Gower Street, London WC1E 6AH Tel: 0171 387 8033

The Computability Centre, PO Box 94, Warwick, Warwickshire CV34 5WS Tel: 01926 312847 Fax: 01926 311345

The Employment Service, Head of Disability Services Branch, Level 3, Steel City House, c/o Rockingham House, 123 West Street, Sheffield S1 4ER. Tel: 01742 739190

The **HYPIT** and **EDIT** projects: Toucan, 27 Ardwick Green North, Manchester M12 6FZ Tel: 0161 273 5122 Fax: 0161 273 5122 Email: 100321.1620@compuserve.com. Contact Jean Hough

Outset: contact Jean Wiltshire Tel: 0181 692 7141 Fax: 0181 469 2532

DIAL – Disability Information and Advice Line Tel: 01302 310123 Fax: 01302 310404

DissBASE - the Disability Information Database Tel: 01306 742282

Dolphin Systems co-ordinates the fight to remove VAT from equipment for disabled people. Tel: 01905 754 577 Fax: 01905 754 559

Central Computer and Telecoms Agency (which runs the able CDG email listserv), Rosebery Court, St Andrew's Business Park, Norwich NR7 0HS. Contact Richard West Tel: 01603 704791 Fax: 01603 704817 Email: rwest@ccta.gov.uk

Typetalk textphone services contact RNID Tel: 0151 709 9494 Fax: 0171 709 8119

Disability Discrimination Act: Tel: 0345 622633 for a copy or web: http://www.disability.gov.uk.

Teleworking equipment

A note on prices

Technology changes dramatically, and prices with it. Sample prices are only given here where they are considerably higher or lower than you might expect.

Often the prices stated by equipment manufacturers in advertisements are slightly higher than the 'street prices' which you will actually have to pay. To get an idea of the likely street price, check a number of retailers' advertisements for the same product, and take an average. Remember that quoted prices for office products often don't include VAT.

How and where to buy

Different teleworking businesses require different equipment. When you are deciding what to buy, try to get quotes and advice from more than one source, and talk to other users of similar equipment. It may help to consult your local telecottage. The Consumers' Association magazine *Which?* is helpful for basic facts on computers, mobile phones and cheaper office equipment, and is often available from public libraries.

For PCs, *Personal Computer World, Computer Shopper, Computer Buyer* and *PC Direct* magazines are among the best for comparing advertised prices as well as useful information. Some magazines also provide a 'faxback' service for copies of reviews from back issues – most reviews are 3–4 pages, some as many as 10 pages. For Macs, *MacUser* carries thorough product surveys. All are available nationally in newsagents, and some are kept in libraries. Almost all now also have a web presence, including review articles from past editions, which can be useful. It can be well worthwhile to do some library or web research as most of the magazines regularly review the options for computers, printers, and so on. Use the index to the magazine (usually published annually) to find the last time that they reviewed the item you are interested in. Then look up the back number to find out more detail on the technology issues and product reviews. If the back number is missing, most of the magazines have a service for selling copies of back numbers.

Computers and office equipment are available from:

- independent local retailers, who can give you a personal service but may be relatively expensive;
- high-street chains such as Dixons;
- computer superstores such as PC World and Compustore;
- direct mail order from companies such as Dell, AST and Gateway.

If you buy by mail order, using a credit card may protect you against defective goods or suppliers going into liquidation, although interest charges can make this an expensive method of payment if you don't clear your balance quickly. Some magazines are members of the Mail Order Protection Scheme – look for the MOPS logo – which offers you limited protection against problems with advertisers. Bear in mind that, especially for complex items such as computers, a low purchase cost is no bargain if you are getting poor advice or limited after-sales service. Is on-site repair offered, or will you have to bear the expense of returning the equipment for repair? Is there a guaranteed response time? What is the service option beyond the standard guarantee period (usually 60 or 90 days)? Some computer dealers now offer access to technical support through premium rate telephone lines. This arrangement has the advantage that you only pay for what you use in terms of support, but you need to know that the dealer is technically competent and that you are not wasting expensive telephone time.

Another alternative is to insure your equipment against breakdown. Then if there is a problem you reclaim the cost of having it fixed. Be wary, however, of expensive service contracts where you pay a large sum even if no problems arise. High-tech electronics do not go wrong often and some dealers advertising low prices try to crank up their profits with exorbitant service contracts. You don't have to take one at all.

Also consider whether you should rent equipment or buy; the former is more expensive in total cash terms, but your accountant may decide it will save you more tax, and if money is tight at first it reduces your start-up costs. In essence, if you buy, then you pay upfront and you can only claim a percentage of that cost each year (around a quarter) against tax. If you buy you will probably also need to negotiate a loan with your bank to cover the purchase cost. If you rent or lease, the whole amount can be claimed against tax, and you do not have to stump up large amounts of money upfront. However, there are complexities – at the end of a lease, you don't actually own the equipment though there is usually a method of buying it. Leases do provide a degree of security – usually they can't be withdrawn or curtailed by credit squeezes or changes in economic conditions, and are not repayable on demand like an overdraft. Consult your financial adviser or bank manager to work out the best option for you.

Many equipment purchases have hidden costs. Computer printers require expenditure on toner and paper; mobile phones and portable PCs often require extra sets of batteries to maximise their usefulness; if you're travelling in Europe or North America, you'll need power and telecoms adapters for any portable equipment. These costs are often impossible to assess precisely as your use of the equipment will change over time, but an informed estimate will save you some unpleasant shocks.

Telephony

A telephone is the only essential piece of equipment for a teleworker, and the choice of services is growing fast. First, check with your telephone company whether you are on a digital exchange (almost everyone in the UK and Ireland is), and whether ISDN services are available.

Whether you go for ISDN or not, you will probably want a separate telephone line so that you can easily distinguish business and personal calls and monitor business costs. Business lines are more expensive, but usually guarantee a faster fault-repair service and entitle you to a Yellow Pages entry.

You can also improve the flexibility of your telephone with some low-cost enhancements. Different phone companies offer slightly different services. From BT, for example, Call Waiting alerts you when a caller is trying to get through while you're using the phone; you can switch between calls. Call Diversion redirects incoming calls to any other number, so you can receive them at someone else's premises. Three Way Calling lets you talk to two other numbers simultaneously. Caller Line Identification allows you to see on a display who is calling your number. Call Minder sets up a voice mailbox for you on BT's system. The mailbox works like an answering machine, recording messages when you're out or engaged, and playing them back to you through the phone. None of these services requires any extra equipment other than a standard touchtone telephone handset. Many are even free – all you have to do is ask for them.

Featureline is a BT system that can turn a collection of separate lines at one premises into a switchboard using facilities on the local digital exchange. Ordinary phones located within 200 metres of each other can be used as switchboard extensions, with facilities such as call diversion, call transfer between extensions, ring back when free, ring back when next used, call barring, five way call waiting and three way calling. Call answering can be set up in cyclical hunting to ensure even distribution of calls between a set of lines. Featureline costs £45 for a new line, or £15 to upgrade an existing line, plus rental charges of £49.35 per quarter.

If you are looking at installing any kind of conventional switchboard, beware that the vast majority require professional installation and a pre-connection inspection by your telephone company, and have to be maintained by the installing company. Installation can take up to two days. The fee structure is usually arranged for larger businesses, and can be disadvantageous to small businesses needing only a couple of extensions and a very small switchboard. If you move house and want to take your switchboard with you, you could find that moving it will cost as much as installing a new system.

Computer telephony integration is a new set of tools which use the digital facilities now available for telephones in conjunction with computer databases and other tools to manage information for tasks such as telesales

ISDN (Integrated Services Digital Network)

ISDN lines are more expensive to install and rent than standard telephone lines, but the charges for connection time are the same and ISDN is about seven times faster – so it can prove more cost effective if you plan to send very large quantities of computer data. For example, a computer file one megabyte in size can be transferred in two minutes over ISDN, against 13 minutes over standard PSTN lines using 28.8K speed modems. Fax pages are similarly faster, and ISDN is also essential for videoconferencing. ISDN allows simultaneous use of a single connection for data, text, voice and image (up to six different devices can use one ISDN line), but for the teleworker who is mainly using the telephone for ordinary conversations and does not send many faxes or emails, ISDN may well be overkill. Remember that the person you are communicating with also has to have ISDN to make it useful – and not everyone uses this technology yet.

The fees for ISDN connection only supply you with a box on the wall. You still need to buy a terminal adapter or TA. For about £300 you can get a digital phone with an integral TA. Then you need a digital modem... about another £500... and for a small extra sum you can get multiple subscriber numbering, which provides you with a block of numbers you can assign to the devices attached to your TA, including faxes (yes, you also need a special Group 4 digital fax and so does the person at the other end), spare voice lines, videoconferencing and so on.

ISDN is being used increasingly for connecting remote workers to office LANS cost-effectively. A technique known as spoofing allows both the local and remote computers to automatically disconnect during idle moments, saving call charges. When activity on either side requires the re-establishment of the connection this is easily done in a way which is transparent to the user – to the user it appears the machines are constantly connected. Your computer won't necessarily "plug in" to ISDN effectively without a suitable card or TA, and often the speed of systems is limited by your computer's serial port, not by the ISDN capability.

There are also pitfalls with incompatibility between some British and European ISDN systems, and there can be probems with transferring files from one kind of computer to another, such as Mac to PC, using different ISDN software packages.

Pricewise, there are two BT ISDN services. ISDN 2 is intended for small businesses and ISDN 30 is for larger businesses. Both services have mind-blowingly complex charging systems. Roughly, ISDN 2 costs £200 for connection and £134 in quarterly rental with an annual free calls allowance of £105. Each of the two ISDN 2 lines can carry almost seven times as much information as an ordinary phone line. ISDN 30 provides 15 lines with 2mbit/sec capacity on each line – about 200 times as much as a standard phone line. In Ireland, ISDN 2 is called Basic Access and costs £348 for connection plus £29 monthly rental. ISDN 30 is called Primary Access and costs £3480 to connect with a monthly rental of £290.

and telemarketing. Until recently these functions were only available via expensive call centre switchboards and mainframes, but a number of products have recently come on to the market. One is Callbox 200, suitable for an individual teleworker. Callbox will dial numbers stored in a database, or read the caller line identification (CLI) of an incoming caller and pop up associated information about the caller from a database. The Telephone Expense Management System (TEMS) from Utility Solutions provides a solution for logging and billing all calls made by a teleworker who does not have a separate line for work – each call is prefixed by a three-figure code, and consequently a detailed log of numbers and durations can then be printed out for the client.

For directory services, it is worth knowing that you can get the entire UK business subscriber phone catalogue in database format on CD-ROM for a mere £40 from Thomson Directories (01252 555555).

Conferencing

Teleconferencing (also known as audioconferencing) allows you to hold full-scale meetings over the phone. Although large numbers of participants (over 15) can be difficult to handle in practical terms, the technology will support many more. If some only need to listen in without talking, you can have an audience of hundreds on a single call. Telephone companies and specialist teleconferencing firms will set these calls up for you on a one-off basis – the technological bells and whistles are at their end, and participants can use any normal phone.

There are two flavours of audioconference – dial-in and dial-out. For dial-in conferencing, the conference participants dial a special telephone number and are greeted by a receptionist who checks their identity before linking them to the conference. For dial-out conferencing, an operator dials each of the participants and links them together. Dial-out conferences are more expensive for the organiser (you) but free for the other participants. Some telecottages can help to set up teleconferences for you.

Videoconferencing – using video images of participants as well as their voices – is voguish but expensive, although the growth of PC-based videoconferencing systems is making this technology more accessible and more widely used. PC-based systems are replacing expensive dedicated videoconferencing hardware for basic one-to-one applications. PC-based videoconferencing uses a small camera on the top of each participant's PC and displays video images on the screen; the PCs are usually connected by ISDN lines. PC-based videoconferencing systems are available for less than £1000 plus VAT. Older videophones are stand-alone telephone units with a video attachment, and also suitable for one-to-one videoconferencing.

Room or group videoconferencing systems are much more expensive, and best used where there are several people in each location. They can be used to link up international meetings, for example, capturing each meeting table on video. For simple presentations, one way videoconferencing allows an audience to see a speaker, but not vice-versa. If you are involved in a group or one-to-many videoconferences, experts advise having a separate audio (sound only) link as a backup, in case technical gremlins cause problems with the video transmission. Telephone companies and conferencing firms can provide bureau-based facilities for videoconferencing, as can some telecottages; purchasing the equipment can cost several thousand pounds and it is not yet in widespread use for individual teleworkers.

Other technologies for electronic 'meetings' include electronic whiteboards which let participants in different locations work together on a document, with changes or additions made by one participant visible to all, so the group can quickly share and develop ideas. Electronic whiteboards can be used in conjunction with telephone conferencing or videoconferencing.

Portables, mobiles and pagers

Many teleworkers use radio or 'roaming' cordless telephones. Connected to ordinary lines, these portable handsets allow the user to roam around within about 300 metres of the base station. Roaming phones allow the telephone to be answered speedily even when you are not sitting at your desk. Roaming headset phones to free your hands for keyboard work or to reach down to that awkward file are also now available, such as the GN Netcom DECT headset phone, though they are expensive (over £400).

Mobile telephones can be used anywhere there is signal available (although coverage in some rural and mountainous areas is still not great; if you live in an isolated place, do ask to borrow a phone and check the signal before buying). GSM (digital) phones can be used in a number of different countries, while the old-fashioned analogue phones can be extremely cost effective if you don't travel abroad very often. However, the ubiquity and low cost of the phones themselves, which are sometimes even free when you pay for connection, disguise the fact that for everyday communications purposes they remain pricey compared with standard fixed phones. Call charges for mobile phones have fallen and will continue to fall. PCS, an alternative digital service available in some cities, is typically priced cheaper than GSM. The mobile operators Orange and One2One both use the PCS system.

Most major mobile phone services offer a choice of connection or 'airtime' contracts, ranging from a low basic charge with high charges for each individual call, to a high standing charge offset by lower call rates. This is one area too complex and fast moving for detailed coverage in a book, but it pays to be more than usually suspicious of advertising. Try to imagine in advance how many hours per month you'll typically be using a mobile, and calculate costs of the different contracts on this basis.

Mobile batteries need recharging. This is easily done from the mains, but if you rely on a wireless modem and may spend long periods away from a

Videoconferencing

Paddy Moindrot of Telecottages Wales has wide experience of the use of videoconferencing systems. Here he describes a typical PictureTel PCS100 system: "I've used this system several times for remote training, product development and demonstration to a variety of audiences. It runs under Windows 3.1, requires an ISA or EISA bus on a 386 or 486 CPU, about 8 Mb of RAM and two free full length slots in the computer. It has an 'address book' which is badly needed – many videoconference facilities have at least two numbers so easy addressing is essential. It's H.320 compliant, the Euro-ISDN standard. The camera is a separate unit, with hinge and swivel for adjustment, and a privacy shutter, since the autoanswer facility means a caller can get an instant view of your office clutter or state of undress. The same camera can be used to film documents. Standard use of the system gives a sizeable screen from the remote camera, a small shot of what you look like, and a 'chalkboard' screen which can be used with a range of tools for sharing hand-drawn graphic information. These only work with other PictureTel systems. There's a separate conference phoneset with a loudspeaker or handset, and a headset phone is an optional extra."

A new development which could prove interesting is video email over the Internet, using features available on the latest web browsers and multimedia PCs. Suitable digitising cameras which will record a short video message directly into your computer are now available for around £200. The video "window" on screen has to be kept small to provide acceptable quality, but further developments which may provide basic video telephony via Internet seem likely over the next year.

convenient mains supply, check the cost of spare batteries. Some mobiles can also be powered by an adapter in your car.

Bear in mind, too, that some rural areas get poor reception; if you frequently visit remote valleys, a mobile service offering 100% coverage of major cities is of little use. Also think hard before signing service contracts, where the vendors of low-cost mobile phones often boost their profits. And consider whether you really need a mobile. If you spend time in clients' offices, call diversion services offer many of the same advantages at lower cost and with the advantage of a single contact number (answerphone messages giving several alternative numbers will probably just confuse and annoy your client). In the UK, it is also actually illegal to use a phone handset while driving. The magazine *What Mobile and Cellphone* is good for advice.

Recently a new generation of GSM devices which can accept the SMS (short message service) two-way message protocol of up to 160 characters have come on the market. Many delivery companies are using these services in conjunction with GPS (global positioning system) devices to provide the base station with constant updates on the location of vehicles.

However, it can be unwieldy to type in messages on a mobile phone keyboard for one-to-one messaging, which has not taken off to any great extent. Other uses of SMS can be to automatically alert a remote worker when email has arrived in the office, or to cut costs as SMS messaging is considerably cheaper than voice GSM messages. Nokia recently released its 9000 device which provides a complete keyboard inside a mobile phone – the device can send and receive fax and email via the GSM network. Although the device is not cheap (around £300), it looks as though similar devices may replace lugging the laptop around for some mobile workers, despite the tiny keyboards requiring extremely nimble fingers.

If you are moving around a lot but cannot justify the expense of a mobile phone, think about a pager. They are economical and have improved markedly over past years. Pagers store short messages and display them to you on a small screen. Some also offer a voicemail service, so the caller can leave a message which the pager owner receives by dialling into the pager service. Many pager systems do not cost the pager owner anything other than the initial purchase cost – instead, the person calling the pager is charged premium telephone rates – so it can be cost effective for the teleworker, if not for the caller.

Another item to think about if you travel around frequently is a telephone chargecard, offered by most major telephone companies. This can be used both in public cardphones and on any private telephones where you wish the call charge to be made to your own account rather than to that phone. International chargecards are also available though some transfer the bill to your credit-card account rather than your phone bill. Ordinary credit cards can also be used in many British and foreign payphones.

Answering machines

Answering machines can be obtained for less than £50 and every teleworker should have one so that customers can leave a message if you are not available. If possible, buy an answering machine that uses the two-tape system, or holds the outgoing message on a chip. Older (cheaper) single-tape systems are slow because they have to rewind between the outgoing message and the incoming message each time. Some also severely limit the length of message or the number of messages that can be left. One thing to watch out for is answering machines that do not reset themselves in the event of a short power failure. It is infuriating for you and for your customers if a momentary power blip puts the answering machine out of action for a whole day. Remote callback, often using a small bleeper to interrogate the answering machine by phone to see whether messages have been left, is very useful. On some models the same function can be achieved by dialling using a tonephone and entering a password code.

When using an answering machine, it is reassuring to your customers if you leave a daily message stating who you are, when the message was recorded, and when you will next be available, although this does involve more work on your part. If you are away for a long period, it is a good idea to be a little vague about this on the message to avoid arousing the interest of burglars. Some sophisticated machines can be programmed so that the caller can either leave a message, or press a code to be diverted to an alternative number. Similar systems, which amount to personal voicemail systems, can be installed on PCs to answer and redirect calls according to instructions received from the caller by pressing keypad tones. Many people also now take advantage of voicemail systems offered by telephone companies, which act like an answerphone, but store messages on computers at the local telephone exchange, to be picked up by the subscriber dialling in and using a PIN code to access their voicemail box. The major disadvantage of exchange-based voicemail is that there is no little flashing light to tell you that you have a message waiting.

Fax

Fax machines have become as essential as telephones to all businesses, though the increasing use of email and computer-based faxes means more and more fax machines are standing idle. You do not need to have a separate telephone line installed for a fax machine, but if it is likely that you might use the fax extensively a second line should be considered for several reasons:

■ faxes cannot be received while you are talking on the phone. Your telephone usage may expand considerably as you take up teleworking, and both voice and fax callers may not be able to get through if you opt to share a line

■ if you are using Call Waiting, the second call on the line may well be a fax, which can be difficult to handle

■ if you start off with one line and later decide to move the fax on to a separate line, for some time afterwards your customers may be faxing to the voice line causing irritation to both parties and lost business.

However, in case you do decide to stick to one line, many fax machines incorporate automatic line-switching devices which can detect whether an incoming call is fax or voice and act accordingly. Standalone line splitters are also available for older faxes.

Automatic paper feeders and guillotines are standard on faxes now, but consult consumer guides to decide what features you need and how much they will cost. There is a thriving secondhand fax market with the same advantages and pitfalls as any other used product. Some faxes now have preprogrammed cover sheets which save paper and time. Many of the more expensive machines output onto plain paper avoiding the fade and curl problems associated with thermal paper. (If your fax has thermal paper, don't leave the spare roll near a heater or it will blacken. It is possible to buy recycled thermal paper if you are environmentally minded.) Other fax machines can output to your laser printer and so provide plain paper printout.

Fax features to look out for include memories that allow you to feed in a document now but transmit it later (perhaps in the evening for an expensive international call), and polling, which allows your machine to collect messages from other fax machines. It is also possible to set up fax distribution lists, so that the same fax can be transmitted to several numbers without continually posting the piece of paper back into the fax for each number. Most faxes can also act as low quality, low volume photocopiers, although given that fax paper is more expensive than ordinary paper, this is a rather expensive means of doing more than the occasional copy. Remember to allow for the cost of fax paper in your budgets if you expect to receive many faxes.

One feature not to be swayed by is Group 3 compatibility, sometimes touted as a selling point in fax ads. All faxes sold today, and all but the most ancient secondhand models, are Group 3 compatible.

Faxback services

Faxback services are used for a variety of information services: Met Office Weather updates, theatre seat availability, magazine back issue reviews. Faxback involves ringing the information provider on your fax machine's phone, usually over a premium phone line, and following recorded instructions before the information is delivered to your fax machine. The effectiveness of the system relies on the information provider having successfully predicted what information is required and not forcing the user to spend too long going through a series of menus to get a response. If you want to offer a faxback service, it can be rented from a number of providers or provided by buying a PC-based service which also incorporates voicemail, auto-attendant, fax and data features. Contact management software is gradually becoming more complex and moving to provide basic faxback or structure voicemail services from a standard PC, so check out the latest situation and offerings with extra care before purchasing if you need faxback facilities.

Faxing from your PC

You should consider whether a fax card or fax modem would suit you better than a standalone fax. A fax modem is a card that fits into a computer, and allows faxes to be received and sent. Fax cards are of particular value when sending the same message to a group of people, as the computer software can generate a new cover sheet for each recipient. They can also be scheduled to send faxes overnight when call charges are lower, to retry numbers that are engaged, and so on. Programmes such as the Microsoft Outlook Information manager provided with Office 97 integrate calendar, email, contacts databases and fax software into one product, enabling users to easily send a 'fax mailshot' to an entire customer base if required. Fax modems also save time – instead of printing out the page and putting it into

the fax machine, dialling the destination and sending it off, most fax
software is installed as though it were another printer attached to your
computer – you just select the fax modem and click the "print" button to
send it.

Receiving faxes onto a PC is less useful as they can occupy a lot of disk
space and you will often need to print them out anyway, or use OCR
software (see below) to convert them into a text format which you can edit
and incorporate into other documents. Also consider that if you use a fax
card you may need some way of scanning in documents already on paper
(as opposed to those typed into the computer) such as sketch drawings or
maps. This can lead to extra expense.

Computers

Computers change so quickly that it is never the perfect time to buy the
perfect machine, and there are two schools of thought that both claim to
minimise the disadvantages. One is that you should buy the most powerful
computer you can afford as you will always outstrip its capacity during its
lifetime. The other is that if you require your computer to perform relatively
simple tasks, it is not necessary to go for the latest technology, and
secondhand or low specification computers provide a substantial cost
saving. Part of the argument rests on the rapid depreciation of computer
equipment – in accounting terms, a computer which is more than 3 years
old is likely to be worthless. Even when you've only had the machine a
year, and it is still useful to you, in monetary terms its value will have
plummeted. This factor weighs towards the "buy expensive" option – an
expensive computer may still be useful to you after three years, whereas a
cheap computer not only has no financial value but becomes obsolete in
practical terms more quickly because it is old and slow. But on the other
hand, if your resources are limited, you probably have no choice but to go
for the "buy cheap or secondhand" option.

In reality, the easiest way to buy a computer is first to consider the
software you'll need and not the computer itself – the programs with which
you and your PC can actually accomplish something. Decide what task you
want the computer to do, identify the software that does it, and then buy a
suitable computer on which to run that software, at the same time making
sure that it will be easy to add other software, extra memory and other
enhancements to it. This is easy advice to follow if you are using specialist
software such as CAD drafting packages, but if your needs are fairly
general, you will find the major software packages for word processing,
desktop publishing and so on are supported on almost all computers, so
you may still find the choice confusing. Buying firsthand also often means
that you get some quite powerful software bundled in which would cost a
lot to purchase individually.

The good news, though, is that over the past five years different
computer systems have grown so similar that to a large extent choosing on

Year 2000: a guide for the technophobic teleworker

The British Computer Society and the Engineering Council have prepared a layman's guide to the problems likely to arise when the new millennium has its way with computer date chips. The complete guide costs £20, but the main points are:

Macs are already 2000 compliant. Older PCs (pre-1995) may not be. Nearly all versions of DOS and Windows are compliant and will not be affected.

The year 2000 century change is also a leap year, something which only happens every 400 years and which may bamboozle some "2000 compliant" programmes.

Most word processors will cope unless you have written your own non-compliant macros. The same applies to spreadsheets and databases.

To be safe, upgrade all your software to the latest versions during 1999.

You can also try setting the date forward on your computer to see if anything goes wrong but be sure you have a complete backup, and preferably take professional advice before attempting this.

Other equipment which could be affected includes faxes, telephone switch gear, process control and video equipment.

the basis of price, on the basis of a very minor advantage or even because you like the colour or shape of the case is unlikely to lead you to disaster.

The key questions to ask salespeople, or investigate in ads, concern:

■ **the operating system or 'platform'**

This is the software supplied with the computer which manages its basic functions. Most likely, your choice will be between Windows 95 and the Apple Mac OS, though you might encounter Windows NT on a high-powered computer or Windows 3.xx on an older one; or OS/2, which is an IBM offering similar to Windows. The successor of Windows 95 – Windows 98 – should be available from the middle of 1998. Computers which use the Mac OS are usually called Macs for short. Those which use any variety of Windows, OS/2 or the now-outmoded DOS are termed PCs, although confusingly this latter term also applies to all personal computers generically.

The difference between operating systems is a bit like that between regular and diesel fuel – though they do much the same things, they do them in entirely different manners and you can no more use a program written for the Mac OS operating system on a Windows PC than you can run a diesel car on unleaded.

As far as their actual functions go, there is increasingly little to choose between these operating systems. In the past many "newbie" teleworkers

found the easy-to-use Mac OS more straightforward than Windows 95.
Unfortunately Apple has been suffering major loss of market share and
problems with corporate direction recently, leading more and more
computer buyers to opt for Windows rather than Macs, unless they are
focusing on the Mac specialist areas of publishing, multimedia and
education. In general Macs also come in at a slightly higher cost than the
equivalent powered Windows 95 machine.

■ the processor type

The central processing unit (CPU) chip is, to continue the motoring analogy,
the engine of the computer. As with auto engines there's a multitude of
models. If you are buying a Windows PC you want one with a Pentium
processor; if you are buying a Mac, you want one with a PowerPC
processor, and the higher the number (for instance, 604) the better,
generally. Computer magazines give in-depth advice on this complex issue.
The state of the art Intel processor, as this handbook goes to press, is a
266 MHz Pentium II with MMX technology – a 300MHz model is in the
pipeline. Similar PC processors are also available from AMD and Cyrix as
well as Intel.

■ the processor speed

Often ignored, this is as important as the processor type. The processor
speed, measured in megahertz or MHz, is usually quoted alongside the
processor type and here a simple rule applies: the higher the speed, the
faster and more efficient the computer will be. For example, a 266 MHz
Pentium II is considerably better (and more expensive) than a 166 MHz
Pentium, although they are the same type of processor.

■ the RAM or memory

Measured in megabytes (Mb), this along with the processor specification is
the vital determinant of a computer's speed and its capability to run the
latest software. You should not consider a computer with less than 16 Mb of
RAM, and the more the merrier – many PC manufacturers now include
32 Mb of RAM in their standard business products even though this would
have been considered an indulgence 12 months ago.

■ the hard disk size

Again measured in Mb, this dictates how much information you can
permanently store on your computer. Disk space is now a cheap
commodity, and standard business computers are sold with a least a
2 gigabyte hard disk (a gigabyte, abbreviated Gb, is 1,000 Mb). If you
expect mainly to be using word processing software, it is not a particularly
important issue, as plain text takes up little disk space. However, if you are
desktop publishing, you need much more and 500Mb would be a good
baseline to work from. It is straightforward enough to add a larger hard
disk, or additional hard disks or higher-capacity optical disks in the future if
you need them.

Computers are such large investments that it's wise to try before you buy, talk to colleagues, and check that your chosen system will be compatible with clients' equipment when you need to send them disks or files. Often, such real-world experiences will tell you far more about a potential purchase than any number of reviews. In general, three useful rules do stand out:

- Buy for your real needs, not to reach an abstract technological goal;

- At the same time, beware of false economies, such as a cheap computer so slow that you will spend most of your working day waiting for it;

- And if you have the cash, remember that it is usually cheaper to add extra memory or a more capacious hard disk at the time of purchase than later.

The BOON telecottage offers a service to specify, buy and set up computers for teleworkers. According to manager Drew Llewellyn, although teleworkers have to pay for the service, often they find that to do what they want they can buy a substantially cheaper computer than they had originally intended. Because the machine is ready to go from the moment it is plugged in, the time savings also mean that using the service can "save" money over what would have been paid without the advice. BOON's services also usually include relevant task-specific training.

Finally, once you have taken possession of the machine, set aside time to learn about it. Commercial training courses are good for coming to grips with specific software, and it's always advisable to curry favour with computer-knowledgeable friends; nearly all apparent problems can be sorted out that way without a repair bill!

Portable computing

Portables (laptops) are very convenient and can be used anywhere there is space to put them down, but tend to be less powerful than desktops, and more expensive if you want colour. Recharging mobile batteries can become a chore; ask the salesperson how long the batteries will last between recharges, and if you need to use a portable on long trips where you will have no opportunity to recharge, factor in the cost of additional batteries to tide you over. Battery technology and power management software have advanced considerably over the recent past, but even the newest Lithium ion batteries will not last more than a couple of hours on full power.

As with mobile phones, portables are not worth having for their own sake – only if you will genuinely need a computer out of the office. Alternatively, it's worth considering a docking system, which lets you connect a laptop to a full-size keyboard and screen as well as additional devices such as disk drives for working in your office. The portable can then be easily removed, rather like a video casette from a video recorder, for use as a standalone laptop when you're on the road. Although this involves extra cost, it's still cheaper than having separate laptop and desktop computers – and easier, because you don't have to bother transferring data between two machines. It also means that when you're away, there is no computer in your office to attract thieves. For corporate teleworkers, docking stations and PC cards are becoming increasingly popular for "hotdesking" applications where a mobile teleworker wants to "dock" with the office network for a short period. Both 3Com and Intel offer cards which hold both an ethernet connection and a modem, so that in the office, the laptop can be connected using ethernet, and at home via the modem.

Another option worth considering now that the relevant standards (802.11) have been ratified is a wireless LAN. This allows the mobile PC user to return to the office and connect to the network without wires. Don't touch any equipment which does not comply with the standard.

Personal organisers and other pocket-sized electronic information minders remain popular, such as the Psion Series 5, which links to PCs for information exchange. Other well-known brands include the Hewlett-Packard palmtop, the Philips Velo 1 and the US Robotics PalmPilot, which runs a cutdown version of Windows, Microsoft Windows CE.

For those who need to transfer information between laptops, desktops and other computers, you may need software for transferring large amounts of data between machines – the best known offering is Laplink for Windows.

Printers

Buying printers is comparatively simple, though installation is a common headache for first-time buyers (which is where those friends come in). The considerations are the obvious ones, such as paper size, colour versus black-and-white and the number of pages printed per minute.

If you are doing desktop publishing or graphics, you will need a PostScript-compatible laser printer and indeed laser printers are so cheap now that it can be argued no-one should look at anything else. On the other hand, inkjet printers are very economical and provide good print quality, but are usually slower than laser printers. Inkjets are cheaper than lasers, and though slightly more expensive to run, may still work out cheaper over the lifetime of the printer if you do not need to print in large quantities. Dot-matrix printers are very cheap, but noisy, slow and lower in print quality than a good typewriter.

As for colour, if you just want basic coloured graphs, simple pen plotters or colour inkjets will do the trick. The best colour proofs come from dye-sublimation printers which can provide much finer variations in colour intensity but cost considerably more, both to purchase and in consumables. Colour laser printers are also dropping in price and beginning to fall into the affordable price range for those who need good colour proofs. It is now also possible to connect both Macs and PCs to expensive Canon full-colour photocopiers for excellent output. But if you aren't a big user of graphics, consider that for low-to-medium expenditure, you will get a much better black-and-white than colour printer. Is colour essential to you, or could you just use a bureau service occasionally when you need it?

Printers of any kind involve running costs as you need to replace consumables such as paper and toner. Most printer manufacturers quote a typical 'cost per page' of consumables for their models, but unfortunately there is no standard way of measuring this. A full-page sized laser print of a complex logo, for example, uses considerably more toner than a page of double-spaced text.

Consumable costs are most painfully felt with colour printers, which need multiple ink or colour sources as compared with a black-and-white printer's single colour, and may even require special paper. Some replacement cartridges are only sold in packs of the four colours, yet almost all real-life use wears out the black cartridge long before the others. If you are considering a dye-sublimation printer, for example, it is well worth establishing exactly the basis on which 'typical' consumable costs have been worked out; multiplying or dividing these costs to match your anticipated usage of the printer. You could well find that over a period of years the device will cost considerably more than you had expected. On the positive side, it is a joy to have access to a good colour printer when you are working from home, and it substantially increases your presentation standards and image with customers.

Another trend from equipment manufacturers is the addition of extra equipment to the basic printer to create a multi-functional device. For example Hewlett-Packard's OfficeJet combines plain paper printing, faxing, copying and scanning. This allows incoming faxes to be received (up to 24 pages can be buffered) whilst printing.

Scanners

A scanner converts images on paper, including photos and logos, to images on the computer screen which can then be edited, manipulated or inserted into other documentsn. Anyone considering professional level desktop publishing should invest at least in a cheap device; this is useful for 'positional' scans, which give an impression of the finished design, even if the final version is to be done by a bureau using a very expensive, very high quality scanner such as those used by colour magazines. Scanners can be greyscale, meaning that they will only create monochrome images on your PC, even if the original is colour, or they can be colour.

Reasonable colour scanners are now very cheap, starting at around £100. The Umax Astra 600 (a 300 dpi scanner with graphics and OCR software) for example starts at £85 plus VAT. At the other end of the scale, where true colour separation of the scans for four colour printing is required, very few desktop scanners can produce acceptable results – instead the desktop scanner will be used for position scans only.

Scanner resolution is expressed in dots per inch, or dpi. Higher resolutions mean sharper and more accurate reproduction of the scanned image. 300 dpi is acceptable for everyday greyscale use, or 600 dpi for higher quality. Ask about the 'true' or 'optical' resolution of the scanner; many models use a software technique called interpolation to simulate a higher resolution than they actually offer. 300 dpi interpolated to 600 dpi is certainly better than plain 300 dpi, but not as good as true 600 dpi. For colour scanners, the 'bit depth' is also important; the higher this number, the more different shades of colour the scanner will be able to distinguish, giving more accurate reproduction of photographic images. 24-bit colour and 30-bit are common standards. However, higher resolutions and bit depths do produce larger files; if you are planning to do much colour scanning, you will need to invest in optical media (see below), or at least a very large hard disk, to store the scanfiles.

Most desktop scanners are flatbed models: the original is placed on a flat glass surface for scanning, as with a photocopier. These usually cannot handle transparencies unless you buy an extra attachment. Some drum (rotating) scanners (traditionally the preserve of the printing industry, with five-figure price tags to match) are now available in desktop models, but they are still expensive and only justifiable for those involved in professional publishing.

At the bottom end of the market, handheld scanners are fine for small images such as signatures, logos or passport photos, but inadequate for most publishers or designers. Specialist barcode scanners are also available.

Optical character recognition (OCR) software lets you scan printed material, such as a book or typescript, and turns it into text that you can edit in a word processor, by 'recognising' each character. This is useful if you have very large quantities of clearly printed text that you need in an editable form, but OCR is usually more trouble than it's worth for smaller quantities or for badly printed text which the software will find difficult to read. Impressive-sounding claims such as '99% accuracy' disguise the fact that 1% inaccuracy means one in a hundred characters will be wrong – at least one error every 20 words. The time saved on typing may be lost in proofreading the scanned text.

CD-ROM

Many computers sold today have CD-ROM drives built in. These let you access information on CD-ROMs, which use a similar technology to audio CDs to store enormous quantities of data: one CD-ROM holds the equivalent of about 450 floppy disks. Software (especially multimedia software), games and reference works such as encyclopaediae are often sold on CD-ROM. You can also use CD-ROM drives to play audio CDs.

If your PC is not supplied with CD-ROM, you can easily buy an external player for around £80. The key thing to look out for is speed: recent CD-ROM players are 'sixteen-speed', *ie* sixteen times the speed of the first ones, and some new CD-ROM titles will not function properly on slower players. All new drives are compatible with Kodak's PhotoCD standard. The latest in this technology area is the Digital Video Disk, or DVD, which plays conventional CD-ROMs as well as DVDs. DVDs can store and playback, broadcast quality full screen video. The first PCs with DVD drives are just becoming available after a two-year standards and marketing wrangle.

Ordinary players don't let you store your own information on CD-ROM, however. To do that you need a CD-Recordable drive. These have plummeted in price to around £500 – one of the cheapest is the Mitsumi CD-Recordable which provides a 2x reader and a 6x writer for around £225 plus VAT. An 8x reader and 4x writer will cost more, but should still come in at under £500.

Multimedia

To benefit from the latest multimedia productions (hypertext documents containing audio and video clips) on CD-ROM and the Internet, your PC needs a sound card, some sort of speakers and support for motion video. It's possible to add these in after purchase but much easier, if you expect that work or leisure will lead you in this direction, to look at the machines advertised specifically as 'multimedia PCs'. Voice recording facilities, which are particularly advanced on the Apple computers, are sometimes used in business where people are exchanging computer-based documents. You can record a voice message to comment on the document, which is then played back when the recipient opens it on their screen.

Digital cameras

There has been an explosion in the range and quality of digital cameras which are now available. These are cameras which store images electronically, and can later download the "pictures" directly to your computer for storage and use. Costs range from around £200–£600 and the key points to watch out for are the amount of storage space in the camera, the picture formats available (eg colour tiff if you want to use them in printed publications) and the quality of the optics. As this area is changing rapidly, you are advised to check computer magazines for latest reviews.

Optical and tape media

If you have great quantities of data to store – perhaps you are scanning and archiving colour photos, or you need to keep backups of a large database – consider an optical or tape drive. Optical drives, common in the Mac world, store information on cartridges and work much like floppy disks, insofar as you insert the cartridge into the drive and can then save files onto it or open the files that are stored there, but they hold far more information, with some cartridges accepting 1.3 gigabytes of data, or the equivalent of more than 900 floppies. Tape drives are intended for long-term backup, rather than your working files. They can store even more data than optical cartridges –

as much as 8 gigabytes, equivalent to almost 6,000 floppy disks – but putting files on tape and retrieving them off the tape can be slow. They are used for regular data security backups, run overnight when the computer is not in use. You will have to chose between two types of tape drive. Digital audio tape is faster, has greater capacity and is more expensive, while the old style quarter inch cartridge (QIC) tape drives can be picked up for as little as £100.

External hard disks and cartridges

If you don't need the capacity of optical or tape media, you might consider adding a second hard disk to your PC. These can be bought separately and are plugged into the PC as simply as any other device. They range in size from about 1 gigabyte to 4 gigabytes. A further option, useful if you need to transport large files, is a cartridge-based hard disk drive, often referred to as a SyQuest (after a well-known manufacturer). This lets you store data on as many cartridges as you like, simply putting one in the drive when you require it; the easily-portable cartridges commonly store 88 Mb, sometimes more. SyQuests are available for Macs and PCs, but are more commonly used in conjunction with Macs. The new kids on the block in data storage terms are the increasingly popular Iomega removable drives. These are fast, convenient cartridges – the Iomega Jaz drive stores up to 1 Gb on each cartridge, while the smaller Iomega Zip drives use cartridges that look like 3.5 disks but hold 70 times more data – about 100 Mb.

Modems

The explosion of interest in the Internet, and the growing acceptance of electronic mail (email), are making modems a central part of many people's computing activity. Yet modems have a reputation, not entirely undeserved, for being among the most arcane of PC accessories and the toughest to set up. Fortunately, there is an easy way to buy a modem – ignore nearly all the technical specifications. There are only a few points you need to check:

■ internal, external or PC card

Internal modems, usually the cheapest, are installed directly into a slot in the back of your PC. It's a slightly tricky job, but it only needs to be done once. External modems plug into your PC as easily as a printer does. This means that, unlike internal modems, they can be moved independently of the PC, for instance if you need a temporary modem connection on a client's computer; but they do require their own power supply. PC card modems are intended for notebook computers and come on small cards which fit into the PC Card slot; unless there is one of these slots on your PC, a PC Card modem is useless. Also available for the widely-roaming teleworker with laptop are expensive GSM modems, usually in the PC Card format, which use the worldwide GSM mobile telephony system to let you make wireless modem calls from a portable computer – the modem equivalent of a mobile phone.

■ modem speed

Here, the truism that you should buy the fastest you can afford is more than ever true, because a slow modem translates into longer periods spent online and a higher telephone bill. Modem speed is measured in bits per second (bps) or baud, which are not strictly speaking the same thing but usually treated as such. Most modems sold today operate at 28,800 bps (V.34); though 56 K modems are now available. (A 56 K modem is not always twice as speedy as a V.34 modem, because any modem can only receive data as fast as the other end of the connection is sending it, or send it as fast as the other end is prepared to receive. So you will occasionally find even a 56 K modem slowing to a snail's pace of 300 bps or less, particularly on busy World Wide Web sites. In this circumstance the difference in speed rating is, sadly, no help to you, but at other times you will find the faster modem lives up to expectations.)

■ Hayes compatibility and BABT approval

Nearly all modems are marked as Hayes-compatible, which means they will work with communications software that employs the Hayes command set – and that means nearly all available packages. But it's worth double-checking, as a non-Hayes-compatible modem may be difficult to operate with your communications package. In the UK, all devices connected to the phone system must be approved by the BABT, a government board; it's illegal to connect a non-approved device, so check for the green BABT sticker on the modem box. (This is not to say that non-approved devices are not widely used.)

■ software

A modem is no help without the software which lets you control it, dial numbers, and send and receive text and files. At least a rudimentary software package should be sold with the modem (or you may have one already without knowing it; examine the software that was sold with your PC). Many modems let you send and receive faxes; see the section on fax above, but you will need the appropriate software package to do this.

Talking via modem: Internet phones

It's also worth keeping a weather eye on the the development of 'Internet phones'. Using microphones and speakers attached to PCs, these convert the spoken voice into a form which can be carried as data over the Internet, and then reconverted into audible voice at the destination. This lets you carry on an international conversation with acceptable voice quality for no more than the cost of a local phone call to your Internet access provider. Demonstrations are available from companies offering this service; try a World Wide Web search for 'Internet phone'. Opinion is divided on whether Internet telephony will challenge conventional "landline" telephony. Some claim it will sweep all before it; others that it is an aberration that will disappear as telecoms tariffs fall worldwide. The reality is probably somewhere in between. Certainly many of the initial limitations to Internet telephony have been overcome – both callers can now talk at the same time, calls can be made from a conventional handset to an Internet phone and vice versa, and voice quality has improved markedly from the initial "dalek" impressions.

Software

Software is as, or more, important than the computers on which it is used, and it would be impossible to do such a complex subject justice here. There are thousands of software programs (often referred to as applications, or packages) in existence, and most are updated regularly. The British computer press covers software thoroughly, as do the specialised trade papers of particular industries.

However, a quick tour of the generic software categories will help you prepare a shopping list. Beyond these, there are many, many packages developed to fill particular niches such as computer-telephony integration (CTI), which are likely to be well known to you if they are relevant to your particular field of business.

■ **word processors**

Word processors are probably the most widely used category of software, and the one that's essential to nearly every computer user. They allow you to write and edit text on the screen, providing facilities such as search-and-replace (for example, changing all references to 'USSR' to 'CIS' instead); style sheets (an easy way to ensure that all your subheadings, for instance, are in the same typeface and size); a running count of the number of words in a document; headers and footers (automatically placing predefined text at the top or bottom of each page); automatic page numbering and cut-and-paste (an easy way to move large blocks of text from one part of a document to another).

Those are just the common features. Many word processing packages also approach the flexibility of desktop publishing, allowing you to mix text with graphics, divide the printed page into columns, and so on. The best known and most widely used word processing packages are Microsoft Word and Corel WordPerfect.

Related to word processing is text entry via voice dictation systems. Teleworking translator Roger Fletcher, who works on Chinese to English medical translations, recently purchased an IBM VoiceType Dictation system. Although Roger can type at 80 wpm, his work often requires both hands free as the Chinese characters are small and detailed, sometimes needing magnification. Fletcher dictates at between 70 and 100 wpm with a slight gap between words. The system "learns" a particular user's voice. "Some perseverance is required at the beginning, but what takes your breath away is the speed at which the package learns. If you just want the odd letter typed, you're not going to invest in this software. But it's really of benefit to anyone who processes large quantities of text, for example authors and editors, so obviously it will put some WP operators out of work." The prices for this class of software have fallen considerably. Dragon's NaturallySpeaking Personal Edition 1.0 now costs under £500 plus VAT – it is also claimed to be the first voice dictation package which can cope with continuous speech.

■ spreadsheets

Spreadsheets are specialised tools for the large-scale manipulation of numbers, usually, but not necessarily, financial. A spreadsheet document is divided into rows and columns, forming an array or table of 'cells'. In each cell, you can enter a number, or you can define the cell in terms of other cells – for example, the cell 'Profit' could be defined as equal to the cell 'Sales' minus the cell 'Costs'. Then, when you enter a new figure in the cell 'Sales', the number in the cell 'Profit' will change accordingly.

Very complex financial models, covering the operation of a large company, can be set up this way – and by changing a single figure, you can easily predict the effect that a change in one aspect of the company's operations would have on other areas. For example, if paper costs rose by 10% but rent fell by 5%, would your firm be more or less profitable? The best known spreadsheet packages are Lotus and Excel.

■ databases

Databases are used to store data in a structured way. Each database is composed of a large number of records, each record is made up of fields. For example, in a database of customers, one record would represent each customer; the fields might include name, address, credit limit, and so on. Once the information has been typed in or imported from another database you can then sort and analyse the data in many ways: what are the names of customers who spent more than £500 in 1997 and live in Guildford? Using some advanced database features takes great skill, so it's worth checking out comparative reviews to find a package that will meet your needs but does not demand that you learn a complicated programming language. Popular packages include Microsoft Access, Claris Filemaker Pro and Borland Paradox.

"I'm a freelance copy editor working from home. Last year I was working for a major international publisher, and the author's disks turned out to include the virus Stoned. To cure Stoned, the author's computer staff sent me a doctor disk that contained the much more lethal virus Flip, which put my machines out of action for months and cost me over £1,000.

The author's company at first refused compensation. "The responsibility is with the end user." The publisher offered a mean advance against future work of £400. Before I could respond they changed track and dropped me altogether - my chief source of copy-editing income for 15 years. When pressed, they said it wasn't due to the virus but because I'd upset an author three years earlier. There was nothing I could do despite support from my professional association, the Society of Freelance Editors and Proofreaders.

The Computer Crime Unit at Scotland yard says passing on viruses is illegal under the 1990 Computer Misuse Act. They confirmed that Flip came from the author's company disks. I then received £500 compensation. The publisher still paid nothing. I subscribed to Dr Solomon's anti-virus toolkit, and the brilliant Pete Edgeler spent hours on the phone talking me through rescue procedures. I think the author's company, which had professional computer staff, should have helped more. Take my advice – don't put any visiting disks into your machine, wherever they come from." [Name and address withheld].

■ **desktop publishing**

DTP software is used to design pages of type and images, for newsletters, books, brochures, forms and any other kind of printed matter. There is great variation between the cheaper packages intended for home or casual use, and the powerful professional systems that can be used to produce a commercial magazine. Pick the right package for your level of expertise and presentation. Widely used professional packages include Quark Xpress, Adobe Pagemaker and Corel Ventura. Home use packages include Microsoft Publisher and Serif Page Plus.

■ **graphics**

Graphics software is slightly different in that it's usually employed to create or manipulate single images, such as logos, rather than entire publications. Again, there is a vast gap between hobbyist and professional-level software, and knowledge of printing processes is required to get best final results. The best known professional packages are Corel Draw, Adobe Illustrator and Macromedia Freehand. For preparing Internet graphics, the most widely used package is Microsoft Frontpage.

■ **presentations**

Presentation software is often similar to graphics software but is used to create presentations that you can display on your computer. Usually these combine text, graphics and images in a series of 'slides'. Few companies use anything other than Microsoft Powerpoint.

■ contact managers, time and calendar managers

Contact managers are specialised databases used for storing personal contact details, often used in conjunction with PC-based fax software, email or telephone control systems. Time managers, likewise, are databases set up to help you schedule your diary. Advanced time management packages, called project-management tools, can be used to plan and schedule ventures involving many people, such as the organisation of an exhibition.

■ accounting

Accounting packages ask you to type in financial data such as your daily expenditures and sales, and then produce summarised accounts for you, saving you the trouble of sorting out which information should go where and adding it all up. It's a good idea to ask your accountant's advice before buying one of these, as not all such packages produce information in a form that's acceptable to banks and tax authorities. American accounting packages, particularly, follow US norms which sometimes differ dramatically from British practice. The two most widely used by UK small businesses are Quicken (Quickbooks) and Sage.

■ CSCW tools (groupware)

Groupware tools are used to help work teams collaborate over a network or over the internet (see also Chapter 2, *Implementing teleworking*). Groupware facilities can include editing of documents by multiple authors, electronic diaries, email conferencing, access to networked databases and electronic forms (*eg* to record customer contacts). By far the best-known package in this area is Lotus Notes, now owned by IBM, which is used by many major corporations. Microsoft Exchange acts as a message centre for fax and voicemail as well as email, as does the Windows NT package Microsoft Outlook. Novell Groupwise has a substantial following too. All of these packages are now tightly integrated with the Internet – Lotus Domino extends Notes to the Internet, with a five-user starter pack costing around £1,000 plus VAT.

When shopping for software, don't ignore shareware: a class of semi-commercial software which is distributed free, or at nominal cost, but for which you're expected to pay the author a small fee if you use it regularly. Shareware doesn't always have all the bells and whistles of the big commercial packages, but the best shareware certainly beats an indifferent commercial product, and often at a fraction of the cost. You'll often find it on the free disks with computer magazines; recommendations from friends, colleagues and user groups are also worth following up. Before buying software, be absolutely sure that it will run on your computer: that it's written for a compatible model (Mac software won't run on PCs or vice-versa), that you have enough RAM to run it, and that you have a compatible monitor. All the requirements should be printed on the box in which the software is sold.

Computer security

Most fears of computer crime and computer viruses are exaggerated – but then we buckle our seatbelts even though we're unlikely to crash. Here are some security issues you should consider, which are also covered in the Chapter 8, *Staying safe and legal.*

Do you have **virus-screening** software to ensure that the floppy disks you use or receive are virus-free? Such software is available free or at nominal cost from bulletin boards and user groups, and there are well known commercial packages such as Dr Solomon's AntiVirus tools, Symantec's Norton Utilities and utilities from McAfee Associates. Viruses are very rare, but a single occurrence could damage vital data and, if you passed it onto a client via a disk, could cost you your good name.

Do you allow anyone to dial in to your computer by modem? Consider operating a **password/callback** system to prevent unauthorised access. With Internet access becoming commonplace, you are less likely to need to provide dial-in facilities; information can be exchanged relatively safely using the Internet as an intermediary. However, there is a widespread virus which is spread through Word files sent across the Internet, and it is likely that in future hackers will turn their attention to other viruses that can be spread across the Internet.

Are you worried that an employee might set up in **competition** to you? Use password protection systems on your computer or network. Keep a close eye on what is being taken in and out of the office.

Do you keep anything on your computer that you would lock up if it was on paper? Get an **access-control program** which can lock files and directories unless the correct password is given.

If you work at home, do **children** have access to your computer? Access-control software is needed again – it's easy for play to accidentally delete or alter files.

Do you keep **stationery** that could be misused? (For example, you might have a pharmaceutical company's headed paper that could be used to obtain samples of controlled substances.) Keep a check on paper stocks. Lock them up if necessary.

Have you **backup systems** in place in case your computer or network crashes? Institute a regular backup system. Consider storing some of the backups elsewhere in case fire, theft or flood destroys both computers and backups.

Are you at risk from **theft?** Computers, being portable, anonymous and high-value, are favoured targets of thieves. Protect them physically as you would anything else worth thousands of pounds yet so easily pinchable.

Network security

The following information on technical methods of securing computers and data was provided by Teddy Theanne of Annixter Distribution.

The most commonly used security solutions – listed in order from the least to the most secure -- are incoming call ID, callback, PAP, CHAP, dynamic password authentication servers, encryption and perimeter firewalls. Dynamic password authentication systems, used in conjunction with other security methods, provide the highest level of security available.

Restricted access is a first line of defence that keeps unauthorised users from accidentally gaining access to your network. It works by programming into your central site access equipment a list of remote node addresses (PC addresses) that can dial into the network. Incoming calls from an address not on the list are rejected. The advantage is that this protects against accidental access by users dialling an incorrect number. But the disadvantage is that restricted access validates the equipment, not the user – so stolen equipment can be used to gain network access.

Incoming call ID security checks a teleworker's authorised phone number, which is programmed into the central site equipment, against the phone number provided by the telephone company's network switch when an access attempt is initiated. If the numbers match, the user is allowed access to the system. Incoming call ID is a special service provided by the phone company. To use it, your central site access equipment must also support incoming call ID. Incoming Caller ID – also called Calling Line Identification or CLID – is very secure, since defeating it requires tampering with the phone company's central office switch. A drawback is that this service not available in all areas.

With **callback**, a teleworker dialling into a terminal server or remote LAN access server must supply a password or identification number. The server then automatically terminates the connection and calls back the user at a telephone number that has been programmed into the server. This is reliable for verifying a call from a particular site, such as a teleworker's home but it doesn't work for mobile workers calling in from locations such as client sites or hotel rooms. It also adds a delay to the process of establishing a network connection and can be bypassed using call forwarding. Nor does it protect against the unauthorised use of a computer at an authorised location.

Password Authorisation Protocol (PAP) – a simple password protocol that is part of the Internet Engineering Task Force Suite of protocols – transmits a user's name and password across a phone line to a central server for authentication. PAP's password database on the server is encrypted, but PAP does not encrypt the ID number or password as it travels across the network link. The downside is that as the password is transmitted unencrypted, it is very easy to snoop the line and pick up passwords.

When a teleworker dials into a server that uses **Challenge Handshake Authorisation Protocol** (CHAP), the server sends a random challenge (key) that the software in the teleworker's modem, bridge or router uses to encrypt the password and return it to the server. Since CHAP encrypts the password when it travels across the network, snooping is very difficult. This secures against eavesdroppers but since CHAP's password database is in plain text form, as with PAP, it is also vulnerable to snooping.

Dynamic password authentication servers are third-party products that consist of software that runs on workstations and two-factor password generators that produce dynamically-changing passwords. Password generators can be software-based or hardware-based 'tokens' the size of credit cards that teleworkers carry with them. Both kinds of password generators use two-factor authentication, a method that requires the user to provide something known, such as a password or personal identification number and something held: the software password generator or token.

There are two types of two-factor authentication systems: time-based and challenge-response. Time-based authentication systems generate a password every 60 seconds that is valid for only one minute. This means that a user must send the password over the network within that time period in order to gain access to the system.

Challenge-response systems generate a Data Encryption Standard (DES) encrypted password good only for a single use. DES is harder to defeat than other security methods since passwords are dynamic and they are good for travelling workers who are not statically located and may use different computer equipment. A disadvantage, however, is that third-party products may cause compatibility problems in multi-vendor environments unless managed by the RADIUS protocol.

RADIUS (Remote Authentication Dial-In User Service) from Livingston Enterprises Inc., now in the Internet Engineering Task Force standards-definition process, provides management services to authentication servers on a distributed network. RADIUS functions as an information clearing house that stores authentication information about all of a network's users as well as complete user profiles comprised of access restrictions, destination-specific routing, packet filtering and billing information. Used in conjunction with Kerberos, CHAP, NetWare Directory Services or other third-party authentication servers, a single RADIUS database server can administer multiple security systems across complex networks and maintain security profiles for thousands of users.

When users request access to a RADIUS-managed network, their request is passed directly from the remote LAN access server that answers the call to the RADIUS server. The RADIUS server looks up the user and passes the authentication request to the authentication server that contains information about that user. Once the user has been authenticated, the RADIUS server passes the authentication information back to the remote LAN access server, along with user profile information contained in the RADIUS database. The user is then granted access to the network according to the parameters contained in the RADIUS profile.

RADIUS performs two important functions. It simplifies security administration by allowing a central database to manage authentication services for all users on a network, regardless of their location. It also allows remote access products to inter-operate with third-party security systems from different vendors on the same network. In order to take advantage of RADIUS' capabilities, look for password authentication server vendors and central site access equipment vendors that are incorporating support for this emerging standard into their products.

Encryption Methods

Used in conjunction with other security mechanisms, encryption plays a critical role in a network security scheme. Encryption systems in use today consist of two types – private-key encryption and public-key encryption.

With private-key encryption, a single unique key is used to encrypt and decrypt data. Private-key encryption is an effective method for encrypting small amounts of data such as passwords, and transmitting them between a single device such as an integrated remote access server and a large group of users.

Data Encryption Standard (DES), an encryption scheme developed and maintained by the Institute for Computer Science and Technology for the Nation Bureau of Standards, has become the non proprietary standard for private-key encryption.

Public-key encryption uses two different keys for performing encryption. One is a private key that individual users use to encrypt their own messages. The other is a public key that users distribute to the recipients of their message. The public key will only decode messages sent by the user holding the corresponding private key. Public-key encryption is typically implemented in electronic mail systems to protect messages as they are sent over wide area communication links.

Perimeter Firewalls

With internet usage soaring at a rate of around 1.5 million users a month, the number of hackers staging attacks from the Internet is increasing. If your network has links to the Internet or to any remote network it needs firewall protection. Firewalls are the only mechanism that can adequately guard your computing resources against thieves and vandals.

Perimeter firewalls are barricades that you erect at the edge of your company's network to keep intruders from entering. Think of a firewall as a giant door blocking the only entrance to your castle. Friends and foe, alike, must knock on the door to request admittance. When foes knock, the door recognises them as intruders and repels them immediately before they ever set foot inside the castle. But when friends request entry, the door opens and admits them at once. To friends, the door to the castle is invisible.

Most commercial firewall products are stand-alone, or managed component, firewall applications. These systems usually require the following elements:

- Specialised firewall software
- Firewall configuration and management software
- Dedicated hardware to run the applications
- A router to establish a connection to the Internet or other remote network.

The cost of purchasing a firewall solution can amount to as much as £30,000 or more. Because of this high price tag firewalls make deployment throughout the network too expensive for most companies, leaving remote sites vulnerable to hacker attack. Since firewalls are installed behind the router itself, they also leave your router exposed to attacks.

Perimeter Firewall Technologies

There are two types of firewall technologies available toda –; static packet filtering and dynamic firewalls. Static packet filtering and dynamic firewalls can be implemented as either stand-alone devices or integrated into routers or remote access servers.

Static packet filters examine every packet passing through the network interface to see if it meets pre-established requirements about source and destination IP addresses. However, static packet filters do not monitor the 'session-state' – the real time events involved in sending and receiving data during a TCP session.

Because they do not perform session state monitoring, static packet filtering limits your control and potentially places your network at risk. During an FTP session – since static packet filters don't know which port number a remote caller and a FTP server have negotiated for a file transfer – they keep open all the high numbered ports from 1,024 to 65,535. This makes thousands of ports vulnerable to probing attacks from unauthorised users for the duration of the FTP session. If all the ports are open, intruders can break into your network. If all the ports are closed, even authorised users are prevented from entering the network.

Dynamic firewalls are an intelligent, next generation firewall technology that provide a more secure solution than static packet filters. They give more granular control over users entering the network because they use state-of-the-art technology to create dynamic rules and adapt them to changing network traffic in real time. These rules can be modified to accept or reject conditions depending on specifications such as applications, protocols, network addresses, session state or direction. Once a session has been initiated, dynamic firewalls monitor requests to open ports between terminating points. They open only designated ports and keep all others closed. When the session has ended, the ports are immediately closed, eliminating the potential for hackers to infiltrate the network and your company's sensitive data.

AXENT Technologies reckons it simplifies the enterprise-wide security equation by solving more pieces of the security puzzle than any other vendor. The company's OmniGuard product suite provides a framework that consolidates security functions and enables organisations to adhere to security policies that support business goals and objectives. OmniGuard allows organisations to manage information security centrally while providing access control, data confidentiality, user administration, intrusion detection and user authentication across the enterprise, the Internet and intranets. The product line supports 25 platforms including UNIX, Windows NT, Windows 95, Windows 3.x, Netware and mid-range systems.

Other equipment

There are a number of items of non-computer and telecoms equipment that you may need depending on the teleworking services you are offering. If you cannot justify purchasing the equipment outright, consider using it at a telecottage, or a printshop. It is a good idea to try out equipment at these facilities so that you can work out what you require before you purchase.

Photocopiers

The best advice here is to consult consumer guides on the machine best suited to your needs. Estimate how many copies you make a month and check out maintenance contracts carefully. If you are entering into a service agreement, check what breakdown guarantees are being given and how quickly your photocopier will be returned to working order. Bear in mind that in the computer age, fewer photocopies are needed. The new buzz word is mopying – multiple original copying – using sophisticated laser printers. You may alternatively be better off using a local photocopying bureau. However, there are some bargains to be had on the secondhand market because many older photocopiers are physically bulky despite their good quality and so are being replaced. Look into charge cards if you are running a photocopying bureau service. You sell a prepaid card to the customer which entitles them to a number of copies. There are now a number of peripherals which combine fax, scanning, printing and photocopying such as the HP OfficeJet, and colour photocopiers have come down substantially in price recently.

Tape recorders

Tape recorders fulfil several purposes. Pocket memo machines can be used for recording thoughts or verbal 'notes' when you're away from the office, perhaps for transcribing later by an audio typist. Telephone recording devices are often used by journalists to record phone interviews and can be useful to others; even where a recording is not needed as a legal precaution, preserving a complicated, technical conversation this way can be more reliable than using hastily scrawled notes. Small acoustic devices which connect a handset to an ordinary tape recorder cost a few pounds from specialist electronics shops, though they are not high-fidelity.

Be aware that the legal position surrounding telephone recording is complex; generally, attaching a device to the innards of the telephone (as opposed to an acoustic microphone affixed to the outside) is not allowed, but ask the phone company if you are in any doubt.

Transcribing machines are vital for audio-typing services. There are three main tape sizes, and each has different transcribers, so be sure that you know what size tapes you will be sent and that you have the correct transcriber size. The sizes are: C-size standard audio cassettes, Philips minicassettes and Dictaphone minicassettes. Transcribers usually have a pedal which controls the tape, and headphones, although if you are working alone it is great to be able to switch the transcriber on to its loudspeaker and dispense with those infuriating headphones.

Postal equipment and services

If you expect to send a large volume of mail, consider getting a franking machine which can also be used to enhance your corporate image with a pre-printed logo. Post offices will also frank bulk mailings for you by prior arrangement, without the need for investing in a franking machine, and can give you details of Freepost services (which only cost you if the reply is used) to increase reply rates to your mailings.

Other useful services include:

- **Special Delivery and Registered Post** (Mon–Fri) guarantees delivery by 12.30 pm next working day to "virtually anywhere in the UK". A signature is required for both and each offers an enquiry line to check on whether delivery has been achieved. The main difference is the level of compensation offered in the event of loss; Special Delivery offers compensation of up to £50; Registered Post up to £500. Special Delivery costs £3.20 for the first 100g or £3.50 for up to 500g. Registered Post costs £3.50 for the first 100g and £3.80 for up to 500g. Up to £2,200 can be insured for with registered post costing £4.85 for up to 500g.

- **Recorded Delivery** is for when you simply want proof of delivery. A signature msut be taken from the delivery address. Items are not tracked by an enquiry line. The service costs 60p in addition to normal posting, and the signed receipt can be requested by asking for Advice of Delivery when posting, for an additional 33p.

- **Swiftair** provides fast express airmail to overseas destinations. The service costs £2.70 on top of normal airmail postage, but the delivery times cannot be guaranteed. On average they are:
  Germany 2.3 days
  Ireland 2.6 days
  Belgium 2.3 days
  US 5.1 days
  NZ 5.5 days

- **Parcelforce and Parcelforce Datapost** provide deliveries for larger packages where cost depends on the speed of delivery required. For a

10 kg package, delivery by 10 am next working day using Parcelforce Datapost costs £21.70, but for delivery within 48 hours (Parcelforce 48), you only pay £9.80 for the same package.

Whichever service you are selecting, check with your local post office about cut-off times. Often services such as Datapost are collected earlier – say 4.30 pm – than normal last collection times.

Binding and print-finishing equipment

If you think you will be preparing reports and prospectuses and manuals, look into binding equipment such as guillotines, large staplers, large hole-punchers, comb binders, and laminators, which provide a protective plastic covering for covers and certificates.

Fittings and furniture

You can be almost certain that you will run out of electric sockets by the time you have equipped your home office. It is safer and more effective to have the home office rewired to provide extra sockets. If this is not possible, buy proper 4-way multisockets, available at any hardware or DIY shop. Do not use "towers" of 2-way adaptors plugged together and powered from one socket. This is a serious fire risk.

If you can afford it, have a surge-suppressed socket fitted for the computer to prevent the computer crashing in the event of fluctuations in the mains electricity, or voltage spikes caused by lightning.

Don't neglect the mundane – do you have suitable desks, and chairs? You will need a proper typist's chair if you are going to sit for long hours at the computer. Some people find kneeling chairs great for back pain. Have you got filing cabinets? Drawers and shelves? Can you reach everything easily? People in information-oriented jobs, such as editors and market researchers, usually find they run out of space for papers and reference materials.

Make sure that the office lighting is good, and that you have your eyes tested if you are not used to working with computers. Computers can produce considerable heat in a small room. Do you need fans or air conditioning?

Try to avoid pets near computers – pet hair does not agree with disk drives, and air intakes for fans can also become clogged with fur. Think about security. If everyone outside can see your expensive computer equipment, do you need to do something about preventing vandals and burglars?

Smoke alarms are always a good idea, especially if you are a smoker. A fire extinguisher may be required by local regulations in some business premises, as may a basic first-aid kit. Water and foam extinguishers are suitable for different fire risks; the fire safety office at your local fire station will be happy to advise. In larger premises, or if you store many valuable paper documents, a sprinkler system could be considered. All these investments, particularly fire extinguishers, need to be regularly checked and regulations or insurers may require you to have them checked by an outside service firm.

Contacts

BT Featureline 0800 400 400

BT telephone sales and services information 152 (Tollfree UK only)

Voice dictation systems IBM VoiceType 01705 492249

Callbox 200 CTI system Contact John Chapman at Singleton Corporation Tel: 01600 714478 Fax: 01600 716451.

Telephone directory on CD-ROM. Contact TDS 01345 697630.

For those considering a PC security device, a good starting point is the Loss Prevention Certification Board's list of Approved Fire and Security Products and Services Tel: 0181 236 9600.

Telecoms Solutions (TEMS billing system) Tel: 01527 547720 Fax: 01527 547730 Contact: Peter Billings

Videoconferencing

Picturephone direct (vendors of videoconferencing systems) have pages at http://www.picturephone.com

RSI systems provides its videoconferencing via a separate box attached using a SCSI interface, rather than inserting a card into the computer. http://www.rsisystems.com

A cheap and cheerful system is Connectix QuickCam for about £150. http://www.connectix.com

At http://goliath.wpine.com/cudownload.htm you can find out about the CU-SeeMe software which can be downloaded from the Internet

The Vivo Telework-5 comes recommended by the European TeleConferencing federation. It's H.320 standards compatible and uses an IBM WaveRunner ISDN card, a Logitec video Xcaputre card with microphone and speaker, all for about £1500. Collaborative computing software for use with the system costs about £100, and your computer will need to be something like a Pentium 133MHz or similar for really good results.

Internet phones

Quarterdeck £49.95 plus VAT Tel: 0645 123521 Email: qsupport@qdeck.com

Digiphone http://www.digiphone.co.uk/d2/home.html

Training for teleworkers

As a teleworker, you must take responsibility for your own knowledge and skills. In planning training, focus on the goal of the learning – to make your services more saleable – and feel free to use any method to get the information you need, including online references, exchanges of information with colleagues, bought in technical support services *etc.* At the moment, you don't know enough to enable your business to survive for the next five years. You have to get that knowledge while continuing to run a business. There are gaps in your knowledge, skills and understanding; you may be able to identify some of those gaps now, but others won't become apparent for some time to come. This chapter aims to help you:

- identify gaps in your learning
- plan to plug those gaps
- look forward, manage and anticipate your learning needs.

It is contributed by Brian Goggin of Wordwrights, a virtual company which works to prepare training courses including distance and open learning material.

Who are you?

The amount you need to learn depends to some extent on your role:

- employee in telecottage or telecentre
- employed telecommuter
- self-employed service provider
- manager or employer of others.

If you're an employee, you may be able to depend on your employer to provide all the training you need for your present job. You probably won't have to worry about any gaps in your portfolio of knowledge and skills – at least until the next round of redundancies comes along. You might, however, think it wise to take an active role in managing your own learning and increasing your knowledge and skills; that way, you'll be better prepared for:

- changing demands in your existing job
- promotional opportunities in your current employment
- changing to other employers
- becoming self-employed
- employing others.

Thus the material below should be as important to you as it is to others, but you can choose to be a passive rather than an active learner if you wish.

If you're responsible for managing a business (self-employed, employing others or managing others), you don't really have a choice: you have to learn and keep on learning.

At this stage, you can choose what you want to do with this chapter:

- put it away until you need to think seriously about training
- put it away forever
- skim through it
- work through it.

Working through it means getting a pen and some paper and making some notes; those notes should help you to draw up a realistic training plan. If you want to try that, here's your first assignment:

- Divide your piece of paper into two columns. In the first, write a list of the main work-related things you've learned in the past year. In the second, say where and how you learned each of those things.

Things I have learned	How I learned them

Learning things

Look back on your list of where and how you learned. How much of your learning occurred on formal courses? And how much occurred outside them? Where and how did you learn:

- how to use WinZip?
- how to attach files to your emails?
- how to install an internal modem?
- how to embed CorelDraw graphics in Word 6 files?
- how your best customer likes to receive finished work?
- what your bank manager considers a reasonable overdraft limit?
- how to reduce your tax payments?
- where you can find a cheap, reliable graphic designer?

The point is that you learn a lot outside of formal training or educational courses. So there's no point in confining this discussion to formal training and education – or in getting hung up on formal definitions. For teleworkers, training means learning stuff, irrespective of how you learn it.

Useful knowledge

It's 11.00 pm on Sunday night. You've completed a major job for an important new client whom you're keen to impress. It's due to be on the client's desk at 9.00 am on Monday and, for one reason or another, it's a last minute job. (Of course that never happens to you, but just pretend for the moment.)

You've finished the work; the file is ready for transmission. You dial your Internet service provider... and suddenly your modem starts making funny noises. One hour later, it's still doing the same thing; you've finished the whiskey and you're tempted to use the empty bottle to smash the computer.

At that moment, the clouds roll back and a Voice speaks. It offers you a choice: you can have free enrolment on a two year full-time MBA programme at a leading management college or you can have a five minute conversation with someone who knows how to fix modems. Which do you choose?

You may be tempted to say that MBA-holders don't have last minute problems with faulty modems and that good management would have avoided the difficulty, but an MBA-holder is more likely to be the Voice than the humble mortal struggling with the modem. For many small businesses (teleworking or other), especially those starting up, there's such a huge amount to be learned that you have to ration the time and money allocated to learning.

In general, that means a preference for relevance. It's no doubt very worthy to invest in Developing Human Potential by enrolling (or helping

> **Reclassifying your learning**
>
> One way of reducing the learning load is to reclassify some tasks. For instance, rather than learning the basics of double-entry bookkeeping, you might reclassify the task as "Get and learn accounts software". If you use a cheap package like Quick Books for simple accounts, you won't have to learn much accounting at all. You may have to argue with your accountant (because Quick Books won't really do a trial balance), but you'll have a simpler task and the benefit of Quicken's excellent built-in training.

employees to enrol) on degree courses in Sanskrit, Sociology or Psychology, but you've got to be sure there will be an immediate return to the business. Furthermore, you've got to remember the opportunity cost: if you're funding a BA (Sanskrit), you may not be able to afford to send someone on a course on fixing modems.

There are two further lessons from the modem story. First, qualifications and awards are not, in themselves, important. It's better to go on a non-accredited course that teaches exactly what you want, than to take an NVQ, SVQ or National Certificate that doesn't really meet your needs. Remember, the fact that a course is accredited doesn't necessarily mean that the content is exactly what you want – or that the teaching is any good.

Second, some knowledge is time-bound. Before 11.00 pm on that Sunday night, you didn't need to know about the class of modem problem you encountered; once you'd fixed the problem, you probably wouldn't ever need to know about it again.

Need to know?

There's a lot of knowledge and skills that you might need to have available. Take five or six sheets of paper; start writing down as many things as you can think of – things you don't yet know. You might like to use a separate sheet for whichever of these subject areas is relevant to you:

- your own specialism (accountancy, design, sales consultancy or whatever it is)
- entrepreneurship, business and management
- computers (hardware and software)
- communications technology (modems, Internet, phones, faxes *etc*)
- the management of virtual organisations (including working with others, project teams *etc*).

Add a sheet for any other area you can think of. The first time you try this, you won't be able to think of everything. So keep the sheets somewhere convenient (maybe stick them on the wall) and carry on adding stuff to them. Ask friends, colleagues, customers, employees or contractors for suggestions and ideas.

Look ahead. Think about how your business is going to go; think how your customers' demands will change. What about the technology? What will you have to do to keep up? And how about your competitors? How will you counter their devious plots? Think about the little things. It's all very well knowing how to develop an ongoing corporate finance strategy, but you also need some basic information like:

■ which customers are likely to pay on time

■ which suppliers you can squeeze by delaying payment

■ what new industries (potential clients?) are moving into the area

■ how your customers' purchasing procedures work

■ where you can order cheap stationery by phone for overnight delivery.

That sort of thing isn't usually covered in training courses, so you may not think of it as training. But that's no reason to ignore it: you need to know. Training providers may not be able to help you, but you should still make a deliberate effort to learn these things.

Keep your lists; keep reviewing them, adding to them and crossing things off when you've provided for them.

Delegate some learning

You've categorised your learning needs in one way, by grouping them in five or six subject areas. Now it's time to do a bit more sorting. At this stage, transfer to a separate list anything that you can get other people to know for you. Dr Johnson said:

"Knowledge is of two kinds. We know a subject ourselves, or we know where we can find information upon it."

Rough guide to teleworker training needs

• training in specialisms
A wide variety of skills can be teleworked; many, such as accounting and graphic design, have existing, well-established training routes. Information on courses is normally available from professional bodies.

• training in small business management and entrepreneurship
There are many courses available, both state and commercially run. One of the hardest areas in practice for startup teleworkers seems to be producing viable business ideas; this can be seen in the survival struggles of some of the rural telecottages. Here workshops with business and marketing advisers are probably the best approach – if such an initiative is not available in your area, contact other local teleworkers and approach local development agencies as a group to request help.

• training in basic computer skills
There is substantial provision in existing training structures for computer skills – the problem is finding it. Information about the available courses is often widespread – consult local training bodies, the Yellow Pages, colleges and schools to check provisions in your area. One topic is currently poorly served by existing courses – the area of "housekeeping" and administration of computers, such as correct use of data backup, installation of software and conversion of data from one format to another. Teleworkers often receive data in one software package and then need to convert it to another package, add value and information and perhaps export it back to the client in a third file format. Many of these problems need to be handled as they are encountered and fall into the area of provision of technical support to teleworkers. This area is often avoided on conventional training courses delivered via low-specification educational PC networks because the last thing the average educational computer suite needs is twenty students messing with its internal workings.

• training in communications technology *eg* use of the Internet
Internet training is still generally only available from the commercial sector. An approach which mixes conventional basic "hands-on" training with technical support/mentoring is likely to be most successful. Related to the technical use of communications technology is the area of communications (interpersonal) skills, such as listening techniques. Such skills are best imparted via workshop sessions.

• training in the management of virtual organisations
This need is clearly recognised by those who have been teleworking for a number of years. The subjects that need to be covered include project management, effective use of email, videoconferencing, groupware tools, file transfer, recruitment and management of staff at distant locations and the conduct of face-to-face meetings between teleworking teams. This area can be productively tackled through workshop-based programmes.

Certified courses

Certified courses are those which provide you with a certificate at their conclusion. They are not always the most appropriate for the fast-changing world of the teleworker, but it is always worth considering what is on offer.

RSA, City & Guilds, BTEC (EdExcel)

These bodies award certification for further education vocational courses. RSA has a largely secretarial bias and is well-respected by employers for its insistence on high levels of accuracy. City & Guilds has a wider remit, covering subjects from photography to IT. BTEC (EdExcel) is aimed at 16+ full time education normally to intermediate GNVQ level (one year courses equivalent to GCSE) or advanced GNVQ (two year courses equivalent to A-levels).

NVQs

NVQs are not the same as GNVQs. They are vocational training courses which emphasise on-the-job training, taking into account existing skills plus some classroom and private study. NVQ students normally build up a portfolio of documentary evidence of their skills in order to achieve certification. The TCA has drawn up a Teleworking VQ, which may be developed to become a full NVQ (see separate box).

Degree courses and extramural studies

Degrees in themselves may or not be useful to a teleworker – it depends on the individual's skills and profession, though few would doubt the value of an MBA for any business owner if you have the time, intellect and money to obtain one. Many universities and colleges also offer shorter, non-degree courses. On these courses, students do not become full members of the institution and therefore may not have to meet normally stringent entrance requirements. Extramural courses, like NVQs, often award credits for existing skills. They are also modularised, like NVQs, with modules building towards the final certificate, and can often be "moved" from one college to another if the student needs to move.

Flexible or open learning

This is learning at your own pace, often using a workbook or taskbook. You complete an assignment and hand it in for assessment. Increasingly, such courses also make use of CD-ROM and computer-based training, as well as of the Internet and email.

Commercial courses

These are normally required for software or hardware skills. They are unregulated, but many manufacturers, including Microsoft, Adobe and Hewlett-Packard, run accredited trainer programmes. Use accredited trainers wherever possible.

For instance, how much do you really need to know about taxation? It's important, sure, but (unless you're offering tax-related services to your customers) you can get by with

- a system for ensuring you obey the law
- expert advice on call whenever you need it.

Professional advisers and consultants

You can get the system and the advice from your accountant. Using consultants or professional advisers means paying somebody else to know things for you. This handbook will have shown you many of the areas in which there are things to be known.

Go through your lists and remove (to separate lists) anything you can delegate to professional advisers or consultants. As well as tax and accounting, you might include planning, law, the drawing up of documents and so on.

Obviously you'll have to go through the lists of delegated items and decide what you can afford. But remember, you pay someone else so that you can save your own time. Your accountant may, in five minutes, give you an answer that you'd otherwise spend a day finding. If you have a lot of time on your hands, you may be able to investigate everything for yourself. If you have lucrative work to do, get on with it, and pay other people for professional advice.

Colleagues and staff

In their early days, many self-employed people do have to learn a lot of things themselves, because they can't afford to pay the professionals. Later, if their businesses grow and they take on colleagues or employees, they may feel they should still be omniscient. That's a mistake.

In large organisations, the Chief Executive isn't expected to know everything. A squad of accountants is employed to know about accounting; a squad of designers knows about designing; a squad of cleaners knows about cleaning. The same should apply in small businesses. If you take on a partner or colleague, there's no point in getting someone who knows exactly the same things that you do. Instead, you want someone who knows what you don't know; you want division of the labour of learning.

As well as colleagues or partners, you may have junior employees or contractors. They know things too – things that you don't know. And they have the capacity to learn more. As you'll see below, you don't have to send them on expensive training courses to get them learning. At the very least, they can learn from their everyday experience and from the materials around them, but you'll probably be able to go further. If you are working in a virtual company or network of teleworkers, it may be worth discussing barter arrangements on training costs. For example, Jane wants Sally to improve her HTML authoring skills, but Sally is a part-time worker with young children and no funds available for training. Jane might offer to pay

Cumbrian Genesis aims at training for all

A £42 million pound scheme supported by Cumbria County Council aims to use ISDN, the Internet, an electronic library and videoconferencing techniques to link twelve learning facilities around the county.

The project aims to do away with the need for "chalk and talk" in schools and to replace it with 20 access points where education and information are available at the touch of a button. Support for the project is widespread, including local councils, business and industry, Rotary clubs, trade unions and the WI. The Department of the Environment is to provide £4 million, with a further £15 million bid under consideration by the Millennium commission.

Project director Joe Hendry explains: "The student of the future will no longer need to travel to a particular location. Instead, this new technology will be imported to the student where he or she is located." The plan is for Genesis to cater for 6,000 full-time students and up to 20,000 distance learning students.

for the training course on the understanding that Sally will do free work to the value of half the training course over a period of months. That way, the expense is made manageable for Sally, while Jane gets access to the skill she needs. And Sally has an incentive to put her new knowledge to work.

So go back through your lists again. This time, remove (to separate lists) anything that your colleagues or staff already know or could be encouraged to learn.

Your network

By this stage, your list of things to be learned should be getting shorter. Your next step is to find things that members of your network know and can help you with. In practice, your network is anyone you know. So when your modem breaks down at 11.00 pm on Sunday night, you start thinking who might be able to help:

- that affable person you met at the teleworking conference
- your friendly computer-supplier
- the village nerd
- your sixteen-year-old nephew who knows how to program the video
- the woman you worked with on that project last year; the one who seemed to know everything about modems and the Internet and stuff
- your competitor in the next town
- the wild-eyed nutter in your customer's computer department (the one who said "Call me anytime")
- the supplier's web page… if only the modem was working!

You probably have many more sources of help available to you than most small businesses have. And it's likely that at least some of them will be working on Sunday night. OK, they may not be delighted to hear from you, but they'll probably help.

Of course if you keep ringing people up at 11.00 pm on Sunday night, they're going to get a bit fed up with you. So maybe you should think about an agreement of some kind, formal or informal: you promise to provide expertise on printers in return for help on modems, or a commercial arrangement with a competent computer dealer.

For many teleworkers, such arrangements are both helpful and unthreatening. This week, you and the telecottage in the next village may be competing for a contract; next week they may be employing you; the week after you may be employing them. You do them a favour this week; they reciprocate next week. With shifting alliances and temporary project teams, cooperation is sensible and non-threatening.

So go through your lists again; remove (to separate lists) anything for which you already have a knowledge-sharing arrangement. Then mark anything for which you might be able to set up such an arrangement. Remember, there has to be something in it for the others as well as for you.

When do you need to know it?

Now that you're dealing with a shorter list, you can do some more categorisation. This time, think about when you'll need to know each remaining item on your lists. For instance, you might find some items like these:

What you need to know about	When you need to know it
Using email	Next week
Selling your services to large corporations	Three months' time
Interviewing applicants for jobs	Next month
Fixing modems	In an emergency
Windows NT	Immediately a client asks for it
Ratio analysis	When the end-of-year accounts are ready
Delegating	As soon as possible
Drawing up a web page	Whenever there's time

Your list will no doubt be longer, but you get the general idea. The important thing is to avoid classifying everything as "Immediately" or "Next week". You just can't do it all at once, so don't even try. You've got to categorise your learning needs. Postpone anything that can be postponed: yes, it would be nice to know all about Windows NT, but if your customers don't care, why should you? And rank the rest in order of importance – maybe you should learn how to take on (and train) the new staff member first and then learn about delegating afterwards.

The KITE approach: a pyramid and a circle

At the KITE telecottage in Enniskillen, four years of experience in teleworker training has given Managing Director Sheila McCaffrey a clear idea of how training and telecentre operations work hand in hand.

KITE's original mission was to use a virtuous circle of training, childcare and commercial work to provide employment in rural Co. Fermanagh. The telecottage received funds from the European Social Fund amongst other sources to provide a comprehensive initial training period for 8 teleworkers, including software skills, personal development and business administration. A number of modules were run on site at KITE by the local Fermanagh College. Because most of the teleworkers were women, they could not have attended the rigorous full time course without access to KITE's registered childcare facility. And from the start, Sheila was determined to ensure the KITE workers were trained not just in the skills, but in the practical application of the skills, doing real work for real commercial customers, so that they could understand and reinforce the training they were receiving.

Sheila believes that it takes around two years of full-time training and work experience to train a teleworker with no previous experience, but who had previously received second level education to age 18. The problem is, this is a very long lead-time for a growing business like KITE. Also some of the students will, through natural wastage or discovering teleworking isn't for them, drop out of the training process. So now Sheila is adding in the idea of the training pyramid.

At the bottom of the pyramid, KITE is offering personal development and assertiveness training as a prerequisite to basic computer training in word processing and spreadsheets for around 180 people in the local area, funded through the European Social Fund. From this broad base, she expects about 30 people to move up a level and show sufficient interest and aptitude to go forward to the teleworking VQ qualification. Of these, perhaps 8–10 will reach the top of the pyramid and go on to work at the telecottage or other local hi-tech businesses. Sheila hopes to repeat these activities, constantly feeding in to the bottom of the pyramid, and at the top offering employment to those who "make the grade".

Unfortunately, such a forward-looking approach is difficult for funding authorities to understand, and grants for the pyramid are proving problematic. Sheila emphasises the importance of personal development modules to ensure students understand why they are doing a course and what they want to get out of it, right down to how many hours a week they are prepared to work if they do get a job. Analysing and building up motivation are crucial for the teleworker training to succeed in the long run. Because the KITE students also see and assist with the commercial operation of the telecottage from an early stage, they understand the goal of their training, which gives the KITE course a special hands-on flavour and also ensures that no irrelevant training is given.

You will have to provide for some emergency items. Even if you intend to rely on someone else for expertise on modems, you may need to know some of the basics yourself, just in case there's nobody available on Sunday night.

For some items, you may find it best to prepare now to learn later. You may not need to know, right now, how to fix your modem or how to use Windows 95, but you may be able to prepare so that you can learn the moment the need arises. So, for instance, you might buy some learning materials (see below) about modems or Windows. You then know where you can find information on the subject; you have a resource to hand. When your modem crashes, you can start learning straight away. And, at 11.00 pm on Sunday, it may be easier to find your book than someone to help.

Training needs analysis

By this stage, you've done a training needs analysis, not just for yourself but for your whole organisation (if any). You've set out what you, your colleagues and your staff are going to learn and when they're going to learn it. You've also identified some things that you're not going to learn because you'll rely on other people; in other words, you're going to make good use of your scarce resources of time and money. The next step is to work out how you're going to learn the things you need to know about. Now jot down every learning opportunity you can think of.

Learning opportunities

The phrase 'learning opportunities' is used here because it encourages you to think of a wide range of ways of learning. You may have done your own list by this stage; here are some possibilities to consider.

Experience

Much of your success will depend on your work skills (honed through experience) and your knowledge of your market (gained through experience). It's possible to get better value from experience by managing it. Imagine the scene once more. It's 11.00 pm on Sunday night – but you remember the story... only this time, you want to hit yourself with the bottle, because this is the second time this has happened. You got the problem fixed last time, but how? Nervously you lift the phone and start looking for someone to help. Finally, you get a disgruntled mate who says "Not again! I fixed that for you six months ago."

You, your colleagues and your staff and your contractors need to keep logs, recording significant events and what you learned from them. You might include:

- computer problems and how they were fixed
- stroppy clients and how you dealt with them
- financing problems and how they were overcome

- designers, good and bad, you've worked with
- safety problems, their causes and their cures.

and anything else of interest. Yes, you might be able to remember some of this stuff, but a lot of useful knowledge will be lost, unless you record it on paper, card or computer.

Planned experience

While the last category covered learning from ordinary everyday happenings, planned experience means arranging something from which you (or someone else) can learn. Some examples:

- getting two of your staff to swap jobs for a week so each can learn about the other's work (and thus be better able to provide cover for absences)
- going on a round of visits to potential clients to learn what they want (before going back to sell your services to them)
- trying the beta version of a new software package to see whether it would suit your business
- visiting your competitors to see what you can learn
- assigning someone to a different business in a different location to pick up new ideas.

Those are just a few possibilities; there are lots more. Apart from the planning, the essential point is that you have to extract the learning afterwards. That may mean a debriefing session, a written report or a seminar, but in some way you record whatever (good or bad) has been learned. This sort of activity is very cheap and can be very productive.

Magazines

There is a huge number of magazines, most of them quite cheap, on a vast range of topics. Several of the computer magazines come with demo disks so you can learn about new software; there are also reviews, ads and feature articles.

Treat such magazines as part of your learning provision. Don't just put them in the reception area; read them yourself and circulate them to everybody else. The cost is small (much cheaper than training courses) so you'll be able to keep up with developments with very little trouble.

Books

Books are amongst the cheapest learning resources available, covering practically any subject you care to mention, to any depth you care to mention. They're much easier to read than anything comparably detailed on the World Wide Web.

Go and buy books. Set up a basic library: books on computers, accounting, marketing, employment and so on. Add to your library every year; keep it up to date. If you have a local library, borrow other stuff when you need it. Encourage staff to consult the books. And read them yourself!

Funding the training

Higher education courses of two years or more qualify for grants to cover fees and living expenses for anyone who has not already taken a degree or HND.

Unfortunately, this only applies to full-time study. No grants are available for part-time study. However, a number of telework-related courses are funded through the European Social Fund (see Chapter 14, The *European perspective*). Usually to qualify for these you have to fall into a category of disadvantage (unemployed, women returner, rural dweller). Your local TEC will probably have free courses for anyone starting a small business, regardless of their status.

Vocational courses can qualify for Career Development Loans. These are available from certain banks and are guaranteed by the Department for Education and Employment. They are interest-free during the course itself.

Training and Enterprise Councils can give you information on any funding in your local area, as well as on the range of courses available.

If you are attending adult education or college of further education courses, you will normally receive a discount on fees if you are unemployed, a pensioner or a student.

For self-employed teleworkers, fees paid on training courses can be claimed as a business expense. The situation for employed workers is slightly more complex. According to Mark Dyer of Accountants thru' Internet, the cost of a "qualifying course of vocational training" can be set against taxable income (assuming that you paid for the course, not your employer). Such courses include those which count towards National or Scottish Vocational Qualifications, and it may be possible to obtain basic rate tax relief "at source" by paying a lower amount to the training provider. Higher rate tax relief has to be reclaimed through your tax return. The expenses must be incurred "wholly, exclusively and necessarily" in conjunction with your employment. Generally it is difficult to convince the Inland Revenue that the costs were "necessarily" incurred unless there is a clause in your contract of employment or other contractual arrangement for you to undertake the specified training.

In Ireland, only courses run by certain publicly-funded colleges with a duration of over two years can be claimed by employed teleworkers. The situation for the self-employed is the same as for Britain – training courses can be claimed as a business expense. The state training agency, FÁS, provides a number of free training courses for the registered unemployed.

The TCA Teleworking Vocational Qualification

The Teleworking VQ is certified by City and Guilds, and was developed under the Teleworking for Europe project, a partnership between Staffordshire TEC, Leek College and Staffordshire County Council. It was part-funded by the EU under the Euroform programme, and developed at the Moorlands Telecottage. Like most vocational qualifications, it is competence-based. This means students can supply evidence to show their previous experience proves they are already capable of performing skills required by a particular module, and also that the tutor is free to design modules however they like, as long as the result is that the students can perform the required elements for certification. Students create a portfolio of evidence on their skills and competence.

The VQ gives a good basic grounding in relevant skills. It should be recognised that the VQ, reflecting the fact that teleworking is not in itself a skill or profession, but rather a way of working, is intended to equip the candidate with a platform of competence on which a service or skill can be overlaid. The competence acquired may be put to use in a conventional job, as well as for teleworking. On this basis, the Moorlands Telecottage has claimed that 95% of its trainees get some form of work or placement after completing their course.

For many unemployed or low-skilled returners to the workforce, the VQ offers one of the few opportunities for grant-aided training relevant to telework. It is hoped that the existing qualification will be updated shortly and converted into a National Vocational Qualification (NVQ).

Existing teleworkers may find it interesting to read the course outline and check which units they think they could "pass" with their current knowledge.

Unit 1: Set up and configure computer system
Install hardware ready for use. Reconfigure or upgrade system.
Unit 2: Look after and operate computer system
Ensure equipment is maintained in good working order. Ensure data integrity is maintained. Oversee third party system maintenance. Diagnose and respond to problems.
Unit 3: Control media usage and security
Ensure all data storage media are stored correctly and securely. Control and record use of data storage media.
Unit 4: Telecommunications and data transmission
Process incoming and outgoing telephone calls using a multiline or switchboard system. Transmit and transcribe recorded messages. Transmit and receive copies of documents electronically.
Unit 5: Communicating information
Process incoming and outgoing business telephone calls. Receive and relay oral and written messages. Supply information for a specific purpose. Draft routine business communications.

Unit 6: Data processing
Produce alphanumerical information in typewritten form. Identify and mark errors on scripted material for correction. Update records in a computerised database.

Unit 7: Mail handling
Receive, sort and distribute incoming/internal mail. Prepare for despatch outgoing/internal mail.

Unit 8: Health and safety
Operate safely in the workplace.

Unit 9: Storing and supplying information
Maintain an established filing system. Supply information for a specific purpose.

Unit 10: Information processing
Process records in a database. Process information in spreadsheets. Access and print hard copy reports, summaries and documents.

Unit 11: Text processing
Produce a variety of business documents from handwritten or typewritten drafts.

Unit 12. Self management
Identify personal aspirations and needs. Time management.

Unit 13: Project/team working
Project management. Team working.

Unit 14: Teleworking
Teleworking development

Unit 15: Business development
Compile a profile of personal strengths and weaknesses. Identify and determine business resources. Establish marketing and financial viability. Establish legal entity of a proposed business venture.

Unit 16: Obtain finance for a small business
Develop and produce a business plan for a start-up business. Identify and access sources of finance.

Unit 17: Set up small business
Produce a marketing plan. Produce a sales activity plan. Plan operational running of a small business. Establish commercial and administrative procedures. Set up a financial record keeping system. Establish business relationship network.

Unit 18: Audiotranscription
Produce a variety of business documents from recorded speech.

Unit 19: Shorthand transcription
Produce a variety of business documents from dictated material.

Unit 20: Desktop publishing
Initiate software and create/edit file. Publish documents. Print and distribute job output.

Units 1–17 are mandatory while units 18–20 are optional. However, units 15–17 are optional for the basic teleworker, and units 12–14 are optional for the freelance, or self-employed teleworker.

Libraries

Some libraries are starting to include CD-ROM and other sources of electronic documentation such as WWW sites in their collections. Even if your library does not offer this level of sophistication, talk to your local librarians about your information needs – they may well be able to help you access a wealth of relevant documents. In the UK, well over half of all public libraries provide online searching and CD-ROM facilities.

Seminars and conferences

In this sense, a seminar is a drink after work on Friday. Try to meet people in other businesses. Swap experiences and insights. Learn from them. Build your network. Go to relevant conferences – good ones will reinvigorate you, teach you new things and increase your network of contacts.

Working with others

If you can, try to work on projects with other teleworkers. Every time you do that (no matter who leads the project), you'll learn more. And you'll have more people you can talk to, more networkers you can ring when you have a problem.

Customers

Your customers possess a lot of information. Some of it could help you to gain more business: if you knew their needs better, you could develop products to meet those needs. But there's also information about operational procedures, standards, equipment and so on, information that may not translate immediately into sales but that could help to improve your business. Being in touch with personnel movements – promotions, retirements *etc* within your customer companies can prove vital knowledge.

It's also worth remembering that most people are glad to help if they can

---

Learn while you shop at Gateshead's Learning World

Learning World is a computer training centre located at Gateshead's Metro shopping park which is open for 84 hours a week, over seven days, allowing students to combine shopping and learning. The project is a joint venture between the University of Sunderland and Gateshead College. Courses offered range from introductory to degree level.

Chief executive Pat Robertson explains: "With so many demands on time and the increased emphasis on training and qualifications, we strive to offer a really flexible programme of learning making it easy to integrate learning into life. Our short courses and weekend programmes are perfect for fitting into a busy schedule". Take-up has been high – about 1,000 were expected to sign up in the first year, but over 3,000 have enrolled.

Feedback from the students has been excellent, borne out by a 90% retention rate for coures. Most students go on to take at least three courses. There is also a video link to Newcastle University for careers advice.

– try ringing other organisations that you think may have had a similar problem and asking for advice or information on how they coped.

See what you can learn from your clients. Pick up information during your visits and discussions. Ask about their vendor assessment (before they ask you – see Chapter 10, *Quality for teleworkers* for more information on vendor assessment). Show a willingness to adapt to what you learn and make sure you document your learning.

Daytime courses

Much of the education system is based on ancient technology: put students in one end of a room and a lecturer in the other; get the lecturer to talk to the students. As Adam Smith said in 1776:

"The discipline of colleges and universities is in general contrived, not for the benefit of the students, but for the interest, or more properly speaking, for the ease of the masters".

Despite those wise words, there are still plenty of institutions that force you to attend lectures or training sessions at 9.00 am on wet February mornings, when you'd prefer to be in bed. You probably don't have time for full-time education courses. It's likely, therefore, that any daytime courses you attend will be short training courses. But before you sign up, ask yourself whether there's a better way of covering the course content.

There's no doubt that interpersonal skills and similar topics require work with a trainer and with other participants. Thus, for courses in training skills, management, selling and such topics, a good conventional course is almost essential. But for learning about such subjects as marketing, software and accounting, you may be better off with a distance learning course, perhaps supplemented by some classroom tutorials and telephone support.

It's also worth remembering that the vocational qualification (VQ) approach, although widespread, is controversial within the training sector. On the one hand, courses such as the TCA's teleworking VQ fit well with the British government's funding structure and offer the only training designed for teleworking skills. The modular nature and practical approach of VQs are often much easier to handle for those who do not enjoy conventional courses or who have been out of the jobs market for a period of time. On the other hand other European countries are suspicious of the (N)VQ "competence-based" approach where students collect a portfolio of evidence of their skills. Surveys of British employers also show many feel the (N)VQ approach is limited because it only demonstrates the ability to handle a particular task at a point in time to carry out a task, and not that the trainee has fully understood the background to the task or committed the task to memory. As with all courses, potential trainees should consider course content and teaching quality, as well as how the course will equip them for subsequent work. One of the best ways to find out about a course is to talk to former trainees.

Your time is precious. For taking in basic information, reading is more efficient than listening to a lecture – reading makes better use of your time. Keep classroom time for subjects that really need it. But do give some time for the management and interpersonal subjects; such courses are valuable even if you get nothing more than an opportunity to reflect on your practices.

Evening courses

Traditionally, evening classes have been devoted to adult education and to study for professional qualifications, degrees and other awards. Practical training-type courses in business-related subjects were confined to the daytime. However, several providers now run such courses in the evenings because that's what suits their customers. It's worth checking out what's available in your area: get as many brochures and prospectuses as you can. Start by ringing your local Business Link or TEC (in the UK) or the adult education organiser of your VEC (in Ireland).

For both daytime and evening courses, you can take what's on offer from education and training providers or you can commission your own course. You might be able to get together with others in the same area, draw up a list of things you want to learn on a particular subject and get proposals from several local providers.

Distance learning courses

There is an ever-increasing range of distance learning courses in work-related subjects. You can do anything from a two hour course on Lotus to a full four-year professional accounting qualification or an MBA. The courses may use printed workbooks, audio, video, computer disks or multimedia CD-ROMs.

Scottish Professional Development Award in Teleworking

This qualification is accredited by the Scottish Qualifications Authority and is a competency-based award which has been developed and tested by Aberdeen City Council and the Northern College. Instead of aiming at providing a basic level of competency in a number of IT skills (the TCA VQ approach), this award is aimed at people who already have a marketable skill (such as architects, designers, accountants) and helps them to rethink their business to take advantage of teleworking opportunities.

Employees may be encouraged to work from satellite offices. Prospective teleworkers may need help to promote confidence in their clients in the use of teleworkers. The skills required will vary according to the situation of the individual course delegates. The course developers state: "Issues such as self-management and work flow assessment are just as important to the teleworker as keyboarding or knowledge of email."

There are five core modules to be assessed, plus one option taken from a range of four. The core modules are: 1) Enable use of IT solution 2) Maintain IT solution 3) Communicate electronically using the IT solution 4) Contribute to the effectiveness of the work flow 5) Develop self to improve performance. The four options are: 1) Produce documents using IT solution 2) Produce numerical models using IT solution 3) Produce graphical images using IT solution and 4) Maintain data in a computer system. The modules allow considerable latitude so that the competencies assessed are relevant to individual delegates' needs.

For work-related courses, consult the Open Learning Directory (Butterworth-Heinemann, annual). You should also get the brochures of the Open University and the National Extension College. Several professional, trade, educational and training bodies have their own courses, which may not be in the Directory; contact any bodies relevant to your needs and ask what they offer themselves and what they know about.

A good distance learning course is likely to structure your learning (see below): there may be starting and finishing points, help from tutors, get-togethers (tutorials or seminars) with other learners, assignments to check your learning and other helpful arrangements.

The Internet

Some education and training courses and materials are provided or advertised on the Internet. You can spend many happy days searching for them. In September 1997, a search for "training" using Altavista reported over 855,000 finds; by the time you've searched through that lot, and then checked the quality of what you find, you'll probably be ready for retirement. Happy surfing!

That's not to say that there's no good stuff out there. But you'll have to know in advance that it exists – and be sure you know where it is.

Who's in charge?

The earlier suggestions in this section were about growing and cooking your own stuff; the later ideas were about the table d'hôte menu. But there are other approaches. Unless you're more interested in a qualification than in the content of the learning, there's no reason why you shouldn't pick and mix from several providers and add your home-grown goodies as well.

If you had a lot of time and money you could, for instance, plan a year's learning that included:

- a single module of an evening course on marketing at the local university
- a series of briefings from your customers on their future needs
- a two day training course on time management
- a distance learning module on management from the Open University
- a two week assignment to a telecottage offering services complementary to your own
- a reading programme on project management, finishing up with a short training course on MS Project.

If you're taking learning seriously, you have to be in charge of it yourself. You decide what you need to learn; you arrange to learn precisely what you need, when you need it. You don't have to take a package holiday, just because your local TEC or college offers it; it's better to get what you want, even if it's more expensive, than to end up wasting your time on a cheap, but unsuitable, course on (say) computers or entrepreneurship. Learning is worthwhile if it helps your business. Choose your learning experiences based on their quality (fitness for your purposes) rather than on the availability of qualifications or grants.

Structure

A course may be defined as a structured learning experience. At one level, the difference between (say) reading a textbook and studying a distance learning text is that the text may be better structured: you're shown the map of the whole course; you get an introduction and a summary of each unit (chapter) as well as of the whole module; there are various features along the way that are designed to help you to learn.

These days, the distinction between textbooks and distance learning texts is increasingly blurred. Many modern college textbooks, especially the American ones, look very like distance learning texts and use similar learning features.

A properly-run distance learning course is more than just a text (or other materials). A course provides managed learning: there are events of various types to help you to get started, to tell you what's expected of you, to monitor your progress along the way and to assess your performance at the

Cybertraining – using the Internet for distance learning

A number of providers of distance learning courses have been experimenting with offering courses over the Internet. The Open University offers certain management and computing courses via Internet (mainly through the Open Business School), but points out that costs can be a problem for some students, and states that it has no intention of replacing its existing systems of videos, paper materials and tutorial sessions with Internet delivery to any great extent. The OU courses mainly use Internet gateways to the First Class bulletin board system to support students. There is also the Knowledge Media Initiative (KMI) which is working to provide "webcasts" of lectures to OU students. The webcasts can be played back by students, and act as a focus for discussion with tutors. Jerzy Grzeda of the KMI unit says he feels that training the trainers to use the Internet is one of the biggest issues to be overcome.

The FÁS training centre at Cabra in Dublin and the Irish Management Institute have both used the Internet-based WEST tutorial support system for distance learning provision. This is a basic system where course delegates can email each other using a discussion forum and leave messages for tutors, as well as submitting work. One student found using the system a frustrating experience: "Half the time it did not work, and the tutors did not use it actively. If you are already having trouble with the course content, you have no motivation to log on to the system in the first place – it would be better if the tutors sent messages via ordinary Internet email so that you receive a reminder when you pick up your normal email. Also submitting work was supposed to be done online which did not give you a chance to edit your coursework before sending it. We did not get fast feedback on our coursework which was also a disincentive to complete further modules."

Seamus Fox of Dublin City University points to two further limitations on providing training via Internet for teleworkers. Firstly, most existing distance learning institutions focus on certified courses – these courses provide the institutions with income and they have no remit to provide uncertified courses. Secondly, the cost of supporting a student over the Internet, according to US experiments, is at least one and half times the cost of conventional distance learning support. Until funding and certification issues are resolved, Fox believes that courses are more likely to be developed by commercial IT training providers than by distance learning institutions.

end. Much of the cost of distance learning is in this management rather than in the materials. In general, courses that provide a lot of support to learners will have greater success: a higher proportion of learners will stick with the course and complete it successfully.

If you're choosing a long course, look for one that provides significant support, in many different ways, to help the learners. That applies as much to classroom-based courses (are there tutorials? study-group sessions? individual discussions with lecturers?) as it does to distance learning courses.

If you decide to plan some learning from materials like books, videos, magazines or computer-based packages, you should try to provide yourself with structure and support. Just as you plan your work (and perhaps that of employees or contractors), so you should plan your learning. Set goals, monitor progress, assess performance.

Build in some supports. One of the best forms of support is to work with someone else, in your own organisation or elsewhere. Discuss what you've learned. Share your insights. Question each other – and encourage each other too.

The year as a whole

What's true of individual courses applies to the year's learning as well. This chapter has encouraged you to plan for training as for any other aspect of your work. Your solutions don't have to be costly but, if they're to work, they must be organised.

By all means find out what grants and other support you can get. But don't sign on for an unsuitable course just because it's cheap or it's grant-supported. Instead, get your customers to pay for your training. Every time you bid for a contract, include an element to cover anything new you'll have to learn for that contract — and some extra learning as well. Put that money aside; don't spend it on anything but learning.

Focus on what you need. Nobody knows your business as well as you do; the views and recommendations of course providers are their sales spiels and should be treated as such: not dismissed, but not given too much weight either.

Don't sign up for a course just because there's a qualification attached. It may be useful; it may help you to land your next contract or the one after. However, the content and delivery of the course are more important than the qualification.

Keep managing the learning. Note new needs as you come across them; check and revise your lists of needs every week. Work out how best to meet each need, then arrange to do it. And remember to learn from experience; record what happened to the modem and how you fixed it.

Don't try to learn everything yourself, by yourself. Delegate some learning to professionals and more to your colleagues and your staff. Network with others; learn from them and let them learn from you. Make arrangements so you can call on them in time of need, but make sure you reciprocate.

Above all, keep learning.

Bibliography

Open Learning Directory 1995 published by Butterworth-Heinemann, Jan 1995
ISBN 0750623055

How on earth can a computer help my business? available free from Microsoft
Tel: 0345 002000 (expect a wait before connection)

Contacts and URLs

National Council for Vocational Qualifications: 222 Euston Road, London
NW1 2BZ Tel: 0171 387 9898

Information Technology Industry Training Organisation are keen to help train
teleworkers and has some relevant literature Tel: 0171 580 6677

BTEC: Central House, Upper Woburn Place, London WC1H 0HH Tel: 0171 413 8400
Web: http://www.edexcel.org.uk/btec

Making information work for you (Part of the *Managing in the 90s* series) available
at http://www.bnet.co.uk

University of the Highlands and Islands seeks to provide a "virtual university" for
the remotest areas of Scotland and is receiving £35 million on Millennium funding. Its
degrees are validated by the Open University. http://www.uhi.ac.uk/

The **Stanford Learning Organization** website covering information technologies
and organization learning is at http://www.Ieland.stanford.edu/group/SLOW

http://www.icbl.hw.ac.uk/tet/usability-guide/ is a set of guidelines for producing
easy to use computer-based learning systems produced by Carmel Smith
Email: carmel@icbl.hw.ac.uk.

Prepared for the Future – The British and Technology Motorola survey of
take-up of IT: http://www.mot.com

Learning World Units 9–11, Allison Court, MetroCentre Retail park, Gateshead NE11
9YS Tel: 0191 488 3232 Fax: 0191 488 3111

ISI free briefing leaflets:
– How the Internet can work for you
– How networking can work for you
– How email and fax can work for you
– How videoconferencing can work for you
– How EDI (electronic data interchange) can work for you
– How CD-ROM can work for you
– How mobile communications can work for you
Available from the ISI helpline 0345 152000 http://www.isi.gov.uk

City and Guilds of London Institute 1 Giltspur Street London EC1A 9DD

RSA Examinations Board (IT courses and exams including word processing and
dtp, held in high regard by employers because of the level of accuracy required to
achieve the qualification) Westwood Way, Coventry CV4 8HS Tel: 01203 470033

TCA Teleworking VQ Contact: Sarah McBrine Tel: 01538 386674 Fax: 01538 398445
Email: 100336.3353@compuserve.com

In Ireland, **Arthouse** offers training in multimedia and WWW related skills
Tel: +353 1 605 6800 Email: training@arthouse.ie
WWW: http://www.arthouse.ie/training/

In Britain, **ASLIB**, the association for Information Management, offers a number of

Internet related courses from a lihrary/information management perspective.
Tel: 0171 903 0000 Fax: 0171 703 0011 Email. aslib@aslib.co.uk

Open University's Knowledge Media Institute http://www.kmi.open.ac.uk

Henley Management College http://www.henleymc.ac.uk

The European perspective

What's happening out there?

DGXIII of the European Commission, responsible for telecommunications and research, has estimated that around 2 million Europeans are now teleworking. Europe consumed around 29.7% of world trade in information and communications technology in 1996, amounting to a total market of 315 billion ecus (EITO 1997). However, there are large differences between European take-up of teleworking technologies and those in other regions of the world, as well as vast gaps between take-up in different areas of the Union. The EITO 1997 report gives the following table drawn from its own figures, those of IDC and those of the OECD – we've reordered the figures to rank by PCs per 100 white collar workers:

	IT/GDP %	IT spend per capita ecus	No. of PCs/100 white collar workers
Netherlands	2.71	521	118
Denmark	2.76	698	107
Sweden	2.90	630	106
Germany	2.07	460	99
UK	2.55	370	93
Finland	2.31	426	89
Austria	1.80	396	88
Ireland	1.63	217	85
Belgium/Lux	2.25	453	84
Spain	1.18	131	80
France	2.05	417	76
Italy	1.34	214	72
Greece	0.62	50	61
Portugal	1.10	88	58
EU as a whole	2.01	351	88
Switzerland	2.86	942	132
US	3.67	763	104
Japan	2.40	672	24

The Telework 97 report produced by the Commission points out that the US has some 48 million individuals connected to the "global economy" (one in five of the active population) compared to Europe's 25 million (one in sixteen) while the world figures are 95 million (one in a hundred). This report contrasts two aspects of this global economy related to teleworking:

- the tendency for enterprises to shift work to areas that offer the best combination of labour quality and costs
- the opportunity for individuals to widen the geographic scope of their search for work or employment

and builds on the 1996 Telefutures and 1994 TELDET reports with figures relating the percentage of the labour force teleworking to the uptake of telecommunications technology (see opposite). The report goes on to identify a number of other factors that affect telework development:

- geographic conditions (distances, population densities, urban/rural split)
- demographic factors (age distribution of population, migration, education levels, family and social structures, *etc*)
- telecoms and industrial infrastructures
- size and number of large and smaller companies
- cultural traditions, education systems
- computer literacy
- internet access
- presence of telework associations and of EU-supported telework projects
- initiatives by telecoms and IT companies
- catalyst role by individual key activists
- models for telework stimulation previously used (*eg* telecentres, neighbourhood offices)
- other factors such as unemployment rates and government support
- use of English as a second language and/or the availability of the technology/services in the local language

Interestingly, the report makes no specific mention of gender issues such as the level of female participation in the workforce in different countries, despite the preponderance of female telehomeworkers, or of commuting and traffic problems as a driver towards more teleworking in some regions.

Britain's Department of Trade and Industry carried out a survey covering the way in which different countries were moving towards the Information Society, interviewing 500 UK companies plus 200 each in the US, Japan, France and Germany, alongside a telephone survey of Internet usage. The report found that Germany was the most developed in terms of ownership of hardware and access to infrastructure, ahead even of the US in computer penetration, the use of local area networks (LANs) and mobile phones, but that usage of the technology was less intensive than in the US. The US, in comparison was ahead on ownership of PCs with modems, the use of voicemail, and of websites. Nearly double the number of companies in the US have companies using remote access to computer networks (*ie* logging

Country	Labour force	Teleworkers	% teleworking	Phone lines per 100 inhabitants	% labour force with email	% labour force with B-ISDN
Sweden	3,316,000	125,000	3.77%	66.96	43.68	0.56
Finland	2,400,000	60,000	2.50%	55.00	22.00	–
UK	25,630,000	563,182	2.20%	49.42	17.16	0.96
Ireland	824,000	15,000	1.40%	32.78	16.30	0.14
Netherlands	6,561,000	80,000	1.22%	49.94	26.18	0.09
France	22,021,000	214,143	0.98%	53.60	6.86	4.72
Spain	12,458,000	101,571	0.82%	36.43	4.13	0.21
Portugal	4,509,000	25,107	0.56%	31.13	2.61	–
Luxembourg	165,000	832	0.50%	54.11	11.39	0.19
Belgium	3,770,000	18,044	0.48%	43.66	8.12	0.23
Italy	21,015,000	96,722	0.46%	41.75	6.86	0.07
Greece	3,680,000	16,830	0.46%	27.57	2.10	–
Germany	36,528,000	149,013	0.41%	45.69	12.99	5.05
Denmark	2,584,000	9,800	0.37%	58.88	19.17	0.22
Austria	3,278,000	8,195	0.25%	46.50	9.00	–
Total EU	148,739,000	1,484,439	0.10%			
US	121,600,000	5,518,860	4.54%	57.38		
Canada	14,907,000	521,745	3.5%	57.50		

Souce: Telework 97, Euroepan Commission DGXIII/B
Note that the definitions of 'teleworker' used may vary from country to country and thus make comparisons difficult.

Usage of applications %

Country	Email	EDI	Video conference	Intranet	Website	Remote Access
France	32	20	6	3	9	15
US	56	28	7	13	39	50
UK	52	33	11	11	27	33
Japan	51	29	14	15	28	20
Germany	43	30	8	9	16	26

in from a distance, which in many cases will equate to teleworking) than any other country. US citizens are also more inclined to transact business on the Internet. The DTI report warns of fast growth in Japan with an increase in mobile phone penetration of 130%, in a culture which rapidly assimilates new technologies, and of big increases in Japanese PC and Internet usage. France is characterised by slow uptake of mobile communications, limitations caused by lack of French language content on the Internet and low profile by trade and government departments in supporting IT uptake. Britain leads in email, EDI and videoconferencing, but has a long way to go in relation to its smaller companies. Britain performs well in training – only 35% of employees receive no IT training, compared to 52% in France and 51% in Germany.

The DTI survey asked about the percentage of employees working from home at least one day a month, and found the following: US 34%, UK 24%, Germany 14%, France 9%, Japan 8% – lack of space as well as a collectivist culture are likely to militate against teleworking in Japan.

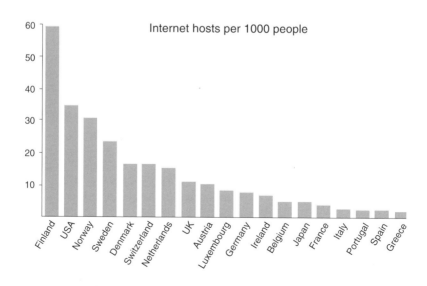

The figures for Internet host computers in different countries also paint an interesting picture. The Nordic countries are ahead in Internet usage, while Germany and France, despite their economic size and strength, are well back in the pack, particularly France, where widespread usage of the Minitel system has restricted Internet growth to date. Of the smaller and less developed countries, Ireland stands out as an intensive Internet user, but

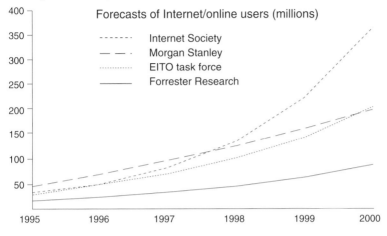

Forecasts of Internet/online users (millions)

- - - - - - Internet Society
— — · Morgan Stanley
· · · · · · · · · · EITO task force
——— Forrester Research

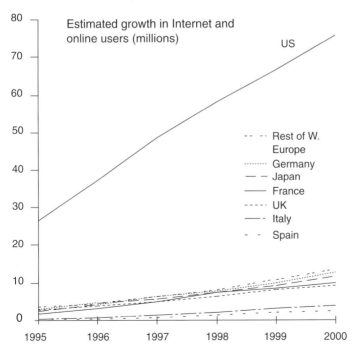

Estimated growth in Internet and online users (millions)

US

- - - - Rest of W. Europe
· · · · · · · · Germany
— — Japan
——— France
- - - - - UK
—— · Italy
- - Spain

this is less surprising when its status as the world's second largest exporter of software products is taken into account. Portugal has a higher Internet penetration than Spain despite its development problems, which may in part be due to its close connections with Portuguese-speaking Brazil, currently leading the world in Internet connection growth. Predictions for further Internet growth vary widely. The EITO 97 report points out that mass market Internet growth in Europe compared to the US is still restricted by higher telephone charges and by the preponderance of the English language in Internet content. However, Internet usage is currently growing faster in Europe than in the US, with the relative proportion of US usage predicted to shrink from 58% in 1995 to 39% in the year 2000 – perhaps not quite as depressing as the graphs seem to indicate. Europe-wide, Dataquest suggests that there are still only 5 million Internet users in Europe in mid-1996, with that figure expected to rise to 40 million by the year 2000.

Social and political initiatives

EU industry commissioner Martin Bangemann has been a key figure in the promotion of teleworking. He placed teleworking at the top of the list of priorities in his Action Plan aimed at greater competitiveness and job creation in 1994. He has also worked hard to achieve liberalisation of Europe's telecommunications laws as early as possible, and in 1997 he announced at the ITU's Telecom Interactive conference that he would:

- push for proper enforcement of the World Trade Organisation telecoms agreement so that telecoms markets will be opened worldwide and telecoms charges thus reduced

- battle against technophobia and computer illiteracy

- publish a Green Paper on the convergence of the telecoms and broadcasting industries

- work towards a European communications and media act covering infrastructure, services, content, intellectual property rights, data protection, digital signatures and harmful content as well as access to content

- consider whether a single European regulatory body to cover this area may be necessary

- work towards an international charter on communications law to establish global interoperability on issues such as digital signatures, but which takes account of diverse cultures, avoiding dominance by a small number of multinational content distributors.

DGV of the European Commission, responsible for social affairs, first published a Green Paper entitled *Living and Working in the Information Society: People First* which was adopted in 1996. The consultation process for this paper was highly polarised between parties who felt telework should evolve naturally, and those who wanted new legislation to protect teleworkers. This was apparent in the consistent editing out of comments from telework practitioners by the rapporteurs in the 1996 Dublin colloquium which kicked off the DGV consultation process. Subsequently a second Green Paper, *A Partnership for a New Organisation of Work* which looks at a wide range of issues relating to changes in work practices has been published. In relation to teleworking, the paper identifies the following issues which it will consult with member states on before developing future policies. These are:

- Contractual status (employed, self-employed teleworking)
- Voluntarism – teleworker's right to return to the company's premises
- Written information on working conditions
- Equality of treatment between onsite workers and teleworkers
- Teleworkers' involvement in information, consultation, participation and negotiation
- Teleworkers' training rights and skills development
- Social security issues
- Data protection issues
- Environmental impact
- Inviolability of home and employer's access to it
- Working time, availability and workload
- Pay systems
- Infrastructure, equipment and expenses
- Teleworkers' involvement in the company's affairs
- Separation of working and living environments
- Health and safety issues – isolation, stress, checking and control
- Social implications of transborder teleworking
- Legal framework applicable to freelance teleworking, including trade union rights

Unfortunately the consultation process is unlikely to reach very many actual teleworkers, being aimed at "public authorities and social partners" and the worry must be that a restrictive directive on teleworking may ensue, where discussion and consultation has been limited to actors and bodies who have little practical knowledge of teleworking. It is noticeable that one of the main practical legal difficulties for teleworkers – planning permission – is not included on the DGV list. A major conference at the beginning of 1998 will discuss all the issues arising from these papers and consultations.

Another Commission document, the communication on *The Social and Labour Market Dimension of the Information Society*, mentions the creation of an adequate framework for telework as a priority. Key actions envisaged include:

- initiate, in the first half of 1998, consultation with the Social Partners on whether and to what extent Community action on the protection of teleworkers is advisable

- continue to cooperate with the European Foundation for the Improvement of Living and Working Conditions to undertake research on the working conditions of teleworkers

- propose to enhance the role of research on technologies supporting telework and related social and employment implications in the 5th Research, Technology and Development (RTD) framework programme

- continue to support awareness-raising activities related to telework

- study how telework can be promoted within the Commission itself.

The Telecommunications and Information directorate, DGXIII is responsible for a number of research programmes directly or indirectly related to teleworking which are covered below. It is also responsible, with DGIII, for the Information Society Activity Centre, which works to raise awareness of the opportunities and impacts of the Information Society. Acitivities include a web site, http://www.ispo.cec.be, a monthly newsletter and electronic forms, a helpdesk and a freephone service. In addition, there is a service to help provide guidance on Commission funding instruments, especially for people who have a good idea but need contacts within the European Commission.

DGXIII also supports an annual European Assembly on New Ways of Working and Telework, and provides some coordination and marketing assistance for European Telework Week activities, although these activities generally don't receive funding from the EU.

Countries and case studies

These sketches have been provided by the national coordinators of the European Telework Development project supported by DGXIII. More detailed information is available in the European Commission's Telework 97 document.

Austria

The majority of companies are still sceptical about the opportunities teleworking can provide. About 19% of companies are "interested" in teleworking but only 2% of employees have already had practical teleworking experience. Vienna hosted the 1996 European Telework Assembly. This year the Austrian Office of Weights and Measures began a project to convert some of their 67 regional offices into public telecentres.

Belgium (and Luxembourg)

During 1995 and 1996, a number of telework trials took place including a satellite office for 90 Belgacom employees in Ghent and a public telecentre in Geel with 15 workplaces. The Belgian Teleworking Association has

Danish digital office trial to expand

The government board for evaluating industrial and workplace injuries undertook a telework trial of a department of 24 employees. This took place at the same time as digitalisation of the department, including scanning of all incoming mail and documents, and the installation of a workflow system. The employees were provided with a full home office including ISDN connections. They were able to carry out the whole range of work tasks as though they were in the office. The project was evaluated as a success, providing productivity increases and greater employee and family satisfaction, and is likely to be extended in the future.

about 110 members, mainly corporate and institutional organisations. BTA has a Brussels office, a website and a newsletter. In Luxembourg the post and telecommunications office is offering facilities for telework trials to private enterprises. There is also a training scheme in the Luxembourg area which lasts three months and guarantees a further six months telework for successful students.

Denmark

There has been more media attention than actual practical teleworking experience in Denmark over the past year. The Ministry for Research and IT published a survey suggesting 250,000 Danes could work from home for two or more days per week. The Transport Council suggested 56,000 to 211,000 employees could telecommute 1–2 days a week, and therefore the effect of teleworking on traffic reduction would be marginal. The government recently abolished tax liability on PCs supplied by employers for home use to promote teleworking. Two white collar trade unions have produced booklets of advice for members considering teleworking.

Overall, government policy is that the Information Society must aim to improve social and living conditions.

Finland

Finland has the highest use of mobile phones, and the greatest penetration of Internet hosts in the world. It also has high unemployment (about one sixth of the labour force), and a deregulated telecoms industry. There is

First hotel office: Helsinki 1988

Digital's Helsinki office designed the first flexible office in 1988. A quarter of the floorspace was devoted to relaxation areas such as a sauna, but despite this 40% of space was saved compared to a conventional office. Ideas such as moveable desk units and filing cabinets and reservation of workspaces through a reception unit all began in Helsinki, and have since been refined into the Hotel Office concept by a number of other multinationals.

Telergos attracts lawyers on the move

Telergos runs a network of five regional offices in France and one in north-east England. Local people work as "telesecretaries" for customers mainly located in central Paris. Dictated texts can be downloaded by high speed playback systems over ISDN. They are typed, and returned as computer files for printing by the originator. Many lawyers now use this service on the move between their offices and the courts where documented evidence is all-important.

lively discussion about the need for restructuring the labour market, in which teleworking is an element, but also a natural concern by those in traditional jobs about future insecurity. The government is actively interested in telework, with contributions from the Ministries of Interior, Labour, Environment and Communications as well as Telecom Finland, local authorities and several universities accessible on the Telework Theme Group website http://www.uta.fi/telework.

France

Paradoxically, France has one of the highest levels of research and innovation but also one of the lowest levels of PC penetration in western Europe. At the same time, most French people are familiar with online services through the Minitel videotext service which many have in their homes, and through the widespread use of home banking services. The metropolitan authority of Paris, CATRAL, has been active in promoting telework to assist with traffic congestion in the city. Telecentres and teleports have been set up in Marseilles, Marne la Vallée, Roubaix, Nice and Vercors, near Grenoble. There are a number of call centres such as the SNCF reservations centre. A telework magazine, *Télétravail,* and the French telework association (AFTT at http://www.aftt.net) have both been launched in the past year.

Germany: teleworking saves an overloaded server

Bönders GmbH has 140 employees and 7 branches in Germany and provides intelligent logistics services to companies in the textiles, chemicals and construction sectors.

In 1993, Bönders faced a crisis with its computer server due to the increased uptake of electronic operations – the server was 180% overloaded, causing delays. By introducing teleworking, Bönders was able to cope without installing a new server. Seven teleworkers who lived over 60 km from the office now telework, using times of the day when the server is not overloaded. The teleworkers have shown productivity improvements of 10–15% compared to office workers, and managers are delighted with the results.

Dell Computers: ordered by Internet, made in Limerick

Dell Computers has a major telemarketing centre in Bray, near Dublin, which employes over 400 people providing technical support and sales for the UK and Irish markets. Recently the company launched an international website where customers can buy computers after checking prices and options online, using a "shopping cart" metaphor. Each country has a section on the site in local language giving prices in local currency.

All sales orders received by phone or Internet are transmitted electronicallly to Dell's European manufacturing centre in Limerick, which employs over 1300 people and has assembled over 1 million customised PCs. Worldwide, Dell sells over $2 million a day over the Internet.

The Vercors Connect centre is a flagship project in the district of Plateau de Villars de Lans. In 1996, the district provided a 500 m^2 cabled office block to become the Teléspace Vercors. The building operates as a demonstration centre, a resource centre and an awareness centre. It has achieved 90% occupation bringing together small businesses, independent consultants and large corporations such as Hewlett-Packard and Schneider. Visitors to the centre include schools, groups of retired people and tourists.

Germany

Most of the teleworking projects operating in Germany follow the "alternative telehomeworking" mode of spending part of the week working from home which was pioneered by IBM Deutschland through a works council agreement signed in 1991. Other companies which have followed suit include Siemens, Deutsche Telekom, LVM Insurers, Integrata, Dresdner Bank, GRZ and Allianz. In contrast to Britain and some other countries, telecentres or "telehaus" are not very common. There is a bi-monthly magazine, *teleworx*, and Berlin hosted the European teleworking assembly in 1994. Regional telework initiatives are taking place in Bavaria, Nordrheinland-Westfalia and Schleswig-Holstein. An information society initiative has been launched by the Ministry of Economics.

Greece

Little firm information is yet available and most of those teleworking are either self-employed, or doing so informally. About 2% of the population has mobile phones, and about 40,000 people have Internet access. The Greek telephone operator has the right to continue its monopoly service offerings until 2003, and to date the telephone network is only about 50% digital.

Ireland

A 1995 report, *Telefutures*, estimates that there are about 15,000 people regularly teleworking in Ireland (including self-employed and mobile teleworkers). A few corporate teleworking trials are taking place, operated

Logos: more than words from Modena

Logos was formed in the Italian city of Modena. Since its inception in 1979 the company has used available technology – first fax, then the Internet – to carry out its translation business. Today Logos is in the top ten league of global translation companies, and has over 1200 translators on its books covering over twenty languages. The translators are freelance, with about twenty full-time employees handling administration. Logos has over five thousand clients worldwide. Quality control is handled by a database which contains every document, task and translated word, as well as information about the translators, their qualifications, specialisations and language combinations. Using the database, Logos can also see which translators have previously worked for which clients, and quickly made a decision on which translator will be most appropriate for a particular job.

by the state telephone operator Telecom Éireann, and by multinationals known for their use of teleworking such as 3-Com, Motorola and Lucent Technologies. The Communications Workers Union has developed a "virtual" membership for teleworkers, including the self-employed, and the employer's organisation IBEC is preparing guidelines for HR managers who wish to implement teleworking in their companies. The Irish government has set up an Information Society Commission to examine how to develop a number of areas including teleworking. Ireland has been active in encouraging European call centre locations though tax breaks and attractive telecommunications tariffs amongst other measures offered by development agencies. The telecottage movement is not as widespread as in Britain due to the lack of funding for IT training through telecottages. Development agency Forbairt has run national roadshows to promote the creation of teleservice businesses, and the LEADER groups and County Enterprise Boards have also been active in providing awareness seminars and training for teleworkers. There is a telework association, Telework Ireland which was founded in 1993.

Italy

Telework is a hot topic in Italian academia, but has yet to filter down fully into the economic and political agenda. A number of companies have negotiated formal telework agreements, including Italtel, Telecom Italia, Dun & Bradstreet, Digital and Seat. These agreements cover about 400 employees to date. The not-for-profit organisation Lavoro & Tecnologia promotes teleworking concepts through its website http://www.mclink.it/telelavoro, and runs an active email discussion list with 450 subscribers. The organisation has proposed a teleworking law which is being considered by the Italian legislature at present. Telecentres are under development in Rome, Bologna and Venezia, and in the villages of Castelnuovo ne' Monti and Piacenza, but are not widely spread yet.

The Netherlands

Teleworking in the Netherlands has been characterised by positive government and private enterprise support. The Ministry of Transport with the Ministry of Economic Affairs and a number of IT and telecoms companies set up the Dutch Telework Platform in 1992, later replaced by a private sector body, the Dutch Telework Forum, which works to stimulate the introduction of teleworking in Holland. A telework magazine, *Telewerken*, has been published for four years. A survey by IDC in 1996 indicated that there are around 137,000 formal teleworkers in Holland (*ie* those with a specific contract, or contract clause, relating to telework). There are also many mobile teleworkers, leading to estimates that around 10% of the working population regularly telework. However, the telework forum reports that tax rules are working against teleworkers since there is no provision for compensation of expenses incurred by working at home.

Portugal

Like Greece, Portugal has an exemption which allows it not to deregulate its telecoms industry until 2003, and high telecoms tariffs compared to OECD countries. The Internet is only recently becoming available to the general public, mostly in the cities of Lisbon and Oporto. Small companies make up a large part of Portugal's economy and in general have a low level of computer literacy. The first report on telework in Portugal was published in 1996, with support from Portugal Telecom. The European Assembly on teleworking and new ways of working will be held in Portugal in September 1988.

Spain

In Spain multinationals have taken the lead in developing telework programmes. IBM Spain has over 1,000 employees who work from home, at clients' offices or while travelling. Teleworking initiatives are planned by Bull, Olivetti, Telefónica and Airtel. Three organisations are working to promote teleworking. The Spanish Telework Association has over 200

Big Blue reports success in major Spanish teleworking trial

IBM Spain began a pilot teleworking project in 1995 for about 100 salespeople and technicians which has since widened to encompass 1,500 staff. Each has a laptop and phone/modem for connection to a company intranet. Information accessible includes company and social news, travelling schedules and diaries for other staff members, "chat" areas and company data such as pricelists and technical specifications. Periodically, each staff member "docks" their laptop with a central facility to ensure that local information is kept up-to-date. Staff satisfaction with the new arrangements is overwhelming particularly for those with a nomadic workstyle. IBM reports careful staff selection, information and preparation have been vital to the success of the new work practices.

Siemens uses teleworking to aid Stockholm relocation

Relocation was the key to a major telecommuting pilot which began in 1994 in Sweden. Siemens Nixdorf Informationssystem decided to relocate to a new site 30 km north of Stockholm in August 1994. Following agreement with trade union SIF, a teleworking programme was piloted in a trial beginning in December 1994. Formal agreement for teleworking was signed in April 1995, and four fifths of the staff are now teleworking, including the managing director and marketing director.

Staff who wish to telework apply first to their manager or supervisor, and that decision is later ratified by the MD. All teleworkers spend at least one day a week at the company's premises. Siemens Nixdorf pays for the cost of equipment (typically including a fax, a PC, a modem and a mobile phone) but employees meet any additional cost of working at home. The company is also opening a neighbourhood office at the town of Nynäshamn, and considering other offices to be located around Stockholm.

members and sponsors and has prepared conferences and a handbook. The Spanish Internet Users Association and the Spanish Association for Documentation and Telework are also active, and there is a Spanish language email discussion list. A project to offer women IT skills through the EU's NOW programme has been operating in Cáceres through the regional government, and an "Infoville" is being created in Villena, a town of 31,000 inhabitants which will install an ISDN network in the town. Over 1,000 home-based PCs will be installed and the project is supported by ATT, Sun, NCR, Microsoft, Netscape, IBM, Oracle and Telefónica.

Sweden

Sweden has a well-developed telecommunications system and good take-up of teleworking technology (eg 32% of employees already use email). Figures for teleworkers vary widely – a recent study suggested up to 25% (around 0.5 million) Swedish white collar workers are teleworking in some form already. Many large companies have formal teleworking programmes including Siemens Nixdorf, Bull, Telia, Skandia, Digital and Ericsson. The white collar trade unions federation has produced a guidance booklet for members on teleworking issues and a model telework agreement. In the 1980s Sweden had as many as 60 telecottages, but these have been consolidated to 23 centres, mainly in rural areas. The Swedish Telecottage Association was founded in 1988 and has over 100 members. A government commission has been established to drive actions towards an information society.

United Kingdom

Early telecommunications deregulation has helped to produce a high level of teleworking development in the UK, alongside the active stance taken by the TCA, which provides information on teleworking to media and general

Scottish Widows counts teleworking pennies saved

Insurance and pension company Scottish Widows has reduced costs by over 45% and increased turnover by 300%, at the same time closing down a network of 25 branch offices. The changes have been achieved by implementing a call centre alongside homeworking for sales and customer contact staff. The company took a step-by-step approach to the new working practices, justifying each alteration with a formal business case. The procedure has saved jobs and will probably lead to job creation. Scottish Widows is the first UK company to actively recruit teleworkers, rather than encouraging existing employees to telework. It has advertised through the TCA's *Teleworker* magazine for suitable candidates.

public alike. The TCA has 2,500 members, produces this handbook and a bimonthly Teleworker magazine. There are currently about 140 telecottages in Britain. British Telecom (BT) has run a number of marketing campaigns supporting teleworking, and had a research team into teleworking technologies for some years. The Department of Trade and Industry has sponsored an umbrella organisation for teleworking development, the TUK Telework Platform, while the Institute of Directors and several trade unions, including MSF, BIFU, UNISON and the CWU have prepared booklets of guidance on teleworking for their members. There has been strong interest in corporate teleworking from the local authority and financial services sectors, with many trials and telework programmes in place.

EU grants and telework programmes

This section has been provided by Richard Warren of Stepping Stones, a consultancy involved in a number of European projects, by Jeremy Millard of the European Telework Development project and by Maarten Botterman of the European Commission, DGXIII/B.

Europe receives revenue through VAT and other levies. These resources are then redistributed into specific funds and budget lines which support actions to promote economic growth and social cohesion in all member states. It is important to understand that these funds and budget lines are agreed upon by representatives from each Member State at a European level, and are designed to supplement, not replace, any existing provision that a particular State may have already established.

The structural funds

The structural funds consist of Regional (ERDF), Social (ESF), Agriculture (EAGGF) and Fisheries (FIFG) and amount to nearly 30 million ecus in funding each year. The European Social Fund (ESF) is the third largest item of Community expenditure and includes action lines to combat youth and long-term unemployment and the integration of the workforce into the changing job market. The structural funds have six priority objectives:

1. development of poorer regions (those with a GDP less than 75% of average)
2. support for regions and urban communities affected by industrial decline
3. combating long-term and youth unemployment and exclusion from employment of disadvantaged groups
4. facilitating adaptation of the work-force to meet new employment challenges
5. support for rural development (5b, vulnerable rural areas)
6. support for areas with extremely low population densities.

The level of funding for activities varies depending upon the level of priority. Thus projects in Objective 1 regions (poor areas) can receive funding equal to 80% of the project's costs whereas only 45% is provided for projects combating unemployment in the better-off areas.

The map of regions is too detailed to reproduce here, but Ireland, Greece, Spain, Portugal and the former East Germany, as well as parts of Scotland and Italy fall into Objective 1, while most of Sweden and Finland falls into Objective 6. Patches of most other member states qualify for Objective 5b and Objective 2. For detailed information on the regional status of your area, contact your local European Information Centre (mainly run in conjunction with local chambers of commerce). A list of EICs is held at http://www.europa.eu.int/index-en.htm.

Mainstream ESF programmes mainly cover local vocational training initiatives. Sub-sections of ESF include the following strands, and funds for projects in these areas normally requires some form of trans-national partnership.

1. The Community Initiative which has three strands (women, disabled and elderly, youth)
2. ADAPT which targets adapting the skills of workers (see below under vocational training)
3. INTERREG which supports cross-border cooperation and certain isolated coastal areas
4. RECHAR, RESIDER, RETEX, and KONVER which support areas involved in coal, steel, textiles and defence industries respectively
5. URBAN which supports depressed urban areas (population 100,000 plus)
6. Special support programme for peace in Northern Ireland and border counties of Ireland which supports a wide range of training and business measures to aid reconciliation between communities.

The structural funds are all managed by national state bodies or agencies. For an individual or a telecottage to make use of these funds they would need to apply through an agency such as a college, enterprise council or charity through whom the funds would be channelled, to the relevant national state body.

The European Social Fund has been used to assist a number of telework training programmes, especially for women returners, through programmes such as NOW (New Opportunities for Women).

Research and development

There are a large variety of research and development funds available throughout Europe, but nearly all of them require pan-European co-operation – you have to create a consortium with people from other member states, and write a proposal which covers your plans and stresses how the European aspect of the research is important. Many of the current funding lines address the needs of new technology and so hold potential for tele-centres which are well established and interested in research. The first step is to become involved at a European level by registering with the Community Research database (CORDIS Partners) to build up working links. There are approximately 92 current research strands the details of which are available through the CORDIS Projects database.

The best known telework-related programmes are the ACTS (Advanced Communications and Technology Services) and TAP (Telematics Applications) programmes. ACTS covers fundamental research into new technologies, while TAP looks at effective implementation of existing technologies.

ACTS supports telework projects through its "general" chain of research, which covers telework, computer supported collaborative software, actions to help SMEs use telework, and work to develop global networks for teleworked services. One ACTS project, the ETD (European Telework Development) programme is aimed at broadening the concept of telework to encompass IT-based cooperation between companies and electronic commerce. ETD operates a large website (http://www.eto.org.uk) and a network of national coordinators in each European country. The ETD project is helping to translate and localise this guidebook for a number of European countries, and is one of the sponsors of the annual IT market survey report EITO (European Information Technology Observatory). The DIPLOMAT project supported by ACTS works to create a series of guidelines which are planned to build into a European Charter for Telework. This charter is intended to help build consensus on teleworking between government departments, professional institutes, employers organisations, unions, business associations and other bodies. DIPLOMAT is also creating a directory of telework champions. (http://www.telework-forum.org/diplomat).

TAP is an extremely wide-ranging programme organised into 9 sectors, which include: urban and rural areas, healthcare, training and education, libraries, disabled and elderly people, administration, transport, research, environment and engineering. It differs from ACTS in that it is aimed at research into the use of existing technologies, rather than the development of entirely new products and services.

Both the TAP and ACTS research programmes are operated by DGXIII, which covers telecommunications and information research.

The ESPRIT programme is mainly involved in developing software, but some of its applications fall into the telework area, especially with regard to software that promotes flexible working and business re-engineering.

The trans-European networks (TEN) programme, also run by DGXIII, contains some actions to encourage EU connections between teleworkers and telecentres in its TEN telework programme. The project aims to encourage transborder connections between individuals at home, virtual corporate networks, WWW and high speed ATM based services, as well as through cellular links to mobile terminals.

As a result of the Bangemann Report and the G7 summits relating to the Information Society, a number of research projects are underway. Some of these are highly technical, involving testing and setting standards for broadband telecoms technologies, but one strand involves helping small companies to reach a global marketplace through teleworking, amongst other techniques.

DGV, Social Affairs, is involved in looking at changes to laws on work practices, health and safety and benefits which may be needed to accommodate the move to teleworking.

DGXXII has been working on an interesting concept of teleplacement, or teleapprenticeship, under which trainees would not go on placements to employers physically, but would work for them from training centres, under the supervision of their trainers.

Other Community Actions

There are a number of actions designed to help European businesses compete on the world market and provide employment opportunities. The programmes listed below are most likely to be of use to small operations such as telecentres and teleworkers. Details of all these programmes should be available through local business centres or National Awareness Partners. Details are also available from your national European Office.

1. The SME INITIATIVE is intended to help small and medium sized enterprises strengthen their competitiveness. Companies with at least 10 employees located in regions eligible for ESF Objectives 1 and 2 funds can apply.

2. SEED CAPITAL provides interest free loans (up to 50%) for entrepreneurs

3. IMPACT (run by DGXIII section E) supports the information services market through grants to SMEs in less favoured regions (Objective 1, 2 and 5 regions), particularly for the development of multimedia and electronic publishing research, and thus involves some telework-related projects.

The EU's Fifth Framework Research Programme

The 5th Framework Programme (5FP for short) will run from 1998 to 2002, with the first call for proposals in the autumn of 1998. The guiding principles of the programme will be to focus on the issues of employment, quality of life and health including the environment, and the globalisation of markets, economic activity and knowledge. In relation to teleworking, the 5FP will attempt to "create a user-friendly information society", and this area is planned to receive 28% of the total funding, likely to amount to around 2 billion ecus. (The entire programme has been earmarked for 10 billion ecus in funding.)

Previous framework programmes have received criticism, particularly from smaller companies, for overloaded adminstrative procedures and bureaucracy, and for inflexibility. The new programme will attempt to be more streamlined and flexible than was the case previously, but proposals will still have to be made by transnational consortia and will be administered on a European, rather than national, basis.

In relation to the information society, it is planned that research will be carried out in the following areas:

- *systems and services for the citizen (eg healthcare, public administration, the environment, transport)*

- *new methods of work and electronic trading (eg flexible and remote working, group working, payment and trading systems, development of suitable security provisions and protections for intellectual property rights)*

- *multimedia content (eg electronic publishing, education and training, new language technologies, managing the information explosion)*

- *essential technologies and infrastructures (eg computing, microelectronics, mobile and satellite related services, telecoms engineering projects)*

There will also be activities aimed at improving research tools in general and supplying research infrastructure.

Another section of the 5FP focuses on assisting small and medium sized enterprises to create innovative enterprises and on providing these companies with access to advanced technologies.

4. CRAFT helps SMEs conduct research by contributing up to 50% of the research costs.

Employment and Vocational Training

Most of the initiatives for education and training involve the active participation of universities or ESF institutions. There is, however, a major new programme that addresses SMEs including telecottages, telecentres and individuals called LEONARDO.

This programme started in 1995 to cover vocational training. It is a transnational programme which includes:

1. transnational pilot projects aimed at improving vocational training systems
2. transnational training or work-placements
3. exchanges for trainers
4. innovative actions in training such as tele-learning
5. demonstration projects using the new technologies for training and job creation
6. language training
7. surveys and studies related to vocational training.

Any organisation involved in vocational training (including companies providing employment opportunities) is eligible to apply for funding. The process is through published calls for proposals from the Commission in Brussels. Details of the current Leonardo, and other, calls are available on the Web (http://www.europa.eu.int/en/comm/dg22/progr.html), or through your local enterprise council or European Office.

The ADAPT programme, which is funded through the ESF, is intended to help the European workforce adapt to industrial change – when jobs in traditional sectors disappear, the new jobs which emerge in new sectors typically require different types of work patterns and organisation. In future there will be fewer young people entering the labour force, and more workers in the 30 plus age groups whose education needs updating. Four types of measures are being supported by ADAPT:

1. training, counselling and guidance
2. anticipating employment creation
3. adaptation of support structures and systems
4. information, dissemination and awareness raising

ADAPT projects must also be transnational (turning potential differences between members states into positive advantages), innovatory, have local involvement from a broad range of actors, exploit results achieved by others and be complementary to other Commission programmes and initiatives. Many of these objectives can be met in teleworker training projects.

Other funding possibilities

There are many other European funding opportunities for a wide variety of social, cultural and political ventures. If you have a clear project, with European benefits, and are unable to access sufficient local funds, it is worth enquiring whether Europe can help. Funds may be simple grants of up to 30,000 ECU to conduct a study or pilot experiment, or larger grants to protect the European environment or heritage. Always remember that these funds are not free handouts but designed to help make Europe a better place to live and work in.

The LEADER II rural development programme contains as one of its objectives the support of projects which use innovation and technology to assist in rural development, and thus can assist with some telework projects in rural areas. It has been involved with telecentre startups, teleworker training and teleservice business support in a number of countries.

Article 10 ERDF funding has been used to support a number of regional information society initiatives (RISIs). These are partnerships of agencies in particular regions to promote information society activities, many of which have teleworking aspects.

Telework Europa forum

Compuserve operates a European electronic forum on teleworking, Telework Europa (GO TWEURO). The forum also has an Internet website http://www.tweuro.com. Much of the forum is devoted to space for European research programmes, but some of the subsections are more directly related to teleworking. The New Ways to Work section provides an "informal international turntable" to stimulate the exchange of ideas, documents and fresh approaches. The Teletools section provides descriptions of new products and services of interest to teleworkers. Telework Europa will shortly spin off a new European Small Business Forum (Eurobus) covering issues such as starting up businesses, legal issues, European marketing, human resources, education and training. Both Telework Europa and the Eurobus forum have foreign language sections.

Ethos website

The Ethos website provides links to many of the telework related Euroepean Research projects. A regular newsletter is also produced by the Ethos project which contains information on the ETD project and many other European activities. http://www.tagish.co.uk/ethos

European Telework Development project (ETD)

ETD is a dissemination project supported under the ACTS programme which amongst other activities develops guidelines – more information is available on page 328.

Bibliography

Teletravail
Editor: Alain Maurice
Source: Sarl Teletravail,14 Rue Yvonne le Tac, 75081 Paris, Fax: +33 142522501, Email: 101572.527@compuserve.com
Comment: French teleworking magazine

Telewerken
Editor: Th Snijders
Source: Kommunikatie Service Nederland, Tel: +31 4853 18008, Fax: +31 4853 13234
Comment: Dutch teleworking magazine

Teleworker Magazine
Editor: Alan Denbigh Tel: 01453 834874 Fax: 01453 836174
Email: teleworker@compuserve.com

Source: TCA Tel: 0800 616008 or 01203 696986 Fax: 01203 696538
Comment: Bi-monthly magazine for TCA members

Teleworx Magazin
Editor: Ulrich Pesch Email: logo-press@compuserve.com
Web:http://www.iwtnet.de/teleworx
Comment: German teleworking magazine

European Information Technology Observatory 97   *Date:* 1997
Source: European Commission DGIII or OECD
Comment: Invaluable source of European IT industry market data and trends

Telework 97   *Date:* 1997
Source: European Commission DGXIII
Comment: Annual review of teleworking status and report of DGXIII/B activities.

TeleFutures – a study on teleworking in Ireland   *Date:* 1996
Authors: Imogen Bertin and Gerard O'Neill
Source: International Services, Forbairt, Wilton Park House, Wilton Place, Dublin 2
Tel: +353 1 660 2244 Contact: International Services – Declan Murphy
Web: http://www.forbairt.ie/telefutures

Europe and the Information Society   *Date:* 1995
Authors: Spikes Cavell & Co on behalf of 3-Com Europe
Source: Spikes Cavell & Co, Benham Valence, Newbury, Berkshire, RG20 8LU, UK

European Guide to Teleworking   *Date:* 1995
Source: The European Foundation for the Improvement of Living and Working
Conditions, Loughlinstown House, Shankill, Co. Dublin Tel: +353 1 282 6888
Comment: General guide from a social issues perspective.

Flexispace/Mobility of work   *Date:* 1995
Source: The European Foundation for the Improvement of Living and Working
Conditions, Loughlinstown House, Shankill, Co. Dublin Tel: +353 1 282 6888

**Employment and economic impacts of advanced communications, and
social trends in use of communications services**   *Date:* 1995
Source: DGXIIIB, European Commission Tel: +322 296 3460
Comment: findings of several EU research programmes, AD-EMPLOY, ACCORDE,
SOCIAL TRENDS, METIER

Legal, organisational and management issues in telework   *Date:* 1995
Source: DGXIIIB, European Commission Tel: +322 296 3460
Comment: findings of several EU research programmes, COBRA, PRACTICE and
ATTICA

Telework and small business networking   *Date:* 1995
Source: DGXIIIB, European Commission Tel: +322 296 3460
Comment: findings of several EU research programmes, WORKNET, EXPERTS
UNLIMITED, TELEURBA

Telework, Telecommuting and Decentralisation   Date: 1995
Source: DGXIIIB, European Commission Tel: +322 296 3460
Comment: findings of four EU research programmes, OFFNET, EVONET, TWIN and
HRM TC

Transnational collaboration from local telework centres   *Date:* 1995
Source: DGXIIIB, European Commission Tel: +322 296 3460
Comment: findings of four EU research programmes, OFFNET, EVONET, TWIN and
HRM TC

Telehomework Case Study   *Date:* 1995
Source: The European Foundation for the Improvement of Living and Working
Conditions, Loughlinstown House, Shankill, Co. Dublin Tel: +353 1 282 6888
Comment: Empirical study on conditions and effects carried out in conjunction with
IBM.

Telematics Applications for Urban & Rural Areas   *Date:* 1994
Source: European Commission DG XIII - C2, Rue de la Loi 200, B-1049 Brussels,
Belgium
Comment: EC publication giving overview of use of telecoms and IT

Contacts and URLs

Teleworkmatica E-zine - send email to webmaster@radiovision.es giving your
name, your email address, your areas of interest and your country of origin to
subscribe.

ECTF is a network of academics and consultants whose discussions have been
supported by the European Commission.

http://www2.echo.lu/ie/en/iehome.html gives details of the language engineering
sector of the EU's Telematics Applications Programme

Portuguese Association for Telework Development – a non profit organisation that
aims to help teleworkers create their own business and provide them with training.
http://www.teleman.pt/apdt

Virtual Workplace, a project to develp teletraining for teleworkers based in Finland
and funded through the EU's ADAPT programme:
http://www.amiedu.net/indexenglish.htm

http://www2.echo.lu/libraries/en/libraries.html gives details of the Libraries sector of
the Telematics Applications Programme with many useful links

http://www.scimitar.terena.nl gives details of the Research sector of the Telematics
Applications Programme

http://www.nectar.org gives details of the Research sector of the Telematics
Applications Programme

http://www.et.westwind.be gives information on the transport and environment
sectors of the Telematics Applications Programme.

http://www2.echo.lu/telematics/education/en gives information on the Education
sector of the Telematics Applications Programme

http://www.ehto.be gives information on the Healthcare sector of the Telematics
Application Programme

http://www2.echo.lu/telematics gives details of forthcoming calls for proposals as
well as information on existing projects operating under the EU's Telematics
Applications Programme

http://www.ispo.cec.be gives access to a listserv which contains information about
information highways and electronic democracy, including the EU's information
society initiative.

http://www.eto.org.uk will feature telework-specific elements of the ISI through the
European Telework Online site. This site also contains information on European
Telework Week 1996.

http://www.RACE.analysys.co.uk. This is the excellent server operated by British
telecoms consultancy Analysys. It contains information on the EU's **RACE** and **ACTS**

programmes. Do not miss the SONAH section which gives succinct, practical useful summaries of the findings of several EU projects

http://www.eema.org is the site for the European electronic message association, a professional group for users of electronic messaging

http://www.tweuro.com gives details of the Urban and Rural Areas sector of the Telematics Applications Programme.

A "site for teleworkers around the world" from Belgium
http://www.ping.be/charly/tvphone.htm

European Commission DGXIII, Directorate B, Advanced Communications, Technologies and Services, Rue de la Loi 200, B-1049 Brussels, Belgium
Tel: +32 2 296 3460 Fax: +32 2 296 2980.

AFTT Association Francaise du Teletravail et des Tele-activites, Telespace du Vercors, Chemin des Breux, 38250 Villard-de-Lans Email: infos@aftt.net
Web: http://www.aft.net.

Stepping Stones (Europe) Ltd, 194 Southcroft Road, Tooting London SW17 9TW
Fax: +44 181 767 8030 Email: 100270.2407@compuserve.com. Services to small businesses including online searches, business training and community training

The Foundation for Development of http://www.fundesco.es:80 Social Function of Telecommunications (Spain).

European Foundation for the Improvement of Living and Working Conditions

The European Foundation is an autonomous body of the European Union which was established in Dublin in 1975 by order of the Council of Ministers after deliberations between the social partners, the governments of the member States and the community institutions. Its aim is to contribute to the improvement of living and working conditions in Europe by providing policy makers with essential knowledge and information. Within the Foundation there is a thematic group co-ordinated by Eberhard Köhler which focuses on Work Organisation and Industrial relations, within which a number of researchers work on issues related to teleworking. The Foundation has published a concise booklet, *The Social Implications of Teleworking*, which summarises the research done in all EU member states by the Foundation for the European commission on three teleworking topics:

■ *legal and contractual situation*

■ *social security position*

■ *health and safety*

The document details the many other working papers on teleworking topics which the Foundation has prepared over the years. The Foundation has also sponsored two Irish teleworking conferences. To obtain the document (ISBN 92–828–0592–1) or other information contact: European Foundation for Living and Working Conditions, Wyattville Road, Loughlinstown, Co. Dublin, Ireland Tel: +353 1 204 3100 Fax: +353 1 282 6456 Email: postmaster@eurofound.ie

European Telework Development Project

European Telework Development (ETD) is a dissemination project supported by the European Commission's ACTS programme, with the objective of helping to build Europe's confidence and competence in key aspects of the Information Society in the linked areas of telework, teletrade and telecooperation. This objective is being realised in three main ways:

1. outreach to citizens, enterprises and institutions, using online as well as conventional methods

2. working with other projects, institutions and communities of interest to develop a shared vision and common understanding of the opportunities and challenges

3. active support to other ACTS projects involved in developing telework technologies and the development of confidence-building guidelines.

ETD is supporting the Telework Handbook by contributing to copyright transfer costs so that versions can be developed and published in other European countries in local languages using locally-relevant material. In this way, ETD hopes to be able to contribute to raisingthe overall level of awareness and practice of telework throughout Europe.

The TCA is the national contact point for ETD Tel: +44 990 502079. The ETD website is at http://www.eto.org.uk. In Ireland there is a Freefone line for ETD – 1800 22 50 70.

UK Telework Platform

The UK Telework Platform was formed following the recommendations of the 1992 DTI report on Telework. It promotes the introduction of Telework in UK businesses to increase their profitability, and realise the environmental and social benefits of reduced travel and pollution. The Platform is funded by Mercury, BT, Cable & Wireless and other major computer and telecommunications suppliers.

It functions as a co-ordinating and funding body for a number of organisations involved in the promotion and development of telework in the UK, including the Telework, Telecentres and Telecottages Association, the Corporate Telework Forum, Telework Special Interest Group, Telework Events, Henley Management College Future Work Forum and others.

Its Telework Promotion Programme integrates activities run by the several organisations.

Telework Promotion Programme

- Central & Local Governement Lobbying campaign underaken by specialist lobbying consultants
- Seminars providing information on state-of-the art practice in particular industries
- Information Telephone Line
- PR Campaign of regular press releases highlighting key telework news items .
- Feedback Seminars providing informed feedback to Government departments
- Market research
- Publications
- Web Pages
- Internet Listserver
- National Teleworking UK conference
- International 3-day Telework Conference and Fair "Tomorrow's Workplace Today"
- Coordination of European Telework Week in the UK

For further information contact +44 990 502079

GCS Telegence

With all the pressures on the environment and changes in the way business is being conducted internationally, very small enterprises and teleworkers are in an ideal position to capitalise on the changing market. GCS Telegence has developed and refined training for teleworkers. We deliver training in our three telecentres for the unemployed over a twenty week period, with the successful students gaining employment in the GCS call centres.

We believe that there is no incentive for people who are unemployed for a long time to enter training without the prospect of employment at the end of the course. GCS has broken the mould in training. We train and we employ (if the trainees come up to standard). We have developed our telecentres into mini call centres, with training at one end of the building and call centre and data processing work taking place at the other end of the building.

We have a professional commercial training division where we deliver training for clients who need to retrain or develop the skills of their staff. Training can be delivered in the client's premises or in one of our well-equipped training rooms.

There is a huge demand for outsourcing all sorts of services, from data processing to telesales and market research – in fact for any service you can provide with a telephone and a computer. So we have developed a division specialising in traininig for the call centre industry as a natural addition to the existing teleworker training. This service is offered both onsite, and at our Scottish call centres, and the qualification is recognised by the Scottish Qualifications Authority.

GCS offer a complete solution for companies including consultancy, presales advice, computer system sales, installation, cabling, implementation, training, support and telephone integration. We also offer support services including telesales, customer care, customer retention and help desks. Our services are available into European countries and we also support North American companies in the UK and Europe.

GCS is changing the way companies work by example and changing the way training is delivered by linking it to real jobs. The secret of the GCS success is to use today's technology to deliver quality work to where people live. Teleworking in call centres, not city centres.

For further information call Roy Guthrie 01234 664164
GCS Telegence, Wood Street, Grangemouth, Scotland FK3 8LH

Lauder College

At Lauder College we pride ourselves on the quality and innovative ways in which our education, training and business services are provided. Lauder has developed from a small community college established at the end of the 19th Century in the town of Dunfermline, through an endowmemt from our founding benefactor Andrew Carnegie, into one of the most successful Colleges of Further Education in Scotland.

Lauder College is a progressive organisation. For a number of years now the College has actively supported flexible learning as a credible method of study for all areas of study. With the development of new communication technology and supporting hardware, Lauder College has embraced its advantages to further improve the flexibility of the College's mode of study.

This support for telework-related technological development, in relation to education and training, has led Lauder College to develop effective education training links between the College, the business community and other support agencies with a view to assisting organisations identify opportunities and suitable methods for implementing teleworking practises.

In particular, the College is trying to raise awareness of teleworking and its potential advantage to businesses, especially small organisations with less than 50 employees. Our Technology Centre within the College offers business managers and teleworkers the opportunity to develop their knowledge of electronic commerce and communication. Employees can use the available resources, such as video conferencing and multi-media to develop and improve their skills in the use of telematics technology.

A consultancy service is also available to help businesses access both training and resource needs. Training programmes can be developed to enable employees to telework effectively and can be customised to the specific commercial and operating requirement of an organisation, and delivered either from our Training Centre or another location, for instance the business's own premises.

Lauder College are actively promoting telematics services - CyberTRAIN, and ways of introducing electronic commerce and communication to business. CyberTRAIN harnesses telecommunications and computing technology to enable users to access training and business services in the workplace, or from an alternative convenient location, for example their home. The service is available 24 hours a day so employees can gain skills without compromising customer care.

CyberTRAIN is an ideal package for accessing distance learning and obtaining one-to-one College tutor support. Training opportunities are available across a wide range of disciplines including:

- construction
- engineering
- information technology
- administration
- hospitality
- management & business

- computing
- languages
- arts & leisure
- european studies
- care and social sciences
- mathematics

Other networked computer services which can be utilised using CyberTRAIN include business banking, internet services and information databases.

Lauder's electronic commerce and communication service (E-commerce) is another exciting new initiative offering expertise to organisations, in particular, who have limited knowledge of E-commerce. Initially activity is focusing upon raising awareness of this technology's potential through organising workshops, seminars and demonstrations to organisations. It will also offer and implement E-commerce solutions to business problems within organisations of any sector.

Lauder College latest initiative has seen it become actively involved in an EU ADAPT funded project to support the first Scottish pilot for the University for Industry. Titled Business Training Networks, the project focuses upon providing training solutions for small to medium sized enterprises using telematics technology.

Business Training Networks will provide a flexible approach to distance learning. Utilising the technological expertise of IBM, a series of linked learning centres will deliver education and training services, supported by a 24 on-line call centre network. Users will be able to access the networked expertise of 13 further education colleges across the UK to develop business and personal skills.

Using the collective expertise of the 13 college partners, CAPITB, IBM and Business Enterprise Scotland, Lauder College will co-ordinate the direction of this leading edge project. This high quality service will utilise new communication technologies and techniques in electronic commerce, telematics and multi-media, to deliver revolutionary new teaching and learning materials which meet the need of business.

The College is also investing in a modern, high technology Business Learning Centre whch will offer a complex range of training and support services to businesses. The centre will contain amongst other things a multi-media production and training facility, information technology and telematics suites, and a Call-Centre training suite.

For more information about Lauder College and its teleworking services contact our business development team on 01383-845000. For information about E-commerce please contact Ruth McGovern on 01383-559055

Lauder College
DUNFERMLINE

Anixter Distribution

Anixter Distribution is part of Anixter International Inc, the world's leading multi-vendor value-added distributor of networking and structured cabling products, focused entirely on communications infrastructure solutions. Worldwide turnover is $2.6 billion, with a European turnover of $480 million. Of the company's 5,600 employees, 1,000 are based in Europe.

Anixter Distribution has over 180 service and distribution locations worldwide, with 45 European centres covering Austria, Belgium, Czech Republic, Denmark, France, Germany, Greece, Hungary, Italy, Netherlands, Norway, Poland, Portugal, Russia, Spain, Sweden, Switzerland, Turkey, United Kingdom and Ireland. Competitive edge is a driving concern for all business areas and is being recognised by many as the single most important issue in maintaining or developing that edge. More and more companies – especially in the small to medium enterprise (SME) sector – are looking to employ technologies that will enable them to apply the sophisticated business systems that are now available to them.

But they are facing a number of questions. Which technologies are most appropriate to their needs? Which communications infrastructure is required to support them? And how can they be sure that it will be implemented and supported effectively? Anixter Distribution is addressing these issues by developing business-led, technology-based programmes and taking them to market through accredited partner channels. It is able to do this effectively by leveraging its unique global resources, skills and relationships, applying them to local business markets. As the world's leading provider of communications infrastructure solutions, Anixter has a unique understanding of the complete system – structured cabling and support, and local and wide area networks. Its supplier partners include the market leading manufacturers in all these areas, so it is able to combine the best technology with the best available product offerings.

Anixter maintains the highest levels of technical support capability demanded by manufacturers to support their products. Its range of training courses – covering everything from generic technologies to specific manufacturer accreditation – helps reseller partners to achieve the skills and level of accreditation that manufacturers demand of them, within the scope of their own business objectives. This is backed up by a range of pre and post-sales technical services to complement or supplement the resellers' own capabilities. Anixter ensures a high quality, technically capable delivery channel that end-users can rely upon.

The Anixter Distribution network of reseller partners includes companies suited to meeting any kind of end-user demand. From the smallest local office, to the largest multi-national corporate roll-out. From a basic cabling installation, to a fully integrated communications network. The combination of Anixter's global and local partnerships, its range of products and services, and its worldwide logistics capabilities, mean that whatever the communications requirement, Anixter can help identify and deliver the optimum solution.

End customers and teleworkers looking to implement remote access computing face tremendous problems when putting their equipment infrastructure together.

Anixter Distribution's response is the RACE (Remote Access Competitive Edge) Programme -- an initiative designed to help deal with the complexity of managing multiple suppliers and components to complete a total remote access solution.

Anixter recognises that designing and deploying such an expansive infrastructure as remote computing is very complex. Companies taking on such a project on their own will generally have to go to different companies to procure all the products, services and expertise that they may need for remote access. This includes public network services, whether ISDN or analogue telephone, home office teleworker equipment inclusive of modems, ISDN access equipment, central site routers, remote access servers, third-party dial-in security, authentication devices, firewall security and remote management software.

Anixter Distribution provides solutions with proven innovative products through partnerships with such leading manufacturers as Bay Networks, 3Com, IBM, Shiva, Cisco, USR, Raptor Systems and Axent Technologies. And this is all backed by quality technical and product support.

Through Anixter and its network of accredited resellers and installers, end users can be confident that the entire process – from initial feasibility studies and design through product selection to implementation and roll-out – will be handled with the highest level of competency.

ANIXTER

DISTRIBUTION

Tolson Messenger
Insurance Brokers

Whether you work from home as a self-employed person, or whether you participate in your employer's teleworking programme, there is a wide range of important issues which will require your careful consideration.

One such issue, where there appears to be a real lack of awareness and understanding, is that of insurance, which until recently has been greeted with little enthusiasm or urgency by the Insurers and their consumers alike.

Many people who work from home are unaware of what implications their activities have on their existing household insurance arrangements, and they are also largely unaware of the additional commercial insurance risks to which they may be exposed, by running a business from home.

Listed below are some of the points you need to consider, either in a self-employed or employed capacity.

- Is your existing Household Buildings and Contents policy affected in any way because you work from home? The vast majority of Insurers will specifically exclude cover for any item of business equipment, and others may go as far as refusing to insure you at all. (Check with your own insurers as they all treat this issue differently.) Failure to do so could mean your household policy being invalidated in the event of a claim.

Some Insurers are now beginning to offer some level of cover for business equipment under their Household Policies, typically up to £5,000. However many of these policies still fail to address the real insurance needs of those people who work from home. For example:

- Cover for portable business items such as laptops and mobile phones, taken outside the home.

- Business Interruption – you may incur additional expenses in running your business following loss or damage. For example, if your computer is lost or damaged, there may be costs involved in hiring a replacement machine, or in reinstating lost data.

- Public liability – If clients visit you in your home, or perhaps more commonly, you visit them, claims may arise where you are held legally liable for accidental damage to property or accidental bodily injury caused to a third party which arise out of your business activities. For example, a consultant working on a client site may spill coffee over a keyboard or may cause accidental damage during installation.

- Employer's liability – This insurance is compulsory by law, and you will require this if you operate as a limited company (and therefore technically an employee), or even if you are merely hiring staff on a casual cash-in-hand basis.

- If your business involves manufacturing and/or distributing stock, you will require cover for such stock held within the home and whilst in transit. You will also require Products Liability Insurance.

As an Employer, you will need to ensure that your existing commercial insurance arrangements are adequate to cover the employees who telework from home. All of the above insurances will need to be reviewed, particularly if, as is becoming increasingly common, such employees are no longer considered to be "employees" as such, but as self-employed contractors, in which case the "insurable interest" where responsibility for insurance will ultimately lie, may be passed on to the "employee" to make their own insurance arrangements.

Over the past four years we have pioneered specific insurance schemes for the growing number of people working from home. Our Home Business policy underwritten by the Commercial Union costs just £124.80 per year (£20 discount to TCA members) and provides a comprehensive package of cover suitable for the vast majority of office-based businesses. Optional extensions are available to cover the "manufacturing" style business. A free business tax and legal helpline is included within the basic cover.

Many self-employed consultants are becomingly increasingly reuired under the terms of their contracts with their clients to carry Professional Indemnity Insurance (PII). Anybody providing a professional service has a responsibility to their clients, and breach of that responsibility might result in a claim that could have a devastating impact on the smaller business. Even a successful legal defence is costly, and the consequences of losing could be a substantial payout to the aggrieved client. In today's climate of high consumer awareness, many will pursue a claim over the slightest grievance. Traditionally, PII has been very expensive and many self-employed professionals feel the amount of cover provided by these policies far exceeds what they actually need. As a result, Tolson Messenger have made available a new PII policy underwritten by Commercial Union which provides lower limits of cover for a more affordable price. Annual premiums start at £125 for £50,000 cover and £155 for £100,000 – less than half the price of traditional PII policies.

Tolson Messenger Limited are Insurance Brokers and Independent Financial Advisers. Members of the British Insurance and Investment Brokers Association, and regulated by the Personal Investment Authority in the conduct of investment business. For further advice and information call free on 0800 37 42 46 fax 0181 741 8361. 148 King Street, London, W6 0QU.

Development perspectives for telework in Europe

In the last few years, we have seen substantial change: firstly, in the adoption of new working practices in the real world of business; secondly, in the technologies now becoming available – notably around the astonishing growth of the Internet, and finally, in the focus of the policy debate at European level on employment – a debate that now cannot ignore the major influence of information and communication technologies and the inevitable transition to a global information society.

It is of course important in a period of change to know where you are, and how much further there is to go. But measuring change is not easy. While we believe there are now over 2 million "teleworkers" in Europe, still less than 2% of the workforce, such a simplistic categorisation is increasingly suspect: it disguises rather than highlights the nature of changes in working practices, the impact of new technologies in business, and the growing disparities between the Member States. Perhaps the best picture of where we now stand is presented by comparative figures of the proportion of businesses allowing remote access to their information networks and the proportion of employees using these remote access facilities to work part-time outside company premises. They now show an increasing proportion of businesses with intranets, with the most advanced European countries at comparable levels of use to the USA. Remote access, intranet use and off-site working are now main-stream practice for larger companies, but there are large differences between the leading and trailing EU countries and between large and small businesses.

We can now recognise new patterns of innovation beginning to emerge – new generations of business and work practices, enabled by new generations of technologies. We are already in a third generation as concerns telework. The first was in the 1980s, typified by remote "log-in" to corporate computers; outsourced work and limited to some thousands of technical experts. The second was in the early 1990's. It involved business re-engineering to cut overheads and involved less than 1% of the workforce being squeezed out to PC-based dial-in access. The current third generation is much more varied and inclusive. It is a part of the shift to networked business activity; it builds on the Internet and World-Wide Web; the rapid growth in mobile telephony; and involves several percent of the workforce; already about 10% of businesses and most large companies in Europe.

It is already clear that a fourth generation will emerge in two to three years. A generation characterised by the global virtual organisation and global small-business networking; held together by a more secure and performant Internet; linked to partners and customers through electronic commerce; and with perhaps 3 to 10% of their workforce more mobile than ever, using multi-media radio and satellite links to work whereever it is most convenient.

The challenges we face concern employment legislation, including health and safety issues, and how to ensure that Europe retains world leadership in the necessary infrastructure deployment and in the mastery of technologies. Building on the resarch already supported at European level, a new structure has been proposed for the 5th European Framework Programme of research and technology development. It identifies a user-friendly information society as one of three top-level themes, within which we propose to refocus support onto four Key Actions. One of these concerns "New Methods of Work and Electronic Trade". This will give greater coherence and visibility to European efforts to lead world developments in this area. It will give a balanced attention to the needs of organisations – both private businesses and public administrations – as well as to the interests of individuals as both employees and consumers. We intend that the technology development will be led by socio-economic analyses which will allow resources to be focused in areas of potential maximum employment growth and of benefit to the individuals' quality of working life as well as business competitiveness.

The European Union is also now able to support the deployment of trans-European Networks. The recent European agreement on 13 key aspects of communications networks and their use, including telework networking, opens the door to more forward-looking network. Transborder working and co-operation will inevitably grow within the single market, and with monetary union.

Finally, beyond these important opportunities to accelerate technology development and use, we must not underestimate the catalytic effect of regulatory change. We can now confidently expect that the Union's Member States will meet the deadlines for liberalisation of telecommunications infrastructures and services. At a time of rapid technological innovation, this will release tremendous creativity and investment in new infrastructure and service offerings. It will enormously increase the choice of services in support of telework, and drive down prices.

However, the convergence of telecommunications, computer networking and broadcasting into a seamless spectrum of digital multi-media services presents new challenges. We will need a coherent regulatory framework for communications, networking and media services which brings together legislation on the provision of services, on content, privacy (and its protection), and on conditions of access. Teleworkers are intense users of services and creators of content. They require clear rules on all these issues. The European Commission will be as vigorous and determined in this next stage of regulatory reform as we have been in promoting choice and fair competition in telecommunications.

Peter Johnston, European Commission, DGXIII/B
9 Avenue de Beaulieu, 1160 Bruxelles Fax: +32.2.296.29.80,
Email: pdg@postman.dg13.cec.be.

Glossary

ACD (automated call distribution): Computer systems used in call centres to distribute calls amongst operators and to monitor statistics such as average length of call, time before calls are answered and so on.

ADSL (asynchronous digital subscriber line): Method of using existing copper telephone lines to transmit high bandwidth signals suitable for video, fast Internet connections and large file transfers.

ASCII (American Standard Code for Information Interchange): Simple data format with no frills used as an "Esperanto" between different computer systems for the exchange of information.

Audioconferencing: using telephone systems to connect up to 20 people at different locations simultaneously for virtual meetings.

Baud rates: speed measurement for modems. Currently most modems purchased have a baud rate of 28,800 (also writtent as 28.8k)

Call centres: businesses for handling work carried out by telephone. The calls can be inbound (e.g. telereservations, technical support) or outbound calls (e.g. telemarketing, telesales). Generally call centres have sophisticated ACD computer systems to distribute calls between a number of operators and provide relevant information such as computerised customer records.

CLI (caller line identification): where digital exchanges and suitable telephones are available, the telephone can pick up the identifying number of the caller. See CTI.

CompuServe: widely used American email and online services system.

CSCW (computer supported co-operative working): software tools and management methods which enable teams to work together from different locations by computer. Examples include electronic diaries, messaging systems, software for tracking updates on multi-authored documents, and videoconferencing tools such as electronic "whiteboards".

CTI (computer telephony integration): computer systems often used in call centres to integrate information between computers and telephones. For example, caller identification codes can be used by CTI systems to bring up the caller's customer record automatically for the operative answering the call.

Cyberspace: science fiction term used to describe the imaginative "space" where people communicate electronically using email and online services.

Electronic commerce: Using electronic mail and/or the World Wide Web to source, order and pay for goods and services.

Email: abbreviation for electronic mail, text messages sent from computer to computer by means of telephone lines.

FAQs (frequently asked questions): files of information often held online for users of email and online services. Many newsgroups and listservs have FAQs which answer the most commonly-requested information on how to use a system, or specialist information related to the topic of the online resource. It is intended that new users should read the FAQs before asking typical "newbie" questions which may irritate more experienced users of the resource.

Fax card: card which inserts into a computer and connects to the telephone line to provide faxing facilities directfrom the PC.

Fax modem: modem which also includes relevant hardware and software for sending faxes. Almost all modems sold through retail outlets are fax modems.

Fax switches: electronic connectors which allow both a telephone and a fax to be connected to one telephone line. When a call comes in, the fax switch detects whether it is a voice or fax call and redirects it to the appropriate device.

Firewall: term for security and isolation measures to prevent hackers damaging or changing data on Internet server computers.

Forum: term used to describe discussion areas of online services, particularly those on the CompuServe online service.

HTML (hypertext markup language): structured language developed from the ISO standard SGML markup language which is used to create hypertext pages for display on the World Wide Web.

Hypertext: computer text pages which contain active areas connected to other pages. By clicking on the active area with a mouse, the user is immediately transported to another page of hypertext. Thus documents can be read by subject of interest, rather than sequentially as when turning the pages of a book.

Internet: the global network of computer networks which is used to send computer messages and files. The internet has around 40 million subscribers worldwide.

Internet phones: development of the Internet to carry voice traffic at low cost. Internet phones have poor audio quality but can provide huge savings on standard international calls. The development is controversial because of its potential to "clog up" the data traffic on the Internet.

ISDN (integrated services digital network): new generation fibre optic telephone lines which allow fast file transfer, videoconferencing, high quality audio telephone lines and fast Group 4 faxing. Up to 8 different devices such as faxes can share one ISDN line.

ISO9000: the International Standards Organisation quality control standard. Companies which are certified to ISO9000 have shown that they have an internal quality system in place and that they can use the system effectively over a period of time. However, award of the ISO9000 standard does not indicate the complexity of the system that is in place – just that it is used as specified in its documentation.

LANs (local area networks): groups of computers connected together so that they can use common resources such as printers, file storage and software packages.

Listservs: mailing lists for specialist topics on the Internet. A message sent to a listserv is read by a human moderator to check the content is relevant and legal, and then redistributed to all those subscribed to that listserv for discussion.

Modem: abbreviation of modulator/demodulator. Electronic device for connecting a computer to a telephone line for the transfer of data.

Netiquette: contraction of two words, network and etiquette, and used to describe acceptable practice and behaviour in the use of online services.

Newsgroups: Email discussion groups sorted by content available over the Internet.

OCR (optical character recognition): software used in conjunction with scanning devices to "read" typsecript into a revisable form on a computer.

OLR (offline readers): software packages used to automate connection to online services. Typically an OLR will log on to the online service, collect any waiting email, and check newsgroups or forums as instructed for new messages. The OLR will also send out any waiting messages from the user, before automatically logging off. OLRs can perform tasks faster and more reliably than human operators, leading to savings in telecoms and online charges.

Portable document format: a data format developed by Adobe which allows documents to be read on different computers regardless of their operating system or the fonts available on each computer.

Sysops and wizops: volunteers who manage forums and bulletin boards, particularly on the CompuServe online system. Sysops perform administrative tasks, answer questions and check files to ensure they are not infected with viruses or contain unsuitable or illegal material. A wizop is a chief sysop or teamleader.

Telecentres: centres where a number of people telework. They can range from small neighbourhood offices with basic computer equipment to sophisticated call centres employing hundreds of people.

Telecommuting: the practice of working at home and connecting to a central office using computers and telecommunications (commuting by telephone, or telecommuting).

Teleconferencing: see audioconferencing

Telecottage: a local centre providing access to low cost computer and telecommunications equiopment, which in turn gives access to information services and work. Some telecottages are community-run, others are commercial operations.

Telemarketing: selling or taking orders for goods or services by telephone, often using ACD and CTI technology in call centres.

Teleshopping: Identifying and ordering goods or services online.

Teleworking: working at a distance from your client, customer or employer and keeping in touch using technology such as telephone, fax and computers.

URL (uniform resource locator): a unique identifier, analogous to a map grid reference, for a resource on the Internet. The most commonly used URLs are those for the World Wide Web, which always begin http://www.

Usenet News: global system of delivering information and discussion messages classified into specific areas via the Internet – also called newsgroups.

User-id: name which identifies a user to a computer system or online service when that user connects or logs in.

Videoconferencing: using video telephony to provide an image of the caller as well as audio communication. Videoconferencing can range from one-to-one calls using inexpensive ISDN equipment to high-level videoconference suites capable of connecting several rooms full of people together on high quality links.

World Wide Web: a user interface providing a consistent organisation to resources on the Internet, including HTML files. Using the World Wide Web, users can browse through different resources held anywhere on the Internet

without needing to see the "nuts and bolts" of Internet usage such as logging in and out of different computers.

Year 2000: generic term for problems likely to occur when the year changes to 2000 caused by the use of computer chips which cannot handle dates greater than 1999.

Zipping files: using the widely-available PKZIP and PKUNZIP utilities to compress computer files before they are sent from one computer to another, and then to decompress them when they reach their destination.

Index

This index is arranged in word-by-word alphabetical order.